THE SOUTH AFRICA
1853 MEDAL

Examples of naming and the original ribbon.

Pte. William Roach, 27th Regt.
Born in 1808 at Templemore Co. Mayo, Roach enlisted in 1826. He served in the West Indies and was in the Cape of Good Hope from 1835 to 1848, being discharged the same year.

Sgt. William King, Royal Sappers & Miners
A native of Plymouth, King enlisted at 13 years of age in 1825. After 9 years in Corfu he went to the Cape in 1845 and distinguished himself at Koonap Hill in June 1852. Discharged in England in 1854 he returned to South Africa where his son served with the Buffalo Vol. Rifles (1877-8) and Landreys Light Horse (1880 Basutoland).

(*Photographs*: John Ormond-King)

THE SOUTH AFRICA 1853 MEDAL

Being the Roll of the recipients and the story of the campaign medal issued for the frontier wars between 1834 and 1853

by
G. R. Everson

The Naval & Military Press Ltd

Published by

The Naval & Military Press Ltd
Unit 5 Riverside, Brambleside,
Bellbrook Industrial Estate,
Uckfield, East Sussex,
TN22 1QQ England

Tel: +44 (0) 1825 749494
Fax: +44 (0) 1825 765701

www.naval-military-press.com
www.nmarchive.com

*In reprinting in facsimile from the original, any imperfections are inevitably reproduced
and the quality may fall short of modern type and cartographic standards.*

Contents

Author's Notes	3	
Publisher's Notes	5	
Acknowledgements	7	

1 INTRODUCTION 9
   The story of the Medal and the ribbon
   Description of the Medal Rolls
   Explanatory Notes
   Bibliography
   Chronology of Military events

2 ROYAL NAVY, ROYAL MARINES, AND
   ROYAL MARINE ARTILLERY 19
   Details of services performed
   Royal Navy Medal Roll
   Royal Marines and Royal Marine Artillery
      Medal Roll
   Notes on recipients.

3 7TH DRAGOON GUARDS 30
   Details of services performed
   Medal Roll
   Notes on recipients

4 12th LANCERS 33
   Details of services performed
   Medal Roll
   Notes on recipients

5 ROYAL ARTILLERY 37
   Details of services performed
   Medal Roll
   Notes on recipients

6 ROYAL ENGINEERS AND ROYAL
   SAPPERS & MINERS 42
   Details of services performed
   Medal Roll
   Notes on recipients

7 2nd REGIMENT 48
   Details of services performed
   Medal Roll
   Notes on recipients

8 6th REGIMENT 55
   Details of services performed
   Medal Roll
   Notes on recipients

9 12th REGIMENT 62
   Details of services performed
   Medal Roll
   Notes on recipients

10 27th REGIMENT 68
    Details of services performed
    Medal Roll
    Notes on recipients

11 43rd REGIMENT 71
    Details of services performed
    Medal Roll
    Notes on recipients

12 45th REGIMENT 77
    Details of services performed
    Medal Roll
    Notes on recipients

13 60th REGIMENT 86
    Details of services performed
    Medal Roll
    Notes on recipients

14 72nd REGIMENT 92
    Details of services performed
    Medal Roll
    Notes on recipients

15 73rd REGIMENT 95
    Details of services performed
    Medal Roll
    Notes on recipients

16 74th REGIMENT 102
    Details of services performed
    Medal Roll
    Notes on recipients

17 75th REGIMENT 109
    Details of services performed
    Medal Roll
    Notes on recipients

18 90th REGIMENT 111
    Details of services performed
    Medal Roll
    Notes on recipients

19 91st REGIMENT 115
    Details of services performed
    Medal Roll
    Notes on recipients

20 RIFLE BRIGADE (1st Battalion) 125
    Details of services performed
    Medal Roll
    Notes on recipients

21 CAPE MOUNTED RIFLEMEN 133
    Details of services performed
    Medal Roll
    Notes on recipients

22 STAFF AND CHAPLAINS 144
    Medal Roll (Staff)
    Notes on recipients (Staff)
    Medal Roll (Chaplains)

Contents

23 'ODD MEN' OF THE REGULAR ARMY 146
   Medal Roll and notes on recipients

24 STAFF MEDICAL SERVICES 147
   Details of services performed
   Medal Roll
   Notes on recipients

25 THE COMMISSARIAT 148
   Details of services performed
   Medal Roll
   Notes on recipients

26 COLONIAL FORCES AND NATIVE LEVIES 150
   Details of services performed
   Medal Roll
   Notes on recipients

27 DIAGRAMMATIC CHART OF MEDALS AWARDED 152

28 THE SIR HARRY SMITH MEDAL 153
   About the Medal
   Roll and notes on recipients

29 THE ROYAL NAVY 1853 154
   Ranks and Rates
   Table of Ranks and Rates in order of Seniority

Author's Notes

The non-fiction book has yet to be written which does not contain an error of fact. Any found here must largely be due to my own lack of care, but while no one relishes being corrected I should welcome being advised of amendments to the rolls and 'notes' which have been substantiated by research. The spelling of place names and of native chiefs differs according to source and I have given more attention to matters of greater importance to medal collectors.

Today, the word Kaffir, which is Arabic for 'unbeliever', has a derogatory connotation and perhaps some will seek to find offence in its use here. Contemporary maps mark the area of the troubles as British Kaffraria and, even if I wished to censor history, I would have found it impossible to totally avoid a term which was commonly used during the 18th and 19th centuries to encompass different native tribes. It is worth reflecting that in India Moslems referred to Europeans as Kaffirs (or Caffyres, etc). The British infidels seem not to have been unduly perturbed and accepted that, to non-Christians, *they* were the unbelievers.

Publisher's Note

This book is the result of nearly 2,000 hours painstaking research by Gordon Everson in spare moments outside his business life, spread over four years.

We feel honoured to have published the work, which must be of great value to students of Military History, and Medal Collectors.

Samson Books

13-19 Jamaica Road,
London SE1 2BY.

Acknowledgements

It takes more than one person to make a book and to no one am I more indebted than John Bristow who did most of the spade work in constructing the rolls for the Royal Artillery, Royal Engineers/Royal Sappers & Miners and the 45th Regiment. John also transcribed and collated the rolls for the Navy and Royal Marines and his ready wit enlivened many a trip to the Public Records Office.

I could always look to Capt Kenneth Douglas-Morris, RN, for expert advice on the Senior Service and he has kindly contributed the information on rank and rates to be found in the Appendix.

Very early in my researches I had cause to be grateful to Maj C. E. C. Townsend whose unrivalled knowledge of our public records was readily placed at my disposal.

My reliance upon Jamie Henderson to offer useful comment on my draft script was wise if sometimes painful, and there is no one better to consult upon matters relating to the 75th Regiment. Other regimental specialists from whom I have sought advice are Major John Samson, Peter Wardrop, David Muir and Jim Boys. Regimental museum curators have been most co-operative in supplying lists of the SA 1853 medals in their collections and I must also express my appreciation to all those enthusiasts who advised me of the whereabouts of existing medals. By appealing for such information I hoped to make an estimate of the survival rate of mid-19th century campaign medals. I am astonished how few have come to light and it is impossible to offer any precise opinion, but I would guess that not less than 75% of the medals of that time have ended in the melting pot.

South Africans Dr Frank Mitchell and 'Bill' Hibbard have been very helpful, while John Jervois permitted me to see the unpublished note books of Capt W. F. Jervois, RE, Norman Collett drew my attention to 'The Philatelist' of September 1974 which included interesting extracts from the private correspondence of Thomas Golding, 45th Regiment and CMR. Special thanks must go to the staff of the Public Records Office, in particular Stan Bickle and Eric O'Dell who were patient and understanding.

My wife Peggy has spent untold hours typing the manuscript and saved me from making too many errors. Certainly I could not have undertaken this task without her assistance. My father chased some loose ends at the British Museum and the Public Records Office and my eldest son Martin helped prepare the map, which was also the work of A. J. Henderson.

Transcripts of Crown-copyright records in the Public Record Office appear by permission of the Controller of Her Majesty's Stationery Office.

Introduction

The South Africa 1853 medal has for too long been underrated. It is not a common medal, just over 10,500 being struck, yet it commands no higher price than the belatedly issued Canadian General Service medal, nearly twice as many of which were awarded and doubtless more than twice as many survive.

The Kaffir Wars did not provide the opportunities for brilliant and memorable cavalry charges, nor were there any large-scale battles to inspire the writer or artist, but then the Fenian troubles in Canada could hardly be said to have added to British military glory when few of those engaged even heard a shot fired in anger! The same could not be said of the men who fought on the South African frontier. Suffering severe hardships in the field the troops faced a savage and pitiless foe whose cruelty towards prisoners equalled anything the North American Indian could devise. The Kaffirs were not armed only with primitive weapons; many possessed muskets and the rebellious Hottentots were often as well equipped as the British or colonial forces.

Reasons for lack of popularity of the medal among collectors are not difficult to find. Although new books regularly appear on other campaigns which were long ago explored to exhaustion, the fighting in what was known as British Kaffraria has virtually been ignored. Memoirs and accounts of the native outbreaks were published during the 19th century but possibly because of the complexities of the campaigns few modern regimental historians deal with them adequately, and until 1974 no author had clearly traced the history of the wars in a single volume.

That identical medals were issued for conflicts which spanned almost 20 years, with the uncertainty of when the recipient earned his award, may also have depressed the interest of collectors in the past.

Some years ago figures were published in Seaby's 'Bulletin' which were intended to enumerate and break down into regiments and campaigns the South Africa 1853 medals issued to the Army. This survey was incomplete and somewhat inaccurate and anyone with an interest in the frontier wars of South Africa must have welcomed the figures given in the 4th edition of 'British Battles and Medals'. Unfortunately, this new look into WO/100/17, which is the Public Records Office reference for the Army Roll, failed utterly to provide for those who campaigned solely between 1850 and 1853 and conveys the impression that the total number of medals issued to the Army was some 7,000 less than that actually awarded. This has led auctioneers and dealers into mistakenly attributing to this uncommon medal degrees of rarity which do not accord with the facts.

To establish a more reliable picture I conducted a 'head count' into the Roll which substantially confirmed the figures given for the 1st and 2nd wars in 'British Battles and Medals' and provided me with the information I was seeking on the 3rd campaign, but during my researches I became increasingly concerned about the accuracy of the Roll itself. I wondered at the disproportion of officers to other ranks in certain units and developed a curiosity over the so-called rarities. These doubts sent me to the regimental musters and the inadequacies of the Roll were soon exposed. Scores of men who are credited with serving in a single war on the Roll were proved to have fought in two and sometimes all three campaigns; most of the rarities were shown to have been falsely created by clerical errors and the spelling of names was disclosed as varying from phonetically arguable alternatives to gross errors.

I discovered also that the bulk of the returns of the ORs for the 45th Regiment, Royal Artillery and Royal Sappers & Miners had been lost, probably well before the turn of the century, and it was clear that nothing short of a complete reconstruction of the Roll would be of any lasting value. It was a daunting prospect but with the aid of the regimental musters, Army lists, public records and other sources, the task was eventually completed. Having gone so far it was a short step to examine ADM/171/18 – the Roll for the Navy. Thankfully, this project did not present the problems of the Army Roll and so here is the complete medal roll for the South Africa 1853 medal as it should have been recorded – or at least as near as it is now possible to determine.

Collectors have always puzzled over certain questions connected with the design of the Kaffir Wars medal and the ribbon. To put an end to conjecture I have taken the opportunity during my researches to unravel the absorbing story of the origins of the medal and its production.

Brief details of the history of the wars and of the particular services of the different regiments will, I hope, provide some understanding of the campaigns and encourage collectors to study the troubles of the South Africa frontier in greater depth.

South Africa 1853

THE MEDAL

Obverse	The diademed head of Queen Victoria with the legend 'VICTORIA REGINA'.
Reverse	A lion depicted crouching in a token of submission in front of a Protea bush. Above are the words 'South Africa' and in the exergue the date '1853'.
Diameter	1·42 inch.
Ribbon	Orange watered with two wide and two narrow blue stripes.
Suspension	Ornamental and swivelling.
Designers	Obverse – W. Wyon, RA. Reverse – L. C. Wyon.
Naming	Indented in Roman capitals as the MGS medal.

Awarded to those who survived and had been engaged in one or more of the Kaffir Wars of 1834–5, 1846–7 or 1850–3, this was the first medal specially struck for military service in the Continent of Africa.

The intention of awarding a medal for the campaign of 1850–3 was established in March 1854, and as Adjutant General, Sir George Cathcart, late Governor of the Cape, had charge of the deliberations. On July 16th he laid the results before the Duke of Newcastle, Secretary of State for War and the Colonies, in a memorandum from the Horse Guards presenting a suggested design for the medal and proposed rules to govern the award. But at that moment, there was already on its way from North America a letter which raised an important issue.

Serving on the Staff of General Rowan in Canada was Sir James Alexander, who in 1840 had addressed a memorial to the Duke of Wellington moving for a medal to be given to survivors of the Peninsula Wars, a proposition which was shelved until the Duke of Richmond took up the cause and obtained the Military General Service medal for Wellington's veterans in 1848. Now Alexander was to play a part in determining the distribution of the Kaffir Wars medal. On July 17th he wrote from Montreal to the Duke of Newcastle, expressing satisfaction that the men who had campaigned in South Africa were to receive recognition of the hardships they had endured. He went on to ask that 'those who served without hope of prize money in 1834–5, 1846–7 at Boemplaats and in the capture of Natal should not be overlooked'.

Mention of the latter actions against the Boers suggests that, with the MGS, Naval General Service and Army of India medals in mind, Alexander* envisaged a similarly retrospective Africa General Service medal. There was need for such an award. The warlike nature of the tribes who had migrated south centuries before and were collectively known as Kaffirs, had brought about a number of armed conflicts with European settlers, and although medal collectors call the troubles in 1834–5 the First Kaffir War, South African history knows it as the Sixth (or Third British) Frontier War. Kaffirs had attacked British soldiers in 1798; they had clashed again in 1811, and there was a major outbreak in 1819 when some 8,000 natives attacked Grahamstown. British troops had fought the Boers in 1795 and 1806 before bringing the Cape under the British flag. They had warred again at Port Natal in 1842 and at the battle of Boemplaats in 1848 and the officers and men who had served in these actions merited recognition no less than those who had campaigned in Kaffirland during 1850–3.

Alexander made it clear he was an interested party, having been an Aide to Sir Benjamin D'Urban during the 1834–5 campaign, of which he wrote an account, and C. Talbot, an Under Secretary at the War Office proffered the opinion that although 'the medal was advisedly restricted I am myself aware of no reason in favour of limitations'. This may mean the wider question of an African General Service medal had already been discussed, but with the assent of Newcastle, Col S. C. Mundy Under Secretary of State for the War Office, referred Alexander's suggestions to Lord Hardinge at the Horse Guards. In his reply on August 16th the Commander in Chief neglected to mention Natal or Boemplaats, which supports the possibility of a General Service medal having been considered and dismissed, but he felt 'it would scarcely be possible to resist the claims of those engaged in two former wars with the same enemy'.

Before approaching the Queen for her approval, Newcastle asked that the additional number of medals involved should be ascertained and on September 28th the Horse Guards requested this information from the regiments concerned. Nearly two months later only the 7th Dragoon Guards, 73rd, 90th and 91st (1st Batt) Regiments and the Cape Mounted Riflemen had responded and so on October 25th Asst. Adj General Wood submitted to the War Office an estimate based on the returns he had received. Wood calculated that some 6,000 extra medals would be required but stressed that several Corps of Levies were also engaged and their numbers could not be assessed without communication with the Colony. This was the first mention of the Levies for it had been intended to reward officers and men of HM Regular Army only, but Talbot did not seize upon the

---

*WO/6/113. The War Department advised a Thomas Hartley that he had been mis-informed as to medals being granted to men present at the taking of the Cape of Good Hope in 1806. Hartley mentions that he had also served in the Nepal campaign (presumably with the 24th Regiment) and it seems that no one advised him that he was entitled to an Army of India medal.

†As this is written primarily for medal collectors my references to the 1st, 2nd and 3rd wars are intended to mean the campaigns for which the medal was awarded.

point, merely noting that the figure was larger than had been anticipated and reminding Newcastle of Hardinge's view. On November 4th the Duke recorded that he had obtained the approval of the Queen but it was not for another 10 days that the C-inC was officially advised the extension had been granted.

The Navy

Now that this matter had been settled, General Order No 634 was issued from the Horse Guards dated 22.11.1854 and laid down that the medal was 'to be conferred on Surviving Officers, non-commissioned Officers and Soldiers of the regular forces, including Officers of the Staff and Officers and Men of the Royal Artillery, Royal Engineers and Sappers and Miners who actually served in the field against the enemy in South Africa'. The Order received the close attention of the late Governor of the Cape Lt Gen Sir Harry Smith, now in command of the Northern and Midland Districts. Sir Harry had always been distinguished by his concern for his soldiers and since his return from South Africa he had addressed a number of vigorous letters to Lord Hardinge and other authorities on behalf of old comrades. But he proved he was not only solicitous of the military for on December 1st he wrote to the Duke of Newcastle and raised the question of eligibility of Seamen and Marines for the medals. Pointing out that a detachment of Marines had served in the field for some months and frequently been engaged with the enemy he continued '. . . as the Commander of that Army during the most eventful period of that campaign (1850–3) as well as Governor of the Colony I feel it is my duty to make to your Grace this representation'.

For the benefit of the Duke, Talbot noted that although a medal had been given to the Navy for the China War (of 1842) 'neither the Nile, Trafalgar, Algiers nor any great naval action has been so commemorated and I cannot concede in all due deference to so high an authority as Sir Harry Smith what services the Seamen and Marines could have rendered during the Kaffir Wars which would justify a departure from the present rule in this respect'. Apparently unaware of the existence of the Naval General Service medal, Talbot's knowledge of things naval was matched by Col Mundy who advised Newcastle 'I conclude medals have been considered incompatible with the dress and duties of sailors for assuredly they have earned honours as well as soldiers'. Perhaps Mundy visualised medals dangling in buckets as the decks were scrubbed!

Newcastle was at this time weighed down with the problems of the Crimean War. The Government was under attack for the deficiences of our military system and the Duke saw himself as potentially the first sacrifice to appease the clamour. With these more critical matters to concern him the War Secretary was content to accept his minion's coolness towards Sir Harry's suggestion but, knowing the old Peninsular veteran was not a man to be easily deterred, the War Department sought to persuade the Navy itself to dismiss the proposition. A letter was sent to the Admiralty of December 8th '. . . to ascertain the opinion of their Lordships as to the propriety of conferring these medals on the Seamen and Marines'. The Navy was used to judging winds and were quick to seize upon a favourable breeze. Choosing to misconstrue the enquiry, Chatham Yard was immediately asked to furnish lists of those officers and men who were engaged in the Kaffir War. The War Office was annoyed upon learning of this precipitate action and the Duke minuted that it had 'better be privately explained' that the measure of awarding medals to the Navy had yet to be decided upon.

If someone did drop a quiet word in a Sea Lord's ear it must have had a negative response, for on December 18th Col Mundy sent a formal letter to the Secretary to the Admiralty. It was made clear that the earlier communication had not been intended to encourage a call for lists of officers and men and their Lordships were left in no doubt as to Newcastle's displeasure '. . . it may be therefore superfluous to observe that his Grace would not feel himself warranted in recommending to Her Majesty that such distinction should be conferred on the Seamen and Marines in the present instance unless the services performed by them were in the estimation of the Lords of the Admiralty of a marked and brilliant character'.

Had the War Office been fully aware of the Navy's contribution, of the difficulties faced and the losses suffered it is difficult to believe they would have been so obstructive, yet the Admiralty made no attempt to detail the services rendered. For the benefit of their Lordships Chatham had already supplied a resume of the activities of various ships at the Cape during the 3rd war and it would have been a simple matter to pass on the information. But the Navy did not feel the need to explain themselves. On December 23rd they replied that their Lordships felt justified in recommending to the Queen that the medal should be extended to Officers, Seamen and Marines who served with the Army. To lend weight to the petition they recalled the award of the Naval General Service medal and enclosed a copy of the letter addressed to the Queen at that time by the First Lord of the Admiralty.

The War Office was perplexed to find the Navy so ready to by-pass them once again but the threat was effective and they made no further attempt at obstruction – at least for the moment. Vexation was expressed in notes which can be seen on the letter copies. The Admiralty had acted 'hastily'; Sir Harry Smith, who had raised the question, is dismissed as '. . . an impulsive person'. Newcastle then washed his hands of the matter, with '. . . it is all the responsibility of the Admiralty'

As the Duke was to resign in little over a month he really had put the Kaffir War medal behind him, but subordinates still in the War Office were determined to salvage something from the defeat. Their influence was brought to bear on Newcastle's successor Lord Panmure and after the Navy finally submitted their lists of officers and men on September 25th 1855 they received a most unwelcome reply from Col Mundy. Under the date October 10th he wrote '. . . Lord Panmure is of (the) opinion . . . that these medals should not be indiscriminately distributed around the whole of the officers and crews of the vessels named, but to such portion of the Naval force only as contributed to the operations by land'. The definition of 'employed in the field' could, according to Panmure's informants, only be met by some 135 to 140 men, but the Admiralty was determined to reward all the crews of vessels supporting the operations.

On August 11th Rear Admiral Edmund Lyons had written to the Admiralty from the Crimea pressing that the medal for the Russian War should not be confined to ships which had seen service under fire. Lyons' view led to the application of less restrictive rules of the award than had been envisaged, and the decision must have influenced attitudes to the Kaffir medal. Certainly it strengthened the resolve of the Navy and they brushed Panmure aside as they had Newcastle. Sir James Graham, First Lord of the Admiralty, went directly to the Queen and on October 30th Mundy passed the Navy and Royal Marines lists to Sir C. E. Trevelyan at the Treasury.

Design of the Medal

The time spent on considering Sir James Alexander's proposal and the discussions with the Admiralty had pushed aside any thought of design or production of the medal. No doubt pressures of the war with Russia also gave the late

native troubles in the Cape a low priority and it was not until an enquiry arose about the ribbons for both the Kaffir and Crimea medals that the Duke of Newcastle was reminded so much had been neglected. In consequence one of his last acts in office was to write to the Lords Commissioners of the Treasury requesting their Lordships to instruct Sir John Herschel, Master of the Mint, 'to cause a drawing to be prepared of the proposed medal. . . .'

As already related it had been the Horse Guards' responsibility to suggest a design for the medal and the memoranda of July 26th 1854 contained their proposals. These had been placed before the Queen without delay and on August 2nd Lord Hardinge was advised that Her Majesty had accepted the counsel and given directions . . . 'that a medal should be prepared to commemorate the success of Her Majesty's Military Forces in the war in which they have lately been engaged against the Kaffir tribes of South Africa. Her Majesty has further been pleased to command that the medal in question should bear on the obverse side the Head of the Sovereign with the words "Victoria Regina" inscribed and on the reverse side a Lion emblematic of Africa in the attitude "Couchant" in token of submission with the words "South Africa" above and the date "1853" underneath to mark the termination of the war. . . .'

This authorisation now faced amendment following the extension to embrace the wars of 1834–5 and 1846–7. The draft of the letter carrying instructions to the Treasury provided for the medals displaying the dates of all three wars, but what, someone must have asked, about men who had served in more than a single campaign? It was obvious permutations would be necessary to cover all dates and the numbers of medals required for each combination was clearly a problem, for the returns from the regiments were still far from complete. The potential increase in costs for extra dies, the difficulties of allocation and perhaps a realisation that the returns had not been accurately recorded quickly persuaded the War Department to take an easy course. Mention of the earlier dates was simply struck from the draft instructions, leaving the original and now meaningless '1853'. How much better it would have been to show '1834–1853'.

Leonard C. Wyon, 'Modeller and Engraver to the Royal Mint' was approached to prepare for the reverse of the medal a design in accordance with the previously mentioned description. 'In respect of the head of the Sovereign for the obverse' wrote Herschel to the designer, 'I propose to adopt the very beautiful one of your late Father which adorns so many of our honorary decorations. . . .' He further asked Wyon for his terms and the time needed to complete and deliver a Matrix and a Puncheon for the production of such Dies as may be required. Accepting the commission, Wyon undertook to complete the work within three months for 100 guineas. His terms were passed to and accepted by the Treasury who authorised rates of payment to the workman of 2½d for each medal executed by ordinary Coining Presses and 3d when produced by the Die Presses. But their Lordships deemed it advisable '. . . for the sake of economy and the speedy execution of this important service that the medals should to the utmost extent be prepared in the ordinary Steam Presses. . . .' It was estimated that the working dies could be manufactured at the Mint for not more than £3 each.

The Duke of Newcastle resigned his office on February 1st 1855 and it was to his successor Lord Panmure that the Mint submitted Wyon's completed design on March 9th, not a drawing as had been ordered, but a wax model on a somewhat enlarged scale. This, it was felt, was 'more adapted to convey the artist's conception'. The graceful illustration of the lion symbolizing Africa is usually wrongly described as stooping to drink and as early as August 1854 the posture of the lion was prominent in the minds of the authorities. Herschel observed that 'the attitude of the Lion is as nearly conformable to the strict Heraldic epithet "Couchant" as consistent with artistic effect and fully conveys the idea of submission intended. The Shrub in the background is Protea Mellifera, abundant in every part of South Africa.' Under-Secretary F. Peel made a note 'I hope the Lion doing penance will not be taken for the *British Lion*'. From a letter by Col Mundy to Maj Gen Sir C. Yorke we know that the Queen had approved the design before March 15th. 'Very beautiful' says a notation, perhaps echoing Her Majesty's own words. Mundy did not hurry himself to advise the Mint, and it was not until the 20th he gave them the go-ahead.

Two days later, W. H. Barton wrote from the Mint to Wyon asking him to proceed with the execution of the dies; adding in a post script 'your model has not yet been returned to the Mint from the War Department; please let me know whether it has reached your hands through another channel'. The designer seems to have waited some six weeks for his model to arrive and when in early May Lord Panmure enquired what progress was being made had to reply that '. . . owing to the loss, at the War Office, of the model of the Kaffir Medal, considerable delay will occur in completion'. He added that he was proceeding to repair the loss and would execute the work as soon as possible.

This stirred the Horse Guards who returned the original model to the Mint on May 22nd. Probably it had not been lost, simply overlooked, but in acknowledging its receipt Wyon could not forbear to comment that as the original had been mislaid at the Horse Guards he had completed another at great inconvenience. This irritated the War Department and it was pompously enquired of the Mint on whose authority Wyon grounded his belief that the model had been mislaid. Herschel could see no profit in this fruitless exchange and to ensure it was not pursued he urged Wyon to complete the dies.

By July the work was finished and on August 14th 1855 a pattern medal was sent to the War Minister for submission to the Queen. This formality being completed, authorisation to begin striking the medals was passed to the Mint and in early October the first medals were at long last ready for distribution.

The Ribbon

In his memorandum of July 26th 1854 to the War Department, Sir George Cathcart suggested that 'the ribbon might be orange colour with a broad crimson stripe down the centre as emblematic of the history of the settlement, originally a Dutch colony, now held as a British Crown possession by right of conquest'. Against the words 'orange colour' Col Mundy noted 'Irish R. Catholics might break heads on this point'. One wonders whether he was being serious.

Following the Queen's approval of the design this description of the ribbon was included in the directions passed to the C-in-C by the Duke of Newcastle on August 2nd and the question of pattern does not occur again in correspondence until January 1855. This was when Her Majesty asked to be shown examples of various campaign ribbons. The request went to Sir John Herschel who forwarded to the War Department specimen ribbons of all medals struck by the Mint, and others he had obtained from India House; but the Mint was baffled by reference to the 'Cape Medal'. 'Should it' asked Herschel with a flash of inspiration, 'refer to the Caffre medal?' When sending the ribbons to the Queen, Newcastle remarked in his covering letter that 'The ribbon for the Kaffir War had not yet been decided upon by your Majesty'. It escaped notice of the War Office that approval had already been given nearly five months before. Less surprisingly Queen Victoria did not recall the matter but some remembrance lingered with the Duke for he added that he believed Cathcart, who had

been killed at Inkermann on November 5th, recommended the colours of the ribbon should be orange and blue. It is a pity the Minister's memory played him false for no doubt the Queen felt she was paying some tribute to the old soldier when, on January 24th, she approved of '. . . the Cape Medal being orange with a dark blue edge, as originally proposed by Sir George Cathcart'. Thus the ribbon colours were decided by a faulty recollection and the failure to refer to earlier correspondence.

Not that the War Office was the only Government Department to be lax in this respect; a similar slip at the Mint helped to slow the laborious procedures. Crook & Son, military tailors of Pall Mall, were being asked by their clients for the ribbons of the Crimea and, as they called it, 'African' medal. Towards the end of February they wrote to the Secretary for War who advised Crook & Son to apply to the C-inC Lord Hardinge. The Horse Guards denied any knowledge of the matter and went back to the War Department. Under Secretary Talbot replied that 'The Master of the Mint has received the necessary directions on the subject through the Lords Commissioner of the Treasury in ordinary course'. From the Mint Herschel professed to know nothing of the ribbon and now Lord Panmure took a hand, perhaps suspecting his department had blundered, but in any case, determining to expedite the matter.

Firstly, he ordered that the Horse Guards should be advised of the ribbon colours and then stirred his Under Secretaries with searching questions about the 'Cape' medal responsibilities. Talbot in turn chased his staff and must have been relieved to be told that the Mint were informed about the ribbon on January 26th. If this was so it says little for the memories of Herschel and his office but why didn't the War Department give Crook & Son a direct answer in the first place?

At the same time that Herschel sent Wyon's design for the medal to the War Office, Panmure asked about the progress being made. The letters crossed, but as the Minister also enquired about the ribbon the Master of the Mint followed up his letter of March 9th to explain that it had not yet been ordered. He continued 'the description "blue with orange border" allows of considerable latitude and the patterns sent have not been sufficiently various'. Herschel had now reversed the colours but it may have been simply a clerical error as it was not noticed by either office.

The firm of J. L. & C. Bankes were commissioned to supply the ribbon. The Queen made her selection from the several patterns submitted but it was felt that the effect was not entirely satisfactory. The manufacturers were consulted and they suggested the appearance would be improved by watering. This was done and the initial order was for 2,000 yards of ribbon at 7d per yard. The stock ran out in July 1857 when another 180 yards was ordered on the same terms.

It is a pity we cannot know whether this second supply was identical in colour with the original for the precise shade of orange of the ribbon is a popular controversy. On one hand it is argued that the blue stripes should be on a bright orange background, as that for the South Africa medal of 1877-9, and on the other blue on pale orange, often described as 'biscuit', an issue which is mis-stated in 'Battles and Medals'. Those who assert that the Kaffir and Zulu war ribbons were identical point to two allegedly specimen pieces of ribbon which can be found in the SA 1853 medal roll. These soiled samples are clearly of the bright orange variety but there is nothing to prove they were put there when the medals were being distributed and in my opinion both pieces are from a spool of Zulu War ribbon.

The similarity of glueing and the uniform grubbiness suggests they were affixed at the same time and while one snip is stuck on an 1853 medal application form the other is on the opening page of the roll, whereupon is written a list of the Kaffir Wars dates and also dates of the Griqua and Zulu campaigns. As all this is in the same hand the sheet could not have been prepared before 1880, and if I interpret correctly a printer's mark, not before 1898, which may be the period at which the various documents in the roll were first bound together.

The illustration in Carter's 'Medals of the British Army' (1861) shows bright orange, but it is recorded that an Army Sealed Pattern of the Kaffir Wars ribbon is or was, 'biscuit' colour. However, in recent years, there have been two important discoveries which surely settle the matter.

In April 1971, M. J. Crook disclosed in the OMRS Journal (No 1 Vol 10) that he had examined an FDC SA 1853 medal with a pale orange ribbon which had, with two other medals, lain apparently undisturbed in the strong box of an Agent since the day they were issued. The medals were still in their original boxes and envelopes. The Kaffir medal had been sent to the Agent on January 19th 1856.

Further evidence emerged in 1972 when London dealer John Hayward came into possession of a large spool of 'biscuit' coloured ribbon which had been found in the vaults of a well known military tailors in perfect condition. Moreover, the inner part of the spool revealed ribbon of exactly the same colouring and thus disposed of any suggestion of fading, which is the favourite argument to account for the pale shade.

Mentioning this to a Lloyd's underwriter, he showed me a superb family collection of medals won in six Victorian campaigns by his naval ancestors. All the medals and ribbons are in 'as issued' condition and an accompanying note unquestionably made generations ago, draws attention to the different ribbons as a means of identifying a 'Kaffir' medal from a 'Zulu' without clasp.

Whether the 1877-9 ribbon was given a brighter orange deliberately or by accident may be difficult to determine but only the most entrenched will deny that the original ribbon presented with the medal of 1853 was blue on *pale* orange.

The story of the medal and its ribbon betrays such prejudice, incompetence and ignorance by Government officials and departments that it seems little short of a miracle a conclusion was ever reached. Some may think things have altered little over the last 120 years!

A Description of the Medal Rolls for the South Africa 1853 Medal held in the Public Records Office

The Roll for the Army; Ref WO/100/17
A specimen medal application form has been bound in the medal Roll for the Army. Besides setting out General Order 634 the form instructed that claims should be addressed to the Board of General Officers, Whitehall Yard; serving soldiers applying through their commanding officers and pensioners through the Staff Officers of Pensions.

Applicants were required to state

1. Rank in which discharged;
2. Date of discharge;
3. Period of service in the field for which he claimed;
4. Regiment, Troop or Company and rank in which he served in each occasion.

A Magistrate, Parochial Minister or Churchwarden had to testify to the identity of the claimant but verification was probably not imperative for claims forwarded from Pensions Officers. As serving soldiers were submitted by their regiments they were automatically endorsed by commanding officers who signed the returns.

The Roll itself provides three columns in which oblique strokes were intended to indicate the campaigns in which a man served. By putting 'ditto' marks in the blank columns the War Office clerks have helped confuse all first time researchers into the Roll and by placing qualifying strokes in wrong columns created false rarities for many regiments. As clasps were not awarded the clerks must have felt it was unnecessary to be too painstaking about dates. We have seen from the evidence in the Colonial Office correspondence that to strike differently dated reverses had at least been considered and although we must regret this was not pursued the decision* saved a great number of officers and men from receiving wrongly dated medals.

Anyone who has sought to confirm an award from the Roll will agree that it is not the easiest to examine. The recipients were recorded in a series of 'reports' in the earliest of which officers and other ranks were segregated. As the flow of claimants diminished this practice was discontinued and an officer slipped in among the ORs can easily be overlooked. Conversely, two senior NCOs are included with the officers as they had been commissioned by the time the medal was issued.

It does not help the researcher that recipients are not presented as entire regiments. All those whose surnames begin with A are shown in order of regimental seniority, then B and so on throughout the alphabet. This is all well and good but as further claimants arrived a second alphabetical list had to be drawn up. But still they came and these later submissions are shown in regimental order without regard to spelling. However, even these patterns cannot strictly be relied upon for both surnames and regiments are sometimes out of sequence. It would appear that War Office clerks made two copies of the lists of applicants as they were received from regiments or when a sufficient number of individuals had made returns to enable lists to be drawn up. One copy they retained and the other was sent to the Mint. Some of the latter evidently were returned and are now bound up in WO/100/17, creating a partly duplicate Roll and unfortunately these lists often contradict one another over spelling, rank and qualifying campaign dates. Although the duplicate lists have caused a considerable number of names to be repeated on the Roll claims for several persons were made from different sources and, boosted by the duplicate lists, these recipients can appear in as many as three or even four places. A few of these men undoubtedly received two medals; some certainly returned one of them, others most likely did not. It was not uncommon for officers who had served on the Staff to be included among the regimental returns as well as being shown as 'Staff'.

The medals of both officers and men had a habit of going astray before reaching the claimants. A note against one man admits his award had been mislaid in the War Office and these occurrences were no doubt responsible for the secondary personal applications which appear.

Holes in many pages show that at one time they were strung together until eventually, shortly before the turn of the century, all the reports were gathered up and bound

*It is not generally realised that very many of the dated clasps of the SA 1877–9 medal do not truly reflect campaign service. For example, the 2/24th only reached the Cape in 1878 and yet were given the clasp 1877–8–9.

together but regrettably a number of documents had already gone astray. GO 690 announced that no claims submitted after December 1st 1858 would be entertained, but this was not observed for they were still being accepted more than 50 years later. However, post-1861 applications were not recorded, apart from a few casual insertions and a number of isolated names which can be traced in the Mint records.

The most serious losses of all are the original returns for ORs of the 45th Regiment, Royal Artillery and Royal Sappers and Miners, for the only men from these regiments to be found on the Roll are later claimants. These documents have not been removed from the Roll after binding as each sheet (i.e. every other page) is number stamped. That the surviving documents were in a sorry condition long before being bound together can be seen by the manner the stamp has been used to avoid tears in the paper.

A naval officer and some marines who engaged in 'special service' under Sir Peregrine Maitland during the 2nd campaign are also listed in WO/100/17 but the main body of Royal Navy and Royal Marine recipients are listed separately in ADM/171/18.

The Roll for the Royal Navy and Royal Marines: Ref ADM/171/18

This slim volume is simplicity itself by comparison with the Army Roll. The recipients came from only five vessels, 'Castor', 'Dee', 'Hermes', 'Rhadamanthus' and 'Styx' and the complement of each ship is entered *en bloc*. Unfortunately, the medals do not bear the name of the vessel and as officers and men are entered without regard to rank or initial, confirmation requires a steady plodding through the Roll.

As submissions were entirely in respect of the 1850–3 war there are no campaign columns to cause complications. The few additions to the original returns were simply tacked on to the appropriate ship's list and no duplicate Rolls survive to confuse us; although a number of men were returned as part of the complement of more than one vessel. Often these double entries were spotted by War Office clerks and a note made alongside the name. Sometimes they escaped detection and no doubt the lucky men collected two medals.

Oddly, nine soldiers from the 45th and 60th regiments who were brought home by 'Castor' in January 1853, 'stowed aboard' the Navy Roll. All were crossed through before the medals came to be distributed but some of the men appear on the Army Roll. Indeed it seems that those delegated the responsibility of compiling the Navy lists had no very clear instructions of what they were about. No one could have explained that only survivors were eligible, for ships' musters disclose that among the returns are seamen who died long before the end of the 3rd war. More extraordinary still, a medal currently in a private collection was issued in the name of a Clerk dying in 1848! Deceased sailors are shown on the Roll with 'DD' against them which means 'Discharged Dead'. Deserters are indicated by the letter 'R' – for 'Run'.

The colourful appellations of the Kroomen make light reading; would you believe 'Prince of Wales'? One might be excused in thinking this was a Victorian joke but the musters show that the gentleman tired of stoking and jumped ship at Shanghai. His medal was returned and re-issued so there is no point in looking out for the piece of a lifetime! For 'odd man' collectors there is the medal to Lt Johann Klocker of the Norwegian Navy who served on 'Castor' and was given a re-named medal in 1862.

Explanatory Notes

A few matters, some already touched upon, and the method of presentation of these revised rolls, require some clarification.

Qualification
It may be noticed that whereas the period of qualification for the 3rd war is tied down precisely to the day, the others are simply stated as 1834–5 and 1846–7. From this it should not be assumed that each of these campaigns lasted for the full two years. The 1st war flared on December 22nd 1834 and a peace treaty was signed on September 17th 1835. The incident which sparked the 'War of the Axe' occurred on March 16th 1846 and the last of the rebellious chiefs had surrendered by December 1847, but when approval was given to accept claims for the earlier conflicts the general dates, by which for ease they had always been referred to in the official correspondence, were slipped into the already drafted wording for GO 634. Consequently failure by the War Office to check on the exact dates unintentionally opened the award, but the number of men to have benefited was negligible.

Civilian Recipients
The decision to permit persons other than those in the regular forces to receive the medal does not seem to have been taken at the very highest levels. Clerks, storekeepers and the like were all part of the Commissariat, but men who served with local forces, civilian doctors and clergymen were accepted as admissible when 'specially recommended by competent authority' and are shown on WO/100/17 to have come 'within the rules acted upon by the late Board of General Officers'. From the Roll it can be seen that claims were supported by Sir Harry Smith, Sir Josiah Cloete, Sir Peregrine Maitland, Sir Charles Yorke and Sir James Jackson. After the Board of Officers was dissolved towards the end of 1855, the secretary Henry Elliot carried on alone dealing with claims until 1858 when they were considered by the Adjutant General or his deputies.

In fact, very few men appear on the Roll as specially recommended and although undoubtedly some who fall in this category received a medal and are not recorded on the Roll, the vast majority of colonists who turned out to defend the frontier had no award to show for their exertions.

Spelling of names
To have slavishly followed the spelling used on the Official Rolls would not always have smoothed the path of collectors and only perpetuated much misinformation. There is evidence that the name on a medal is as likely to conform with the spelling in the regimental musters as with the Roll when the sources conflict. Lt Fairtlough (12th) is on the Roll as Fairlough and the regiment tell me his medal shows Fairclough. The running script handwriting inevitably invites various interpretations. Adonis is not a common surname; if you write it down yourself and see how easily it can be read as Adams you won't be surprised that transcribers misconstrued such lists. Less easy to understand is how Pte Keneybrough, 60th Regiment, came to be shown as Frennyborough but as a note on the Roll tells that a cancelled medal was renamed Keneyborough no difficulty is likely to face any collector trying to trace him. Then again, Pte Rademeyer (CMR) would not have been pleased to be recorded by me as Raddymere, however, his medal was impressed and the numerous phonetical errors may indicate that the names were dictated to the War Office copyists. I feel that by making corrections and giving people their proper, or most likely proper names justice has at last been done to these men who fought and bled in little remembered colonial wars. Where changes have been made footnotes are provided. Since ships' musters were not rewritten every three months, as were the Army paylists, the opportunity for errors was considerably reduced and differences between the Navy Roll and musters are few.

Rank
This has posed a special problem for the Army Roll is inconsistent. All would have been well had every applicant properly answered question four on the official form but as Other Ranks still serving were submitted regimentally the individual soldiers would not even have seen a form. Consequently, their medals were impressed with the rank enjoyed at the time their names were forwarded to the Board of Officers late in 1854 or during 1855 and not, as must have been intended, with the rank held at the close of the campaign. However, as it is impossible to determine the precise dates on which each regiment compiled its returns the musters cannot be quoted incontestably. Not that this would have helped us where ORs who had already been discharged were applying independently or through Pensions Officers. The medals of such men may well be found bearing campaign rank as they are more likely to have completed a form.

The free use of ditto marks, with the numerous alterations and additions made at the time and later, leaves a feeling that the Army Roll was not always intended to mean what it says, but where officers are concerned we can feel more confident. Both current and campaign ranks are mentioned on the Roll and their medals can be expected to display the latter.

I am also aware of medals which I am informed show rank differing from the Army Roll and not supported by the musters of 1854–5. I have not inspected them personally but suspect these medals will be found to have been altered privately to conform with later promotion.

I view of all these factors I have chosen to show Army ranks as they appear to read on the Roll, with but one or two exceptions, about which footnotes are appended. The Roll for the Navy states all ranks very clearly and it seems that where a seaman or marine was demoted his highest rate is usually if not invariably given on the medal.

Regiments
Medals to both officers and men still serving in the Army in 1855 designated the recipient's current regiment, notwithstanding that his entire campaign service may have been with another regiment; *except* where that current regiment was not one of those employed in the frontier wars and then the campaigning regiment is given. It is likely that only four medals, three to the 98th and one to the 62nd display non-campaigning regiments.

Regiments incompletely returned
The loss of the lists submitted by the 45th Regiment, RA and RS&M cannot be remedied but my collaborator, John Bristow, whose idea it was, has reconstructed possible rolls for those regiments from the musters. Even after deleting as many as could be traced of those who died or deserted before the medal was authorised there are still on these lists a considerable number of men who did not claim the medal and, of course, we can never know who they were. Only a very brave man would claim that in researching musters which stretch over some 20 years every eligible man has been detected, but John and I are confident that any who have been overlooked are few and far between. It has not been

practicable to trace the entire career of every individual and rank may be found to differ from that shown on a medal.

Another useful contribution by John has been the identification of the companies in which officers and men of the RA and RE/S&M served, these details not being mentioned in WO/100/17.

Regimental Numbers
The Army Roll, apart from some of the later submissions makes no mention of regimental numbers. To have recorded them all when consulting the musters would have involved much labour for little gain except when confronted with men of the same or similar names. I have sought to identify such soldiers and, to aid any future concentrated research into individual careers, recorded their numbers heedless of whether namesakes gained the medal.

Cancelled medals; deserters and deceased soldiers and seamen
The medals to men who deserted after their names had been submitted were returned and used as replacements or re-named for late applicants.

The next of kin received the medals of seamen and marines who died. As already explained elsewhere some of these men had died years before and should not have been returned by the Navy. No regular course followed the death of a soldier. Some regiments passed the medals to next of kin but others took the narrow view that the award was for survivors only and returned them to the War Office who seem to have been equally happy to send a medal to a soldier's family or have it promptly re-named for someone else. As far as these Rolls are concerned, those who died are shown unless it is certain their medals were re-named. Deserters have not been listed nor a few men whose medals were used as replacements upon their failure to collect the award.

Naming
All medals to the earlier applicants were impressed exactly as the MGS awards. Any other style indicates a later issue or a re-named medal. I have examined an officially re-named medal issued in 1857 which was engraved in upright serifed capitals and it may be that all officially re-named medals were so named. Notations on the Roll show the engraving was carried out by 'H. & R.' which stands for the firm of Hunt & Roskell. A medal to a seaman issued in 1885 is named as the Zulu War medal and, as with all medals of all periods, any very late issue can expect to be named in the style current at that time. A medal to a man in the 27th was issued as late as 1914.

Symbols and Notations
(P) after a name indicates the medal is known to be in a private collection.
(M) shows the medal to be in a museum other than the appropriate regimental museum whose own medals are marked (R).
This information has been derived from collectors, the regiments, dealers' lists and other publications but while members of the Orders and Medals Research Society have usually been scrupulous in describing name, rank, method of naming and whether any alterations have been made, others have been less precise. The information supplied to me has sometimes been presented in a form which has raised questions to which answers could not be obtained without unjustifiable expense of time and money and therefore a (P), (M) or (R) should not be taken as confirmation that the medal is an original issue, is correctly named, and has not been tampered with in any way.
(MRM) means that the medal is listed under WO/100/106–8 as one of those returned to the Mint from the War Office, the regiments and elsewhere. One such medal was 'found by a policeman in the street' and since others were clearly from the personal effects of deceased soldiers we cannot be wholly confident none were reclaimed by the recipient or next of kin and on these grounds I have not deleted them from these rolls.
'See Godlonton', or similar, draws attention to the fact that a recipient is mentioned by the author of that name. The works concerned are listed elsewhere. No such notation has been made against high ranking officers whose names appear freely in most books on the wars.
A symbol thus, △, indicates a campaign qualification as per WO/100/17 and substantiated by the musters. A symbol thus, ○, confirms a campaign which the Roll fails to credit. The total absence of symbol △ against any man establishes that he does NOT APPEAR ON WO/100/17. Any exceptions are notated.

Bibliography

Little purpose would be served by listing all the material I have examined to compile the chronology and provide the information in the notes attached to each regiment. At best a comprehensive bibliography would interest only a few and at worst convey the impression of attempting to swathe this work with a wrapping of academic quality. Nevertheless, besides mentioning those books referred to by author in the 'Notes' I would draw attention to A. J. Smithers' 'The Kaffir Wars 1779–1877' (1973) as an easily available 'plain man's' history of the wars, and some other worthwhile reading.

For detail one must turn to primary sources, but to unravel the complexities of the frontier campaigns from the bewildering number of small actions, shifting allegiances of native chiefs, changes in territorial authority and political manœuvring requires some concentration. 'The Irruption of the Kaffir Hordes' by R. Godlonton (1836) and 'Narrative of the Kaffir War' by Godlonton and E. Irving (1851) have both been re-published by C. Struik (Johannesburg). 'The War of the Axe; the Journal of the Rev J. W. Appleyard' (1971) contains some useful 'notes'.

Memoirs are few and none better than 'Reminiscences of the Last Kaffir War' by James McKay of the 74th Regt (1871). His accuracy with names and events unconnected with his regiment is remarkable. It too has been re-published by Struik. Other accounts are 'Campaigning in Kaffirland' by Capt W. R. King, 74th (1853), 'Records of Service and Campaigning in Many Lands' by Surg Wm. Munro, 91st, 'Camp Life and Sport in South Africa' (1878) and 'Pen and Pencil Reminiscences of a Campaign in South Africa' (1861) both by Capt T. J. Lucas, CMR; and 'Sport and War, or Recollections of Fighting and Hunting in South Africa 1835–1867' by Maj Gen John Bissett, CMR. Extracts from the latter are to be found in Duncan Moodie's 'The History of the Battles and Adventures of the British, Boers and Zulus in South Africa' (1888); re-printed by Frank Cass (London) in 1968.

Treatment of the campaigns in regimental histories varies enormously. With King and McKay to draw upon Col L. B. Oatts' 'Proud Heritage – the 74th Highlanders' (1959) is excellent and Lt G. L. Goff's 'History of the 91st' (1891) gives ample coverage to the wars. Col J. Davis, 'History of the 2nd Queen's Royal Regt . . .' is also good in this respect

but unreliable where individual names are concerned. Royal Artillery historians scarcely give a glance to gunners in the Cape and to find out what they were about one must search out a modest book by James A. Browne, 'England's Artillerymen' (1865). Also consulted were: 'History of the Royal Sappers and Miners and the Royal Engineers' by T. W. J. Connolly (1857); '7th Dragoon Guards, the Story of the Regiment' by P. S. Thompson (1913); 'The History of the 12th Lancers' by Capt P. F. Stewart (1950); 'The Royal Warwickshire Regiment' by C. L. Kingsford (1921); 'History of the 12th (Suffolk) Regt' by Lt Col E. A. A. Webb (1914); 'The Royal Inniskilling Fusiliers' (1934); 'Historical Record of the Forty-Third Regt' by Sir Richard G. A. Levinge (1868); 'History of the 1st and 2nd Battalions The Sherwood Foresters' by Col H. C. Wylly (1929); 'The Annals of the King's Royal Rifle Corps' by Lt Col Lewis Butler (1926); 'Seaforth Highlanders' by Col John Sym (1962); 'A Short History of the Black Watch' (1908); 'The Royal Highlanders . . . Medal Roll' (1911); 'The Life of a Regiment; the History of the Gordon Highlanders' by Lt Col C. Greenhill Gardyne (1903); 'Records of the 90th Regiment' by A. M. Delavoye (1880); 'History of the Rifle Brigade' by Sir Wm Cope (1877).

Apart from the references listed with each regiment other documents contained in the PRO which have proved useful to me are: WO/1/451; WO/3/116-323-325-326-327; WO/6/78-111-112-113; WO/100/106-108.

Mint Records which may be of interest to the researcher are: 21/5, 21/6.

A chronology of military events in Eastern South Africa between 1834 and 1853

DECEMBER 1834
On the 2nd a patrol of the CMR attacked and driven off when attempting to recover stolen horses from Chief Eno.

Two days later, Col Somerset returns with a stronger force to demand compensation and the withdrawal of the Kaffirs to beyond the Keiskamma River.

During the second week a party of CMR under Lt Sutton (75th) clashes with Kaffirs near Fort Beaufort.

Soon afterwards marauding bands descend on settlements and begin to slaughter livestock across the district of Albany.

The depredations grow into widespread murder and pillage. Scattered settlers fall back on Grahamstown or the nearest forts. The garrison of Fort Willshire withdraws to Fort Beaufort and other outposts are abandoned.

JANUARY 1835
After a ride of 600 miles in six days Col Harry Smith arrived at Grahamstown from Cape Town. On the 6th he assumes command, declares martial law and takes control of the confused situation.

A force of 400 men under Major Cox (75th) leaves Grahamstown on the 9th for Eno's Kraal which is destroyed on the 12th. From Fort Beaufort, another column under Major Burney (CMR) joins Cox and attacks are made on the Kraals of Chiefs Tyali and Macomo.

The Governor, Sir Benjamin D'Urban, arrives at Grahamstown on the 20th with an escort of the 72nd, the Highlanders being hurried to the frontier from Cape Town.

FEBRUARY
Smith divides his army into three divisions and with Col Henry Somerset and Col Richard England commanding the flanking columns drives the enemy from the woods and bush of the Great Fish River.

On the 19th, a detachment of CMR and some Kat River Burghers successfully defend their post on the Kat River against an overwhelming horde of Kaffirs.

MARCH
Operations are carried out to clear the fastnesses between the Fish River and the Keiskamma; largely in the neighbourhood of Fort Willshire.

APRIL
With the 75th and some Burgher and Hottentot forces left to defend a line from Winterberg and extending past Forts Beaufort and Willshire to the sea, four divisions are formed by the C-inC Sir Benjamin D'Urban and his Chief of Staff Col Smith. Div 1 is commanded by Col Peddie, Div 2 (Cavalry) by Col Somerset, Div 3 by Major Cox and Div 4 (Cavalry) by Commandant Van Wyk. Singly and in concert they carry out a series of sweeping operations into the foothills of the Amatola Mountains and along the banks of the Gonubi and Buffalo Rivers.

While the 3rd and 4th Divisions continue to harass the enemy the 1st and 2nd Divisions cross the Kei on the 15th to recover stolen property from the country of Chief Hintza.

Following failure of negotiations, war is declared on Hintza and towards the end of the month a cavalry patrol under Col Smith strikes at Hintza's Kraal. Subsequent operations result in the Chief coming into Smith's camp as hostage. Fingo tribesmen, long oppressed by the Kaffirs, ask to be taken under British protection.

MAY
To provide a buffer for the colony D'Urban annexes the territory to the right bank of the river Kei and designates the area Queen Adelaide Province. but this is renounced the following year by Lord Glenelg, one of the most disastrous incompetents to hold Government office.

On the 13th, Hintza is killed whilst trying to escape.

Chief Kreli enters into a treaty on the 24th to end hostilities but Tyali, Macomo and others westward of the Kei fight on.

JUNE
An officer and 30 Provisionals are over-run and killed while patrolling near the Keiskamma River.

JULY
Extensive operations carried out from the mouth of the Kei to Kahoon.

AUGUST
After relentless pursuit by troops under Cox in the Tyumie, Amatola and Keiskamma mountains a meeting is arranged near Fort Cox between Major Warden and dissident chiefs which results in a suspension of hostilities.

SEPTEMBER
Col Smith meets Macomo, Tyali, Eno and others at Fort Willshire on the 8th.

A peace treaty finally ratified on the 17th but on this same day a party of Kaffirs attack herdsmen within 10 miles of Grahamstown and carry off 200 cattle and isolated depredations continue.

MAY 1842
Following trouble between the Boers and natives, Capt Smith (27th) with a force of 263 officers and men and accompanied by some civilians, women and children, makes the second British military occupation of Natal.

Capt Smith defeated by the Boers at Congella on the 23rd.

From May 31st to June 26th the British force is besieged in camp under fire until relieved by detachments of the 25th and 27th Regiments.

APRIL 30TH 1845
The Battle of Zwoortkopjes between British troops and Boers.

MARCH 1846
Some 40 warriors of Chief Tola overpower the escort and release a Kaffir being taken to Grahamstown for trial after stealing an axe at Fort Beaufort. A Hottentot prisoner to whom the Kaffir was manacled is killed.

War formally declared on the 31st following the failure of Chiefs Sandili and Tola to return the prisoner or to surrender the murderers.

APRIL
Two divisions enter Kaffirland under Col Henry Somerset and Col Robert Richardson. They strike at Sandili's Kraal in the Amatolas. The troops find themselves in difficulties against large numbers of the enemy. 61 wagons in a train of 125 are destroyed across Block Drift.

MAY
Elated by their success, savages pour into the eastern district of the colony cutting communication between the forts and outposts along the frontier.

Train of over 40 wagons destroyed by rebels whilst trying to supply Fort Peddie from Trompetters Drift on the Fish River.

JUNE
On the 8th, warriors massed by Chiefs Seyolo and Umhala to attack Trompetters Post are caught in open country by a force under Somerset out of Fort Peddie and suffer severely in what becomes known as the Battle of Guanga.

JULY/AUGUST
Two Divisions are organised. The Right, under Somerset, moves against Chief Pato and the enemy flee before him to the Kei.

Col Hare, commanding the Left Division, moves from Block Drift to the Amatolas to try to intercept Kaffirs being driven by Burgher forces under Sir Andries Stockenstroom, but the enveloping movement fails.

AUGUST
On the 14th a flying column in two divisions under Stockenstroom and Lt Col Johnstone (90th) is organised to punish Chief Kreli who surrenders without fighting and enters into valueless agreements.

NOVEMBER
The feeling that they are bearing more than a fair share of the work leads to resentment by the Burgher forces and their withdrawal from the field, but regular troops are now arriving in increasing numbers and the war seems to be over.

Owing to ill health, Hare resigns his appointment as Lt Governor of the Eastern Division and dies at sea on the way home to England.

JANUARY 1847
Sir Peregrine Maitland is superseded as Governor by Sir Henry Pottinger. Sir George Berkely becomes a separate C-in-C.

MAY
Kaffirs attack supply wagons on the Goolah Heights.

JUNE
Stolen livestock is traced to Sandili's Kraal. A force sent to arrest him is driven off. New and restored posts had been set up in previous months and now forward depots were established in the Amatolas.

JULY/OCTOBER
Constant patrolling reduces the Kaffirs to near starvation.
Macomo surrenders in September and Sandili in October. The axe thief who precipitated the war is also captured.

NOVEMBER/DECEMBER
Similar pressure is now exerted on Chief Pato and he submits on December 19th to the new Governor Sir Harry Smith who has replaced Pottinger; but not before a party of six officers are massacred. Smith declares the country between the Keiskamma and the Kei to be under the Sovereignty of the Queen and named British Kaffraria.

AUGUST 29TH 1848
Battle of Boemplaats between British troops and Boers.

OCTOBER 1850
Following increasingly warlike attitudes being adopted by the Kaffirs Sir Harry Smith travels to the frontier and summons a meeting with the Chiefs. Sandili refuses to attend.

NOVEMBER
Smith deposes Sandili and goes back to Cape Town satisfied that he has quietened matters.

DECEMBER
Depredations increase: Smith returns to the frontier and Col MacKinnon leads a column to arrest Sandili. On the 24th the force is attacked in Boomah Pass and thus begins the 3rd (or 8th) and greatest Kaffir War. over 40 settlers are murdered; Smith is besieged in Fort Cox and after Somerset has made two unsuccessful attempts at relief the Governor breaks out with an escort of 250 CMR. Meanwhile, Col. Mansergh (6th) makes a very gallant defence of Fort White.

JANUARY 1851
The rebel Chief Hermanus killed whilst attacking Fort Beaufort on the 7th.

FEBRUARY
Defection of the Hottentots of Kat River seriously spreads the rebellion even though Somerset captures their stronghold of Fort Armstrong on the 23rd.

MARCH
Operations are still more hampered when over 300 Hottentot Provisionals attached to the CMR desert in a body. Others in the regiment are disarmed.

With a force mainly composed of the 73rd Regiment Sir Harry Smith strikes at the Kaffirs at the Keiskamma on the 19th and then returns to King William's Town on the 25th after scouring the Tab-Indoba Range.

APRIL
A column under MacKinnon marches through the Poorts of the Buffalo and partly penetrates the Amatolas.

MAY
Major Eardly-Wilmot leads a thousand-strong expedition to the base of the Eastern Amatolas.

JUNE
Three converging columns thrust into the Amatolas, seizing cattle and destroying crops as they go.

JULY
Allowing the enemy no respite, Somerset marches into the Waterkloof.

SEPTEMBER
Col Fordyce leads a small force into the Kroome range and clashed with Macomo.

OCTOBER
A larger expedition under Somerset again strikes into the Waterkloof and drives Macomo from his stronghold.

NOVEMBER/DECEMBER
An expedition into the Upper Kei spends weeks in the field in severe weather; driving through Kreli's country heavy casualties are inflicted on the Kaffirs and some 30,000 cattle are captured. Crops are destroyed and the rebels greatly disheartened.

JANUARY 1852
By now the impatient British Government, not appreciating the difficulties of combating an elusive enemy in mountainous, wooded terrain, send a dispatch recalling Sir Harry Smith.

FEBRUARY 25th
The troopship 'Birkenhead' sinks with heavy loss of life.

MARCH
Before relinquishing his command to Sir Geo. Cathcart, Sir Harry Smith accompanies Eyre on a sweep through the re-occupied Waterkloof Mountains. After some hard fighting the back of the resistance is broken and further columns under Eyre and Michel penetrate to the heart of the Amatolas, driving Chief Tyalie before them.

APRIL
Cathcart takes charge and continues the strategy followed by Smith.

JULY/AUGUST
Kaffirs who had been creeping back into their mountain hideouts are harassed by further columns.

SEPTEMBER/OCTOBER
With the Hottentot bands crushed a final mopping up operation clears the Waterkloof and ends all serious resistance.

NOVEMBER/DECEMBER
Mosesh and his Basutos being considered a threat, Cathcart mounts an expedition across the Orange River. But the Basuto horsemen are a different quality of enemy to the rebels in Kaffraria and the battle of Berea comes close to disaster for the outnumbered British force. However, Mosesh promises no further trouble and Cathcart thankfully withdraws.

MARCH 1853
The dissident Kaffir chiefs accept peace terms dictated by Cathcart.

Royal Navy and Royal Marines

Resolved though they were that men of the Royal Navy and Royal Marines should receive the medal for their services during the campaign of 1850-3, the Admiralty lost sight of the fact that a number of seamen and marines were no less deserving of the award for the 2nd war. Some had come within the stricture that recipients should have 'served in the field' and neither their Lordships nor the obstructive War Department can have realised that a handful of officers and men of the Royal Marines had already been accepted without demur by the Board of Officers. With a Lieutenant RN they are shown in the Army Roll (WO/100/17) as having been 'on special service under Sir Peregrine Maitland' during 1846. This was a force which included a detachment of marines from HMS 'President' specially charged to examine the coast east of the Fish River for a new landing place. It was an arduous expedition which penetrated the Buffalo and selected the mouth of that river as a convenient site before falling back on Waterloo Bay in September 1846.

The need to shorten overland routes and improve sources of supply had caused the Navy to establish a landing place at the mouth of the Fish River in June. At that time, 50 marines and a party of sailors had worked under Lt Owen, RE, to construct a boat bridge across the river and throw up a protective earthwork. Garrisoned by marines and seamen and named Fort Dacres after the Admiral commanding the Station, the works were also used as a commissariat store, but the landing lost favour to a small bay a mile to the east after the schooner 'Waterloo' successfully unloaded a cargo on its beaches.

During the campaign of 1850-3, Her Majesty's Ships 'Castor', 'Dee', 'Hermes', 'Rhadamanthus' and 'Styx' were all heavily employed in conveying troops, ammunition and stores from one side of the Cape Colony to the other, and the crews were exposed to great danger in landing soldiers, horses and equipment through the heavy surf. Many men lost their lives by drowning and a letter from Chatham Yard to the First Secretary of the Admiralty, Ralph Osborne, MP (15.12.1854) states that 'Hermes' lost one-sixth of her boat crews engaged in ferrying ashore, but this claim is difficult to reconcile with the number of men shown to be drowned on the ship's musters.

The entire complement of marines on 'Hermes', along with five sailors under a Lieutenant, were put ashore at the mouth of the Buffalo River and used to keep open communications between the Army and the Squadron. It is likely that 'Castor' also provided marines for this purpose for it was from her that the garrison at the base on the Buffalo was drawn. Now named East London, it was fortified and used for commissariat stores as had Fort Dacres. Some 25 marines from 'Styx' are known to have served in land operations, but the 'Dee' did not contribute any of her crew to the field; nor, it would seem, did 'Rhadamanthus'. It was the latter vessel which carried survivors from the ill-fated 'Birkenhead' to Cape Town.

'Hermes' was actively engaged from the outset of the 3rd war and had carried Sir Harry Smith to the frontier in his attempt to avert the uprising of December 1850. It was on 'Styx' that the Kaffir Chief Seyolo was taken as a prisoner to Cape Town towards the end of November 1852.

I would have preferred to show ranks and rates in order of seniority as in the regimental rolls, but few could correctly place them and I am persuaded it is more convenient to list Navy and Marine recipients alphabetically throughout.

The involved and changing systems of rank and rate in the Royal Navy during the 19th century defy clear and simple explanation. Capt K. J. Douglas-Morris wrote on the subject in 'The Army of India Roll' (published by John Hayward in 1975) and has generously provided me with the information to be found later in this work. The lists complement those in the work on the Army of India medal and show the increasing sophistication of the Navy. I believe a complete list of rates for the Crimean period in order of seniority has not previously been published.

ROYAL NAVY

Rank/Rate	Name	Ship	Note
AB	George Adams	Castor	1)
Caulker	John Adams	Styx	
Ordinary 2nd Cl	John Aherne	Dee	
Addl 2nd Master	Christopher Albert	Castor	
AB	Robert Allen	Castor	
AB	James Allison	Castor	
AB	Richard Andrews	Hermes	
Ldg Stoker	Thomas Andrews	Styx	
AB	William Andrews	Castor	(P)
Midshipman	A. G. Annesley	Castor & Styx	
Petty Officer 2nd Cl	Edward Appleton	Castor	
Acting Mate	William Arthur	Styx	
Gunner's Mate	William Ary	Dee	
Boy 1st Class	William Ashbee	Rhadamanthus	
Quartermaster	Charles Ashton	Dee	
Blacksmith	John Atkins	Castor	
AB	William Atkins	Castor	(P) 2)
Midshipman	Henry Baillie	Castor	(P)
Captain's Steward	James Baillie	Hermes	
Asst Engineer 1st Cl	Edward W. Baker	Rhadamanthus	
AB	George Baker	Hermes	
AB	Samuel Baker	Castor	
AB	William Baker	Castor	
Addl Lieut	Henry P. Bance	Castor	
Painter	William Banfield	Castor	
AB	James Barrett	Castor	
Capt Mizzen Top	George Baster	Castor	
Mate	Richard S. Bateman	Castor	
Ordinary 2nd Cl	George P. Bates	Castor	
AB	John Baxter	Styx	
Asst Surgeon	Robert W. Beaumont	Castor	
Gunner's Mate	George Beadle	Hermes	
AB	Charles Beer	Castor	
Master Commanding	John Belam	Rhadamanthus	
Boy 2nd Class	John G. Bell	Styx	
Stoker	John Bellown	Styx	
AB	Charles Belton	Dee	
Boy 1st Class	Thomas Bennett	Castor	
AB	William Bennett	Castor	
Ordinary 2nd Cl	Thomas Bentley	Castor	
Midshipman	Henry Berkeley	Castor	
AB	George Berry	Dee	
AB	Henry Berry	Castor	

ROYAL NAVY

Rank	Name	Ship	
Boatswain's Mate	William Berry	Dee	
Master's Asst	William C. Bicknell	Styx	
Asst Engineer 2nd Class	James W. Bills	Rhadamanthus	
Boy 1st Class	William Binmore	Styx	
Ordinary 2nd Cl	James Bisher	Castor	
Carpenter's Mate	Alexander Black	Castor	
AB	Thomas Blanchard	Styx	3)
Ldg Stoker	Henry Bloice	Rhadamanthus	
Boy 2nd Class	John Bockham	Castor	
AB	George Boden	Castor	
Stoker	William Bolitho	Styx	
Boy 1st Class	Charles Bolton	Castor	
AB	Robert Boorman	Styx	
AB	Edward Bouchard	Castor	
Capt of Hold	Charles Boughton	Castor	
Boy 1st Class	Henry Bowen	Castor	
Boy 1st Class	John Bowyer	Styx	
AB	James Boyd	Castor	
Midshipman	David Boyle	Castor	
Gunner 3rd Class	Samuel Boyle	Castor	
Boy 2nd Class	George Bray	Castor	
AB	Henry Brealey	Castor	
Capt of Mast	Thomas Brenchley	Castor	
Midshipman	Harry W. Brent	Castor	
Acting Gunner	Michael Bresnahan	Castor	
Boy 2nd Class	James Brewer	Hermes	
AB	Stephen Brient	Castor	
Ordinary	George Brigden	Castor	
Midshipman	Julius D. Brockman	Hermes	4)
Boy 1st Class	John Brown	Castor	
Krooman	John Brown	Rhadamanthus	
Capt of Forecastle	William Brown	Castor	
Master's Asst	Edward P. G. Browne	Rhadamanthus	(P)
Boy 1st Class	John Browning	Castor	
AB	George Buckley	Styx	
Petty Officer 2nd Class	Charles Buckman	Castor	
Ordinary	Joseph Budd	Castor	
Ordinary	George Bugden	Castor	
Asst Engineering 2nd Class	Alexander Buist	Styx	
AB	Fraser Bunyan	Castor	
Stoker	Henry Burgess	Hermes	
AB	Arthur Burke	Hermes	
Ordinary	Hugh Burke	Castor	
Stoker	John Burke	Dee	
AB	Paul Burke	Styx	
Ldg Stoker	Charles Burley	Dee	
Capt Mizzen Top	Thomas Burns	Castor	
Ordinary	William Burt	Castor	
Lieut	Robert H. Burton	Hermes	
Midshipman	Charles P. Bushe	Castor	5)
Ordinary	Thomas Butler	Castor	
Landsman	William Buxey	Castor	
Ropemaker	John Cableton	Castor	
Ordinary	John Caley	Castor	
Ordinary	James Callacott	Castor	
AB	James Callaghan	Castor	
AB	William Callar	Styx	
Stoker	Edward Caligan	Rhadamanthus	
Midshipman	William A. Cambier	Castor	
Lieutenant	Thomas M. Campbell	Castor	
AB	James Campin	Castor	
Ordinary 2nd Cl	John Carter	Dee	
AB	Patrick Cassidy	Castor	
AB	James Castles	Castor	
Boy 1st Class	Henry Cavill	Rhadamanthus	
Stoker	Henry Cawston	Hermes	
AB	William Chalker	Castor	
Act Paymaster/ Purser	Edward R. Chamberlain	Castor	
Surgeon	Robert J. B. Chambers	Castor	
Stoker	William Champion	Dee	(P)
Caulker	Henry Chappell	Castor	
Stoker	William Chapman	Hermes	6)
Stoker	William Chard	Styx	
Ship's Corporal	John Charters	Styx	
AB	Joseph Cheeseman	Castor	(P)
Ordinary 2nd Cl	Edward Chevell	Castor	
Gunroom Cook	Edward Chidwick	Hermes	
Ordinary 2nd Cl	Charles Childs	Castor	
Ordinary	William Claringbould	Castor	
Sailmaker's Crew	Daniel Clark	Castor	7)
Stoker	William H. Clark	Rhadamanthus	
Ordinary	Charles Clarke	Hermes	
Captain's Steward	Daniel Clarke	Hermes	
Ordinary	Frederick H. Clarke	Castor	
Carpenter's Crew	George Clarke	Castor	
Ordinary	Henry J. Clarke	Castor	
Boy 1st Class	James Clarke	Dee	
Boy 1st Class	Thomas Clarke	Castor	
Paymaster	Walter Clatworthy	Castor	
AB	Thomas Clemence	Castor	8)
Ordinary	Edwin G. Clements	Castor	
Ordinary	George Clilverd	Castor	
Stoker	William Cockrane	Rhadamanthus	
Capt of Fore Top	John Cockrell	Castor	
Gunner 3rd Class	John Coghlan	Styx	
Carpenter's Crew	John Cole	Castor	
Boatswain's Mate	Joseph Coleman	Hermes	
Ordinary 2nd Cl	Thomas Collett	Rhadamanthus	
Ordinary 2nd Cl	William C. Collier	Castor	
AB	Samuel Collines	Castor	
Midshipman	George M. Comber	Castor	
Ship's Corporal	Daniel Coney	Castor & Styx	
Boy 1st Class	Michael Connor	Castor	
Blacksmith	Henry Cook	Hermes	
Stoker	Richard Cook	Hermes	
Capt of Forecastle	William Cook	Castor	(P)
Midshipman	John R. Cooper	Castor	
Cadet	Chidley Coote	Castor & Hermes	
AB	William Cornish	Castor	(P) 9)
Capt of Mast	Barford Corton	Castor	
Captain's Steward	George Cossar	Hermes	
Boy 2nd Class	William Costen	Styx	
Stoker	John Couch	Styx	
AB	Michael County	Castor	10)
Painter	Thomas Cousins	Styx	
Clerk	John K. Cowley	Castor	
AB	Richard Cox	Castor	
Boy 1st Class	Stephen Cox	Castor	
Capt of Mast	Peter Coxell	Castor	
Krooman	Martin Cozet	Rhadamanthus	
AB	John Craigie	Castor	
Ordinary	James Crane	Castor	
Ordinary	Peter Crane	Castor	
Leading Stoker	James Crapper	Styx	
Ordinary	Charles Crebbin	Castor	
Boy 2nd Class	Robert Creber	Styx	
Ordinary 2nd Cl	Thomas Creber	Castor	
Asst Surgeon	Henry Crocker	Dee	
Ordinary	William Crockford	Castor	
Ordinary 2nd Cl	William Croft	Castor	
AB	John Cross	Styx	
AB	Samuel Cross	Styx	

South Africa 1853 Medal 21

ROYAL NAVY

Rank	Name	Ship	Note
Lieut in Command	William Crowder	Dee	
Acting Carpenter 3rd Class	William Crowhurst	Castor	
Carpenter's Mate	Robinson Crusoe	Dee	
Boatswain's Mate	Stephen Cuer	Styx	
Capt of Mast	Alexander Cumyns	Castor	
AB	John Cunningham	Styx	
AB	William Cunningham	Castor	(P)
Ordinary 2nd Cl	Thomas Curber	Castor	
AB	John Curtis	Dee	
AB	William Daley	Castor	
Leading Stoker	Daniel Dare	Styx	
AB	Joseph Davenport	Hermes	11)
AB	James Davey	Castor	
Sailmaker's Crew	John Davidson	Hermes	
Paymaster and Purser's Steward	William Davidson	Styx	
Boy 1st Class	Thomas Davis	Castor	
Cooper	William Davis	Hermes	
AB	William Davis	Castor	(M)
Ship's Corporal	Robert Dawes	Castor	
Ordinary	Dublin Dawson	Rhadamanthus	
Boy 2nd Class	William Deal	Castor	
Caulker's Mate	John Deddan	Dee	12)
Ordinary	John Dellar	Castor	
AB	Robert Denney	Dee	
Petty Officer 2nd Class	Robert Denny	Castor	
Carpenter's Mate	David Dick	Castor	
Midshipman	John W. Dimond	Hermes	
Boy 1st Class	Joseph Dixon	Castor	
Carpenter's Crew	Joseph Dixon	Castor	
AB	James Donald	Castor	(P)
Ordinary	Jeremiah Donovan	Castor	
Ordinary	Thomas Doole	Dee	
Midshipman	Sholto Douglas	Styx	
Capt of Forecastle	George Dovey	Hermes	
AB	Joseph Downs	Castor & Styx	13)
Boy 1st Class	William Dowse	Castor & Dee	
Quartermaster	Thomas Drake	Hermes	
Capt of Mast	John Dray	Hermes	
AB	Jeremiah Driscoll	Castor	
AB	Timothy Driscoll	Castor	
Midshipman	Alfred Duff	Castor	
AB	John Dukes	Castor	
Sub Officer's Steward	Robert H. Dunn	Styx	
AB	John Durham	Styx	
Ordinary	James Dyer	Castor	
Master's Asst	John Dyer	Dee	14)
Master at Arms	Joseph Dyer	Castor	(P)
2nd Master	Richard Dyer	Rhadamanthus	
AB	Thomas Dyer	Castor	(P)
AB	James Dykes	Castor	
Stoker	Henry Eason	Rhadamanthus	
Acting Boatswain	John Eccles	Castor & Styx	15)
Steward's Boy	James Eden	Hermes	
Boy 1st Class	William Edgar	Dee	
Passed Clerk	Edward Edmeades	Dee & Rhadamanthus	16)
Stoker	George Edney	Rhadamanthus	
Clerk	Edward Edwards	Rhadamanthus	
Boy 1st Class	George Edwards	Castor	
Carpenter's Crew	Thomas Edwards	Hermes	17)
Asst Surgeon	John Elliott	Castor	18)
Boy 1st Class	William Elliott	Castor	
Stoker	George C. Ellis	Rhadamanthus	
Master	Henry Ellis	Styx	
Boy 2nd Class	William Ellis	Hermes	
Ordinary	William Ellis	Castor	
Carpenter's Mate	Walter Elphick	Hermes	
Stoker	Richard Epps	Dee	
Commander's Steward	James Evans	Rhadamanthus	
Capt of After Guard	Luke J. Evans	Castor	
Asst Surgeon	William Evans	Rhadamanthus	
Clerk's Asst	William Evans	Dee	
AB	William Evans	Castor	
Gunroom Cook	James Farquarson	Castor	
AB	James Farr	Castor	
AB	Joseph Farrow	Dee	
Midshipman	Hawksworth Fawkes	Castor	
Capt of Fore Top	Jacob Feabes	Castor	
Boy 1st Class	Richard Feast	Castor	
Capt of Fore Top	Richard Ferrell	Castor	
AB	William Ferry	Castor & Styx	
Boy 2nd Class	William Fettell	Castor	
Blacksmith	James Fiddick	Castor	
Master Commanding	George Filmer	Dee	19)
AB	John Findlay	Styx	
Ordinary	Henry Firks	Castor	
Commander	Edmund G. Fishbourne	Hermes	
Ordinary	John Fitch	Hermes	
Asst Engineer 1st Class	A. Fitzgerald	Dee	20)
AB	William Flemming	Rhadamanthus	
AB	William F. Fogden	Castor	
Gunroom Steward	John W. Foote	Hermes	
Stoker	John Forster	Dee	
Boy 1st Class	Edward Foster	Castor	
Ordinary	Thomas Foundling	Rhadamanthus	
Captain's Cook	Osborne Francis	Castor	
Master	Thomas H. Fraser	Hermes	
AB	William Fraser	Castor	21)
Boy 2nd Class	Thomas Friend	Castor	
AB	Frederick Frost	Castor	
Quartermaster	James Fry	Castor	
Ordinary	George Fuller	Castor	
Sub Officer's Steward	Henry Fuller	Hermes	
Ordinary	Henry Furgurson	Hermes	
AB	George Gamblen	Castor	
AB	James Gardener	Castor	
Boy 2nd Class	William Gibbons	Castor	
AB	Francis Gilbert	Castor	
AB	William Gilbert	Rhadamanthus	
Paymaster/Purser	Samuel Giles	Styx	
AB	George Gill	Rhadamanthus	
Boy 2nd Class	George Gillot	Hermes	
AB	John Glew	Dee	
Clerk	George R. Gliddon	Castor	
AB	James Goggins	Castor	
Boy 1st Class	Thomas J. Goldsmith	Rhadamanthus	
AB	James Golhell	Castor	
Boy 2nd Class	Benjamin Gomier	Hermes	
Quartermaster	James Gordon	Styx	(P) 22)
Lieutenant	William E. A. Gordon	Styx	
AB	William Gorey	Castor	
Lieutenant	Frederick W. Gough	Cleopatra	23)
Quartermaster	Robert Gould	Castor	
AB	Samuel Gouslem	Castor	
AB	Samuel Gowden	Styx	(P)
Carpenter's Crew	John Graham	Castor	

South Africa 1853 Medal

ROYAL NAVY

Rank	Name	Ship	Note
Quartermaster	William Gratwick	Castor	
Lieutenant	Alfred Graves	Styx	
AB	John Gray	Styx	
Acting Carpenter 2nd Class	Samuel Greake	Castor	
Carpenter's Crew	Christopher Green	Castor	
Stoker	James Greenfield	Styx	
Stoker	Robert Greenslade	Styx	
Asst Engineer 1st Class	Benjamin Greetham	Hermes	
AB	John Groves	Castor	
Ordinary	Robert Gunn	Dee	
AB	Jesse Gurnett	Castor	
Sub Officer's Cook	Martin Guy	Styx	
AB	Francis Hall	Castor	
AB	Fraser Hall	Castor	
Capt of Mizzen Top	James Hall	Castor	
Boy 1st Class	John Hall	Styx	
Commander	William K. Hall	Styx	
Stoker	William T. Hall	Dee	
Ordinary 2nd Cl	William Hall	Hermes	
Gunner 3rd Class	James Hambly	Castor	(P)
Cadet	Robert J. Hancock	Castor	
Midshipman	Philip I. Hankin	Castor	24)
Ordinary	John Hannan	Castor	
Capt of Forecastle	Charles Harloe	Castor	
Quartermaster	Henry Harper	Castor	
AB	Samuel Harrighan	Castor	
AB	Charles K. Harris	Hermes	25)
AB	John Harris	Castor	
AB	Richard Harris	Castor	
Capt of Fore Top	Thomas Harris	Castor	
Ordinary	Thomas Hart	Hermes	26)
Chief Engineer	James Harvey	Hermes	
AB	John Harvey	Castor	(P)
Quartermaster	William Harvey	Castor	
Stoker	Francis Hatch	Styx	
Boy 1st Class	Richard Hawken	Castor	
Boy 1st Class	James Hawkins	Hermes	
AB	Francis Hawton	Styx	
Capt of Mizzen Top	James Hawton	Castor	
Acting Carpenter	William Hayman	Hermes	
Ordinary	John Haynes	Castor	
AB	Henry Head	Styx	
Sailmaker	James Heales	Hermes	
Gunroom Steward	Richard Heard	Styx	
Stoker	Patrick Hearne	Dee	27)
Captain's Steward	David Henderson	Styx	(P)
Ship's Corporal	Robert Heriot	Hermes	
Stoker	Henry Hewlett	Hermes	
Stoker	Robert Hext	Dee	
Gunroom Cook	Robert Hiam	Castor	(P)
AB	Elias Hibbs	Castor	
Blacksmith	John Hicks	Styx	
AB	John Higgins	Styx	
Quartermaster	Robert Hill	Dee	
AB	Edward Hills	Castor	
Engineer 3rd Cl	John Hinton	Rhadamanthus	
AB	William Hoare	Castor	
Paymaster	Richard Hocken	Castor	
AB	Edwin Hodge	Castor	
Capt of Mizzen Top	George Hodges	Castor	28)
Master and Pilot	George F. Hodges	Castor	29)
Ordinary	John Hodgson	Styx	
Boy 1st Class	John Hogg	Castor	
Boy 2nd Class	Gabriel Holt	Castor	
Asst Engineer 1st Class	James Hopkins	Styx	
Ordinary	Robert Hopkins	Castor	
Lieutenant	Henry Hoskin	ADC (MRM)	30)
Sailmaker	William Hosking	Castor	
Lieutenant	Anthony H. Hoskins	Castor	
Leading Stoker	John Hough	Dee	
Lieutenant	John H. Howard	Castor	
AB	Thomas Howarth	Castor	
Carpenter	Thomas Howes	Styx	
AB	George Hoyle	Castor	
Paymaster and Purser's Steward	William Hugo	Styx	
Midshipman	James E. Hunter	Hermes	31)
Midshipman	James E. Hunter	Castor	
Asst Surgeon	Thomas Hunter	Rhadamanthus	
AB	Henry Hurrell	Castor	
Second Master	Frank Inglis	Castor	
Boy 2nd Class	James Jackson	Styx	
Boy 2nd Class	James W. Jackson	Styx	
Capt of Fore Top	Thomas Jackson	Styx	
AB	James Jacobs	Castor	
Sailmaker's Crew	Charles Jago	Castor	
AB	Joseph Jaques	Castor	
Boy 1st Class	Joseph S. Jarman	Styx	
AB	John Jarrett	Hermes	
AB	John Jarvis	Castor	
Ordinary	Frederick Jasper	Castor	
AB	Thomas Jasper	Castor	
AB	James Jefferies	Dee	32)
Chaplain	Rev John Jenkins	Castor	
Lieutenant	Robert Jenkins	Castor	
AB	Robert Jennett	Castor	
Quartermaster	James Jennings	Styx	
Stoker	John Jennings	Rhadamanthus	
Gunroom Steward	Antonio Joaquim	Rhadamanthus	
Capt of Mast	Walter Johnson	Styx	
Boy 2nd Class	Charles Johnstone	Hermes	
Chaplain	Rev Henry Jones	Castor	
Acting 2nd Master	James Jones	Dee	
AB 2nd Class	John Jones	Dee	33)
Passed Clerk	John Jones	Styx	
Ordinary	Robert Jones	Castor	
Stoker	William Josling	Rhadamanthus	
Stoker	Thomas Joyce	Rhadamanthus	
AB	John Judge	Hermes	(P)
Ordinary 2nd Cl	John Kaylor	Dee	
Cooper	George Keating	Castor	
Gunroom Steward	Patrick Keefe	Dee	
AB	John Keife	Rhadamanthus	
Ordinary 2nd Cl	Richard Keith	Castor	
Stoker	William Kelleher	Styx	
Captain's Coxswain	Dennis Kello	Castor	
Midshipman	Edward Kelly	Castor	
AB	Richard Kelner	Styx	(P)
Boy 2nd Class	John Kemp	Styx	
AB	William Kennedy	Castor	
Ordinary	Charles Kersey	Castor & Styx	(P)
Sub-Officer's Steward	William Kettle	Castor	
Midshipman	Gilbert J. Key	Castor	
Stoker	Edward Kimber	Rhadamanthus	
Ordinary 2nd Cl	Benjamin King	Castor	34)
AB	James King	Castor	
Carpenter's Mate	William King	Styx	35)
Addl Carpenter's Mate	William Kingdom	Castor	

South Africa 1853 Medal 23

ROYAL NAVY

Rank	Name	Ship	Note
Carpenter's Crew 2nd Class	John Kingdon	Styx	
Carpenter	William Kingdon	Castor	
AB	Michael Kinnah	Dee	
AB	James Kirby	Castor	
Boy 2nd Class	Samuel Kitchener	Styx	
Lieutenant	Johan Klocker	Castor	36)
Stoker	James Knight	Styx	
Sailmaker's Crew	Joseph Knight	Styx	
AB	James Kydd	Hermes	
AB	Richard Lamb	Styx	
Ordinary	William Lambell	Castor	
Ship's Cook	Alfred Lambert	Rhadamanthus	
Ordinary	Richard Lambert	Castor	
Krooman	Isaac Lament	Rhadamanthus	
AB	George Lamerton	Castor	
AB	Frederick Lane	Castor	
AB	John Langford	Castor	37)
Ship's Cook	David Langley	Dee	
Gunner's Mate	Robert Langston	Castor	
Acting Lieut	J. R. Lawrence	Hermes	
Boy 2nd Class	Richard Lawrence	Rhadamanthus	
Ordinary	George Leach	Castor	38)
AB	John Leader	Styx	
AB	William Ledger	Rhadamanthus	(P)
AB	Henry Lee	Castor	
Boy 1st Class	William Lee	Hermes	
Boy 1st Class	John M. Lees	Hermes	
Boy 2nd Class	William Legg	Styx	40)
Captain's Steward	James Leggett	Dee	
Addl Asst Surgeon	Frederick Lekeux	Castor	39)
Paymaster and Purser	Joseph Lewis	Castor	
Paymaster and Purser's Steward	Thomas Lewis	Dee	
Coxswain of Pinnace	William Lewis	Castor	
Passed Clerk	Thomas J. Ley	Hermes	
Midshipman	Frederick C. W. Liardet	Styx	
Midshipman	Neale D. Lillington	Castor	
AB	Jesse Lindfield	Castor	
Stoker	Alfred Linney	Hermes	
Midshipman	Richard Livesay	Castor	(P)
Petty Officer 1st Class	William Lloyd	Castor	
Ordinary	Joseph Lobb	Dee	41)
Armourer	John Lock	Castor	(P)
Quartermaster	David Loft	Dee	
AB	Samuel London	Styx	
AB	George Long	Castor	
Boy 2nd Class	George Longhurst	Castor	
AB	William Longman	Castor	
Clerk	Francis Lory	Styx	
Boy 2nd Class	Henry Louder	Castor	
Ordinary	Frederick Luke	Castor	
AB	George Lundy	Styx	
Ordinary	John Lynas	Dee	
Stoker	William Mace	Hermes	
Surgeon	John Macleod	Hermes	
AB	James Mahoney	Castor	
AB	John Mahoney	Castor	
Captain's Coxswain	John R. Major	Hermes	42)
AB	Thomas Major	Castor	
Sub Officer's Steward	William Mallett	Hermes	
Ordinary	James Maloney	Castor	
Asst Engineer 2nd Class	James Mangnall	Styx	
AB	John Manicom	Castor	
Stoker	Thomas Mann	Hermes	
AB	Robert Manning	Rhadamanthus	
Paymaster and Purser's Steward	Thomas Mansell	Rhadamanthus	
Midshipman	Alfred F. Marescaux	Castor	43)
Caulker	John Marks	Castor	
Stoker	Alexander Marsden	Hermes	
Armourer	William Marsh	Dee	
Commander's Steward	John Marshall	Rhadamanthus	
Master's Asst	Arthur B. Martin	Castor	
Stoker	James Martin	Rhadamanthus	
AB	John Martin	Castor	
Paymaster	Thomas Martin	Castor	
Petty Officer 1st Class	Jacob Matthews	Castor	
Boy 1st Class	William Matthews	Castor	44)
AB	George May	Styx	
Carpenters' Crew	Thomas May	Castor	
Carpenter's Crew	George Mayne	Styx	
Second Master	William J. Mayne	Styx & Dee	
Carpenter's Crew	William Mayse	Castor	
AB	Edward McAlligate	Hermes	
AB	Joseph McCann	Castor	
Second Master	James McClune	Castor	
AB	David McCoskie	Castor	
AB	James McCredie	Rhadamanthus	
Capt of Forecastle	John McDonald	Styx	
AB	William McIntyre	Castor & Hermes	
AB	William McKegg	Castor	
Sailmaker	John McKenzie	Rhadamanthus	
Gunner's Mate	John McKenzie	Styx	
AB	Alexander McLennon	Castor	
Asst Surgeon	William McMahon	Dee	
Capt of Fore Top	Thomas Medhurst	Hermes	
Gunroom Steward	Joseph Mellin	Castor	
Mate	Robert Mercer	Castor	
AB	Peter Merrett	Styx	
Ship's Corporal	Peter Merrett	Styx	45)
Gunroom Cook	George Miller	Styx	
Boy 1st Class	Thomas Miller	Hermes	
AB	Edward R. Millin	Castor	
Engineer 3rd Cl	Augustus Mills	Rhadamanthus	
AB	William Mines	Rhadamanthus	
AB	William Miskin	Castor	
Quartermaster	William Mitchell	Hermes	
AB	William Mitchell	Dee	
Boy 1st Class	Lewis Moise	Styx	(P)
Master's Asst	John Molloy	Castor	
AB	Daniel Moore	Castor	
Boy 1st Class	Henry Moore	Styx	
Clerk	John S. Moore	Castor	
AB	William Moore	Dee	
Stoker	William Moore	Hermes	
AB	John Morey	Castor	
Boatswain's Mate	John Moriarty	Rhadamanthus	
Sub Officer's Cook	William Moss	Castor	
Capt of Mast	Joseph Muchmore	Styx	
Stoker	Samuel Mugford	Styx	
AB	John Mulcock	Rhadamanthus	
Gunner's Mate	William Mullice	Castor	(P)
Stoker	Peter Mundin	Hermes	
Ordinary	Charles Mungean	Castor	
AB	William Munro	Castor	
AB	David Murphy	Castor	
Ordinary	Patrick Murphy	Castor	

24 South Africa 1853 Medal

ROYAL NAVY

Rank	Name	Ship	Note
AB	Edward Murrant	Castor	
AB	Owen Murther	Castor	
Capt of Mizzen Top	Joshua Mutton	Castor	
Quartermaster	John Myhill	Castor	
Ordinary	James Naggs	Castor	13)
Capt of Forecastle	Thomas Napier	Hermes	
Boy 2nd Class	James Neary	Castor	46)
AB	John Nelson	Hermes	
AB	William Newham	Castor	
Boy 2nd Class	Frederick Norris	Hermes	
Ordinary	John Norton	Hermes	
Ordinary 2nd Cl	John Nye	Castor	
Midshipman	James W. L. Oakes	Castor	
Ship's Corporal	James Oates	Castor	
Ordinary	William Ocock	Hermes	
Boy 1st Class	Abraham Odgers	Castor	
AB	William Olden	Castor	
Stoker	Thomas Oliver	Rhadamanthus	(P)
Lieutenant	Montague F. O'Reilly	Castor	(P)
Ship's Cook	Thomas Owen	Hermes	
Leading Stoker	William Owen	Hermes	
Boy 1st Class	William Owen	Styx	
Yeoman of Signals	Henry Owens	Castor	
AB	William Paddon	Styx	
Carpenter's Crew	William Paddy	Styx	
Stoker	Charles Palmer	Dee	
Ordinary	William Parke	Castor	47)
Stoker	Charles Parker	Hermes	
Leading Stoker	John Parker	Hermes	
AB	William Parker	Hermes	
Boy 1st Class	Gilbert Parr	Castor	
AB	John Parr	Castor	
Ordinary	John Parry	Castor	
AB	Thomas Parry	Castor	
AB	Richard Pascoe	Styx	
Quartermaster	James Paterson	Rhadamanthus	
Acting Mate	John C. Paterson	Castor	
AB	William Pattison	Dee	
Gunner's Mate	Thomas Pearce	Rhadamanthus	
Boy 1st Class	Edward Peters	Castor	(P)
AB	Charles Peterson	Styx	
Leading Stoker	Thomas Physick	Styx	(P)
AB	John Pickles	Castor	
Leading Stoker	James Pickman	Rhadamanthus	
Boy 1st Class	William Pike	Castor	
AB	Samuel Pinhorne	Castor	
Ordinary	Edmund Pink	Castor	
Captain's Steward	John J. Pitcher	Castor	
Clerk	George F. Pocock	Dee	
Stoker	Joseph Polkinghorne	Styx	
AB	James Pollard	Castor	
Ordinary	Robert Popham	Castor	48)
Paymaster and Purser's Steward	John Potvine	Rhadamanthus	
Gunner 1st Class	John Powell	Castor	
AB/Diver	Robert Price	Castor	
AB	Thomas Price	Castor	
Passed Clerk	Thomas Price	Castor	
AB	Isaac Prickett	Hermes	
AB	William Prior	Hermes	
AB	John Prout	Styx	
Boy 2nd Class	John Pryle	Rhadamanthus	
Gunner	William Pugh	Castor & Styx	49)
Stoker	Leonard Pyne	Styx	
Boy 1st Class	Morris Rabbick	Styx	50)
Boy 1st Class	Edward Rackett	Styx	
Second Master	William Rainbott	Rhadamanthus	
Capt of Mizzen Top	Thomas Raverty	Castor	
Second Master	Frederick Rea	Rhadamanthus	
Cooper	William Rea	Castor	51)
Carpenter's Crew	Alfred Redman	Rhadamanthus	52)
Captain's Cook	William Reed	Styx	
Caulker	Thomas Reid	Hermes	
Acting Boatswain 3rd Class	Edward Reilly	Hermes	(P)
Boy 1st Class	John Reilly	Rhadamanthus	
Midshipman	James S. Reynell	Hermes	(P)
Stoker	Reuben R. Reynolds	Rhadamanthus	
Asst Engineer 3rd Class	R. C. Reynolds	Hermes	
Capt of Main Top	Thomas Reynolds	Castor	
Leading Stoker	William Rich	Dee	
Secretary	Charles Richard	Castor	
Ordinary	George Richards	Castor	
Acting Boatswain 2nd Class	John Riddett	Castor & Hermes	
Ordinary	John Riley	Dee	
AB	George Rixon	Hermes	
AB	Thomas Roberton	Castor	
Boy 2nd Class	Robert Roberts	Styx	
Engineer 2nd Cl	Robert Roberts	Dee	(P)
Capt of Fore Top	George Robinson	Styx	45)
Boy 2nd Class	Thomas Robinson	Castor	
Asst Engineer 2nd Class	W. L. Robinson	Hermes	
Carpenter's Crew	James Rootes	Castor	(P)
Ordinary	John Rose	Rhadamanthus	
Asst Surgeon	John T. Ross	Castor	
Carpenter's Crew	Francis Rowe	Castor	
Stoker	Thomas Rowe	Styx & Hermes	13)
Clerk	William N. Rowe	Castor	
Capt of Mast	John Russell	Castor	
Master	James T. Russell	Castor	
AB	James Rutland	Castor	
AB	John Sampson	Castor	
Gunroom Steward	James Santop	Castor	
Capt of Fore Top	Richard Saunders	Castor	
Surgeon	William McK. Saunders	Styx	
AB	William Saunders	Styx	
AB	Charles Savage	Castor	
AB	Josiah Saxby	Styx	
AB	Robert Scott	Castor	
AB	Owen Seacome	Castor	
AB	John Seaton	Dee	53)
Asst Engineer	Thomas Seccombe	Hermes	
AB	William Shaw	Rhadamanthus	
Quartermaster	Daniel Shay	Castor	
AB	James Shea	Castor	
Capt of Mast	Thomas Sherley	Castor	
AB	Robert Sherlock	Rhadamanthus	
Stoker	Thomas Shore	Dee	(P)
Ordinary	John Short	Castor	
Capt of After Guard	George Simms	Styx	
Master's Asst	Francis O. Simpson	Hermes	
Second Master	Francis Skead	Dee	54)
AB	William Skoyles	Castor	13)
AB	James Slyne	Castor	
Ordinary	Edward Smith	Hermes	
Carpenter's Crew	Frederick G. Smith	Hermes	
Captain's Coxswain	James Smith	Styx	

South Africa 1853 Medal

ROYAL NAVY

Rank	Name	Ship	Note
AB	John Smith	Castor	
AB	Joseph Smith	Styx	
Ropemaker	Richard Smith	Hermes	
AB	Richard Smith	Castor	
Ordinary	Robert Smith	Castor	
AB	Thomas Smith	Castor	
AB	James Snow	Dee	
Ordinary	Henry Sobeg	Styx	
Asst Surgeon	John Sole	Dee	
Master's Asst	William L. Southey	Rhadamanthus	(P)
Master's Asst	Thomas H. Spence	Styx	
AB	William Spencer	Styx	
AB	John Spiller	Castor	34)
Boy 2nd Class	Thomas Springate	Styx	
AB	James Spurling	Castor	
Ship's Cook	Robert Stafford	Castor	
Cooper	George Stanbury	Styx	
Midshipman	Francis P. Staples	Castor	
Ordinary	William Staples	Rhadamanthus	
Quartermaster	Thomas Stares	Castor	(P)
Ordinary 2nd Cl	Thomas Starkey	Dee	
AB	Thomas Startup	Castor	
Boy 2nd Class	Henry Stephens	Hermes	
AB	William Stephenson	Castor	
Capt of Main Top	John Stevens	Styx	
Leading Stoker	Daniel Stewart	Hermes	(P) 55)
Lieutenant	Frederick Stirling	Castor	
AB	William Stokes	Styx	(P)
AB	David Stoneham	Castor	
Boy 1st Class	William Storey	Styx	
Leading Seaman	John Strawbridge	Hermes	56)
Gunroom Steward	Robert Stredder	Hermes	
Captain's Cook	Hickson Sturgess	Dee	57)
Midshipman	Francis W. Sullivan	Castor	
Midshipman	George L. Sullivan	Castor	
Gunner's Mate	George Sullivan	Dee	
Boy 1st Class	John Sullivan	Styx	58)
Boy 1st Class	John Summers	Castor	
Boy 2nd Class	Ambrose Sutton	Hermes	
Second Master	Edward Swain	Dee	(P)
Leading Stoker	Richard Swale	Hermes	59)
Carpenter's Crew	William Swarbrick	Hermes & Dee	
Second Master	John Switzer	Styx	
Sailmaker	George Tallack	Castor	
Acting Carpenter 3rd Class	Charles Taylor	Hermes	(P) 60)
Boy 1st Class	Robert Tee	Castor	
AB	John Terry	Castor	
Boy 1st Class	Charles Thomas	Dee	
Caulker's Mate	George Thomas	Castor	
Carpenter's Crew	Joseph Thomas	Castor	61)
Capt of Mizzen Top	Joseph Thomas	Castor	
Acting Carpenter 2nd Class	William F. Thomlinson	Castor & Hermes	(P)
AB	Henry Thompson	Hermes	
Mate	Sackville Thompson	Castor	
Carpenter's Mate	William Thompson	Castor	
Capt of Forecastle	William Thompson	Styx	
Cooper's Crew	Edmund Thorne	Styx	
Capt of Forecastle	William H. Thornton	Hermes	
Boy 2nd Class	Henry Thorpe	Castor	
AB	William Tickner	Castor	
Capt of After Guard	Isaac Tinker	Castor	
AB	Patrick Tobin	Dee	
Boatswain's Mate	William H. Toms	Castor	
Stoker	Patrick Toomey	Rhadamanthus	
AB	Edward Trattle	Castor	
Capt of Mizzen Top	Charles Treathy	Styx	
Stoker	George Tregelles	Styx	
AB	Thomas Tregurtha	Styx	
Carpenter's Mate	Nicholas Trenaman	Rhadamanthus	
AB	James Trigg	Castor	
Ship's Corporal	Thomas Trueman	Castor	
Stoker	George Tucker	Styx	
Sailmaker	William Tucker	Styx	
Acting Asst Surgeon	William Turner	Styx	
Boy 1st Class	William Turner	Dee	62)
Boy 1st Class	William Turrell	Castor	
Ordinary	James W. Tutten	Styx	
Mate	Ernest A. Tweedale	Hermes	
AB	Michael Twohig	Hermes	63)
AB	James Tye	Castor	
AB	William Underhill	Castor	
Clerk	Arthur B. Usher	Castor	
Capt of Hold	Stephen Veale	Castor	
AB	Samuel Venning	Castor	
Boy 1st Class	Henry Wadge	Castor	
AB	George Walker	Castor	
Boatswain's Mate	James Walker	Hermes	(P)
Carpenter's Mate	Samuel Walker	Dee	
AB	Charles Waller	Dee	
Boy 2nd Class	Joseph Walton	Styx	
Carpenter's Crew	Charles Ward	Hermes	
AB	Joseph Ward	Castor	
Leading Stoker	John Warman	Dee	
Quartermaster	Joseph Warwell	Rhadamanthus	
Sailmaker	James Watford	Dee	64)
Master's Asst	James S. Watts	Dee	
AB	Philip Webb	Styx	65)
Boy 2nd Class	William Webber	Styx	
Passed Clerk	George A. V. Welch	Castor	
Ordinary	John Welch	Styx	
AB	Stephen Welch	Castor	
Ordinary 2nd Cl	George Welshford	Dee	
Lieutenant	Henry West	Dee & Hermes	(P)
Boatswain	John West	Styx	
Boy 2nd Class	William G. West	Rhadamanthus	
Capt of Hold	Thomas Westerman	Castor	
AB	William Whatley	Castor	
AB	Anthony Whitby	Styx	
AB	Samuel Whitcombe	Styx	
Clerk	Benjamin C. White	Dee	(P) 65)
Ordinary	Thomas White	Castor	52)
Ordinary	George Whitehead	Hermes	
Ropemaker	William Whiter	Castor	(P)
AB	Andrew Whitlocks	Castor	
AB	William Widger	Rhadamanthus	
Capt of Forecastle	James Wild	Castor	
Ordinary	James Wilkinson	Dee	67)
Ropemaker	William Willcocks	Styx	
Boy 1st Class	Daniel Williams	Castor	
AB	John Williams	Hermes	
AB	John Williams	Castor	64)
Asst Engineer 1st Class	John T. Williams	Dee	
AB	George C. Wills	Styx	
Midshipman	John C. Wilson	Castor	
Capt of Mizzen Top	William Wilson	Castor	
Acting Gunner	William Wiltshire	Hermes	(P)
AB	William Winch	Hermes	
AB	John Wingham	Dee	
Paymaster and Purser	George H. L. Wise	Hermes	(P)

26 South Africa 1853 Medal

ROYAL NAVY

Rank	Name	Ship	
AB	Henry Wise	Castor	
Carpenter's Mate	William Withers	Castor	
Acting Asst Surgeon	Charles G. Wolfenden	Castor	
Boy 2nd Class	Richard Wood	Castor	
AB	Thomas Wood	Castor	
Asst Engineer 1st Class	Thomas W. Woodcock	Dee & Hermes	
Painter	Frederick Wormington	Hermes	(P)
Acting Second Master	James Worsley	Castor	
Yeoman of Signals	William Worsnip	Castor	68)
Boy 2nd Class	William Worsnip	Castor	68)
AB	William Worthington	Castor	
Clerk	John Wotton	Rhadamanthus, Castor & Dee	69)
Chief Engineer 3rd Class	William G. Wratton	Styx	
Stoker	George Wright	Rhadamanthus	
Quartermaster	John Wright	Castor	
AB	Thomas Wright	Castor	
AB	William Wright	Styx	
Gunner's Mate	William Wyatt	Dee	
Lieutenant	Thomas M. M. Wynyard	Styx	(P)
Captain and Commodore 2nd Class	Christopher Wyvill	Castor	
Boatswain's Mate	Thomas A. Yates	Castor	
Armourer	Thomas Yeo	Styx	
Boy 2nd Class	James Yeoman	Styx	
Fifer	George Youlton	Castor	
Boy 1st Class	Robert Yule	Styx	

ROYAL MARINES

Rank	Name	Ship	
Private 1st Class	John Allan	Castor	
Private	John Ardstall	Castor	
Corporal	John Armstead	Castor	
Private	George Baker	Castor	
Gunner 1st Class	William Barbrook, RMA	Styx	
Private 3rd Class	Samuel Barker	Castor	
Sergeant	James Barrott	Castor	
Private 1st Class	William Bateman	Castor	
Private	Henry Bazeley	Castor	
Private	Syrus Bennett	Castor	
Private	Thomas Bennett	Castor	
Private 1st Class	William Berell	Castor	(P)
Sergeant	Charles Berry	Rhadamanthus	
Private	James Birch	President	70)
Gunner 3rd Class	Walter Bonning, RMA	Hermes	
Private	George Bovatt	Rhadamanthus	
Gunner 3rd Class	George Breckenridge, RMA	Styx	
Private	Charles Brown	Castor	
Gunner 3rd Class	William Brown, RMA	Styx	
Private	William Burr	Castor	
Private	Thomas Bush	Castor	
Private 3rd Class	John Cage	Castor	
Private	William Carpenter	Castor	
Gunner 3rd Class	Joshua Chambers, RMA	Styx	
Gunner 3rd Class	James Clarke, RMA	Styx	
Private	Matthew Clipsham	Castor	
Private	Abraham Cole	Castor	
Private	William Conningsby	Rhadamanthus	
Private	James Cook	President	70)
Private	John Cooper	Castor	
Private	William Cooper	Castor	(R)
Gunner 3rd Class	William Cooper, RMA	Styx	
Private	Samuel Copsey	Castor	
Private 3rd Class	John Corder	Dee	
Gunner	Daniel Cornely, RMA	Hermes	
Colour Sergeant	Charles Cousins, RMA	President	70)
Private	William Coye	Rhadamanthus	
Gunner	Benjamin Crocker, RMA	Hermes	
Private	James Dale (alias William Walker)	Castor	
Private	William Davey	Castor	
Private 3rd Class	Alfred Deacon	Dee	
Private 1st Class	John Denman	Castor	
Private	William Digby	Castor	
Gunner 1st Class	James Dowd, RMA	Styx	
Captain	James Dowman	President	70)
Gunner	Andrew Dunlop, RMA	Hermes	
Gunner 3rd Class	William Eamey, RMA	Styx	(R)
Gunner 3rd Class	Josiah Edge, RMA	Styx	
Gunner	Richard Elliott, RMA	Hermes	
Lieutenant	Charles J. Ellis	President	70)(R)
Private	Cook Feary	Castor	
Private	William Fisher	Rhadamanthus	
Gunner	John Fox, RMA	Hermes	
Corporal 1st Class	George Francis	Styx	45)
Sergeant	William Frost	President	70)
Private	James Fuell	Castor	
Gunner	Elijah Gardner, RMA	Hermes	
Gunner	William Guy, RMA	Hermes	
Lieutenant	Philip Harris	Castor	71)
Private	Amos Harrod	Castor	
Private	Daniel Hilder	Castor	
Private	Samuel Hocking	Castor	
Private	James Horsenail	Castor	
Gunner	George Hurle, RMA	Hermes	
Gunner 3rd Class	George Jackson, RMA	Styx	
Private 3rd Class	George Jones	Castor	
Private	William Keenan	Castor	
Gunner	Charles Ketteridge, RMA	Hermes	
Drummer	John King, RMA	Styx	
Drummer	Solomon Knowles, RMA	Hermes	
Gunner	Charles Kylo, RMA	Hermes	
Private 3rd Class	William Ladyman	Castor	
Private	Miles Lawin	Castor	
Gunner	William Lee, RMA	Hermes	
Private	Edward Lepard	Castor	
Gunner	Jabez Levitt, RMA	Hermes	
Private	Henry Lewis	Castor	
Gunner	Charles Lonnow, RMA	Hermes	
Private	Jabez Luddington	Castor	
Sergeant	Essau Marchant	Castor	

South Africa 1853 Medal 27

ROYAL MARINES

Rank	Name	Ship		Rank	Name	Ship	
Private	Daniel Manning	Castor		Lieutenant	John Reed	Castor	72)
Private 3rd Class	Charles McAuley	Dee		Gunner	James Rhodes, RMA	Hermes	
Private	Peter McCarthy	Castor		Private	Charles Robinson	Castor	
Gunner 3rd Class	John McCormick, RMA	Styx		Gunner 3rd Class	Thomas Rowsell, RMA	Styx	
Private	Isaac Meaddows	Castor		Private	Anthony Scott	Castor	
Private 3rd Class	Robert Melluish	Dee		Gunner 3rd Class	Henry Scott, RMA	Styx	
Private 1st Class	William Middleditch	Castor		Corporal	George Screes	Dee	
Sergeant	William Milliard	Hermes		Private	Charles Shorter	President	73)
Private	John Mills	Castor		Sergeant	John Smith, RMA	Styx	
Private	Stephen Monk	Castor		Private	William Smith	Castor	
Gunner	Charles Morant, RMA	Hermes		Private	Jesse Sollors	Castor	
Private	Christopher Morcombe	Castor		Private	William Stock	Castor	(R)
Gunner 3rd Class	Thomas Morris, RMA	Styx		Gunner	William Sudbury, RMA	Hermes	
Private	James Morrison	Rhadamanthus		Colour Sergeant	John Syms	Castor	
Private 3rd Class	John Moseley	Dee		Gunner	George Taylor, RMA	Hermes	
Sergeant	Francis Naylor	Castor	(R)	Private 1st Class	John Thompson	Castor	
Private	Charles Paul	Castor		Private	John Thomson	Castor	
Private 3rd Class	William Pards	Castor		Private	Thomas Trowton	Rhadamanthus	
Gunner 1st Class	Abraham Phillips, RMA	Styx		Gunner	John Tulk, RMA	Hermes	
Private	John Pike	Castor		Private	Martin Wade	Castor	
Private	William Portman	Castor		Corporal	William Watts	Castor	
Corporal	Henry Prescott	Hermes		Private	Thomas Webster	Castor	
Private 3rd Class	James Quin	Dee		Private	Robert Wesson	Castor	
Gunner 3rd Class	William Randall, RMA	Styx		Private	John Willis	Castor	
Private	William Read	Castor		Private	William Wilson	Castor	
				Gunner 3rd Class	James Withers, RMA	Styx	
				Drummer	John Wood	Castor	
				Sergeant	Richard Wood	Castor	

ROYAL NAVY AND ROYAL MARINES NOTES

1. Died at sea 17.10.51.
2. Alias Aitken.
3. Died 11.9.55.
4. Became an Ensign in the 86th Regiment in 1855.
5. Received a re-named medal.
6. Died of wounds 19.4.52.
7. Clarke on Roll but signed his name without the 'e'.
8. Drowned in the Buffalo River 3.4.51.
9. The medal in a private collection is engraved and either a late issue or replacement.
10. Drowned 1851.
11. Drowned December 1853.
12. Wrongly shown as a carpenter on Roll and name given as Dedden.
13. Twice entered on Roll.
14. Drowned September 1850.
15. Twice entered on Roll, once as Boatswain's Mate.
16. Twice entered on Roll. Died and medal sent to father.
17. Drowned 7.1.52.
18. Shown as Acting Surgeon on Roll.
19. Died; medal sent to widow.
20. Died 13.9.51.
21. Frazer on muster.
22. Was among the original returns but a note on the Roll says 'sent 21st October 1881' and the medal in a private collection is engraved in the style of that period. Possibly the originally impressed medal was returned to the Mint when no attempt was made to collect the award.
23. Returned on the Army Roll. Served with Sir Peregrine Maitland's force late in 1846.
24. Twice entered on Roll, once as Hawkin.
25. Possibly the same man from 'Castor' who is shown as 'Run'.
26. Drowned December 1853.
27. Hearn on muster.
28. Died April 1851.
29. Second initial shown as 'J' on Roll.
30. Naval ADC to the Army and entered only on the Army Roll.
31. The 'Castor' medal was signed for by the recipient in 1856. The 'Hermes' medal was collected by a Henry Smith in 1866.
32. Jefferes on Roll.
33. Died of fever 24.6.50.
34. Died; medal to father.
35. Died 20.4.55.
36. An observer from the Norwegian Navy and received a re-named medal in 1862.
37. Died December 1852.
38. Leache on Roll.
39. The Navy List confirms the Roll spelling but the musters show Lereux.
40. Died 22.8.54.
41. Drowned 14.9.50.
42. Drowned December 1853.
43. Maresceaux on Roll.
44. Died 14.1.51.
45. Died.
46. Signed his name Nearey.
47. Died 17.11.53.
48. Roll altered to Pophem but muster confirms original entry.
49. Twice entered on Roll, once as Gunner's Mate.
50. Died 11.3.55.
51. Shown as Red on Roll.
52. Twice entered on Roll, once as 'Run'.
53. Twice entered on Roll where his name could be read as Jeaton.
54. It is likely that the Sir Harry Smith medal in the Africana Museum SA named to 'Capt. Skead R.N.' belonged to this man.
55. Died 11.9.53.
56. Died 18.5.51.
57. Died. Sturges on Roll.
58. Died 24.11.54.
59. Died; medal to mother.
60. Died 21.7.52, medal to widow.
61. Alias Thomas Lazelle.
62. Died July 1850.
63. Received re-named medal originally prepared for Stoker 'Prince of Wales'.
64. Twice entered on Roll, once as Ordinary.
65. Received a re-named medal.
66. Died 5.12.60.
67. Drowned 14.9.50.
68. Possibly father and son. Both were born in Devon, one in 1805, the other in 1835.
69. Twice entered on Roll, once as Passed Clerk.
70. Returned on the Army Roll. Qualified 1846–7.
71. Commanded a RM detachment with Mackinnon's force on the Fish River September 1851.
72. Read on Roll; Reed in Hart's.
73. A late applicant whose name only appears on the Mint records. Qualified 1846/7.

PRO References: AD/38/2821 – 4597 – 7772 – 7948 – 8277 – 9113.

THE ARMY

There were compelling reasons to show the rolls for seamen and marines alphabetically but I have indulged my own personal preference by listing soldier recipients in order of rank. The possibility that the rank given on a medal may not conform with these rolls has already been explained in the 'Explanatory Notes'.

7th (The Princess Royal's) Regiment of Dragoon Guards

Upon their arrival at the Cape in 1843, part of the regiment was sent to take charge of horses which had been purchased for them, while the remainder went by sea to Algoa Bay and then marched to Grahams Town. The wild young horses were ridden and led 500 miles to the frontier and the re-united regiment proceeded to Fort Beaufort.

Heavy cavalry were a branch of the army ill suited for service in the terrain in which they were expected to operate. Dragoon trappings were much too cumbersome for their little Cape horses and it was foreseen that the troopers might be employed as mounted infantry. The men were given arms that had formerly belonged to the 60th Rifles and were taught infantry drill, including fixing bayonets. Loading a rifle on horseback was a difficult exercise and before the horses had been fully trained the regiment was called upon to help protect the Griquas against the Boers. After marching 300 miles they participated in the action at Zwart Koppies in April 1845 and returned to Fort Beaufort until the outbreak of the War of the Axe.

Under Col Richardson (the hyphen Robertson was added a few years later), the 7th DG took the field in April 1846 with a force which tried to pursue Chief Sandili and was brought into action on the 16th when strenuous resistance was met on Seven Kloof Mountain. Meanwhile, Capt Bambrick's troop had been part of the camp guard left at Burns Hill under Major Gibsone. The laager came under attack and, endeavouring to retake cattle captured by the enemy, Bambrick, a Waterloo veteran, was killed. The following day, Gibsone was ordered to bring up the wagons but at a narrow point in the track the Kaffirs made an onslaught on the centre of the train. The Dragoons were concentrated at the rear of the column to protect the ammunition wagons and were compelled to return with them to Burns Hill. Sixty-one wagons, nearly half the total, were captured and burnt by the enemy. Among the property lost was the baggage and mess plate of the 7th DG.

The whole expedition was then withdrawn to the Tyumie River where Lt Butler, with his men dismounted, held the banks while the troops crossed at Block Drift.

The 7th DG were sent to Post Victoria, and as the Kaffirs swept down upon the settlers four troops under Col Richardson went to Fort Peddie. It was from here that a squadron was ordered to join the force which subsequently failed to give aid to Fingoes under siege at Beka Mission Station. Uncommitted Kaffirs were thereby encouraged to rebel, and twice Dragoons were sent from Fort Peddie in early May; once going to the assistance of a party looking for cattle and then to rescue some settlers' wagons. On the 27th, while with infantry protecting a wood gathering detail, the Dragoons found an opportunity to get among Kaffirs who were pressing upon the wagons and killed and wounded some 40 of them.

Two squadrons were among the raiding column under Somerset which burnt Chief Stock's Kraal on June 8th. As the force sought a camping ground scouts unexpectedly found a considerable body of Kaffirs on the march under Chief Seyolo. Over-confident, the natives were in open country and the British commander was quick to seize his opportunity. After artillery had not altogether successfully played upon the enemy the 7th DG led the only cavalry charge of the wars. Wielding their heavy sabres the Dragoons scattered the Kaffir masses and the carbines of the following Cape Mounted Riflemen did great execution.

The battle of Guanga, as it came to be called, cost the enemy some four hundred warriors. Casualties to the 7th DG were one officer killed and two wounded, and nine ORs wounded. The engagement was a turning point in the rebellion and the last major action. During the next 18 months the regiment was engaged in some minor excursions and were in at the death by being paraded at King Williams Town when Sir Harry Smith presided over the ceremony of surrender in December 1847.

They had not much longer to serve in South Africa and sailed for home on April 13th 1848.

			Kaffir Wars		
			1	2	3
LIEUTENANT COLONEL					
Robert Richardson-Robertson	1)				△
MAJOR					
John C. Gibsone	2)	(R)			△
CAPTAIN					
Arthur C. Bentinck	3)	(P)			△
John Campbell		(P)			△
Charles E. Petre	4)				△
Thomas Smales					△
LIEUTENANT					
Allen N. Adams					△
Antoine S. Butler	5)				△
Philip M. Bunbury	6)				△
Nicholas De la Cherois					△
Annesley P. Gore		(P)			△
J. Hamilton Gray					△
Thomas M. Riddell					△
Pearson S. Thompson	7)				△
CORNET					
John T. Cramer					△
CORNET/ADJUTANT					
John Gray	8)	(P)			△
CORNET					
Robert Johnston	9)				△
Charles J. B. Plestow					△
QUARTERMASTER					
Henry Magill					△
VETERINARY SURGEON					
Benjamin C. R. Gardiner					△
SERGEANT MAJOR					
Robert Howard					△
TRUMPET MAJOR					
Robert Banks					△
TROOP SERGEANT MAJOR					
George Gillam					△
William Sutherland					△
SADDLER SERGEANT					
William Prytherch					△
SERGEANT					
John Coleman					△
Robert J. Crow					△
David Dunbar					△
John Gillam	10)				△

South Africa 1853 Medal

Name	Note		Kaffir Wars 1	Kaffir Wars 2	Kaffir Wars 3
John G. Hamilton					△
John James					△
Philip H. Morrell					△
George Nicholson					△
George North	(P)				△
John Nowlan					△

CORPORAL

Name	Note		Kaffir Wars 1	Kaffir Wars 2	Kaffir Wars 3
William Banks					△
Henry Barnes					△
Joseph Clement					△
Robert Davidson					△
Henry Glover					△
William Green					△
John T. Knox					△
John McBryan					△

TRUMPETER

Name	Note		Kaffir Wars 1	Kaffir Wars 2	Kaffir Wars 3
John Bottomley	11)				△
Joseph Elston					△
Michael Fox					△
Thomas Marshall					△

PRIVATE

Name	Note		Kaffir Wars 1	Kaffir Wars 2	Kaffir Wars 3
William Adams					△
David Adcock					△
John Albert					△
James Anderson					△
David Beck	(P)				△
Joseph Bennett					△
Robert Benneworth	12)				△
Edward Billis					△
Edward R. Binckes	13)				△
James Blake					△
William Bolton					△
Josiah Brown	(P)				△
Edward Bull					△
Richard Campbell					△
John Chambers					△
Edward Clarke					△
Thomas Clegg					△
Henry Cobbett	(R)				△
Edward Cole	14)				△ O
William Coleson					△
Patrick Conlan					△
John Connally					△
John Connell	15)				△
James Cook					△
William Coultrop	16)				△
William Coveny	27) (P)				O
Henry Cramp					△
John Curtis					△
William Davis					△
Hugh Dennis					△
John Dilkes					△
William D. Duffield					△
James Dunne (1)	17)				△
James Dunne (2)	17)				△
Miles Dwyer	(R)				△
Henry Elston	(P)				△
Conrad E. Fairbrass					△
Robert J. Fairbrass					△
Michael Finn					△
Patrick Finnigan					△
William Foley					△
Mark Frearson					△
John Fuller					△
Thomas Gallagher					△
Robert Garland	18)				△
Robert Getty					△
John Girling					△
Francis D. Gourley					△
Charles Griffin					△
George C. Griggs					△
John Harper					△
Joseph Harris					△
Henry Hartley					△
George Hirst					△
Alfred Hogben					△
Henry Hogben					△
James Hudson	(P)				△
William Humphries					△
Thomas Jackson					△
Robert Jennings					△
Robert Johnson					△
George Jordan					△
Alexander Keath	19)				△
James Kershaw					△
George King					△
George Knight					△
James Lance					△
William H. Lawson					△
William Lee	(MRM)				△
George Legg					△
Henry Lewis	(P)				△
George Lott					△
Stephen Luff					△
James Magher					△
John Mathews					△
James McCrisikan					△
Daniel McDonald					△
Marcus McGuire					△
Alexander McNamara					△
William McVitty					△
William Metcalf					△
Henry Millington					△
Charles Morrice					△
Thomas Mullan	20)				△
David Murdoch					△
James Murray					△
Richard Nash					△
William Nash	(P)				△
John O'Connell					△
Henry O'Neill					△
William Owen					△
Richard Parker	(P)				△
Frederick Potbury					△
Thomas Ratcliffe					△
George Regan					△
Absalom Richards					△
Thomas Richards					△
John Scrivens					△
Samuel Sharpe	21)				△
Peter Sheerin					△
James Simpson (1)	22)				△
James Simpson (2)	22)				△
Dawson Slater					△
Thomas Smith					△
David Tait	(P)				△
Thomas Taylor					△
John Thompson					△
William Thornill	23)				△
Henry T. Turney					△
Timothy Toohey	24)				△
John Usher					△
Alfred R. Vize					△
James Wall					△
Henry Waller					△

32 South Africa 1853 Medal

PRIVATE		Kaffir Wars					Kaffir Wars		
		1	2	3			1	2	3
James Wells					George Wise				△
Joseph C. Whitehurst				△	William Woollen				△
John Whittingham				△	David Yewdell	26)			△
John R. Wickenden				△					
Henry Wieman				△	△ = campaign qualification as WO/100/17.				
John Winton	25)			△	O = campaign which the Rolls fail to credit.				

7TH (THE PRINCESS ROYAL'S) REGIMENT OF DRAGOON GUARDS NOTES

1 Commanded the expedition against the Boers across the Orange River in 1845. See G and I.
2 Led the charge at Guanga. Wrongly shown as Gibson on Roll and medal. See Bissett.
3 Attached to CMR for most of the campaign.
4 Peter on Roll.
5 Commanded the rearguard during the attack on the wagons at Burns Hill. See Bissett.
6 Wounded at Guanga.
7 Was at Guanga. Author 'The Story of the Regiment'.
8 Regtl Sgt Major until commissioned Cornet 1.1.47.
9 Although on the original returns he did not receive his medal until 28.4.63.
10 Behaved gallantly at Burns Hill. See Thompson.
11 Bottomly on Roll.
12 Benniworth on Roll. A Farrier.
13 Bincks on Roll.
14 No 60 is given against his name on the Roll but his Regt No is 550. During the third war he served with the CMR.
15 Given a re-named replacement in 1858.
16 Also Coultrup on musters.
17 Nos 204 and 240, one of which is in a private collection.
18 Lost original and received re-named replacement.
19 Also Keith on musters.
20 Also Mullen and Mullin on musters.
21 Sharp on Roll.
22 Nos 591 and 640.
23 Also Thornell on musters.
24 Toohy on Roll.
25 Alterations on the Roll give the impression that this man's name was either Winter or Winterton, but musters prove it to be Winton.
26 Also Yewdale on musters.
27 I have been unable to trace this man, who may have won his medal with another unit. The date cannot be confirmed.

ADDENDUM – It is believed that there is also a medal to Farrier Major C. Dennis. If genuine, it is probably a later issue, for it does not appear on the Roll, but in any eventuality was not properly earned. He was with a draft which reached South Africa in September 1847, but the musters show he did not leave Cape Town until February 1848 and by that time peace had been declared.

PRO Reference WO/12/425/6/7.

12th (The Prince of Wales's) Royal Regiment of Lancers

The 12th Lancers was one of the regiments sent to South Africa as reinforcements in 1851. Given short notice before embarkation in the 'Birkenhead' and 'Charlotte', those on board the latter ship had a miserable voyage. Lt Jary recorded 'no convict ship was worse' and the passage to Cape Town took a month longer than that of the 'Birkenhead' but by mid-October the entire regiment was at East London.

The small Cape horses provided as mounts were no better suited for Lancers than they had been for heavy dragoons and when severe weather and short rations pulled them down many died from sickness.

Weapons too were hardly ideal for the warfare which faced them but the men's lances made useful ridgepoles when makeshift tents were required! Their flintlock pistols were cumbersome and Lt Col Pole ordered all officers to carry carbines or rifles while his advance guards used double barrelled carbines.

For Somerset's campaign beyond the Kei during November/December 1851 and January 1852 the bulk of the 12th Lancers was attached to Col Mackinnon's column, but a detachment under Maj Tottenham marched with Col Eyre to relieve Kaffir pressure on Butterworth before joining with Somerset. Large numbers of cattle and other livestock were captured in the operations in the area of the Little Kei and T'somo rivers and within a few days of returning to headquarters at King William's Town the regiment received new orders. They were posted to Kabousie Nek on January 25th to implement the scorched earth policy; capturing or killing cattle, burning Kraals and destroying crops. The patrols in pursuit of these ends brought on some minor skirmishes but did little to subdue the enemy and the troops suffered badly from severe weather.

As part of the plan to clear the Waterkloof stronghold the 12th Lancers were stationed at Eland's Post. Their duty was to intercept the natives flushed out by columns under Michel, Eyre and Napier, which had advanced on March 10th. After five days in the mountains a great number of cattle had been gathered by Lancer patrols and the Kaffirs were pursued to the Tyumie River. An extension of the operations, during which the regiment was diverted between Eyre's and Michel's columns, swept the enemy to the Kei and inflicted heavy casualties.

During the following months the Kaffirs gradually filtered back to their old haunts and in August operations were begun which again cleared the Waterkloof. But this time further drives were made on the Kroome Range and eventually the Amatolas. The Kaffir insurrection was now all but at an end and the 12th Lancers could hardly have expected their greatest test was to come.

When Cathcart moved against the Basuto chief Mosesh in November 1852 his force included two squadrons of Lancers and after a hard march a camp was established at Platberg in mid-December. An attempt to extract a fine of cattle was largely unsuccessful and on the 20th December three columns set out to punish the Basutos on the Berea Plateau. A detachment of the regiment under Lt Gough moved with Cathcart's column around the base of the south and western sides of the plateau; 11 Lancers acted as escort to Eyre, who was to climb to the summit; and the remainder of the 12th – 114 rank and file – accompanied Napier's troops to watch the north and eastern approaches.

Cathcart soon met the enemy. Gough formed his men in extended order and with the aid of the guns drove off the Basutos. Eyre lost a few men in crossing the plateau and, as he descended, was surprised by well mounted enemy horsemen wearing caps and lances captured from Napier's column. After a sharp action he joined Cathcart and a square was formed until canister dispersed their attackers.

Napier had been in some more serious fighting. Finding his maps inaccurate he determined to move across the Berea. At first the column met only slight opposition and the Lancers and CM Riflemen gathered up a vast herd of cattle as they went. Suddenly they were charged by a host of Basuto horsemen who had been concealed in dead ground. Tottenham and the men acting as rearguard were enveloped by the enemy. Many were cut down, for in close work nine-foot lances were no match for assegais and the light axes which could be used as swords or throwing weapons. With the support of some of the Cape Mounted, Tottenham rallied the survivors and enabled Napier to carry off the cattle. At the bottom of the hill a troop of the 12th Lancers charged the Basutos and killed several before the remainder turned their attention to the 74th who were protecting the crossing on the Caledon River. It was the infantry who finally beat off the enemy and James McKay of the 74th wrote 'It was painful to see the 12th on their return.... During the desperate charges in which they had been engaged many had their lances broken, and only retained the blade half in their hands; some had no lances at all; others were without caps, but had handkerchiefs tied around their heads, besmirched with blood; and some were horseless, showing the severe struggle they had with the enemy.'

Besides those Lancers lost with Tottenham several men with Capt Oakes and a troop of the CMR had been cut off early in the action. Desperate riding saved most of them but some had ridden into a morass and were butchered. Altogether 27 NCOs and men of the 12th were killed.

No doubt to Cathcart's relief Mosesh thereafter adopted a conciliatory attitude and the British troops, having narrowly escaped a disaster, were able to withdraw honourably.

With peace once again on the frontier the regiment remained in South Africa for another year, when they sailed for India and campaigns of larger proportions.

		Kaffir Wars		
		1	2	3
LIEUTENANT COLONEL				
Edward Pole	1)			△
MAJOR				
William H. Tottenham	2)			△
CAPTAIN				
Edward B. Cureton				△

		Kaffir Wars		
		1	2	3
John A. Digby				△
George C. T. Durant	(R)			△
John W. Fox				△
David A. Monro	3) (P)			△
Thomas G. A. Oakes	3)			△
John De M. M. Prior	(P)			△
George Whittingstall				△

34 South Africa 1853 Medal

LIEUTENANT

Name	Notes	Kaffir Wars 1	2	3
Chandos F. Clifton				
Charles F. Fuller				△
George T. Gough	3)			△
Robert H. Jary				△
John K. Lennox				△
Charles Marr				△
John E. Swindley	3) (P)			△
Arthur W. Williams				△

CORNET

Name	Notes	1	2	3
Valentine Baker				△
Ralph S. Bond	4)			△
Edward Brown				△
Valentine D. H. C. Elwes				△

SURGEON

Name	Notes	1	2	3
George Anderson				△

ASSISTANT SURGEON

Name	Notes	1	2	3
Dudley C. Wodsworth				△

PAYMASTER

Name	Notes	1	2	3
Blayney Walshe				△

QUARTERMASTER

Name	Notes	1	2	3
Michael Blake				△

VETERINARY SURGEON

Name	Notes	1	2	3
William Thacker				△

SERGEANT MAJOR

Name	Notes	1	2	3
Joseph Sefton				△

TROOP SERGEANT MAJOR

Name	Notes	1	2	3
Joseph Cummins				△
Dennis Evans				△
John Milligan				△
James Pronger				△

FARRIER MAJOR

Name	Notes	1	2	3
John Fryer	(P)			△

TRUMPET MAJOR

Name	Notes	1	2	3
Benjamin Laing	(P)			△

SERGEANT

Name	Notes	1	2	3
Joseph Bailey				△
John Basher				△
Thomas Elliott				△
Daniel Ferris				△
John Gibson				△
Stephen Gibson				△
Francis Gormley				△
William Green				△
Edward Hyde	(M)			△
Henry Mimmack				△
William Pye				△
John Rogers				△
William Taylor				△
William Thompson				△

CORPORAL

Name	Notes	1	2	3
Frederick Bailey				△
Charles Cross	5) (R)			△
Barry Dennehy				△
Henry Field				△
Patrick Fitzgerald				△
Cornelius Glennan				△
James Innes				△
Henry Leeland				△
Thomas McVeagh				△
James Moreton				△
Mark Munson				△
Samuel Ordidge				△
Edwin Overton				△
Stephen Perkins				△
John W. Smith				△
Edwin Stott				△
Charles Wabe				△
William Whitfield				△

TRUMPETER

Name	Notes	1	2	3
John Earson				△
John Gleason				△
John Henderson				△
Joseph Phipps	(R)			△
Henry Rayner				△
William Towsend				△
John Walsh				△

PRIVATE

Name	Notes	1	2	3
William Adams				△
John Allingham				△
Robert Anderson				△
Josiah Arch				△
Thomas Arms				△
Thomas Armitage	7)			△
John Ashley				△
John Banaghan	8)			△
William Barber				△
William Barnes				△
George Basdell				
William Beck				△
Robert Bell				△
George Bendy				△
Thomas Berne				
Joseph Bevan				△
John Bingham				△
Patrick Birmingham				△
William Blower				△
Dennis Boardman				△
William Bollingbroke	9)			△
Henry Bolton				△
Joseph Booth				△
John Bosworth				△
James Bowes				△
John H. Box	(P)			△
Henry Bragg				△
James Braithwaite				△
Walter Bramwell				△
Robert Brewer	(P)			△
Richard Bristol				△
John Brooker				△
Robert McMullen Brown				△
James Brown	10)		△	△
Thomas Brown				△
William Brown				△
William Brownley				△
George Bryant				△
Francis Buck				△
William Buck				△
Michael Buggy				△
William Bullock				△
Charles Bundock				△
Patrick Burey				△
Richard Burke	11)			△
Robert Butler	(P)			△
John Campbell				△
Edward Canderton				△
James W. Cannings				△
John Capper	(R)			△
William Capper				△
William Carley				△
James Cates				△
Thomas Cavanagh				△
Edward Caulfield				△

		Kaffir Wars					Kaffir Wars		
		1	2	3			1	2	3
Richard Chantlin	12) (R)			△	Thomas Hampton				△
George Cheadle				△	John Harper				△
Thomas Clarke				△	James Harris				△
Ralph N. Cleghorn				△	Mark Hartnell				△
Samuel Cock				△	John Harvey				△
Francis Coles				△	John Haws	(P)			△
John B. Coles				△	John Healey	18) (M)			△
Daniel Collins				△	William Hedges				△
John Conran				△	George Helliwell				△
Charles Conroy	(P)			△	Daniel Hemmings				△
William Cook				△	Joseph Hickey				△
Edward Cooper				△	Walter D. Hickman				△
Eli Cooper				△	William Hill				△
Jeremiah Couglin				△	Elijah Hodgkins				△
Henry F. Cullen				△	George Holl	19)			△
Michael Cullen				△	Garrett Holloway				△
Samuel Cumberledge				△	James Holmes				△
James Dalton				△	John B. Holmes				△
Edward Danton				△	William Holmes				△
William Dawson				△	Humphrey Home	20) (R)			△
Cornelius Delaney	13)			△	Thomas Hood				△
George J. Devereaux				△	Charles Horne				△
James Devitt				△	William Houldsworth	(P)			△
George Devonport	14) (P)			△	Alfred G. Hughes				△
Thomas Dignam				△	David Hughes				△
Stanley Dixon				△	William Hunt				△
Thomas Dodd				△	John Hutchinson				△
Miles Donegan	(P)			△	Charles Ivers				△
Francis Donnelly				△	Josiah James				△
Patrick Doyle				△	William Jenner				△
James Duffy				△	William Jessop				△
Thomas S. Eads				△	James Johnston				△
Joseph Edwards				△	James Jones				△
Patrick Egan				△	John Jones				△
George Ellis				△	Walter Jones	(R)			△
William Ellis				△	Edward Keates				△
Thomas Elliss				△	Charles Keating				△
John English	(R)			△	George King				△
George W. Ensor	15)			△	Arthur Kirby				△
Charles Evans				△	Edward Kirby				△
William Evans				△	William Knight				△
James Falvey				△	James Lane				△
George Featherstone				△	Joseph Lee				△
James Flanagan				△	Luke Leeds				△
Andrew Foggo				△	Robert H. Lofthouse				△
Thomas Foster (1)	16)			△	George Long				△
Thomas Foster (2)	16)			△	J. H. P. Luscombe				△
Thomas Foulkes				△	Thomas Lye				△
James Fowler				△	Patrick Magahey				△
John Fox				△	James Magarity				△
James Freeman				△	Hugh Maguire				△
John Freeman	(P)			△	Jude Mallender	21)			△
John Frost				△	John Mardling	(P)			△
James Gallop	(P)			△	James Martin				△
Edward Gamble				△	Jonas Martin				△
Edward Garnett				△	John Matthews				△
John Gibbons				△	James McBride (1)	22)			△
John Gibson				△	James McBride (2)	22)			△
George Gilbert				△	James McCann				△
James Gilluly				△	John McCarthy				△
William Goldstone				△	William McCullock				△
John Gorman				△	Patrick McCrate				△
Jathro Grace				△	Duncan McDavid				△
Moses Gregory				△	Robert McGowan				△
Edward Griffin				△	John McGregor	(P)			△
John Hall (1)	17) (R)			△	James McLoughlin				△
John Hall (2)	17) (MRM)			△	Michael McManus				△
Joseph Hampton				△	John Mee				△

36 South Africa 1853 Medal

PRIVATE		Kaffir Wars 1 2 3			Kaffir Wars 1 2 3
John Metcalfe	(R)	△	Benjamin Scholfield	4)	△
Thomas Miller		△	Samuel Scholfield		△
Joseph Mills		△	Walter McD. Severier		△
Joseph Mitchell		△	William Sharpe		△
John Moon		△	James Shaughnessey		△
Philip Mooney		△	William T. Shaw		△
William Moore		△	James Shotter	(MRM)	△
William Morley		△	Joseph Smith (1)	26)	△
John Morton		△	Joseph Smith (2)	26)	△
Isaac Moss		△	Patrick Smith		△
John Mulhern		△	John Smyth		△
Michael Mulloy		△	Edward Sprowell		△
Thomas Munro		△	Edwin Staddin		△
Charles Murphy		△	William Stafford		△
John Murray		△	Henry Starr	27) (R)	△
Peter Murthi	(MRM)	△	James Steer		△
George Naylor		△	David Stickley		△
Samuel Neidham	23)	△	William H. Sutcliffe		△
Frederick Nellor		△	Joseph Sutton		△
Thomas Newall		△	Thomas A. Swaysland		△
John Newnham		△	George Tailby		△
Andrew Nicholson	(P)	△	John Tailby		△
Edmund O'Ryan		△	Robert Teasey		△
William Osmond		△	Francis Thompson		△
John T. Palfreman		△	William Thompson		△
Richard M. Parkinson		△	Henry Tillier		△
Samuel Payne		△	William Toesland		△
William Payne	24)	△	John Toole		△
James J. Pearce		△	William Trevis		△
Edward Peers		△	Bartholomew Trevors		△
Henry Pengally		△	Edwin Troughton		△
Andrew F. Phillips		△	George Turner		△
George Pike		△	William Turville	28)	△
Joseph Pinchback		△	Samuel Ufton		△
Walter Pitcher		△	Daniel Underwood		△
Thomas Pound		△	William Uzzell		△
Charles Powell		△	Thomas Walsh		△
Thomas Pryce		△	John West		△
Alfred Rawlins		△	William West		△
William Redburn		△	Samuel Whalley		△
Pressland Reeve		△	Isaac Wheeler	(P)	△
William Rice		△	Joseph White		△
James Rickey		△	James Whitehead		△
John Rider		△	Luke Whitehead		△
Thomas Rider		△	William Whitehead		△
Edward Roberts		△	James Wickens		△
William Roberts		△	John Wickens		△
William Rodgers		△	William Wickens		△
James Rowley		△	Thomas Williams		△
John Russell		△	Henry Wright		△
Thomas Sampey	25)	△	Samuel Wright		△
George Sawyer		△	△=campaign qualification as WO/100/17.		

12TH (THE PRINCE OF WALES'S) ROYAL REGIMENT OF LANCERS NOTES

1. Commanded the cavalry and artillery during Somerset's expedition beyond the Kei, November, December 1851.
2. Struck on the head with a knobkerry at Berea. See Moore; McKay.
3. Present at Berea.
4. A survivor from the 'Birkenhead', February 1852.
5. The Regimental Museum has a medal which I understand is named to F. Cross. Two men named Cross served with the regiment. Robert, who went to the CMR and Charles; the latter's second christian name began with F, and I conclude the medal was his.
6. Munsen on Roll.
7. Armytage on Roll.
8. Bannaghan on Roll.
9. Boilingbrook on Roll, variously spelt on musters.
10. Served with the 73rd during the 2nd campaign.
11. Burk on Roll.
12. Chantler on Roll and medal, the latter also wrongly bearing the initial 'H'.
13. Delany on Roll.
14. Devenport on Roll; medal may show Cpl Davenport.
15. Appears to be Enson on Roll.
16. Nos 601 and 603.
17. Nos 1087 and 1117, either of which could be the medal in the Regimental Museum.
18. Healy on Roll.
19. Also Hole on musters.
20. Medal wrongly named Horne.
21. Mallendar on Roll.
22. Nos 872 and 1122.
23. Neiddam on Roll.
24. Paine on Roll.
25. Sampry on Roll.
26. Nos 924 and 1343.
27. Star on Roll, but medal correctly named.
28. Christian name correctly altered on Roll from Henry.

PRO References: WO/12/1059/60/1/2.

Royal Artillery

Until the war of 1846-7 a single company was required to stretch itself from Cape Town to the most forward posts and before the outbreak of 1834 the allocation of Gunners to the frontier was just 20 men. Throughout the period of the wars the artillerymen were so scattered that it was not uncommon for a bombardier to command a detachment. Such men possessed a freedom of action experienced by few non-commissioned officers of those days.

Unfortunately it is not always possible to be certain from the musters whether a man saw service in the field against the Kaffirs and therefore this Roll, which has had to be constructed from the musters, shows all the men who served in South Africa with the RA during the wars but excluding those known to have been killed, died or deserted and others who undoubtedly did not qualify for the medal.

In 1851 Major H. R. Eardley-Wilmot, OC, the 4th Co 5th Btn wrote – 'I cannot persuade the people here that guns are of no use for this sort of work, as guns drive Kaffirs away and our object should be to get near them ... artillery is of no use in this country except when escorting wagons, in a camp or in forts.'

Perhaps if Eardley-Wilmot had not been killed in action on New Year's Day 1852 his views might eventually have gained acceptance but commanders persisted in employing artillery on offensive operations to the very end of the war. That their columns made slow progress while the guns and limbers were laboriously hauled across wooded and mountainous terrain seems not to have discouraged them and when the enemy resorted to felling trees along the paths of retreat artillerymen had to lift the guns bodily over the obstructions.

But when employed defensively cannon played an important role. Heavy losses were inflicted on Kaffir and Hottentot forces gathering to attack the posts and forts and at times may have been crucial in the outcome.

Five different companies of the RA saw service in the Kaffir campaigns. At the outbreak of the 1st war the **8th Co 8th Btn** were the only artillerymen stationed in South Africa and to reinforce their numbers on the frontier some 50 men of the 75th Regiment were hastily trained to serve the guns. Under Capt J. S. Bastard 8th Co had been in the continent since 1831, based at Cape Town and then Grahams Town. During 1835 they appear to have seen little action and the only fatal casualty was an unfortunate corporal who fell to his death from a cliff. The 8th/8th tour of duty in the Cape lasted until December 1841 and they were replaced by the **5th Co 4th Btn** who had reached Cape Town the previous August commanded by Capt Pallisser.

Eighteen men of the Company were with Capt Smith's expedition in Natal in 1842. Twelve were killed or wounded at Congella and the relieving force included eight artillerymen under Lt Maclean.

The larger part of the 5th/4th were in the Cape Town garrison or at Simons Town during the period of the 2nd war. At the same time a detachment of 17 men was in Natal for operations against the Zulus under Capt Faddy (3rd/7th) but an officer and 36 men were sent to serve on the field. The company returned home in January 1850.

It was the **3rd Co 7th Btn** who bore the brunt of the gunners' work during 1846-7. They had landed at Simons Bay in July 1843 commanded by Capt Shepherd and moved promptly to Grahams Town but during 1846-7 were also centred at Post Victoria and Fort Beaufort. For the whole of their 10 years in South Africa they were on or near the frontier. A detachment of the 3rd/7th was at Boemplaats and the company saw considerable service in 1850-3, their headquarters being at Grahams Town. Capt Burnaby succeeded Shepherd and the 3rd/7th eventually sailed for Europe in November 1853.

The **4th Co 5th Btn** OC Capt Lethbridge arrived at the Cape in October 1849. Thirty officers and men went promptly to Natal and as the situation deteriorated on the frontier some 60 officers and men under Capt Eardley-Wilmot were sent to King William's Town in December 1850. A year later Eardley-Wilmot was killed at the Fish River and Capt Devereux commanded for the remainder of the war, following which the 4th/5th was reunited at Fort Napier, Natal.

After returning to England with the 5th/4th Capt Faddy sailed again for South Africa, this time with the **4th Co 8th Btn**. At the Cape by the end of August 1851 the company lost little time in marching to the scene of operations and were at Grahams Town in October. From July to September 1852 they were centred at Fort Beaufort and then returned to Grahams Town for the remainder of the war.

The loss of the major portion of the returns of the Royal Artillery other ranks has necessitated a reconstruction from the musters. Listed here are over 500 officers and men who qualified for the medal but for one reason or another, less than half of them actually claimed the award. Mint records show that 195 medals were earmarked in the first batch for the regiment and with subsequent issues I estimate approximately 225 medals altogether were presented to artillerymen.

				Kaffir Wars		
			Co/Btn	1	2	3
BREVET MAJOR						
Hon. George T. Devereux	1)		4/5			△
Peter P. Faddy	2)		4/8			△
CAPTAIN						
Charles H. Burnaby	3)	(R)	3/7		△	△
William M. King	4)	(P)	3/7		△	
Stapylton Robinson	5)		4/8			△
Henry F. Slater			8/8	△		
LIEUTENANT						
Patrick J. Campbell	6)		4/5			○
Alfred W. Drayson			5/4		△	
Edward E. R. Dyneley	7)	(R)	3/7		△	
Thomas S. Field	8)		4/5			△

				Kaffir Wars		
			Co/Btn	1	2	3
James M. Hill	9)		3/7		△	
R. Horsley R. Rowley			4/8			△
ASSISTANT SURGEON						
Hugh C. Walshe			Ord Med Dept		△	
Stanhope H. Fasson	10)		Ord Med Dept		○	○
SERGEANT MAJOR						
James Scott		(P)	8/8	○		
COMPANY SERGEANT						
John Bowie			8/8	○		
George Cowen			8/8	○		
James Hook	11)		3/7		○	○
James Lennox	11)		3/7		△	

38 South Africa 1853 Medal

Name		Co/Btn	Kaffir Wars 1	2	3
COMPANY SERGEANT					
Robert Lucas		4/5			O
Reuben Stubbs		5/4	O		
Elijah Swan		8/8	O		
Alexander Watters		4/8			O
John Wharin		3/7	O		
William Wilson		8/8	O		
SERGEANT					
George Dallas		5/4	O		
John Dallas		5/4	O		
Alexander Denning		8/8	Δ		
John Flanagan		8/8	O		
John Good		3/7	O		
Gavin Greenlees		8/8	O		
James Hopkirk		4/5			O
William Jarvis		4/5			O
William Lee	11) (P)	3/7	O	O	
Henry Lord		5/4	O		
Roderick Mackenzie	(P)	4/5		Δ	
Andrew Main	12)	4/5	O		
William McAdam		5/4	O		
Patrick Meehan		4/8			O
James Midgley		3/7	Δ		
Edwin Morris		4/8			O
Henry Oliphant	11)	3/7	O		O
John Scott		4/8			O
William Turner		3/7	O		O
Thomas Wells		4/8			O
CORPORAL					
Alexander Bennett	(P)	3/7	Δ	O	
Joseph Campbell	11)	3/7	O		O
James Castles		4/8			O
John Creggan		5/4	O		
James Davenport		5/4	O		
John Dawson		4/5			O
Robert Dunlop		5/4	O		
Joseph Hamilton		3/7	O		
Matthew Harris		3/7	O		
Thomas Hassall		4/8			O
William Hayter	11)	3/7			O
Hugh Keenan		4/8			O
Adam Lawson		8/8	Δ		
Patrick Lunney		4/8			O
John Martin	(P)	4/5		Δ	
John McArthur		8/8	O		
William Morton		8/8	O	O	
George Moscrop		8/8	O		
James O'Connor		3/7	O		O
John Rogers		4/5			O
Henry Wilson	11)	3/7	O	O	
John Wilson		3/7			O
James Woolley		4/5			O
BOMBARDIER					
James Aiken		3/7	O		
Henry Atkins		4/8			O
Richard Barlow	(P)	3/7	O		O
Frederick Black	13)	4/8			O
John Campbell		5/4	O		
James Carter		8/8	O		
John Flanagan		5/4	O		
John Glen		3/7	O		O
Edward Harvey		5/4	O		
Robert Hogg		8/8	O		
Thomas Hume		8/8	O		
Joshua Kelly		4/8			O
Thomas Lyness		4/8			O
William McGee		4/8			O
George Merchant	14)	3/7	O		O

Name		Co/Btn	Kaffir Wars 1	2	3
Alexander Moore		3/7	O		O
Walter Perryman		4/5			O
Walter Sim		4/5			O
Robert Smith		4/5			O
James Wallace		4/8			O
James Wright		4/5			O
Robert Wright	11)	4/5			O
DRUMMER/TRUMPETER					
Jacob Binns		5/4	O		
James Cuthbert		4/5			O
John Divine		3/7	O		
James Kirk		3/7			O
Francis McManners		8/8	O		
Benjamin Mitchell		4/5			O
James Orr		4/5			O
Archibald Paterson		5/4	O		
Henry Rollands		4/8			O
Charles Stewart		8/8	O		
George Wilson		4/5			O
Richard Worger		3/7			O
GUNNER/DRIVER					
Charles Albaster	15)	8/8	O		
Benjamin Airey		3/7			O
Alfred Allen		3/7		Δ	
Joseph Allen		5/4	O		
James Anderson		5/4	O		
John Anderson		5/4	O		
Frederick Andrews		3/7			O
James Armstrong		8/8	O		
Robert Armstrong		4/8			O
John Ashworth		8/8	O		
Ralph Astley		5/4	O		
John Atkinson	(P)	8/8	O		
James Attenborough		4/8			O
William Auld		3/7			O
Thomas Aylmore		3/7	O		O
Thomas Bamford		5/4	O		
James Barker		4/8			O
Samuel Barnard		5/4	O		
Thomas Barnby		4/5			O
James Bashforth		3/7			O
James Baxter		4/8			O
Dickson Beaton		5/4	O		
David Beattie		5/4	O		
Thomas Bennett		8/8		O	
John Best		3/7	O		O
James Bishop		8/8	O		
Thomas Bissett		4/8			O
Peter Black		3/7	Δ		O
Robert Blair	(P)	4/8		Δ	
George Bonning		5/4	O		
Robert Borthwick	11)	3/7	O		O
Benjamin Braithwaite	16) (P)	4/5			O
John Brice	11)	3/7	O		O
John Bright		5/4	O		
James Britton		4/8			O
Edward Brown		4/8			O
John Brown	17) (MRM)	?			?
Patrick Brown		3/7			O
Richard Brown		8/8	O		
Robert Brown		3/7			O
John Brucher		5/4	O		
Thomas Burke		3/7	O		
John Burns		5/4	O		
Thomas Butterfield		8/8	O		
James Cairnes	(MRM)	4/8			O
William Calwell		4/5			

South Africa 1853 Medal 39

Name		Co/Btn	Kaffir Wars 1 2 3
Alexander Cameron		3/7	○ ○
John Campbell		4/5	○
R-. Carmichael		3/7	○
James Carroll		3/7 & 4/8	○ ○
Hance Carson		3/7	○
Thomas Carson		4/5	○
William Cawley		4/5	
John Chapman		8/8	○
William Chapman		3/7	○ ○
William Chest		5/4	○
George Child		4/5	○
William Clacker		4/5	○
William Clayton		4/8	○
SHOEING SMITH			
Francis Clegg	11)	3/7	○ ○
GUNNER/DRIVER			
Thomas Clues		5/4	○
Thomas Coalston		3/7	○ ○
Isaac Colcraft		4/8	○
Edward Collier		3/7	○
William Collins	11)	3/7	○
Edward Connolly		3/7	○
George Cook		8/8	○
James Corell		5/4	○
William Cottrell (1)		5/4 & 3/7	○ ○
William Cottrell (2)	18)	8/8	○
James Coulter		4/5	○
Abraham Cousins	(P)	4/8	○
Richard Crampion	11)	3/7	○ ○
WHEELER			
John Crawford		4/5	○
GUNNER DRIVER			
James Cross	19)	8/8	△
Edmund Crowe		3/7	○
James Cunningham		3/7	○ ○
Bernard Curley		8/8	○
John Curley		8/8	○
Patrick Curley		8/8	○
Thomas Curley		8/8	○
Emerson Cuthbert		4/5	○
John Daley		4/8	○
FARRIER			
William Darling	11)	3/7	○
GUNNER/DRIVER			
Henry Davie		5/4	○
James Davis		3/7	○
John Davis		5/4	○
Thomas Daw		5/4	○
Thomas Day		8/8	○
Boyd Dewar		4/5	○
William Dewhurst		3/7	△ ○
Dominic Diamond		5/4	△
Robert Diamond		5/4 & 4/8	○ ○
Caleb Dickens		4/8	○
James Dickson		8/8	○
William Doloughan		5/4	○
William Donachie		8/8	○
Bernard Donnelly		4/8	○
George Donnelly		3/7	○
Bernard Dorkin		8/8	○
Thomas Downey		5/4	○
Peter Doyle		3/7	○ ○
SHOEING SMITH			
John Duncan		4/5	○
GUNNER/DRIVER			
Nelson Duncan		3/7	○
James Dunn		4/8	○

Name		Co/Btn	Kaffir Wars 1 2 3
John Dunn		4/8	○
Pierce Dynes		4/5	○
John Edis		4/5	○
Andrew Edmondston		8/8	○
Richard Entwistle		8/8	
William Ellis	(P)	4/5	○
Edward Evans		3/7	○ ○
David Ferguson		8/8	○
Thomas Ferns		3/7	○ ○
William Findlay		4/8	○
William Findlayson		8/8	○
Daniel Flanagan		4/8	○
John Flanagan		4/5	○
Michael Foins	20)	3/7	○ ○
William Follay		5/4	○
John Fraser		4/5	○
John Fulton		3/7	○ ○
John Galletly		8/8	○
George Gibbs		5/4	○
Edward Gibson		8/8	○
Robert Gibson		5/4	○
Hugh Gileese	(MRM)	4/8	○
John Giles		8/8	○
Lewis Gillett		3/7	○ ○
Alexander Gilpin	21)	4/5	△
James Gilpin		4/5	○
William Gilpin		4/5	○
John Glass	18)	8/8	○
John Glenn		4/8	○
William Goforth		4/5	○
Charles Goodbrand		3/7	○ ○
Terence Goodwin		3/7	○
Alexander Gould		4/5	○
David Gourlay		4/8	○
William Graham		4/5	○
James Grant		5/4	○
John Grant		5/4	
Philip Gratton		3/7	○
Henry Gray		4/5	○
Thomas Gray		5/4	○
James Gribben		3/7	○
John Gribbon		4/5	△
James Griffiths		3/7	○
John Hall		4/5	○
John Halstead		8/8	○
Thomas Hamilton		8/8	○
Robert Hancock		4/5	○
Henry Handbridge		3/7	○ ○
Patrick Hannigan		4/8	○
John Harcombe		4/8	○
George Harvey		5/4	
Andrew Haxton		3/7	○ ○
Robert Hay		4/5	○
COLLAR MAKER			
John Henry	(P)	4/8	
GUNNER/DRIVER			
John Hetherington	(P)	4/5	○
John Heywood	22)	3/7	○ ○
William Hobell	(P)	4/8	
James Hodgkins		3/7	○
Thomas Holden	11)	3/7	○ ○
Charles Holland		4/8	△
Benjamin Hollingsworth		4/8	○
Hartley Holt		5/4	○
William Hooper		5/4	○
Peter Horner		4/5	○
Matthew Hosie		4/8	○

40 South Africa 1853 Medal

Name	Note	Co/Btn	Kaffir Wars 1	2	3
GUNNER/DRIVER					
William Howarth	23) (P)	8/8 & 3/7	O	△	
Samuel Hudson		4/5			O
Maurice Hughes		5/4		O	
Stephen Hughes		4/8			O
Andrew Illingworth	24)	8/8	△		
William Illingworth		8/8	O		
Alexander Irvine		4/8			O
George Jackson		4/8			O
William Jackson		4/8			O
George Jeffries		5/4		O	
Thomas Jeffries		5/4		O	
Alexander Jervis		3/7		O	O
James Johnston		8/8	O		
Robert Johnston		8/8	O		
Samuel Johnston		3/7		O	O
Thomas Johnston		5/4		O	
Charles Jones		4/5			O
George Jones		3/7			O
John Jones		4/5			O
Thomas Jones		3/7			O
Joshua Judd		5/4		O	
Daniel Kelly		5/4 & 3/7	△	O	
William Kennedy		8/8	O		
James Kenny		4/5			O
John Kenny		4/5			△
William Kent		3/7			O
Robert Keone		4/8			O
Elias Kidd		4/5			O
James Kiggan		4/5			O
Henry Kinder		4/8			O
James Kirk		5/4		O	
John Kirkbride		4/5			O
David Knight	(P)	4/5			O
George Knight (1)		3/7			O
George Knight (2)		4/5			O
Joshua Lakin		3/7			O
William Lamb	11)	3/7		O	O
John Lancaster		8/8 & 5/4	O	O	
George Leaper		4/5			O
John Lecknam		5/4		O	
James Ledingham		3/7		O	
John Leonard		8/8	O		
Matthew Lewis		5/4		O	
Robert Lindsay		8/8 & 5/4	O	△	
James Lipton		4/8			O
John Litley		5/4		O	
David Little		4/5			O
Robert Little		4/5			O
John Logan		3/7		△	O
WHEELER					
William Long		4/5			O
GUNNER/DRIVER					
William Lucas (1)		3/7		O	
William Lucas (2)		4/8			O
John Ludlam		4/8			O
Patrick Lunney		5/4		O	
John Lyde		4/5			O
Joshua Lyness		4/8			O
Bernard Maguire		4/8			O
John Malone	(P)	4/8			△
Hugh Maroy		4/5			O
Henry Marriott		4/8			O
James McAdams		4/5			O
James McAleese		4/5			O
John McCawley		4/8			O
John McConkey		4/8			O
Miles McCough		3/7		O	O
Robert McCrea		4/8			O
David McDole		4/5			O
Edward McDonagh		4/8			O
Donald McDonald		4/5			O
Malcolm McDougall		8/8	O		
Peter McEteer		4/8			O
John McGee		5/4		O	
Robert McGhie		4/5			O
William McGladdery		5/4		O	
Turbett McGonagall		4/5			O
Francis McGovern		4/8			O
William McGrath		4/5			O
Alexander McGuinness		3/7		O	
Philip McGuinness		4/8			O
Edward McGuirk		4/8			O
Alexander McKay		8/8	O		
Donald McKay		4/8			O
William McKeown		4/5			O
James McKittrick		5/4		O	
John McKittrick		5/4		O	
William McLaughlin		4/5			O
John McLean		8/8	O		
John McLeay		8/8	O		
James McMullen		4/5			O
Samuel McMullen		4/5			O
James McQuilkin		3/7		O	O
John McQuilkin		3/7		O	O
James Melroy	11)	3/7		O	O
Dennis Mihan		5/4		O	
Joseph Miller		8/8	O		
William Mitchell	18)	8/8	O		
John Moffatt	11)	3/7		O	O
Charles Monahan		4/8			O
Patrick Mulgrew		4/8			O
James Mulholland		4/5			O
Thomas Murdoch		4/8			O
William Murdoch		3/7		O	
James Murray		3/7		O	
John Murray		4/5			O
George Musgrove		4/5			O
Samuel Neilson		3/7		O	O
Matthew Nielson		5/4		O	
Francis Nolan		3/7		O	O
John O'Connor		3/7		O	
James O'Donnell		4/5			O
Eli Palmer		4/8			O
William Parry		4/8			O
Richard Pasmore		4/8			O
James Patterson		3/7		O	O
Henry Pawley		4/8			O
Abel Penfold	(P)	4/8			O
Adam Perry		3/7		O	O
James Piper		4/5			O
William Pippin		8/8	O		
William Pollard		8/8	△		
William Polson	(M)	4/8			O
George Pooley		4/5			O
Adam Potter	(P)	4/5			O
George Prince		3/7		O	O
Andrew Purdie		5/4		O	
Patrick Quinn		4/8			O
Thomas Redding		4/5			O
John Reed		4/8			O
George Reid		3/7			O
William Reid		4/5			O
James Rennick		4/5		O	
John Rice		3/7		O	O
Joshua Rice		4/8			O

South Africa 1853 Medal

		Co/Btn	Kaffir Wars 1 2 3
Robert Rintone		3/7	O O
Dominic Rivron		5/4	O
Hector Robertson	(P)	4/8	O
George Robinson		3/7	O
Alfred Rodham		5/4	△
Alexander Rose		4/8	O
David Ross		3/7	△ O
Alfred Rowe		5/4	O
William Russell	11)	3/7	O O
John Rylands		8/8	O
Amos Selley		4/5	O
Isaac Sheen		4/5	O
Thomas Shepherd		4/8	O
William Shepherd		8/8	O
Richard Siddle	(P)	5/4	O
John Simpson		4/5	O
James Skelly		5/4	O
Luke Slavin		3/7	O
Michael Slavine		4/8	O
James Small		5/4	O
George Smallman		5/4	O
Edward Smith	(P)	5/4 & 4/5	O O
George Smith (1)		8/8	O
COLLAR MAKER			
George Smith (2)	(P)	3/7 & 4/5	O O
GUNNER/DRIVER			
Henry Smith		4/5	O
Joseph Smith		5/4	O
Joshua Smith		5/4	O
Patrick Smith		4/8	O
Thomas Smith		8/8	O
Thomas Spink		4/5	O
James Stephenson		4/5	O
George Stewart		8/8, 5/4 & 3/7	O O O
Henry Stewart	(P)	4/8	O
John Stewart		8/8	O
George Stinson		4/8	O
John Stoops		5/4	O
Thomas Stoops		5/4	O
Henry Stubbs		5/4	O
John Sutherland		4/8	O
Isaac Talbot		4/8	O
Frederick Taylor		4/8	O
George Taylor		3/7	O
John Taylor	18)	8/8	O
Thomas Tetley		4/8	O
Charles Thompson		3/7	O
Hugh Thompson		8/8	△
William Tilley		4/8	O
James Tomkinson		3/7	O O
Edward Toomey		4/8	O
Robert Totten		5/4 & 4/8	△ O
John Tracey	11)	3/7	O O
Joseph Turner		4/5	O
Daniel Tyler		4/5	O
Job Vains		3/7	O
Thomas Valentine	(P)	4/8	O
William Wadsworth		4/8	O
James Walker		8/8	O
William Walker	(P)	4/8	O
Thomas Warwell		3/7	O
Alexander Watson		4/5	O
James Watson		3/7	O O
Robert Watson		8/8	O
John Watt		4/5	O
William Watt		3/7	O O
Alexander Webster	(P)	3/7	△ O
James Weir		5/4	O
Alexander Wells		5/4	△
James Wheaton		4/8	△
Job White		5/4	O
John White		5/4	△
Thomas Whitaker		8/8	O
Thomas Whitsett		3/7	O
Charles Wilkinson		4/8	O
William Williams		8/8	O
SHOEING SMITH			
James Willison	(MRM)	4/5	O
GUNNER/DRIVER			
Andrew Wilson		8/8	O
Charles Wilson		5/4	O
James Wilson		5/4	O
Robert Wilson		8/8	O
Charles Wones	(MRM)	4/5	O
David G. Wright		4/5	O
Robert Wright	25)	3/7	O
John Young		3/7	△

△ = campaign qualification as WO/100/17.
O = campaign which the Rolls fail to credit.

ROYAL ARTILLERY NOTES

1. At Berea. See Moodie.
2. Commanded the RA against the Zulus in Natal 1846. Engaged in the Waterkloof expedition against Macomo in March 1852. Served at Berea.
3. Commanded the RA on the frontier during the 2nd and 3rd campaigns. Commandant of Grahams Town in 1851. See G and I; Bissett.
4. Commanded the artillery in defence of Fort Peddie 27th/28th May 1846.
5. At Berea. See Moodie; McKay.
6. With Michel's force on the Fish river September 1851. With the Waterkloof expedition, October 1851.
7. A later claimant who was given a re-named engraved medal. Served at Boemplaats. See G and I.
8. With the Waterkloof force October 1851. See McKay.
9. With the force at Burns Hill, April 1846.
10. Not on Roll but Harts confirms. See King.
11. Served at Boemplaats.
12. With the expedition against Mosesh and the Basutos, November 1852. See McKay.
13. Only appears on Roll as a note against a cancelled medal showing him to have received a re-named engraved medal, perhaps as a replacement.
14. Was in charge of the RA detachment of 24 pounder Howitzers during the attack on Fort Hare, 21st January 1851. Served at Boemplaats. See G and I.
15. Also Alblaster on musters.
16. Medal wrongly shows christian name initial as 'R'.
17. Only appears on Roll as a note against a cancelled medal. I have been unable to trace him on musters.
18. Served at Waterloo.
19. Servant to Lt Levinge who died from an overdose of opium in 1854.
20. Also Foines on musters.
21. Earned his medal with the 45th Regt from whom he transferred in April 1853.
22. Also Haywood on musters. Served at Boemplaats.
23. Servant to Lt Slater.
24. Wrongly shown as Ellensworth on Roll.
25. Not to be confused with Bombardier Robert Wright. See also note 17.

PRO References: WO/10/1723-1739-1774-1778-1779-1804-1807-1823-1831-1846-1858-1884-1896-1897-1939-1967-1968-1998-1999-2000-2025-2026-2049-2050-2076-2077-2083-2091-2099-2109-2110-2117-2139-2140-2141-2147-2155-2173-2174-2175.

Royal Engineers/Royal Sappers and Miners

The expertise of the Royal Engineers was rarely tested during service in South Africa. The Corps was employed mostly upon routine peacetime occupations of surveying, road making, camp construction, bridge building and the like and it was considered that only a token number was sufficient to meet the needs of the Cape Colony. But as artisans, the men of the Royal Sappers and Miners were highly valued and in an attempt to increase the half company which was there in the early 1830s the point was made that, on the frontier, 'scarcely a bricklayer or mason could be found ... (who was) ... not only unskilful and indolent but generally drunken and dissipated.'

During the periods of rebellion their specialist work altered little; there were no defences to breach, mines to lay, heavy gun emplacements to prepare nor any work of the kind which was soon to fall to them in the Crimea. As regular troops were at a premium during all the campaigns, the Sappers were often called upon as infantry and during the 2nd and 3rd wars numerous detachments saw action on all parts of the frontier. But in 1835 the few men from the **2nd Company** (possibly only 30) stationed in the area of the troubles were occupied in building defensive works.

After the restoration of order the men of the 2nd Company in the Cape were replaced by the **10th Company**. It was the 10th that provided the party of sappers which accompanied Capt Smith (27th) on his expedition to Natal in 1842 where they suffered several casualties when besieged by the Boers.

The **9th Company** went to the Cape from Mauritius in August 1845 and during the next eight years saw more action than most infantry regiments. One of its NCOs Cpl Castledine, a man of exceptional calibre, was involved in one of the first skirmishes of the 'War of the Axe' when he successfully beat off an attack on a wagon in which he was travelling with a gunner and two natives. Shortage of artillerymen caused sappers to serve 9-pounders and $5\frac{1}{2}$-inch howitzers at Grahams Town as well as at other forts along the frontier, and they also manned some of the guns in the retreat from Burns Hill on April 16th/17th 1846.

On April 23rd, 50 men of the 9th Company under Lt Bourchier repulsed a night attack on their encampment near Fort Brown at the Great Fish River and killed 30 of their assailants. Bourchier's command inflicted further casualties on marauders while patrolling during May and June.

Aided by seamen, 10 sappers of the 10th Company under Lt Owen built a boat bridge across the Fish River to reopen communications with Fort Peddie and then constructed protections for the camp which had been established at Waterloo Bay. With a small detachment, Lt Stokes took part in the July operations at the mouth of the Keiskamma and in the action at Chief Dodo's Kraal. Stokes and six men then participated in Sir Peregrine Maitland's attack on the Amatolas while 38 sappers from the 10th under Lt Howarth served with the 1st Division which restored Fort Cox.

In May 1847 the strength of the Corps at the seat of the war was brought up to 155 officers and men by the reinforcement of Lt Jesse and a draft of 35 men for the 9th Company but operations were now petering out and it was a detachment of the 10th Company under the redoubtable Capt Walpole that took part in activities beyond the Kei which saw out the last few weeks of the campaign.

A strong contingent of sappers was on the frontier between the 2nd and 3rd wars. The 10th had been replaced by the **15th Company** but only a small party, a sergeant and six men of the 9th Company, were at the battle of Boemplaats. By 1850 some 200 men of the Corps were scattered among 15 posts. Five men under Capt Tylden were engaged in surveying in the Whittlesea district when, at the end of the year, Kaffirs began attacking the settlers and Tylden took the initiative in raising a local levy which did much to resist outrages in the area.

During March 1851 80 sappers on patrol in Seyolo's territory were in a skirmish which resulted in casualties on both sides and detachments of similar strength operated on the Keiskamma and in the Amatolas during April and May. Capt Robertson and 81 other ranks from the 9th and 15th Companies, serving with a force under Lt Col Burns performed gallantly at Committy's Hill on September 1st by driving the enemy from the bush.

After sailing from Mauritius the **17th Company** arrived at King William's Town in December and 19 of its NCOs and men were almost immediately despatched on patrol duties under Lt Siborne. The numbers of RS&M in the Cape now stood at 276 men of all ranks and few had any rest. They were attached to Eyre's column across the Keiskamma at the end of January 1852 and with Kyle's Division in Seyolo's country. Others participated in the Waterkloof operations which took place in March and 60 sappers under Capt Moody were with Eyre the same month.

But the bloodiest single action for the Corps occurred on June 12th. Moody, with 34 NCOs and men of the 9th Company had left Grahams Town to escort nine wagons to Fort Beaufort and on a hill near the Koonap River the convoy was ambushed by rebel Hottentots. Four of the advance guard were killed by the first volley and with women and children to protect, the soldiers fought from wagon to wagon. With seven men, one woman and a youth killed and nine wounded the survivors withdrew to a nearby ruined house and held their attackers at bay until the sounds of firing eventually attracted assistance. The rebels made off with 36 Minie rifles and 3,000 rounds of ammunition. Two of the wounded sappers later died.

From that point on matters were very much quieter for the Corps until November, when Siborne and 14 men were ordered to join Cathcart's force sent against Mosesh. The detachment did not become involved in the subsequent fighting with the Basutos and only one man was present at the action at Berea.

Nearly four years later, while the SA 1850–3 medals were awaiting distribution, the Corps of Royal Sappers and Miners was denominated the Corps of Royal Engineers, thus ending the anomaly of the officers and men being separated into two distinct corps.

As in the case of the Royal Artillery this Roll has had to be reconstructed from the musters and unavoidably lists many men who did not receive a medal. Records at the Mint show 219 medals were prepared for the RS&M. With those for the Royal Engineers and late applicants I estimate that approximately 265 medals were issued to the Corps.

South Africa 1853 Medal

		Co	Kaffir Wars 1 2 3
LIEUTENANT COLONEL			
Pennel Cole	1)		△
John Walpole	2) (R)	10	△
CAPTAIN			
Thomas Fenwick	3)	17	△
Richard Howarth	5) (P)	9	△
William F. Jervois	6) (P)	10	△
Charles Robertson	8)	15	△
Joshua K. Smith		15	△
William C. Stace			△
SECOND CAPTAIN			
Eustace Bourchier	9)	9	△
Charles Gibb	4)	10	△
William H. Jesse	10)	9	O △
Hampden Moody			△
Henry Owen	7) (P)	10	△
John Stokes	12)	9	△
Richard Tylden	13)	9	△
LIEUTENANT			
Edward Belfield		9	△
Charles Fowler		15	△
Thomas Inglis	14)	9 & 15	△
Herbert Siborne	15)	17	△
Edward Stanton	16)	9	△
Montgomery Williams	17)	2	△
COLOUR SERGEANT			
James Gardner		10	O
Charles Hawkins		15	O
John Hopkins		10	O
James Lewis		17	O
John Mealey	18)	15	O
Philip Ness		15	O
George Pringle	19)	10	△
James Robertson		15	O
Alexander Spalding	20)	9	O O
James Young	21)	10	O
SERGEANT			
Charles Beer		17	O
William Burridge	22)	10	O
Thomas Cook	23)	9	O
George Dadswell		17	O
Robert Down		10	△
Alexander Drysdale	(P)	10	O
Joseph Ireland	24) (R)	17	O
William King	25) (P)	9	O O
William Lean		2	△
James Leonard		9	O
Edward Luke		9 & 10	O
Edward Lynn		9	O O
Hugh McIntyre		9	O O
Alexander McLeod	26)	9	O O
James Marshall		17	O
Thomas Passmore		2	O
John Poole	27) (R)	10 & 9	O O
William Ralph		2	O
John Smith		2	O
Alexander B. Wright	(P)	10	△
CORPORAL			
Edward Barnicoat	28)	9 & 15	O O
John Campbell	23) (P)	10	O
Benjamin Castledine	29)	9	O O
George Colwell		2	O
Thomas Cook		10	O
James Cumming		9	O O
Christopher Dart		9	△
Noah Deary	4)	9 & 10	O
Joseph Dunbar		2	O
Benjamin Godfrey		10 & 9	O O
George Grubb	30)	17	O
James Hampson		9	O
Edward Henderson	31)	17	O
John Howatson		10	O
William Levens	(P)	9 & 17	O O
Donald McFarlane		9	O O
William McLintock		15	O
John McMurphy		10 & 9	△ O
James Ponton		17	O
William Read		9	O
John Saul		15	O
James Scott		9, 10 & 15	△ O
Henry Smith		17	△
Edwin Scrimshaw		15	O
Edward Stone		10	O
Patrick Tully		9	O
William Walters		15	O
Edward Wilmore	32)	9	O O
SECOND CORPORAL			
James Adams		10	O
William Cameron		15	O
Howell Clarke		17	O
Alfred Cossins		17	O
Henry Culhern		15	O
Archibald Cumming		10	O
John Frampton		10 & 9	O △
John Gardiner		10	O
Charles Gardner		9	O O
Stephen Hawkins		2	O
John Landrey	33)	15	O
George Lendrum		17	O
Peter Luxton		17	O
William Marshall		9	O
William McGrigor		10	O
William Roberts	34) (P)	15 & 17	O
John Shaw		9	O △
David Simpson		9	O
William G. Smart		9 & 15	O O
Patrick Walsh	(P)	9	O
James Wilson	35)	15	O
BUGLER			
Richard Bullock		9	O O
John Easterbrook		17	O
Harry Oldham		9	O O
Henry Palmer		15	O
Henry Quinn		17	O
David Sinclair		2	O
David Williamson		15	O
PRIVATE			
John Adams		15	O
Alexander Allen		10	O
Andrew Anderson	18)	10	△
Colin Anderson		17	O
David Anderson		10	O
Hugh Anderson		15	O
Frederick Andrews		17	O
John Andrews		17	O
Alfred Baker		15	O
William Baker		17	O
John Balmer		10	O
Charles Banbury		10 & 9	O O
William Bannerman		10	O
William Barnes		9	O
Thomas Barrable		9	O △
Isaac Barrett	36)	15	O

44 South Africa 1853 Medal

PRIVATE		Co	Kaffir Wars 1 2 3
William Barrett		15	○
Thomas Beard		15	○
John Beattie		10	○ ○
George Birch		17	○
Robert Blair		9	○ △
Thomas Bleakey		15	○
Hugh Boag	37) (P)	9	○
Alfred Boucher	(P)	15	○
Nicholas Bowers		10	△
Richard Bowers		17	△
John Bradley		15	○
Donald Bremner		10	○
Thomas Brooking	38)	9	△ ○
Alfred Brown		17	○
David Buchan	39)	9	○ ○
William Bullock		9	○
Edward Burnell		9	○ ○
William Burrows		15	○
John Cameron		10	△
Edward Casey		17	○
William Chandler		17	○
Robert Charters		15	○
Joseph Chesham		10	○
Alexander Christie		2	○
Henry Chubb		10 & 9	○ ○
William Church		17	○
John Cloggie	32)	9	△ ○
Thomas Coffey		15	○
William Collins		10 & 9	○ ○
James Collocott		9	○ ○
Patrick Conroy	40)	15	○
John Cook		2	○
William Cooke (1)		2	○
William Cooke (2)		17	○
Richard Cossentine		9	○
Hosick Cowen	28)	9	○ ○
William Cox		15	○
William Crawford		10	○
John Crawley		17	○
James Crighton		17	○
Thomas Cross		10	△
Patrick Crow		15	○
James Cuthbert		10 & 9	○ ○
Thomas Dadswell		17	○
William Denham		9	○ ○
Owen Devaney		15	○
Christopher Digweed		9	○
Samuel Dixon		15	△
John Donaldson		10	○
Thomas Downing		10	○
William Duckman		17	○
George Duddy		17	○
Andrew Duncan		10	
Robert Dunlop	18)	15	○
Robert Dunning	41) (R)	9	○
Richard Ellis		9	○
John Evans		10 & 9	○ △
Charles Fear		10	○
John R. Fee		9	△ △
John Fennell		15	○
Richard Fenton		17	○
Thomas Finch		2	○
George Fletcher		17	○
Joseph Flint	38)	9	○ ○
Charles Foot		9	○ ○
Frederick Ford		17	○
John Forrester		2	○
William Frame		9	○ ○
George Fraser		17	○
John B. Furze		10 & 9	○ ○
William Gabriel		9	○ ○
William Garland		15	○
James George		10	△
Angus Gibson		17	○
William Gilbert		15	○
Daniel Gilchrist	42)	10 & 9	○ ○
John Girvan		9	○
William Goldsmith	43)	2	△
Philip Gould	32)	9	○ ○
Archibald Graham		9	○ ○
William Graham		17	○
Donald Grant		17	○
John Green		9	○ ○
William Grierson	(P)	9	△ ○
John Griffiths		17	○
James Guthrie		15	○
John Guthrie		15	○
Edward Gwyther		17	○
William Haley		2	○
James Hall		17	○
John Hamill		2	○
John Harman		17	○
James Harrison		17	○
Joseph Hassett		15	○
John Hawkins		15	○
Thomas Hayward	18)	9	○ ○
William Henderson		9	○ ○
John Hendrick		10	○
Morris Hicks		15	○
Peter Hill		15	○
William Hill		17	○
Robert Hilton		17	○
Henry Hoblin		17	○
Robert Hodgson		9	○ ○
William Hodskins		9	○ ○
James Holton		10	○
William Hopgood		17	○
Andrew Horne		17	○
Thomas Houlgate		2	○
Job Houlston		17	△
William Howarth		17	○
Robert Hume		9	○
Thomas Hunt		15	○
Charles Ingerson		15	○
Hugh Ingles		10	○
Thomas Inglis		15	○
James Intifolm		17	○
James Ireland		9	○
Alexander Irvine	44)	10	△
John Irvine		10	○
William Jackman	45) (P)	17	○
Thomas Jago		17	○
George James		9	○
Thomas James		15	○
Charles Jarvis	46)	9	○
George Jarvis		10	○
John Jarvis	47) (P)	10 & 9	○ ○
George Jeffry		17	○
John Jelley		15	○
Alexander Johnston		17	
John Johnston		10	○
Henry J. Jones		10 & 9	△ △
Thomas Jones		10	○
James Kearley		2	○
Colin Kelly		15	○

South Africa 1853 Medal

Name	Notes	Co	1	2	3
Alexander Kerr	(P)	17			O
Thomas Kneebone		9		O	O
Robert Knight		10			O
William Knott		10			O
Daniel Laird		9			O
John Landry		10			O
John Lawler		17			O
Elijah Lear		15			O
Thomas Leask		2	O		
Philip Lewis		10		O	
Joseph Lockwood		9		O	O
William Love		17			O
John Lucas	(MRM)	15			O
Charles Luker		15			O
George Lyon		15			O
Hugh Mallen		9		O	O
Stephen Mallen	48)	17			△
Thomas Manners		2	O		
William Mark		15			O
George Martial	(R)	17			O
James Martin		10		△	
Thomas Matthews		17			O
Joseph Maycock		9		O	O
Alexander McAndrew		2	O		
James McBain		10		O	
William McCain		2	O		
James McCreery	(R)	17			O
Allen McDonald		9		O	O
Duncan McDonald	(P)	17			O
Peter McDonald		15			O
Thomas McGrigor		10		O	
Roderick McKenzie		2	O		
Alexander McIntosh		9 & 10		O	
Alexander McIntyre		9		O	O
William McKay		9		O	O
William McLintock		10		O	
James Mealey		15			O
John Milford		2	O		
David Miller		17			O
Lewis Miller		17			O
Thomas Mitchell		17			O
William Mitchell		2	O		
James Moncur		10 & 9		O	O
David Moore		9		O	
Isaac Moore		15			O
Jonathan Morey		17			O
Robert Morgan		15			O
George Mountcastle		15			O
William Moxey		9		O	O
James Muir		17			O
James Murdoch		10		O	
John Murphy	49)	9		O	O
James Murray	50) (R)	15			O
Robert Mustard		2	O		
James Newton		10		O	
William Novell		15			O
William O'Brien		17			O
Edward Oldfield		10		O	
Frederick Oldham		2	O		
John O'Reilly	51)	9		O	O
Owen O'Rourke		17			O
John Pace		17			O
Henry Palmer		2	O		
Simon Parsons		17			O
Edward Paton		10 & 9		O	O
John Patterson	44)	2 & 10	O	O	
Thomas Patterson		9			O
John Paul		10 & 9		O	O
Thomas Paul		9			O
John Pearce		9		O	O
Thomas Pearce		17			O
John Pearson		9		O	O
James Peat		15			O
Thomas Perrin		9		O	△
Alexander Phillips		9		O	O
Robert Phillips		2	O		
Charles Pitcher		10		△	
Richard Potter		17			O
William Powell		10		△	
James H. Prance		2	O		
Robert Purdy		10 & 9		O	O
John Puston		15			O
James Ralph		17			O
John Rapson		9		O	O
Samuel Redward		15			O
William Reese		17			O
James Reid		15			O
John Reid	52)	10		O	
James Reynolds	32) (P)	9		△	O
Thomas Riddle		10			O
William Ring		15			O
Charles Roberts	(P)	17			O
Joseph Roberts		9		O	O
Thomas Robertson		15			O
William Rogerson		15			O
John Ross		15			O
John Rowe		10		O	
Edward Rowse		15			O
George Rumsby		15			O
Edward Saunders		17			O
Stephen Saunders	53)	10		O	
Robert Saward		10		O	
David Scott		10		O	
Henry Scott	32)	9		O	O
Peter Scott		9		O	△
Seth Scotton		17			O
John C. Searle		2	△		
Thomas Seaman	32)	10 & 9		O	O
John Seath	54) (R)	15			O
William Shabrook	55)	9		O	O
Duncan Sharp		10		O	
John Shopland		2	O		
Samuel Siddons		2	O		
Richard Sleeman		2	△		
James Smallridge		15			O
William Smart		9		O	
Thomas Smeaton		10		O	
Alfred Smith		15			O
John Smith		17			O
William Smith		15			O
John Spencer		2	O		
Robert Spinks		15			O
Thomas Squires		17			O
George Stephens		15			O
William Stephens		15			O
John Steptoe		9		O	O
Matthew Stevens		9		O	
Alexander Stewart		10			O
Thomas Stillaway		17			O
George Stocker		17			O
Charles Stockman		17			O
Archibald Storrie		15			O
Henry Strivens		17			O
Edward Strong		15			O
Alexander Stuart		9			O
William Stuart		9			O

46 South Africa 1853 Medal

PRIVATE		Co	Kaffir Wars 1	2	3			Co	Kaffir Wars 1	2	3
John Sutherland		9	O			Thomas Weatherly		15			O
William Symons		15			O	Henry Wells		17			O
Daniel Swann		15			O	John Wells		17			O
Henry Targett		15			O	William Wells		15			O
Henry Taylor	(R)	17			O	John J. West		9			O
Samuel Taylor		17			O	George Wharram		9		O	O
William Thomas		17			O	Henry White		2	O		
Archibald Thompson		10	O			George Williams		17			△
Richard Tibbs	56)	10	O			James Williams		15			△
George Tickner		15			O	George Wilson	57)	9		O	O
William Tidy		10	△			Isaac Wilson		2	O		
Charles Tommy		15			O	John Wilson		15			O
James Tosch		17			O	William Wilson		15			O
John Triggs		15			O	William Wimbleton	(R)	17			O
George Trueman		17			O	George Wingham		17			O
William Trusk		2	O			Thomas Winsbury		17			O
Philip Tucker		15			O	William Winsor	(P)	15			O
Francis Tyrell		10	O			Henry Wood		10	O		
John Vance	18)	10	O			James Wood		15			O
James Wallace		9		O	O	Robert Wooldridge		15			O
Edward Ward		9		O	O	John Wright (1)		10	O		
Josiah Ward		10				John Wright (2)		9		O	△
John Watt		15			O	Robert Wright		10	O		
Joseph Watts		2	O			John Yule		2	O		

ROYAL ENGINEERS/ROYAL SAPPERS AND MINERS NOTES

1 Commanded the RE in the Cape during the 3rd campaign.
2 Commanded the Corps during the 2nd campaign. Twice wounded, which is not surprising since although being short-sighted he would stalk the enemy in the bush on foot. See Bisset; Moodie and others.
3 Took part in the Waterkloof operations March 1852.
4 Served with Capt Smith's (27th) force on the expedition to Natal in 1842.
5 Commanded the Sappers who were with the force which restored Fort Cox.
6 An officer vastly experienced in surveying and map making. He was responsible for laying out the site at the Buffalo Mouth and accompanied patrols into the Amatolas late in 1847. Jervois was present at the surrender of the Chiefs to Sir Harry Smith on 23.12.47. Some of his water colours, plans and diaries made during his years in the Cape are in possession of the family.
7 Supervised a construction of the boat bridge over the Fish River.
8 'As gallant a fellow as ever lived' according to Sir Harry Smith. Commanded a column at Isel Berg and Sapper detachment in the attack on Committy's Hill on 1.9.51. See G and I; Connolly.
9 Commanded the small force of sappers which successfully defended their camp near Fort Brown in April 1846.
10 Served on the Staff as Asst QMG during the 3rd campaign. See King.
11 With Eyre's Division on March 1852. Commanded the Sappers' escorting wagons which were attacked at Koonap Hill 12.6.52.
12 Served on the Staff during the 3rd campaign, see G and I; Bisset.
13 Commander of Cradock and North Victoria. He raised a levy at Whittlesea early in 1851 which blunted depredations in the district. 13 times he defeated and put to flight large concentrations of rebels. See G and I; King.
14 See G and I.
15 With Robertson into the Isel Berg and on Cathcart's expedition against Mosesh. See Moodie; King.
16 Attached to the QMG Staff during the operations against Mosesh and was present at Berea. See King.
17 See Godlonton.
18 See Connolly.
19 Commended by Sir Harry Smith for his bravery at the Mooi River in 1848. See Connolly.
20 Distinguished himself during the attack on the wagons at Koonap Hill 12.6.52. See Connolly.
21 Served on Capt Smith's expedition to Natal in 1842.
22 Fired the first shot when Capt Smith engaged the Boers at Congella on 23.5.42, and was subsequently wounded. See Connolly.
23 Distinguished himself when patrolling during May and June 1846. See Connolly.
24 Served on Cathcart's expedition against Mosesh, November 1852.
25 Present at the engagement at Committy's Hill, 1.9.51, and was commended for leading repeated bayonet charges in attempting to drive off the enemy in the ambush at Koonap Hill in June 1852. See Connolly.
26 A 'particularly active and zealous' soldier who served at the battle of Boemplaats in 1848. See Connolly.
27 Killed two rebels when surprising cattle thieves. See Connolly.
28 Name spelt variously on musters. On 24.10.47, Barnicoat and 7 men with a 3-pounder faced 350 rebellious native levies but missionaries intervened before fighting broke out. See Connolly.
29 Commended by Somerset and a soldier of whom Col Sutton wrote 'I have not met Cpl Castledine's superior in his position'. He was in charge of a Howitzer at Fort Beaufort and when Sutton was absent took command of the post, being made Garrison Sgt Major. See Connolly.
30 Commanded a small detachment with Kyle's division. See Connolly.
31 The only sapper at Berea, where he was attached to the Rocket section of the RA as Medical Orderly to Surgeon Fasson.
32 Wounded during the attack on the wagons 12.6.52.
33 Present at the engagement at the Fish River September 1851, and took part in the operations in the Waterkloof November 1851. Also joined the expedition across the Kei the following year. After serving with the Land Transport Corps in the Crimea (as a Cornet) became a Q/Master in the CMR.
34 Commanded the 10-man Sapper detachment with Eyre's column across the Kei in February 1852.
35 A resourceful soldier who shot 6 of the enemy whilst on cattle guard. See Connolly.
36 Also Barratt on musters.
37 Also wrongly shown as Brag on some musters.
38 Wounded at Committy's Hill 1.9.51.

39 One of the wagon escort ambushed at Koonap Hill 12.6.52.
40 Killed an enemy at 300 yards on Committy's Hill. See Connolly.
41 The medal in the Corps Museum is engraved and was once in the collection of Lt Col Ll. Palmer in 1914. A comrade of Dunning told the Colonel that the original medal had been lost at sea. Dunning also possessed a Sir Harry Smith medal – a re-strike from a cracked die.
42 Present at the battle of Boemplaats in 1848.
43 Medal claimed by his son in 1911.
44 Killed a Kaffir scout in June 1846. See Connelly.
45 Lost an eye while stone cutting.
46 Wounded in March 1851.
47 Medal may be named Jervis.
48 Mallon on Roll.
49 Killed a rebel who was about to shoot Capt Moody at Koonap Hill. See Connolly.
50 Performed gallantly at Committy's Hill 1.9.51. See Connolly.
51 Also Reilly on musters. One of the wagon escort attacked at Koonap Hill 12.6.52.
52 Accompanied Capt. Jervois on a mapping expedition to Natal in 1846.
53 Also Sanders on Roll.
54 Medal believed to be wrongly named Seall.
55 Also Shobrook on musters.
56 Wounded when serving with Capt Smith in Natal in 1842.
57 Killed two of the enemy during the skirmish in Seyolo's country in March 1852. See Connolly.

PRO References: WO/11/71-74-77-80-83-87-108-112-116-120-124-128-132-133-136-137-140-141-144-14.

2nd (The Queen's Royal) Regiment

Six service companies of the Queen's embarked from Ireland for the Cape during June 1851. They were in three contingents; the largest suffered a series of mishaps in the 'Birkenhead' but reached Simon's Bay by August 8th. The smallest party had an uneventful voyage in HMS 'Cyclops' but fire broke out on the 'Sumner' and the companies aboard did not disembark at East London until September 12th. By then the regiment had sustained its first casualties.

Marching at once for King William's Town the first contingent had soon been ordered out after reaching the frontier. On September 1st 180 officers and men of the 2nd, with detachments from several other regiments, were sent to patrol the Committy's Hill under Lt Col Burns. Finding themselves confronted by a large body of Kaffirs the 2nd light company extended in skirmishing order and the whole patrol was gradually brought into action. A heavy fusilade from Kaffirs concealed in clumps of trees and the bush wounded several men of the Queen's, three mortally. Some of them were bandsmen who had been given arms but were wearing their white regimental jackets and were singled out by the enemy who supposed them to be of superior rank. The engagement continued until Burns withdrew his inadequate force which was protected by a rearguard of Armstrong's Horse.

Within a week another column was formed to disperse the increasing number of rebels gathering in the bush of the Fish River. The 2nd were part of the mixed force of 1,200 men commanded by Col Mackinnon and on September 9th were sweeping along the line of the river. Before dawn the Grenadiers and No 2 Company under Captains Oldham and Smyth had been ordered into a deep kloof to fire some native huts. They killed a number of Kaffirs and Hottentots but as it grew light the enemy became aware of the small number of troops against them. In the desperate fighting which followed Oldham and 24 men of the 2nd were killed and 23 other ranks wounded before the 6th Regiment came to their aid and they were extracted. Six of the wounded subsequently died. But this was not the total list of the regiment's casualties for eight men of Capt Addison's company were missing and never returned. They had been engaged some miles from the main action and never received the word to retire after it was decided not to sound a bugle.

Before the end of the year the 2nd took part in the operations in the Kroome and Waterkloof mountains and lost one man killed on October 27th. They also engaged in the expedition against Kreli in January 1852 and then replaced the garrisons at Forts Cox, White and Hare. Their patrolling in the areas commanded by the forts was not entirely successful as the Kaffirs attacked Fort Cox and managed to make away with wagons and much of the stock.

In November the Queen's, with four companies of the 74th and one Rifle Brigade company composed the 2nd Infantry Brigade on the expedition against Mosesh. It was an arduous march before a camp was established at Platberg and eventually the men of the Queen's must have wondered whether the hardships were worth while since they did not become embroiled in the fighting at or near the Berea plateau.

Although the campaigning was at an end the regiment stayed on in South Africa and saw eight year's service in the Cape before being sent to China for the war of 1860.

			Kaffir Wars		
			1	2	3
MAJOR					
Thomas W. E. Holdsworth	1)				△
Oliver Robinson	2)				△
CAPTAIN					
Thomas Addison	3)				△
Frederick Connor		(P)			△
Demetrius W. G. James					△
Frederick Mathias	4)				△
Edward Selby Smyth	5)				△
LIEUTENANT					
Francis L. Atty	6)				△
John Chalmers	4)				△
John Croome					△
William H. Grimstone					△
Lord Charles E. Hay	4)				△
Robert Holdsworth					△
LIEUTENANT/ADJUTANT					
Simon F. Jacson		(P)			△
LIEUTENANT					
William W. Martin					△
LIEUTENANT/ADJUTANT					
James H. Rocke					△
LIEUTENANT					
Robert C. Thomson	7)				△
John Tolcher					△
John C. Weir	4)	(P)			△
ENSIGN					
William H. Spencer	4)				△
SURGEON					
Henry C. Foss	4)	(P)			△
ASSISTANT SURGEON					
John E. Moffatt					△
PAYMASTER					
Oliver Nicholls					△
QUARTERMASTER					
John Mansfield					△
SERGEANT MAJOR					
William Adams		(P)			△
QUARTERMASTER SERGEANT					
William Mackie					△
COLOUR SERGEANT					
William Brook					△
John Carruthers					△
William Clarke	8)				△
George Davis					△
John Ferguson					△
John McAlary					△
DRUM MAJOR					
John R. Darkin	9)				△
SERGEANT					
James Barkus					△

South Africa 1853 Medal 49

		Kaffir Wars		
		1	2	3
Henry Barnes				△
Thomas Benning				△
David Brown				△
Thomas Campking				△
Abraham Dawkins				△
William Field				△
Michael Garrett				△
Joseph Irwin				△
Charles Jones				△
Samuel Jones				△
Patrick Kilduff	(P)			△
Daniel McDonald				△
Joseph McNamee				△
Robert Moore	10)			△
James Ousbey	11)			△
Henry Randall	12) (P)			△
Absolom Roberts				△
De Booth Rowbottom				△
Abel Sidwell				△
George Stowell				△
Godfrey C. Tunbridge	13)			△
Thomas Turner				△
William Watkins				△
John Worthington	14)			△
CORPORAL				
Benjamin Attree				△
Caleb Batten				△
James Clark	15)			△
James Coghlan				△
George Dibbin				△
William Dines				△
William Dobbin				△
Edward Doonan	16)			△
William Greenwood				△
John Hargan	18)			△
Martin Harvey				△
Edward Heath	17)			△
Michael Hoare				△
William Horton				△
John Law	19)			△
John A. Murray				△
George Orr				△
William Ramsbottom				△
William Read				△
John Richardson				△
Thomas Ryan				△
William Sayer				△
James Schofield				△
Andrew M. Taylor				△
James Varndell				△
John Walsh				△
John West				△
Thomas West				△
Charles Whicher				△
John Willis				△
DRUMMER				
John Conniff	20)			△
James Corrigan				△
Peter Davis				△
Frederick J. Farringdon	21)			△
Henry J. Gowers				△
James Hill				△
George Manning	22)			△
James McGuire				△
John Pearson	(P)			△
Richard Ralph				△
Thomas Reid	23)			△
William Upton				△

		Kaffir Wars		
		1	2	3
PRIVATE				
Alfred Adams				△
William Alderman				△
Andrew Alexander				△
William Anderson	(MRM)			△
William Antill				△
George Arnell				△
Andrew Arthur	24)			△
Charles Ash	(R)			△
Thomas Ash	(P)			△
James Attree				△
Peter Aves	(R)			△
Jacob Bacon				△
James Badcock				△
Daniel Bailey				△
John Baird				△
John Barnes				△
William Barnes				△
Joseph Barnett				△
Thomas Barry				△
George Bartlett				△
William Bateman				△
James Bates				△
Thomas Baxter				△
John Beek	(MRM)			△
Michael Bell				△
George Bennett				△
Lawrence Benson				△
James Betterton	25)			△
Meshach Bew	26)			△
Richard Binning				△
William Bird	(P)			△
James Blackwell				△
James Bloice	27)			△
John Blunden				△
William Boatman				△
William Bond				△
Frederick Bostock				△
John Bowden				△
James Boyden	28)			△
John Bradley				△
Robert Bradshaw				△
Thomas Brannon	29)			△
William Braund				△
Thomas Breffitt	30)			△
John Brewer				△
John Brien				△
Michael Brien				△
Henry Brindley				△
James Britcher				△
Solomon Broadbent				△
James Broderick				△
David Brooks				△
James Brown				△
William Browne				△
John Bryan				△
Edward Buck	31)			△
John Buckingham				△
George Budd	(MRM)			△
Daniel Burch				△
George Burcher	(R)			△
James Burns				△
Allen Burroughs	32)			△
John Burt				△
Henry Butcher				△
William Butler				△
Patrick Byrne				
James Cadden				△

50 South Africa 1853 Medal

PRIVATE	1	2	3 (Kaffir Wars)
Daniel Caffrey			△
Thomas Cakebread			△
John Callaghan			△
Patrick Callaghan			△
James Cannin			△
James Canty			△
Patrick Carbery	33)		△
Richard Carlisle			△
Patrick Carney			△
Thomas Carr			△
William Carroll			△
Jeremiah Carty			△
William Carty	34)		△
Frederick Carvell	35)		△
Joseph Caton			△
Peter Cavanagh			△
Joseph Chadwick	36)		△
William Channon		(MRM)	△
James Chilton			△
Daniel Clark	37)		△
James Clark	38)		△
Patrick Clarke			△
John Clowes	39)		△
William Cochrane			△
Samuel Cockrane	40)		△
Robert Coe			△
John Colahan	41)		△
John Cole			△
Thomas Cole	42)		△
James Connelly			△
Thomas Connelly			△
Thomas Conners			△
William Cook			△
Denis Cooney			△
Patrick Cooney		(MRM)	△
James Copeling			△
Charles Cornish			△
George Couzens			△
James Cox		(P)	△
Thomas Cox			△
John Crawley			△
William Croughan	43)		△
Denis Cronen			△
Samuel Crook			△
Ezekial Crowder		(MRM)	△
James Cunningham			△
John Cunningham			△
Michael Cunningham			△
John Damery	44)		△
Robert Davis			△
Snowden Davison			△
William Dawson			△
John Delany			△
William Deverell			△
John Devine			△
James Devlin			△
James Dobbie			△
Hugh Donaldson		(P)	△
Michael Donohoe			△
Richard Dootson			△
Edward Douglas	45)		△
Richard Dow	48)		△
Patrick Doyle			△
James Duffy		(MRM)	△
John Duig			△
William Duke			△
Daniel Dukes			△
Timothy Dumphy			△
Richard Dunne			△
Thomas Dwyer			△
Daniel Earl			△
Charles B. Elliott			△
John Ellis			△
Robert Ellis			△
Thomas Ellis			△
Richard Elsworth	47)		△
William Embleton			△
Thomas Esling	48)		△
John Farnden	49)		△
Thomas Feasby			△
George Feely			△
Michael Feely			△
James Fell			△
Thomas Fellows			△
Peter Fitchard			△
John Fitzcharles			△
Thomas Fitzgerald			△
Joseph Fitzjohn			△
John Flanaghan			△
John Flavel	50)		△
Edward Foden			△
James Forrest			△
William Forth			△
James Foxwell			△
Hugh Foy		(MRM)	△
George Francis			△
John Fraser	52)		△
Nicholas Furlong	51)		△
Robert Gallaway			△
John Gallivan			△
James Gane			△
John Gannon			△
John Garnett (1)	53)		△
John Garnett (2)	53)		△
Robert Gaskell	54)	(MRM)	△
James Gilday	55)		△
Robert Girling			△
Michael Gleeson			△
Patrick Gleeson	56)		△
Henry Goddard			△
John Gorey	57)		△
John Gould			△
William Grace		(MRM)	△
George Graddon			△
Hugh Graham			△
James Gray			△
John Gready			△
John Greenhalch	58)		△
Nathan Griggs			△
John Groome	59)		△
James Groves			△
Michael Gunn			△
Absolom Hale			△
William Hale			△
Samuel Hales	56)		△
John Hall		(MRM)	△
James Hamilton			△
George Hammond			△
Henry Hammond			△
Thomas Harris			△
William Harris	60)	(P)	△
John Harrison			△
Edward Harwood			△
Joseph Haughton			△
Patrick Haydon			△

South Africa 1853 Medal 51

Name	Note	Kaffir Wars 1 2 3
William Haynes		△
William Heathcote		△
Francis Heney	61)	△
David Hennessy		△
Joseph Herrington		△
John Hindley		△
David Hirst		△
Robert Hodson		△
Thomas Hogan		△
Jacob Hollingsworth		△
Henry Hollis		△
George Holmes	(R)	△
Richard Holmes		△
John Honeyball		△
John Hope		△
Edward House		△
John Howard	62)	△
William Howard		△
George Hubber		△
John Hughes		△
Thomas Hughes		△
William Humberstone	63) (MRM)	△
William Humphrey		△
Patrick Hunt (1)	64)	△
Patrick Hunt (2)	64) (MRM)	△
William Hunt		△
Joseph Huskins	65)	△
Martin Hynes		△
James Hyson	66)	△
George Irish		△
Thomas Irwin	67)	△
Job Islin	(MRM)	△
Edward Jackson		△
John Jackson		△
William Jackson		△
Edward Jeffery		△
Henry Jeffery	(MRM)	△
John Jeffery	68)	△
Orlando Jennings		△
Arthur Johnstone		△
Charles Johnstone (1)	69)	△
Charles Johnstone (2)	69)	△
Robert Johnstone		△
John Jones		△
Spencer Jones		△
David Joslin		△
James Kaveney	70)	△
Edward M. Kay	71)	△
Thomas Keen		△
Michael Keleher		△
Francis Kelly		△
Owen Kelly		△
Thomas Kelly		△
William Kelly (1)	72)	△
William Kelly (2)	72)	△
Michael Kennedy		△
James Keogh		△
Patrick Keon		△
William Ketteridge		△
James Kidd		△
John Kiernan		△
Frederick King		△
George King		△
George Kingstone	73)	△
George Kite		△
James Kough		△
James Kynes		△
Joseph Lamb		△
Henry Lambert		△
William Lambert		△
James Laracy	(P)	△
Edward Lavery	74)	△
James Law		△
Michael Lee		△
Patrick Lee		△
Thomas Lee		△
John Leech		△
Thomas Leech		△
John Lever	75)	△
George Lewis		△
John Lewis		△
Nicholas Lewis		△
Frederick Lincoln		△
George Livings		△
Reuben G. Locke		
Henry Long		△
Robert Long	17)	△
Thomas Lowrie		△
Thomas Lunnon		△
John Lynch		△
Terence Lynch		△
Patrick Magee		△
Edward Maguire	76)	△
Edward Main		△
James Main		△
Michael Malley	77)	△
William Mannion		△
John Martin	(MRM)	△
George Mason		△
John Mason		△
William Maw		△
John McCann		△
Justin McCarthy		△
Patrick McCarthy	78)	△
Stephen McCarthy		△
Michael McCormick		△
Patrick McCreary	79)	△
Michael McDonald	(P)	△
John McDonough		△
John McGhee		△
John McGill		△
Dominic McGrail		△
John McGrath		△
Patrick McGrath		△
Patrick McGreal		△
James McGuire		△
Patrick McGuire (1)	80)	△
Patrick McGuire (2)	80)	△
John McKay	(P)	△
Robert McKey		△
James McLean		△
Patrick McLoughlin		△
James McMahon		△
John Meer		△
Roger Meiklam	81)	△
James Mellor		△
William Melvin		△
Robert Michael		△
Alfred Mills		△
James Mills		△
William Mills		△
Charles Mitchell		△
Edward Mitchell		△
Henry Mole		△
Thomas Molloy	82)	△
Henry Moon		△

52 South Africa 1853 Medal

		Kaffir Wars 1 2 3			Kaffir Wars 1 2 3
PRIVATE			Frederick Russell		△
Francis Moore		△	John Ryan		△
James Moore		△	Stephen Ryan		△
John Moore	83)	△	Joseph Sanderson		△
William Moore		△	John Sands	99)	△
Thomas Moran		△	George Scott		△
Archibald Morgan		△	Thomas Seaman		△
James Mortimer		△	Giles Searle		△
Samuel Mottershead		△	Daniel Seerey		△
William Moulder		△	Henry Selwood	(MRM)	△
James Mullins	(P)	△	George Shaeen	100)	△
Thomas Murphy		△	Michael Shannahan	17)	△
Timothy Murphy		△	Henry Shaver		△
John Murray		△	Robert Sinclair		△
Alfred Mutlow	84)	△	Edward Sleater		△
John Nelligan		△	Patrick Sloane		△
Thomas Newman		△	Andrew Smith		△
William Newman		△	Charles Smith		△
William Nicholas		△	James Smith		△
William Noonan		△	John Smith (1)	101)	△
Reuben Nottingham		△	John Smith (2)	101)	△
William O'Brien		△	John Smith (3)	101)	△
Samuel Ogilvie		△	William Smith		△
James F. Oliver		△	John Smyth		△
John Owen		△	George Stafford		△
Robert Page	85)	△	William Staton		△
James Parker		△	George Stillwell		△
Oliver Parker		△	Nicholas Stokes		△
William Parker		△	James Stoppard	102)	△
Robert Peake	(P)	△	George Storey		△
Charles Pearce	86)	△	Robert Stott		△
Stephen Pedley		△	Dennis Sullivan		△
Thomas Pendry		△	Florence Sullivan		△
James Perron	87)	△	Jeremiah Sullivan		△
John Perron		△	John Sullivan		△
George Perry (1)	88)	△	Patrick Sutton		△
George Perry (2)	88)	△	Charles Syrett		△
John Peters	89)	△	Robert Tallinson	103)	△
Patrick Peters	89)	△	George Taplin		△
John Picket		△	Jonathan Taylor		△
John Plunkett	90)	△	Joseph Taylor		△
John Pocknell	91)	△	Samuel Thacker		△
Michael Pounde		△	William Thomas		△
Patrick Power		△	Ewing Thompson		△
Henry Pratt		△	James Thompson		△
John Primsole		△	John Thompson (1)	104)	△
Edward Pruen		△	John Thompson (2)	104)	△
John Pullen	92)	△	John Thompson (3)	104)	△
Joshua Purkiss		△	William Thornton	(MRM)	△
John Quigley	93)	△	Joseph Thorogood		△
William Raine		△	Reuben Tipping		△
Samuel Ramsden		△	John Toft		△
Samuel Rayner	94)	△	Charles Tomblinson		△
Joseph Reeves	17)	△	Richard Tooze		△
Thomas Reid	95)	△	Josephus Toozes		△
Samuel Rendell		△	John Torrence		△
Joseph Rhodes	96)	△	Peter Treacy	105)	△
William Richards		△	Joseph Trevitt		△
Charles Richardson		△	John Trewsell		△
Emmanuel Rigby		△	Henry Tributt	106)	△
Charles Roberts		△	James Turner		△
William Roberts		△	John Turner		△
Henry Robinson		△	Thomas Turner		△
George Rodgers	97)	△	Henry Veazey		△
William Rolph	98)	△	William Venus		△
John Rowles	(MRM)	△	William Vermin		△
Richard Rowson		△	Henry Vernon	107)	△
James Rudlin		△	William Wainwright	(R)	△

South Africa 1853 Medal 53

		Kaffir Wars				Kaffir Wars		
		1	2	3		1	2	3
John Walker				△	Charles Williams			△
Alexander Wallace				△	George Williams			△
Alexander Walsh				△	William Williamson			△
Francis Walsh				△	William Wilson	110)		△
Robert Watkinson				△	Thomas Windass	111)		△
Charles Webb				△	Thomas Wings			△
George Webb				△	Edward Winter			△
James Webb	108)			△	Thomas Winter			△
James West				△	William Wood			△
Charles Whitaker				△	Benjamin Woodall	112)		△
Richard Whitaker				△	John Woodworth			△
John White (1)	109)			△	Edward Young			△
John White (2)	109)			△	John Young	(R)		△
John White (3)	109)			△				
Joseph Wilkinson				△	△ = campaign qualification as WO/100/17.			

2ND (THE QUEEN'S ROYAL) REGIMENT NOTES

1 Commanded the 4 companies engaged in the expedition against Mosesh.
2 Twice returned, once as Staff. Served as Asst. QMG of the 2nd division.
3 Severely wounded 14.10.51. See McKay.
4 With the force against Mosesh.
5 Served against Mosesh. DAQMG of the 2nd division. See McKay.
6 Attye on Roll.
7 Thompson Roll. Served against Mosesh.
8 Clarke on Roll.
9 Also Darken on muster. His wife and child were survivors from the 'Birkenhead'.
10 No 947. A survivor from the 'Birkenhead'.
11 Ousby on Roll.
12 Spelling as on medal and musters. Randal on Roll.
13 Medal returned for alteration after being wrongly named Trowbridge.
14 Worthing on Roll. Wounded September 1851.
15 No 1459, also Clarke on musters.
16 Saw his campaign service with the 74th.
17 Severely wounded September 1851.
18 Horgan on Roll.
19 Llaw on Roll.
20 Coniff on Roll.
21 Farrington on Roll.
22 No 1009.
23 No 2334; Not the same man as Pte Thomas Reid.
24 No 2663. A survivor from the 'Birkenhead'. Christian name given as Adam on Roll.
25 John on Roll.
26 Meshae on Roll.
27 May have received two medals as he was also returned by the CMR to whom he transferred.
28 No 2665. Boydon on Roll. A survivor from the 'Birkenhead' who acquired the nick-name of 'Jack Straw' as he floated to safety on a straw bale. See Davis, McKay and others.
29 Also Brannan on musters.
30 Breffit on Roll.
31 Received 13 gunshot and assegai wounds 9.9.51.
32 Burrows on Roll.
33 Carburry on Roll. Severely wounded September 1851.
34 Also Carthy on musters.
35 Cawell on Roll.
36 No 1526, a survivor from the 'Birkenhead'.
37 Also Clarke on musters.
38 No 2094, also Clarke on musters.
39 Clowers on Roll.
40 Cochrane on Roll.
41 Also Colohan on muster.
42 Coles on Roll.
43 Croghan on Roll.
44 Dammery on Roll.
45 Also served with the 6th.
46 Consistently shown as Done on musters until altered by depot memo dated 27.6.54.
47 Ellsworth on Roll. Wounded 9.9.51. See Davis where his name is wrongly spelt Ebsworth.
48 Eslington on Roll but last three letters deleted.
49 Farndon on Roll.
50 Also Flavell on musters.
51 Michael Forlong on Roll.
52 Frazer on Roll
53 Nos 1492 and 2212. Various spelling on musters.
54 Gaskill on musters.
55 No 1801. A survivor from the 'Birkenhead'.
56 Disembarked at Simons Bay two days before the 'Birkenhead' foundered.
57 Twice entered on Roll.
58 Greenalch on Roll.
59 Also Grome on musters.
60 Saw his campaign service with the 43rd.
61 Henry (altered to Francis) Henly on Roll.
62 James on Roll.
63 Humberston on Roll.
64 Nos 2254 and 2420, either of which could be the medal returned to the Mint.
65 Huskin on Roll.
66 I have been unable to trace this man and am of the opinion it is a mistake for James Higson No 1779.
67 Irvin on Roll. Later to the 73rd.
68 Jeffrey on Roll.
69 Nos 1322 and 2316. On the Roll one is spelt Johnson and the other Johnston.
70 Kaveny on Roll.
71 Key on Roll. Muster shows christian names as E. Malcolm.
72 Nos 2120 and 2429.
73 Kingston on Roll.
74 Alias Lowry.
75 Also Leaver on musters.
76 McGuire on Roll. Corrected by depot memo 20.6.74.
77 Mally on Roll. No 2671, a survivor from the 'Birkenhead'.
78 Medal in auction in 1918 accompanied by a Zulu War medal to P McCarthy, King William's Town Vols.
79 No 2674. A survivor from the 'Birkenhead'.
80 Nos 897 and 2305.
81 Meeklan on Roll.
82 John on Roll.
83 Twice entered on Roll.
84 Muslow on Roll.
85 No 2089, a survivor from the 'Birkenhead'.
86 Altered on Roll from Peass.
87 Also Perren on musters.
88 No 2614 and 2700.
89 Nos 2586 and 2684 respectively, both survivors from the 'Birkenhead'.
90 Medal sent to widow 12.2.64.
91 A late claimant who may have earned his medal with another regiment.
92 Also Pullin on musters.
93 Quigly on Roll.
94 Raynor on Roll.
95 No 2330 and not the same man as Drummer Reid.
96 Rhoades on Roll.
97 Rogers on Roll.
98 Ralph on Roll.
99 No 2430.
100 Shaen on Roll. Spelling corrected by depot memo 27.6.54.
101 Nos 1382, 2431 and 2659, who was a survivor from the 'Birkenhead'.

54 South Africa 1853 Medal

102 Stopperd on Roll.
103 Talinson on Roll.
104 Nos 1290, 2112 and 2207. A medal to J. Thompson is in the Regimental Museum.
105 Tracey on Roll, but depot memo 27.6.54 corrects spelling.
106 Tribut on Roll.
107 No 2298, a survivor from the 'Birkenhead'.
108 Alias Lee.
109 Nos 1324, 2907 and 1989, a survivor from the 'Birkenhead'.
110 Received a re-named medal.
111 Windlass on Roll.
112 No 1705, a survivor from the 'Birkenhead'.

Note: – Capt Henry Reynolds, 2nd Regt served as a volunteer during the war of 1846–7. The medal Roll shows him as 'unattached' and presumably his medal does not mention Reynolds' connection with the 2nd.

PRO References: WO/12/2057-2058-2059-2060-2061.

6th (Royal Warwickshire) Regiment

The regiment left Cork aboard two transports on August 28th 1846. After calling at Cape Town the troops disembarked in Algoa Bay on November 11th and 21st and moved forward to join Somerset's 2nd Division on the frontier. They were employed on patrolling until January 1847 when a detachment took part in an expedition across the Kei River. With Lt Col Michel in command of the infantry the troops were out for nearly three weeks and the atrocious weather which hampered the operations had a very bad effect on soldiers who were little more than recruits.

Upon their return, the 6th were moved to Fort Peddie and when the C-in-C Gen Sir Geo Berkeley inspected the regiment in May he was not impressed. As a result of his report detachments from the Warwicks were only made to posts not far afield from headquarters and as soon as the frontier emergency would allow, the regiment was ordered to Cape Town. This came about at the turn of the year and when the 6th was reviewed by Governor Sir Harry Smith in June 1848 he gave a measured approval of the improvement that had been made. The soldiers were, he said, 'animated by the characteristic spirit of Britons'. There can be no doubt that while their fighting qualities were evident the drill and discipline of the men left something to be desired. There was a high rate of desertion but the 6th came to earn the respect of other regiments and, because of the large number of Irishmen in their ranks, were known as the 'Daring Doylers' – but this was not yet.

Held in Cape Town until May 1850 the regiment was then called upon to relieve the Rifle Brigade at King Williams Town. On the spot therefore at the outbreak of the 3rd war, 244 officers and men, under Capt Robertson provided most of the infantry for the force which moved out of Fort Cox to try and capture chief Sandili on December 24th 1850. The column came under heavy attack in the Boomah Pass and 10 men of the 6th were killed with five wounded before they fought through to Keiskamma Hoek. An ex-Warwick, then with the CMR, recorded that his old comrades had not behaved well but when the force returned to Fort Cox 68 men under Capt Mansergh were left to hold Fort White and they fought bravely enough to repulse furious attacks on the post during January. Two companies were in Mackinnon's convoy which carried supplies to Forts Cox and White the following month and in May a detachment under Capt Crowden clashed with the enemy.

Early in September the 6th were part of Col Mackinnon's force which swept the bush along the Fish River and then accompanied Somerset's expedition to the Kroome Mountains. Michel commanded a brigade and the 'Doylers' suffered a number of casualties during the drawn out operations. They were in the field for nearly a month without tents and protected against the sleet and rain only by blankets.

But the regiment was allowed little rest. A patrol caught up with a band of Kaffirs on the Blinkwater in November and at the end of the month the 6th joined Mackinnon's column in the sweep beyond the Kei. Starting from King William's Town the regiment particularly distinguished themselves on December 9th by storming a Kaffir strong point with the bayonet.

Back in camp by the middle of the month the troops rested until late January 1852 when the whole regiment was put to work devastating crops and Kraals. Lt Armytage was wounded and a man killed before they returned at the end of February.

On March 30th they crossed the Kei once again to take the war to the Waterkloof and Blinkwater. This successful operation was followed by further patrols in the Amatolas throughout the ensuing months until in August the 6th were involved in a larger raid into chief Kreli's country.

The round of minor raids and skirmishing continued until the last of the chiefs submitted in 1853 and the Warwicks could justifiably claim that no regiment had been more heavily employed during the war. Their appearance showed hard usage. An eye witness described them as having long beards; red coats patched with leather, canvas and cloth of all colours; straw hats, wideawakes and tattered trousers while their broken boots revealed stockingless feet.

For the next two years the 6th worked on road construction to open up the Keiskamma Hoek and were constantly on the frontier until the outbreak of the Indian Mutiny.

			Kaffir Wars 1	2	3
LIEUTENANT COLONEL					
John Michel, CB	1)			△	△
John Stuart	2)				△
MAJOR					
Robert W. M. Fraser					△
Randal Rumley					△
BREVET MAJOR/CAPTAIN					
Thomas Powell					△
CAPTAIN					
Godfrey Armytage	3)			△	△
Henry Balguy					△
Andrew Barnes		(R)			△
Edward Blanckley	4)			△	△
Charles P. Catty	5)				△
Edmund J. Cruice					△
Frederick W. Gore	6)			○	○
Henry P. Gore					△
Morris J. Hall					△
John C. Mansergh	7)	(P)			△
J. Elphinston Robertson	8)				△
Thomas H. Somerville					△
Edward Staunton	9)	(P)		○	△
Richard Thompson	10)			○	△
LIEUTENANT					
Hon Augustus G. C. Chichester					△
John Dawson				△	△
Charles H. Dowker		(R)			△
John Elkington	11)			△	△
Henry J. N. King	12)				△
LIEUTENANT/ADJUTANT					
William Lee					△
LIEUTENANT					
Edward Lloyd		(P)			△
Francis W. H. McClelland				○	△

56 South Africa 1853 Medal

		Kaffir Wars					Kaffir Wars	

Rank / Name	Note	1	2	3	Name	Note	1	2	3
LIEUTENANT					William Silver			O	△
William Robertson				△	John Stokes			O	△
Nicholas Spoor				△	John Sweeney			△	△
Robert Unwin				△	Joseph Threadgold			O	△
George G. Webb			△		James Walker			△	△
ENSIGN					John Wilson			△	△
Hugh F. Crofton	13)			△	**CORPORAL**				
Hon Hercules Rowley			△		William Baker	22)		△	△
SURGEON					John Betts				△
John Murtagh			△	△	Henry Boon			O	△
Egerton J. Pratt				△	David Bryan				△
ASSISTANT SURGEON					James Clarke			O	△
Henry Bindon	(R)		O	△	James Cole	23)		O	△
PAYMASTER					Patrick Daly				△
Sidney J. Timbrell				△	John Darcey			O	△
QUARTERMASTER					Thomas Donovan			O	△
John C. Croker	14)		O	△	John Egan	24)			△
SERGEANT MAJOR					Samuel Foot			O	△
William Wastle	15)		△	O	Edward Gilmore				△
QUARTER/MASTER SERGEANT					William Glover	(R)		△	△
James Cranney			O	△	Thomas Hardacre			O	△
STAFF SERGEANT					Samuel Hellewell			O	△
John Nichol	(P)		△	△	James Hendry	(MRM)			△
COLOUR SERGEANT					Richard Hixson	25)			△
Thomas Burgess			O	△	Martin Hogan			O	△
Henry Bradley			O	△	Thomas Johnson	26)		O	△
Thomas Clarke	16)		△	△	Michael Kirby			O	△
Charles Dunlap			O	△	John Kitson	27)			△
Emmanuel Newman			O	△	John Mahoney				△
James Wood			O	△	Simon Maynard	28)		O	△
SERGEANT					John McKay				△
Francis Armstrong			△	△	Robert Million				△
David Barry			△	△	John Mires				△
George Beadle	17) (R)		O	△	William Pink			O	△
Abraham Beale			O	△	James Smith			△	△
Thomas Bennett			O	△	George Walker	29)			△
Thomas Bush			O	△	Robert Warren			O	△
James T. Brown	18)		△	△	William Whittaker	30)			△
Joseph Brown			O	△	John Woodall			O	△
Robert Campbell			△	△	**DRUMMER**				
Nicholas Canney			O	△	James Barkwith			O	△
Jeremiah Cansidine				△	John Barry	31)			△
George Davis			O	△	Stephen Carrack	32)			△
William Day			O	△	Michael Connell				△
John Dunlap				△	Robert Ellis			O	△
George Feather			△		William Haddon				△
Henry Franks	19)			△	Edward Kelly			△	△
Benjamin Harper			O	△	John Trotter			O	△
George F. Haywood				△	**PRIVATE**				
Patrick Hughes			O	△	Charles Adair			O	△
Lawrence Johnstone			O	△	Hugh Alexander			O	△
Mark Jollife	20)		△		George Alexander				△
John Keen			△	△	William Allen	(R)			△
Charles Lea			△	△	William Allsop			△	△
Joseph Lunn			△		Owen Anderson				△
George Manning			△	△	William Andrews			O	△
Michael McGann			△		Henry Armstrong				△
William Monoghan			△	O	John Arnold			△	△
James B. Murray	21)		O	△	Benjamin Ash			△	△
Thomas Noble			△	△	John Ashbridge	(MRM)		O	△
David Oldham			O	△	William Ashworth				△
Joseph Salmon			O	△	James Atkins			O	△
Stephen Shepperley			O	△	Thomas Atkins				△
					Walter Atkins				△
					William Atkins			O	△
					John Austin	33)		O	△

South Africa 1853 Medal

Name	Note	Kaffir Wars 1	Kaffir Wars 2	Kaffir Wars 3
John Bamford			O	△
John Barstow	34)		O	△
Samuel Barstow	34)			△
Robert Bartlett				△
Thomas Bates			O	△
George Baxendine			O	△
William Beaumont			△	△
James Bennett				△
Terence Bennett				△
Matthew Bergin	35)			△
Michael Bergin	35)			△
George Betts				△
Michael Bird				△
Peter Bird			O	△
James Blakey	(MRM)			△
John Boneham	36)		O	△
Joseph Boss				△
Thomas Bostock				△
William Boyes	37) (MRM)		O	△
John Brennan			△	△
John Brian	38)			△
Edward Brighurst				△
Edward Broadbent			O	△
James Broom			△	△
David Brown			O	△
George Brown			O	
James Brown				△
John Brown			O	△
Thomas Bryson				△
Charles Buchanan			O	△
John Buckley	(MRM)			△
George Bullock			O	△
Patrick Bulman				△
Thomas Burley			△	△
Daniel Burns	39)			△
William Bush	40)			△
Michael Byrnes				△
John Caffrey	41) (P)			△
Patrick Cahill			△	△
Jeremiah Cahill	42)		O	△
Matthew Cairns	43)		△	△
Michael Carney				△
John Carrington			O	△
John Carrock	44)		△	△
James Cartledge			O	△
James Cartmell	45)		O	△
George Caswell				△
John Cavanagh	46)		O	△
John Ceene			O	△
Bryan Ceirey	47)			△
John Chadwick			△	△
Theophilus Chamberlain				
Jesse Chandler	(MRM)		O	△
Charles Charley			O	△
Joseph Charley			△	△
John Chippendale				△
Joseph Chittuck			O	△
George Chusick				△
Richard Clarke				△
William Clarke	48)		O	△
George Clarkson			O	△
William Clarkson			O	△
Henry Cleft	49)		O	△
John Coates	50)			△
James B. Coe				△
Thomas Coe	51)			△
Timothy Cokely	52)		O	△
James Cole			O	△
James Coleman			O	△
Patrick Coleman				△
William Coleman				△
James Collins			O	△
Patrick Comerton	53) (MRM)		O	△
Patrick Connell			O	△
Thomas Connell			O	△
Henry Connor				△
Stephen Conroy			O	△
Edward Conway			O	△
Samuel Cooper				△
Henry Copley	54)			△
John Costello (1)	55)			△
John Costello (2)	55)		O	△
William Costley				△
John Cotton			O	△
John Coupe			O	△
Robert Cowell			O	△
Frederick Craven			O	△
Charles Craythorn			O	△
Dennis Cronan	56) (P)			
James Cook	57)		O	△
Roderick Cummins			O	△
Thomas Currie	58)		O	△
Michael Curtin				△
Jonathan Dackus			O	△
John Dain				△
Cornelius Daley				△
Dennis Daley				△
Matthew Daley				△
Michael Daley				△
John Daley	59)		△	△
James Darcey (1)	60)		△	△
James Darcey (2)	60)		△	△
Joseph Darcey			△	△
Patrick Darcey			△	△
James Dawson			O	△
William Dawson				△
Stephen Deloughey				△
Edward Dickerson	61)		O	△
Michael Dinneen	62)		O	△
Rutherford Dodd			O	△
George Dogherty			O	△
Patrick Dolan			O	△
John Donohoe				△
Peter Doovan				△
Charles Dovey				△
Thomas Dovey			△	△
James Downey			O	△
Thomas Duckett			O	△
Patrick Duffy			△	△
David N. Duggan	63)			△
David Duggins	64)			△
John Duncan			O	△
Patrick Dunn	65)			△
Richard E. Dunne			△	△
Richard Durance			O	△
William Dyer			O	△
William Eades			△	△
Michael Early				△
William Eckersley			O	△
Henry Edmondson	66)		O	△
Thomas Edon			O	△
Daniel Edwards			O	△
William Eglestone	67)			△
William Ellis			O	△
Joseph England	(MRM)		O	△
John English			O	△

58 South Africa 1853 Medal

Name	Note	Kaffir Wars 1	2	3
PRIVATE				
James Ennis	(MRM)		O	△
John Eskett				△
Henry Evans			O	△
Joseph Evans	(MRM)		O	△
Thomas Evans			O	△
Robert Everett			O	△
Robert Farmer			O	△
Matthew Farrell			O	△
John Farrier			O	△
Henry Fay			△	O
John Field	(MRM)		△	△
Jonas Field			△	O
George Fieldwick			△	△
Joseph Fiern	68)		O	△
William Finlay	69)		O	△
Thomas Finn			O	△
William Fitch			△	△
Patrick Fitzpatrick				△
William Flannigan	70)		O	
John Flax			O	
Patrick Flemming	71) (P)		△	△
James Flint			O	△
Patrick Flood				△
Daniel Flynn				△
Francis Flynn				△
John Flynn (1)	72)			△
John Flynn (2)	72)			△
Robert H. Flynn				△
Henry Foot				△
John Ford		△		
George Fowler			O	△
William Freeson				△
William French			△	△
William Geoghan			O	△
Peter Gilford	73)			△
Charles Gilks				△
Edward Gipson	74)		△	△
Peter Glavey			△	△
Joseph Goldsmith			O	△
Thomas Gorham	75)			△
John Gorman	76)			△
Michael Gorman	76)			△
Joseph Gorry				△
George Grant	(MRM)		O	△
William Green			O	△
John Gregson	(R)		O	△
John Gutridge	77)			△
Edward Hadley				△
William Hadner	78)			△
Squire Halden	79)		O	△
Frederick Hall	(MRM)		O	△
John Hall				△
Richard Hall	80)			△
James Hallas	81)		O	△
Peter Hammond				△
Stephen Hammond	82)			△
Thomas Harker			O	△
George Harris	83)		O	△
Patrick Hart			O	△
Henry Harwood				△
Henry Hawkins			O	△
Stephen Hayford			O	△
Isaac Head			O	△
James Healy			O	△
William Heath	(P)		O	△
Richard Herbert	84)		△	△
John Herrick	85)			△

Name	Note	Kaffir Wars 1	2	3
Nicholas Hess				△
John Hewitt				△
William Hicks			△	△
Benjamin Hiorns	86)		O	△
John Hodgin			O	△
John Hogarth			O	△
Allen Hollingsworth			O	△
Joseph Hollingsworth				△
Edward Hollis			△	
John Holmes				△
Solomon Howe			△	△
Isaac Horton			△	△
James Houlden	87)		O	△
John Hudson	88)		O	△
Joseph Hughes				△
James Humphries			O	△
Richard Hunt	89)			△
Thomas Hunter			O	△
Thomas Hurle			O	△
Henry Hyde			O	△
William Ingram			△	O
Thomas Isherwood				△
George Jacobs				△
James Jacocks			△	△
Charles James	(MRM)		O	△
William Jelly	(P)		△	△
Joseph Jenkinson				△
William Jenkinson			△	△
William Jobson			O	△
Thomas Johnson	90)		O	△
John Jones	91)		O	△
Joseph Jordan	92)		O	△
Richard Jordan	92)		O	△
Michael Judge			△	O
Daniel Keefe				△
Michael Keelan			O	△
Edward Keenan				△
James Keenan			O	△
Benjamin Kellett			O	△
Patrick Kelly (1)			O	△
Patrick Kelly (2)	93)		O	△
William Kenney	94)		O	△
John Keoghan	95)		△	△
John Keon	96)			△
James Kerrigan				△
Thomas Kerwin	97)		△	△
Darby Kidney				△
Patrick Kilday			△	△
George King	98)		O	△
Henry Kingston				△
Thomas Kingston	99)		△	△
Robert Knowles			O	△
Thomas C. Lamb			O	△
John Lavin				△
James Lawler	80)		O	△
Michael Lawler	100)		O	△
George Leake	101)		O	△
James Lealy			△	
James Lee	(P)		O	△
Henry Leek	102)		O	△
William Leonard			O	△
Robert Leroy				△
Peter Linnen				△
John Lister	103)		△	
Richard Lomasney				△
Thomas Loughan	104)		△	△
John Love			△	△
William Lupton			O	△

		Kaffir Wars				Kaffir Wars
		1 2 3				1 2 3
John Macklin		△	John Nowlan (1)	114)		○ △
John Maguire		△	John Nowlan (2)	114)		△
Michael Maguire		○ △	John O'Brien			○ △
John Malden	105)	○ △	Michael O'Brien (1)	115)		○ △
Henry Mann		○ △	Michael O'Brien (2)	115)		○ △
John Manning		△	Patrick O'Leary			○ △
Jeremiah Maroney		△	David Ormond			○ △
John Maroney		△	Robert Otley			△
William Marsden		△ △	Peter Owen			○ △
Joseph Marshall		△	William Parker			○ △
John Masterton		△	Thomas Parnum			○ △
Michael McCann	(MRM)	○ △	David Paterson			△
James McCanna (1)	106)	○ △	James Patterson			○ △
James McCanna (2)	106)	△	Charles Pearson			○ △
Darby McCarthy		△	Joseph Percy			△
Samuel McCawley	107)	○ △	John Perry			○ △
Charles McClean		○ △	Samuel Petteth			○ △
Edward McClean		△	John Pinnock			○ △
James F. McClelland		△	Henry Plummer			○ △
Patrick McCormick		○ △	James Poole			△
Patrick McCranney	108) (MRM)	○ △	Patrick Power			△
Francis McCullen		○ ○	John Purcell			○ △
Bernard McGee		○ △	John Queen			△
James McGuire		△	Patrick Quinn	116)		○ △
John McGuire		○ △	Richard Ralph			○ △
Andrew McHugh		○ △	David Ramsey	117)		○
John McHugh		○ △	John Reddington			△
Peter McHugh		△ △	John Reeves		(R)	○ △
Thomas McKeone		○ △	Thomas Reid			○ △
John McKurrell	43)	△ △	Michael Reynolds			○ △
Francis McLoughlin		△	Richard Reynolds			△ △
Lucis McMahon		△	James Rice			△
James McNabney		○ △	William Rigby			△
Martin McNamara		△	William Ritchie			△
James McNicol		○ △	Thomas Roach	118)		○ △
John McWilliams		○ △	William Roach	118)		○ △
William Mee		○ △	Thomas Roak			○ △
Patrick Meehan		○ △	James Roberts			○ △
Robert Merryman		△ △	William Ronsdale			△
William Mills		△ △	William Roundhill			○ △
Abraham Mitchell		○ △	Charles Rowley			○ △
Robert Mitchell		△	William Rudd			○ △
Robert Mitton	109)	△	Martin Rush			○ △
Frederick Moon		○ △	Robert Rutter			○ △
John Moore	110)	△	James Ryder		(P)	△
William Moores	111)	○ △	Robert Ryder			○ △
Alexander Moran	(MRM)	△	Abraham Saunders	119)		△
Michael Moran		△	James Savage			△
William Moran		○ △	Thomas Savage			△
James Morrow		△	Hugh Scott			△
George Moseley	43)	△ △	John Scott			△ △
William Muires	112)	○ △	William Scott			○ △
Richard Mulhall		△ △	John Seddon	(MRM)		○ △
Alexander Mulholland		○ △	Peter Sessnan			○ △
Thomas Mullen		△	Timothy Sessnan			○ △
Charles Mulligan		△ △	Patrick Sharp			△
Michael Murphy		○ △	Alfred Shaw			○ △
William Murphy		△	William Shaw			○ △
James Murray	113)	○ △	Silvester Sheehan			○ △
Michael Murray		○ △	Thomas Sheeran	120)		○ △
Joseph Nelson		○ △	John Sheppard		(R)	○ △
George Nelson		△ △	Thomas Sheppard		(P)	○ △
Daniel Newman		○ △	James Shields			○ △
Thomas Newman		○ △	William Sime			△
Henry Nibbs		○ △	John Simmons	121)		○ △
William Noblett		○ △	Benjamin Simpson			△
John Norman		△	Thomas Skehan	122)		△
William Norvin	(MRM)	○ △	George Slarke			△

60 South Africa 1853 Medal

PRIVATE		Kaffir Wars 1 2 3			Kaffir Wars 1 2 3
Patrick Slohan	123)	O △	William Turner		△
Hugh Smith		O △	Cornelius Verboon		△
Isaac Smith		O △	Charles Vincent		△ △
John Smith		O △	George Vivash		△
Patrick Smith		△	James Wade	128)	△
Thomas Smith		△	Thomas Wade		△
William Smith		O △	John Wakefield		O △
John Stansfield		O △	Henry Walker	(R)	O △
John Stebbings		△	John Wallis		△ △
Alexander Stephenson		O △	Joseph Walls	(MRM)	O △
William Stephenson		△	Dennis Walsh		△
Joseph Stockman		△	Edward Walsh	129)	△
John Swalthy		△	Patrick Walsh		O △
Dennis Sullivan	(P)	O △	Thomas Walsh (1)	130)	O △
Patrick Sullivan		△	Thomas Walsh (2)	130)	O △
Stephen Sullivan		△	William Walsh	131) (MRM)	△
John Summerton		△	Edward Ward		△ △
Thomas Surmon		O △	William Warner		O △
Henry Sutcliffe		O △	Daniel Watkins		△
Henry Sutton		O △	George Watts	(MRM)	O △
Edward Swift		△	Simon Webster		O △
George Symes		△	William Westwood		O △
Frederick Tabor		△	George Whatmough	132) (MRM)	O △
Joseph Tafe		△	Edwin Wheeldon		△
Charles Tamage		O △	John Whitchell	133)	
John Taylor		△	John White		△ △
Isiah Teale	124)	△	Samuel Whitehead		O △
Henry Tester	(P)	O △	Luke Whiteworth		O △
John Thompson		△	Henry Whitterick	134)	△
George Thompson		△	Robert Williams		△
John S. Thorley		△	Henry Wilson	(MRM)	O △
John Thornton		△	James Wilson		O △
William Thrasher	125)	O △	John Wilson		△
John Tierney		O △	Samuel Wilson		△
Thomas Tierney		O △	John Witter		△
Patrick Timms	126)	O △	Benjamin Wood		O △
Samuel Timms	126)	O △	James Woods		O △
William Timson		O △	Atkinson Wray		O △
William Toach		△	John Wrigglesworth		O △
George Tolan	127)	△ △	John Young		O △
Hugh Tolan		△	George Young	(R)	O △
John Toner		△	Thomas Yarwood	(P)	△
Robert Toole		O △	James Farrell		△
Isaac Triston		O △	Richard Oddy	135)	△ △
James Trollope		O △			
Michael Tuite		O △	△ = campaign qualification as WO/100/17.		
Joseph Turner		O △	O = campaign which the Rolls fail to credit.		

6TH (ROYAL WARWICKSHIRE) REGIMENT NOTES

1. One of the most experienced and prominent regimental commanders of the wars.
2. See G and I.
3. Severely wounded 28.6.52.
4. Commanded the regiment during an action on 29.6.51 when forming the rearguard of the division.
5. Severely wounded 24.12.50 when Field Adjutant at Boomah Pass. For 13 months from May 1851, commanded an irregular corps of Europeans known as 'Catty's Rifles' which was engaged in nearly every patrol of the 2nd division. Catty took part in the expedition against Chief Kreli and was commander of Fort Grey during the later stages of the 3rd war.
6. Only appears on the Roll as a note against a deserter of the 91st recording that Gore received the cancelled medal re-named.
7. At Boomah Pass and in command of Fort White during the attack of 3.1.51. Also on two expeditions to the Waterkloof. 'One of the best officers I have ever known' – Bissett. See also G and I.
8. Commanded three companies of the 6th and one of the 73rd in the engagement at Boomah Pass. Commanded the two companies attacked between Fort Cox and Fort White on 6.2.51. Appointed commandant of Fort Elizabeth and the Uitenhage district in March 1851. See G and I.
9. Commandant of East London during the 3rd war.
10. Present at the operations in the Waterkloof in September 1851 and March 1852.
11. Commanded the Light Company. Present at operations on the Fish River, in the Amatolas and across the Kei.
12. Wounded 9.6.51. See G and I.
13. Engaged in the Boomah Pass action and present at the attack on the Amatolas in June 1851.
14. Adjutant in the expedition beyond the Kei in January 1847. Field Adjutant at the beginning of the 3rd war, he was acting Brigade Major in July 1851 and DAQMG of the 1st Brigade in February 1852.
15. Wastell on Roll. Later commissioned.
16. Clark on Roll.
17. Also Beedle on musters.
18. No 1688.

19. An Armourer Sergeant.
20. Received a re-named duplicate to replace lost original.
21. No 2679 and not to be confused with No 1574.
22. With the 73rd during the 2nd campaign.
23. No 1229. Cale on Roll.
24. Also Egin on musters.
25. Hixon on Roll.
26. No 1036.
27. No 3297, a survivor from the 'Birkenhead'.
28. Maynord on Roll.
29. Earned his medal with the 12th regiment.
30. No 2743. I have not traced his war service which may have been earned with another regiment.
31. Berry on Roll.
32. Carrick on Roll.
33. Austen on Roll and later musters.
34. Bastow on Roll.
35. Bergan on Roll.
36. Bonham on Roll.
37. Also Boys on muster.
38. Bryan on Roll.
39. Burnes on Roll and later musters.
40. No 1489, a survivor from the 'Birkenhead'.
41. Caffery on Roll and also Caffray on later musters.
42. A boy soldier during the 2nd campaign.
43. Earned his medal with the 91st Regiment.
44. Carrick on Roll and also Carrack on later musters.
45. Cartmill on Roll.
46. Cavenagh on Roll.
47. Ceiry on Roll.
48. No 1845. Clark on Roll.
49. Clift on Roll.
50. Coales on Roll.
51. No 3310, a survivor from the 'Birkenhead'.
52. Coakley on Roll.
53. Cunnerton on Roll.
54. Coupley on Roll.
55. Nos 2878 and 2606 respectively. One shown as Costelow on Roll; various spellings on musters.
56. Cronnan on Roll, Cronin on medal.
57. Crooks on Roll.
58. Served with the 90th during the 2nd war.
59. Daly on Roll.
60. Nos 2548 and 2605. Various spellings on musters.
61. Dickisson on Roll.
62. Dineen on medal; both spellings on musters.
63. No 2986, Duggin on Roll and later musters.
64. No 1102.
65. Dunne on Roll and later musters.
66. Also Edmonson on musters.
67. Also Eagleston on musters.
68. Feirn on Roll.
69. Finley on Roll.
70. Flanagan on Roll.
71. Twice on Roll, once as Fleming, each showing a different campaign. To the CMR in 1855.
72. Nos 3036 and 3139, the latter earned his medal with the 60th Regiment.
73. Guilford on Roll.
74. Served with the 27th during the 2nd campaign.
75. No 2974. The christian name Thomas has been altered to James on the Roll, but this may be a confusion for James Gorman No 2845, who seems to have qualified but does not appear on the Roll.
76. Gormon on Roll.
77. Gutteridge on Roll.
78. Hadnor on Roll.
79. Haldon on Roll.
80. Subsequently to CMR.
81. Also Hallis on musters.
82. Also Hammont on musters.
83. Harras on Roll.
84. Medal was returned to have christian name altered from Edward.
85. No 3287, a survivor from the 'Birkenhead'.
86. Hirons on Roll.
87. Houlding on Roll.
88. No 1527.
89. No 3320, a survivor from the 'Birkenhead'.
90. No 1997.
91. No 1420
92. Jordon on Roll.
93. Nos 2272 and 2575.
94. No 2043. Also Kenny on musters.
95. Keighan on Roll. Also Kaghan on musters.
96. I have not identified this man. It is probably John Keene No 2029.
97. Also Keirwin on musters.
98. Served with the 90th during the 2nd campaign.
99. Kingstone on Roll.
100. Discharged 6.4.50 but re-joined and served in the 3rd campaign before going to the CMR in 1855.
101. Leek on Roll.
102. Also Leeke on musters.
103. Lester on Roll.
104. Logan on Roll.
105. Maldon on Roll.
106. Nos 2347 and 2704, one of which was returned to the Mint.
107. McCauley on Roll.
108. McCannay on Roll.
109. Medal may be found to be altered from Milton.
110. Moores on Roll.
111. Also Morres on musters.
112. Mures on Roll.
113. No 1574.
114. Nos 2488 and 1687.
115. Nos 1902 and 2533.
116. No 2366.
117. Shown as qualified for the 3rd war on Roll but was discharged 29.7.50 before it began.
118. Various spellings on musters.
119. Sanders on Roll.
120. Sheran on Roll.
121. Simmonds on Roll.
122. Skeean on Roll.
123. Slowhan on Roll. Ex-CMR.
124. No 1491, a survivor from the 'Birkenhead' – when a sergeant.
125. Also Thresher on musters.
126. Tims on Roll.
127. Twice shown on Roll, once as Jolan.
128. No 1963, a survivor from the 'Birkenhead'.
129. No 3294, a survivor from the 'Birkenhead'. See McKay.
130. Nos 1593 and 2505.
131. No 3277, a survivor from the 'Birkenhead'. See McKay.
132. Watmough on Roll.
133. Witchell on Roll.
134. Witterick on Roll.
135. Twice on Roll; once as Sgt.

PRO References: WO/12/2415-2416-WO/12/2421-2422-2423-2425.

12th (East Suffolk) Regiment (Reserve Battalion)

Having sailed from Mauritius in the 'Hermia', six companies of the Reserve Battalion disembarked at Port Elizabeth on August 24th 1851. They were soon at Grahams Town where one company remained while the rest set out on September 6th to join Somerset's 1st Division at Rietfontein. A detachment to Fort Brown under Major Horne was first into action; on October 2nd they scattered a large body of the enemy, killing 10 and capturing some cattle.

The 12th was one of the regiments which made up Somerset's force of some 4,000 who moved out of Fort Beaufort to attack Kaffir strongholds in the Waterkloof. During the attack on the heights above Hermanus' Kloof they were expected to cover the rear of the 74th and 91st Regiments, but their inexperience found them in some disorder which displeased the other regiments. By mid-November they were on the Blinkwater and from there marched to Lower Albany to form part of the screen to protect Grahams Town and the western part of the colony.

Constantly employed on patrolling until March 1852 the regiment provided most of the troops which, commanded by their Colonel, John Perceval, operated against Kaffir and Hottentot camps along the Fish River, and then combined with Lt Col Michel's force in clearing the Amatola basin. The various columns then assembled at Fort Cox before moving off again; the 12th to scour the forests of the Buffalo Poorts and Peri bush. Two companies under Capt Gillman were detached with a party of CMR near the Tab Indoba mountain when attacked by an overwhelming number of Kaffirs. Fortunately the rest of the division was attracted by the sounds of firing and extracted Gillman from his predicament. The force then moved into the Keiskama Hoek in early April; the 12th being detailed to escort livestock captured there to King William's Town. When returning to the Albany the division searched the territories of rebel chiefs Stock, Tola and Seyola before camping at Botha's Hill and bringing to a close an operation which had lasted 46 days. During that time the troops marched nearly 1,000 miles, killed 124 of the enemy and captured some 1,500 cattle. The Suffolks lost two men killed and only one badly wounded.

In June the Reserve Battalion was employed in keeping open communications between Grahams Town and King Williams Town. When Capt Moody and his sappers were attacked and cut off with their convoy whilst travelling to Fort Beaufort, Lt Bagnell set out from Fort Brown to their relief with 50 of the 12th and some of the CMR. Lt Studdert with 30 men and a troop of lancers also moved to the sappers' aid from Governors Kop but they were not in time to prevent the convoy waggons being ransacked.

During a punitive expedition to the Fish River in August, Gillman and only 15 men encountered nearly 100 rebels and managed to kill several before driving them off and capturing some 300 cattle.

The 12th formed camps at Line Drift, Fort Peddie, Botha's Hill, Koonap and several other posts from which patrols were made almost daily, but these activities had little result until January 8th 1853 when a detachment under Capt Espinasse clashed with a party of Hottentots near Jantjies Kraal and killed 18 of them. The Reserve Battalion lost one man killed and another wounded in this action; the last casualties they suffered in the war; but it was another five years, by which time the Reserve Battalion had become the 2nd Battalion, before the regiment returned home.

		Kaffir Wars 1 2 3			Kaffir Wars 1 2 3
LIEUTENANT COLONEL			Julius Stirke		△
John M. Perceval, CB	1) (R)	△	James F. Sweeney		△
MAJOR			James D. Travers	(P)	△
Arthur Horne		△	**SURGEON**		
CAPTAIN			William Dick		△
Thomas Dundas		△	Robert V. George	5)	△
James Espinasse		△	**ASSISTANT SURGEON**		
Bennett W. Gillman	2)	△	John Small		△
Francis G. Hamley	(P)	△	**QUARTERMASTER**		
LIEUTENANT			Alexander Nesbitt		△
Frederick Bagnell		△	**SERGEANT MAJOR**		
Samuel Fairtlough	3) (R)	△	John Sankey	6)	△
LIEUTENANT/ADJUTANT			**DRUM MAJOR**		
Edward H. H. Foster		△	Richard Haggan		△
LIEUTENANT			**COLOUR SERGEANT**		
Thomas Garner		△	James Gartland		△
Edward Herrick	(R)	△	Samuel Madge	(P)	△
Robert N. Irving	(P)	△	William Park		△
John R. Palmer	(M)	△	Richard Slater		△
G. L. Studdert	4)	△	**QUARTERMASTER SERGEANT**		
ENSIGN			John Crowe	(P)	△
Benjamin S. Adams		△	**ARMOURER SERGEANT**		
Frederick C. Barclay		△	John Edwards		△
George Gibson		△	**HOSPITAL SERGEANT**		
George Robertson		△	William Fairbanks		△

South Africa 1853 Medal

		Kaffir Wars		
		1	2	3
SCHOOL MASTER SERGEANT				
William Davidson				△
SERGEANT				
Samuel Baddock				△
James Cavanagh				△
Thomas Cave				△
William Cherry				△
Thomas Corbett				△
Benjamin Crompton				△
Michael Crowe				△
Patrick Daly				△
John Davis	7)			△
Peter Fox				△
Charles Gulston	8)			△
John Henderson				△
William Hillman				△
Daniel Hourigan				△
Dennis Keighry	9)			△
Bernard Laughlin				△
Samuel McCauley	10)			△
William Montgomery				△
Thomas Morgan				△
John Mulvogue	(MRM)			△
John Pearton				△
Patrick Penrose				△
Edward Scanlen	11)			△
Lewis B. Smith	12)			△
Charles Spruce				△
John Sullivan	13)			△
Thomas Sullivan	13)			△
Thomas Worsnup				
CORPORAL				
Aaron Bennett	(P)			△
Richard Berry				△
William Brooks				△
Christopher Byrne				△
Cornelius Carroll				△
John Carroll				△
Francis Doyle				△
John Foulkes				△
Thomas Hall				△
John Herriron	14)			△
John Judge				△
George Keene				△
Mark C. Kelly				△
John Kyle				△
Benjamin Laws	15)			△
Alfred Mann				△
John McGee				
James Mulroy				
Thomas Mulvogue				△
Edward Needham				△
Matthew Noon				△
Edward Pickess	16) (P)			△
William Quantrell				△
Simon Reardon				
John Reilly				△
William P. Smith				△
Matthew Travers				△
DRUMMER				
William Berry				△
Edward Cavanagh				△
James Crane				△
John Doughan	(P)			△
James Eagan	17)			△
Thomas Frost				△
Frederick Hinton				△
Josiah Howarth				△
Robert Jackson				△
James McNulty	(MRM)			△
Hans Murphy				△
William Murphy				△
Francis Stainburn				△
PRIVATE				
John Acheson				△
William Allcock				△
Joshua Allen				△
Isaac Allport				△
George Andrews				△
John Andrews				△
Jonathan Appleyard				△
David Armstrong				△
Samuel Ashton				△
William Ashton				△
Henry Aspden				△
James Baguley				△
John Bailey				△
Henry Bain				△
Joseph Barker	18)			△
James Baldry				△
Edward Bales				△
James Banks				△
Thomas Barber				△
James Barlow				△
Henry Barnard				△
Thomas Barne				△
John Bartholomew				△
George Bateman				△
George Beckett				△
John Beeley				△
William H. Berry				△
Thomas Bishop	19)			△
Joseph Blackburn				△
George Bligh				△
William Blow				△
George Bowden				△
Patrick Boyde	20)			△
John Brady				△
Thomas Brady				△
James Brennan	21)			△
John Bridgeman				△
John Bridges	22)			△
John Brindley				△
Joseph Brindley				△
Samuel Broadbent				△
Michael Broughton				△
Thomas Brown				△
William Brown				△
John Buckley				△
William Bulger	23)			△
Charles Burke				△
Charles Burns				△
Thomas Butcher				△
Lawrence Byrne				△
James Campbell				△
John Capstick				△
Cornelius Carlton				△
James Carpenter				△
William E. Carr				△
George Carruthers				△
Major Carter				△
William Cash				△
Robert Charlton				△
Enoch Clarke				△

South Africa 1853 Medal

PRIVATE		Kaffir Wars 1 2 3			Kaffir Wars 1 2 3
George Clarke		△	John Filbin		△
Thomas Clarke		△	Luke Finnegan		△
William Clarke (1)	24)	△	Patrick Fitzgerald		△
William Clarke (2)	24)	△	James Fitzharris		△
George Claydon		△	Thomas Fitzpatrick		△
William Clements		△	James Fitzroy		△
William Coates		△	James Flemming	32) (R)	△
Daniel Coffee		△	Patrick Flynn		△
James College		△	James Ford	33)	△
Thomas Colvin		△	Thomas Foster	34)	△
John Connor		△	Richard Foxcroft	34)	△
Patrick Connor		△	Joseph France		△
Michael Connors	25)	△	John Fuller	35)	△
Thomas Conroy		△	William Furgis		△
John Constable		△	Michael Gallagher		△
William Conway		△	William Galley		△
Frederick Cooke		△	John Gardiner		△
Samuel Cooper		△	Matthew Gardiner		△
William Cooper		△	William Gearey	36)	△
Alexander Crawford		△	John Gee		△
Michael Creedon		△	Thomas Gelling		△
John Cresswell		△	Richard Gibbs		△
John Crooke		△	James Gilby	(MRM)	△
John Crothers	26)	△	John Giles	(M)	△
George Crowe		△	Henry Gillard		△
Michael Crown		△	Richard Glanville	37)	△
George Crowther		△	William Glenane		△
Brian Cullen		△	William Godhard		△
John Cullinan		△	Stephen Gradidge		△
Henry Cunliffe		△	James Graham	(MRM)	△
James Curley		△	Peter Grant		△
James Curtis		△	William Greathead		△
Robert Curtis	(MRM)	△	John Green	38)	△
Benjamin Dardrey	27) (R)	△	Thomas Green		△
Charles Darlton		△	Edward Griffin	(MRM)	△
Edward Davis	28)	△	George Griffin		△
William Davis	28)	△	William Groom		△
Shadrach Davis		△	John Guirey		△
John Dawson		△	George Hackett		△
Thomas Dawson		△	James Hall		△
John Day		△	William Hallings		△
Thomas Demeary		△	James Hammond		△
William Denny		△	John Handlon		△
Patrick Devine	(P)	△	William Hanks		△
Henry Dipple		△	John Hardman		△
David Dixon		△	James Harran		△
John Dolan		△	Timothy Hart		△
Michael Dolan		△	Jeremiah Hartley		△
Patrick Dolan		△	William Harvey		△
Charles Dolby		△	Daniel Hastings		△
Robert Doolan	29)	△	William Haswell		△
Patrick Doorass		△	Matthew Hawksworth		△
Thomas Doughan		△	James Haxell	(R)	△
Francis Dowde	(MRM)	△	John Hayes		△
Michael Downes		△	Thomas Healey		△
Patrick Dugan	(MRM)	△	Thomas Hearne		△
Joseph Dunn	30)	△	Sidney D. Herbert		△
Edwin Dunstan		△	Thomas Higgins	39)	△
Thomas Eagle		△	Thomas Hill		△
Joseph Etchells		△	Patrick Hilliard		△
Samuel Ever		△	William Hives		△
James Farlon		△	Abraham Hodgson		△
Henry Farnes		△	Jonathan Hollingshead		△
Timothy Farrell		△	Job Holt		△
Henry Farrier		△	Matthew Hood		△
Edward Faucett	31)	△	James Hopwood		△
William Field		△	James Howatt		△
			Joseph Hughes		△

South Africa 1853 Medal

Name	Note	Kaffir Wars 3
Peter Hughes		△
Robert Hurn		△
Robert Hutchen		△
Charles Hutton	(P)	△
John Hynes	(R)	△
Thomas Isherwood		△
Charles Jackman		△
Frederick Jeffery		△
Joseph Johnstone	40)	△
William Johnstone		△
Michael Joyce	41) (MRM)	△
John Jones		△
Samuel Jones		△
William Jones (1)	42)	△
William Jones (2)	42)	△
George Joy		△
John Kaye		△
Edward Keegan		△
Robert Keenan		△
Michael Kennelly		△
Patrick Kevill	43)	△
Richard Kilcoyne	44)	△
Patrick Kilcullen		△
John Killeen		△
Charles Kilgour	45)	△
Francis Kimmitt		△
Matthew Kirkham		△
John Kitt		△
Luke Knight		△
Henry Knock		△
Patrick Lally		△
Joseph Lambert		△
Daniel Landers		△
Thomas Langan	46)	△
Thomas Large		△
John Lawson		△
James Lee		△
Michael Lee		△
Andrew Leitch		△
John Lennon		△
Charles Lewis		△
George Liees		△
Joseph Lindsey	47)	△
Thomas Line		△
James Lloyd		△
Thomas Loader		△
James Long		△
Isaac Lougheed	48)	△
Samuel Lowe	49)	△
Michael Lynch (1)	50)	△
Michael Lynch (2)	50)	△
John Malonie		△
William Manham		△
Edward Manning		△
James Markland		△
Thomas Marsden		△
Robert Marsh		△
George Mason	51)	△
Thomas Mathers		△
Joseph Matley		△
William Maxwell		△
William Mayo		△
Andrew McCann		△
Robert McCann		△
Dennis McCarthy		△
James McDonald	52)	△
Michael McDonald	(R)	△
Patrick McDonald		△
John McGuire	(MRM)	△
Patrick McLear		△
John McLoughlin	(P)	△
Hugh McMorray	53)	△
James McNally		△
John McNally		△
Hugh Mealey		△
Abraham Middleton		△
Peter Miller		△
Henry Mills		△
John Mitchell		△
James Monaghan	54)	△
John Moore		△
John Morgan		△
William Morgan	55)	△
William Morley	56)	△
Henry Morris		△
John Mullally		△
James Mulvey		△
Michael Murphy		△
James Navin	57)	△
John Newett	58)	△
John Nightingale		△
George Nunn		△
Henry Oakley		△
Hugh O'Beirne		△
Gilbert O'Dea		△
James O'Donnell	59)	△
Henry O'Donnell		△
Charles Oldridge		△
John Owen		△
Henry Page		△
James Page	(R)	△
Stephen Palferman		△
William Pallant		△
Charles Palmer		△
Gregory Palmer	(P)	△
Joseph Parker		△
William Parker		△
Joseph Partington		△
Charles Paul		△
Charles Perry		△
John Petted		△
Michael Phelan		△
William Pitt	(MRM)	△
James Plummer	(R)	△
John Postles		△
James Poulton		△
Stephen Pragnell	60)	△
John Prestwich		△
Henry Price		△
Richard Priest	61) (P)	△
George Prince		△
Charles Pugh		△
Henry Pye		△
Daniel Quinn		△
Edward Quinn		△
John Quinn	62)	△
William Quinn		△
Samuel Rainbird		△
John Ralphs	63)	△
Thomas Rawlings		△
Anthony Reddington		△
John Rees		△
Charles Rew		△
Philip Reynolds		△
Charles Rhodes		△
Levi Riddler	64)	△

66 South Africa 1853 Medal

PRIVATE		Kaffir Wars 1 2 3			Kaffir Wars 1 2 3
Jeremiah Riley	65)	△	John Thorn	(R)	△
Roger Rooney		△	John Tick	79)	△
William Roper		△	John Timon	80)	△
Robert Rose		△	John Tobin (1)	81)	△
James Rubley		△	John Tobin (2)	81)	△
Thomas Runion	66)	△	James Todd		△
Josiah Rushworth	67)	△	William Tombling	82)	△
James Russell		△	Stewart Townshend	83)	△
James Rutherford	68)	△	Elijah Troth		△
Patrick Rutledge		△	Thomas Vest		△
Patrick Ryan		△	Philip Viles		△
Francis Rye		△	James Viner		△
Joseph Sanderson	69)	△	Thomas Walker		△
Joseph Satchwell		△	William Walker		△
Robert Scorrell		△	Henry Wallace		△
Thomas Scott (1)	70)	△	John Walmsley		△
Thomas Scott (2)	70)	△	John Walsh	84)	△
Henry Senior		△	Richard Ward		△
Charles Seymour	(R)	△	William Warren		△
John Shaw (1)	71)	△	Daniel Wartes	85)	△
John Shaw (2)	71)	△	James Watts		△
Matthew Shawcross		△	George Wellum		△
Michael Sheedy		△	Thomas Whalley		△
Hugh Sherry		△	Thomas Whatton		△
James Sill		△	Joseph Wheeler		△
Ralph Skinner		△	John Whelan		△
Matthew Slater	72)	△	William Whelan		△
William Slough		△	James White		△
Edward Smith	73) (MRM)	△	William Whitehead		△
Henry Smith		△	Henry Williams		△
Jeremiah Smith		△	John Williams (1)	86)	△
John Smith (1)	74)	△	John Williams (2)	86)	△
John Smith (2)	74)	△	Thomas Williams (1)	87)	△
William Smith (1)	75)	△	Thomas Williams (2)	87)	△
William Smith (2)	75)	△	John Wilkinson		△
William Smith (3)	75)	△	John Willshaw		△
John Spencer		△	John Wilson		△
John Stafford		△	Thomas Wilson		△
Edward Stanford		△	Matthew Wise		△
John Steele		△	Joseph Wood		△
John Stevens		△	Thomas Wood		△
Henry Stewart		△	George Wright		△
Robert Stewart		△	William Wright	(P)	△
James Stott	(MRM)	△	Thomas Wright	88)	△
Edward Sullivan	76)	△	Israel H. Rowe		△
Maurice Sullivan	77)	△	Joseph Wyatt		△
Ralph Suthers		△	John Yale	89)	△
James Sweeney	78)	△	Samuel Yates		△
Matthew Sweeney	78)	△	James Yea		△
William Swinscow		△	Robert Binns		△
Richard Thistlewaite		△			
William H. Thomas		△	△ = campaign qualification as WO/100/17.		

12TH (EAST SUFFOLK) REGIMENT (RES BATT) NOTES

1 Percival on Roll.
2 Gillinan on Roll.
3 Fairlough on Roll; medal said to show Fairclough.
4 Served with the CMR in the 1850-2 campaign.
5 Present at Berea.
6 Sanky on Roll.
7 Davies on Roll.
8 Gulstone on Roll.
9 Keighrey on Roll.
10 Also McCawley on musters.
11 Musters show various spellings.
12 Wounded 15.10.51.
13 Sulivan on Roll.
14 Harrison on Roll.
15 Lawes on Roll.
16 Prickess on Roll.
17 Egan on Roll.
18 Baker on Roll.
19 Also Bisshop on musters.
20 Boyd on Roll.
21 Two men on musters Nos 2115 and 2142.
22 Brydges on Roll. No 2703, a survivor from the 'Birkenhead'.
23 Bugler on Roll.
24 Nos 1969 and 2041.
25 Connor on Roll.
26 Crothars on Roll.
27 Dardry on Roll, Davdy on medal.
28 Davies on Roll.
29 No 2667, a survivor from the 'Birkenhead'.
30 Also Dunne on muster. 'Dead' on Roll.
31 Fenset on Roll.
32 Fleming on Roll.
33 Also Forde on musters.

34 'Dead' on Roll.
35 Also Joseph on musters.
36 Original medal was lost and recipient paid for a re-named replacement.
37 Medal wrongly named Granville.
38 Two men on musters No 1780 and 2444.
39 No 2672, a survivor from the 'Birkenhead'.
40 No 2727, a survivor from the 'Birkenhead'.
41 Joice on Roll.
42 Nos 2291 and 2313.
43 Also Keivil on muster.
44 Also Kelcoyne on muster.
45 Also Killgour on musters.
46 No 2721, a survivor from the 'Birkenhead'.
47 Lindsay on Roll.
48 Loughhead on Roll.
49 Lawe on Roll.
50 Nos 1710 and 2128. One of these medals is in a private collection.
51 'Dead' on Roll.
52 No 2612, a survivor from the 'Birkenhead'.
53 McMurray on Roll.
54 John on Roll.
55 Two men on musters Nos 2607 and 2670.
56 Also Moreley on musters.
57 Two men on musters Nos 1823 and 2510.
58 Newitt on Roll.
59 O'Donald on Roll.
60 Prangnell on Roll.
61 Also Priests on musters.
62 Two men on musters Nos 2386 and 2666.
63 Ralph on Roll.
64 Ridler on Roll.
65 Reilly on Roll.
66 Runnion on Roll.
67 Joshua on Roll.
68 Wounded 11.4.52.
69 Saunderson on Roll.
70 Nos 2366 and 1803.
71 Nos 2010 and 2468.
72 Ex-45th Regiment.
73 No. 2511.
74 Nos 2266 and 2638.
75 Nos 2562, 2614 and 2636, a survivor from the 'Birkenhead'. One of these medals is in the Regimental Museum.
76 Sulivan on Roll.
77 Morris on muster.
78 Sweeny on Roll.
79 Thick on Roll.
80 No 2704, a survivor from the 'Birkenhead'.
81 Nos 1740 and 2214.
82 Tambling on Roll.
83 Townsend on Roll.
84 'Dead' on Roll.
85 No 2682, a survivor from the 'Birkenhead'.
86 Nos 1231 and 1571.
87 Nos 1470 and 1853.
88 'Dead' on Roll.
89 No 2638, a survivor from the 'Birkenhead'.

PRO References: WO/12/2968–1969–1970–3007.

27th (Inniskilling) Regiment

Embarking at Cork the six service companies of the Inniskillings reached Cape Town on August 18th 1835. They proceeded at once for Algoa Bay and then on to Grahams Town, arriving at the time the peace treaty was being ratified. Depredations did not cease overnight and the 27th were split up in detachments to relieve troops who had borne the brunt of the warfare at the various posts along the frontier. By November matters had quietened sufficiently to allow the grenadier and light companies to be ordered back to Cape Town, but it was another 18 months before the remaining companies under Major McPherson were also recalled.

In November 1838 the 27th returned to the frontier. Patrolling from the chain of forts was generally monotonous work and the occasional expedition to punish cattle raiders held little hope that such retaliation was effective.

And so it went on until 1842 when, to keep the peace between the Boers and native tribes in Natal, Capt T. Charlton Smith was directed to Port Natal (now known as Durban) to act as commandant.

On April 1st Smith set out from the Umgazi River with 263 officers and men, a howitzer and two six-pounders. His force consisted of two companies of the 27th, a troop of the CMR and detachments of the RA and RE/S&M and, as they were accompanied by women and children, clearly had no notion of the difficulties which faced them. Following a hard march through wild country they reached their destination on May 4th and Smith found the Boers in belligerent mood. Pouring in from their farms they set up an armed camp just outside the port at Congella (or Kongella), and seeing the Boers were determined to fight Smith decided to make a pre-emptive attack on the night of May 23rd. It failed disastrously; two light guns were lost and 50 officers and men killed or wounded. Within a few days the British force was surrounded and under siege; both sides were well dug in although during the following weeks the troops made sorties against Boer positions they lacked the strength to break out. Their enemies had not the purpose to overwhelm them by direct assault and sought to starve Smith into surrender but in the final week of June a relieving force of men from the 25th Regiment and Capt Durnford's Grenadier Company of the 27th reached Natal by sea and brought to an end a very gallant defence which deserves to be better known.

Two companies were stationed in Natal until 1845 when they were re-united with their comrades on the eastern frontier and at the outbreak of the War of the Axe the Inniskillings and the 91st were the only regular infantry at the call of the Lt Governor, Col Hare.

The 27th had been left to man the forts and blockhouses when Hare moved against Sandili in June 1846. The expedition ended in failure and upon the Inniskillings fell much of the responsibility to stem the tide of exultant Kaffirs as they invaded the settlements. After the enemy had been forced back into their own territory the 27th was very active on patrols ranging out from Block Drift and allowed the Kaffirs little rest. There was a fruitless attempt to surround them in the Amatolas during August and Lt Col Johnstone commanded one of the columns which organised against Kreli, but the wily chief surrendered before any serious fighting and the troops returned through country severely burned up through drought. These conditions hampered operations but pressure was kept up until Sandili surrendered at Fort Hare. During 1847 the Inniskillings were continually employed in the desultory warfare of patrolling and in common with most other regiments their once bright red tunics were a tattered maroon by the time peace was concluded in December.

Their long service in South Africa had been arduous and unrewarding, but the regiment had not long to wait before embarking for England and they set foot ashore at Gravesend in April 1848.

		Kaffir Wars 1 2 3			Kaffir Wars 1 2 3
LIEUTENANT COLONEL					
Montague Johnstone	1)	△ △	ENSIGN		
MAJOR			William Crozier		△
Duncan McPherson	(R)	△	SURGEON		
CAPTAIN			William N. Irwin	5)	△
William Amsinck	2) (P)	△	Thomas Mosteyn		△
Walter Butler		△	PAYMASTER		
George Durnford	3)	O △	Victor Raymond		△ O
Richard Fawkes		△	QUARTERMASTER		
John Maclean		△ △	George Thompson		△
Sir Robert Stanford	(P)	△	COLOUR SERGEANT		
Andrew V. Watson		△	John Armstrong		O △
Usher Williamson	4)	O	Maurice Barry		△ O
LIEUTENANT			Michael Foley	8) (R)	O △
Henry W. Cholmeley		△	John Gardiner		△
Lewis C. Irwin	5)	△	Patrick Kavanagh		△
John S. Manly	(R)	△	William McDonald	(P)	O △
LIEUTENANT/ADJUTANT			Benjamin Moore		△
Benjamin Midgley		△	James Reilly	9)	△
LIEUTENANT			John Trenor	10)	△
Edward N. Molesworth	6)	△	DRUM MAJOR		
Bartholomew Tunnard	7)	△	James Kilday	11)	△

South Africa 1853 Medal 69

		Kaffir Wars						Kaffir Wars		
		1	2	3				1	2	3
SERGEANT					Bernard Dolen	24)			△	
John Acton			△	O	John Doonan				△	
John Atkinson			△	O	Hugh Douglas				△	
James Barry			△		Hugh Duffy				△	
John Bolster			△	O	Patrick Dunn	25)		△	O	
Francis Burgess			△		Bernard Dyer			△		
Peter Cadden			△		William Eccleston				△	
Thomas Guy	12)				David Edgar			O	△	
Stephen Hester			△	O	John Edwards			O	△	
William Kavanagh	13)		O	△	Matthew Egan				△	
John Murphy			O	△	William Elliot (1)	26)		△		
John Perryman			O	△	William Elliot (2)	26)			△	
Thomas Ralph			△		John Farmer				△	
James Taylor	14) (P)		△		Matthew Farmer				△	
Michael Walsh		△			Patrick Feeney	27)			△	
Anthony Woods		△	△		Robert Fenner			△		
					Walter Ferguson				△	
CORPORAL					James Fitzpatrick	28)		△		
Bradshaw D. Bell		△			John Fitzpatrick				△	
Patrick Boyland		△			John Fitzsimons				△	
Thomas Campion	(P)	O	△		William Flannagan			△	△	
Michael Delaney			△		George Fleming			O	△	
William Dunn	15) (R)		△		Matthew Flynn	29)		△	△	
John Farrelly		△	O		Michael Flynn	30)		△	△	
Alexander James			△		Michael Foley	31)		△	△	
Owen Gunning		O	△		William Gilchrist			O	△	
John McBarron		O	△		Michael Gilgan	(R)			△	
John Nowlan			△		Patrick Gilleese	32)			△	
Edward Prendergast			△		Thomas Ging				△	
James Ryan	(R)		△		Patrick Glenn	33)			△	
					William Gorley			△	O	
DRUMMER					John Graham	34)			△	
Abraham Fisher			△		John Gregory			△	△	
William Kane	16)	O	△		Joseph Grier	35)		△	O	
Thomas Kearnes		O	△		Thomas Gunn			△	△	
Robert Kemp			△		John Halpin				△	
George McVey	17)	△	△		Archibald Hamilton	(R)		△	△	
					James Hamilton			O	△	
PRIVATE					George Haycock			△		
James Adrian	(R)	O	△		John Higgins				△	
Richard Allingham		△	△		Richard Hinds				△	
John Beattie			△		Joseph Hughes			△		
Samuel Bolster	18) (P)	O	△		Edmond Hynes			O	△	
William Booth			△		Martin Hynes				△	
Robert Burchell		△			Thomas Hynes	36)		△	△	
David Burke		O	△		William Johnstone				△	
Charles Brady	(R)		△		John Kildea				△	
James Breen		△	△		Thomas Kilpatrick	37)			△	
James Campion		O	△		Edward Lawler	38)			△	
John Campion			△		Hugh Lynn	39)		O	△	
Richard Carey		△			James Macnamara			O	△	
William Carmichael	(R)	△	O		Thomas Maguire			△	O	
Richard Carroll		△	△		Thomas Mallon				△	
John Casey		O	△		James McCabe			O	△	
Patrick Casey		△			Edward McCaffrey			O	△	
John Cathcart			△		Owen McCaffrey	(R)			△	
Patrick Cavanagh	19)	△	△		Patrick McCaffrey			O	△	
James Clark		O	△		Henry McCluskey	40)		O	△	
William Cluff		△	△		James McConnell				△	
James Corrigan		△			Thomas McClenagh				△	
John Coyle			△		John McDonagh				△	
Thomas Cutler		△	△		Patrick McGivney			△		
James Daly	20)	△			William McGolrick			△	O	
William Deegan	21)	△			James McGowan			O	△	
John Derwin	22)	△			Edward McGuire	(MRM)		△	O	
Edward Devaney		O	△		John McGrath	(P)		△	△	
Thomas Devine			△		John McHugh			O	△	
Thomas Devitt			△		Patrick McHugh			△	O	
Peter Devlin		△								
John Dolan	23)		△							

70 South Africa 1853 Medal

		Kaffir Wars		
		1	2	3
PRIVATE				
Andrew McKenna		○	△	
William McKenna	41)	△	△	
Edward McLoughlan	42)	△	△	
John McMahon	43)	○	○	
James Moane	44)	○	△	
Francis Monaghan		○	△	
John Moynagh		△	○	
Maurice Mulcare			△	
Bartley Mulligan			△	
Thomas Murphy		△	○	
William Murphy		○	△	
James Murray		○	△	
Thomas Murray	(R)	△	△	
William Nixon			△	
Cornelius O'Brien		△	△	
John O'Neill			△	
John Ovens		○	△	
William Ovens			△	
Henry Patterson			△	
William Patterson		○	△	
Thomas Perkinson	45)		△	
Thomas Pickens	(R)		△	

		Kaffir Wars		
		1	2	3
Joseph Purcell		○	△	
John Regan	46)		△	
John Reilly			△	
William Roach		○	△	
John Rutter			△	
James Ryan	(R)		△	
John Scannel		○	△	
Frederick Shelton			△	
James Smith	47)		△	○
Matthew Sorohan	48)		△	
Thomas Stewart			△	△
David Sullivan			△	
William Tomilty		○	△	
John Tredway	49)		△	
Christopher Vaughan		○	△	
Robert Wanson	(MRM)		△	
Thomas Welch	50)		△	
Samuel Wilson		△	○	

△ = campaign qualification as WO/100/17.
○ = campaign which the Rolls fail to credit.

27TH (INNISKILLING) REGIMENT NOTES

1 Johnston on Roll. Column commander against Kreli. Entrusted with the dangerous mission of visiting Sandili at his kraal in September 1846.
2 Amsink on Roll.
3 With the force which relieved Smith in Natal 1842.
4 Not on Roll, but regimental history states that he received the medal. Musters confirm qualification.
5 Irvin on Roll.
6 With Smith's expedition to Natal 1842.
7 Severely wounded in action against the Boers 24.5.42.
8 No 378.
9 No 945.
10 Later made Quartermaster and is listed among the officers on the Roll.
11 No 1111; shown as Kildea on Roll.
12 A late claimant who received a re-named medal. He has proved elusive on the musters and may have qualified with another regiment.
13 No 545; Cavenagh on Roll.
14 No 1085; not to be confused with Sgt John Taylor.
15 Dunne on Roll, Dunn on medal.
16 Keane on Roll and shown as a Bugler.
17 Roll simply shows 'Pte McVey'. The only man of this surname serving during the period of the wars was George McVey – at that time a drummer.
18 The medal in a private collection is a replacement, presumably issued when Bolster was a sergeant as it bears that rank as well as his regt No. 800.
19 No 504 and not to be confused with Sgt Kavenagh.
20 Daley on Roll.
21 Deigan on Roll.
22 Darwin on Roll.
23 Two men of this name are shown on the musters. Nos 1424 and 275, who also served during the 1st war.
24 Dolan on Roll.
25 Dunne on Roll.
26 The Roll gives one Elliott qualified for 1846–7 and the other for both campaigns. Musters show No 702 served during the 1st war and No 1352 in the 2nd.
27 Also Feney on musters. Roll wrongly credits both campaigns.
28 Two men of this name served during the 1st war, Nos 263 and 650.
29 Flinn on Roll.
30 No 792.
31 No 598.
32 Gilleece on Roll.
33 No 1159; Glynn on Roll.
34 No 1299 and not to be confused with No 273 who served in the 1st campaign.
35 Greer on Roll.
36 Served with the 45th during most of the 2nd war.
37 'Dead' on Roll.
38 Lawlor on Roll.
39 Linn on Roll.
40 McCloskey on Roll.
41 Served with the CMR during the 2nd campaign.
42 Also McLoughlin on musters.
43 Medal was applied for in 1914 and Roll wrongly credits 1850–3 campaign, besides giving the name as Mahon.
44 Moan on Roll.
45 Perkison on Roll.
46 Reegan on Roll.
47 No 269.
48 Soroghan on Roll.
49 Tredways on Roll.
50 Walsh on Roll and presumably No 2143 who probably qualified with another regiment.

PRO References: WO/12/4355-4356-4366-4367-4368.

43rd (Monmouthshire) Regiment

The regiment disembarked at East London on December 17th 1851 and upon arrival at King William's Town they were given instruction on the principles of bush fighting. It had taken a long time for the lesson to be learned that shining brasses, pipe clay and parade ground drills would not help to subdue their Kaffir enemies. Officers wore civilian clothes or patrol jackets of the same pattern as their men with fustian trousers dyed the colour of the bush; which would seem to pre-date the claim of the 2nd Batt Ox & Bucks Light Infantry (then 52nd Foot) to have introduced Khaki during the Mutiny.

The 43rd soon saw service in the field for in early January four companies were ordered to escort provisions to Eyre's force beyond the Great Kei. Eyre's troops had spent some six weeks on operations in severe weather; their clothing was in tatters and the 43rd stayed with them for a while before returning to King William's Town on Janury 18th.

Intent upon crop destruction, five companies of the regiment joined with the 73rd upon a raid into the Amatolas on January 27th. When returning to the force after collecting supplies from King William's Town, Capt Bruere's company, with some men of the 73rd, were ambushed in a pass near Baillies Grove and Surgeon Davidson was killed. Skirmishing the following day brought further casualties to the regiment, two men being wounded, and whilst scouring the forests of Fullers Hoek and Hermann's Kloof on March 15th, Lt Wrottesley and two men were killed.

Part of Eyre's brigade on the Kei in March, the 43rd participated in a successful cattle raid across the river but in a brisk fight near Mount MacThomas Capt Gore was killed. A man was lost during patrolling duties in mid-April and the following month five companies were engaged in patrols into Seyolo's country. On May 20th they surprised a considerable party of Kaffirs while in their laager and routed them for the loss of three wounded.

Until October the regiment was employed on building houses and huts on the Keiskamma Hoek and from there the 43rd joined the pursuit of Sandili into the Amatolas. Commanded by Maj Phillips, three companies of the regiment served in Cathcart's expedition against Mosesh. They were not heavily engaged at Berea but one officer and six men were wounded. Meanwhile the remainder of the 43rd suffered more severely from an extraordinary thunderstorm which struck their camp at Keiskamma Hoek and lightning exploded an ammunition store; killing two men and injuring 19.

The 43rd stayed on in the Cape after the close of the 3rd war, but only until December 1853, when they embarked for Madras and a spell of service which would take them through the Indian Mutiny.

			Kaffir Wars		
			1	2	3
LIEUTENANT COLONEL					
Henry Skipwith	(P)				△
MAJOR					
Robert N. Phillip		1)			△
CAPTAIN					
Henry Booth					△
Frederick Bruere					△
James A. Dick					△
Cornelius Dawson Greene					△
Lumley Graham					△
Percy E. Herbert					△
William Milnes					△
James M. Primrose					△
Hon Henry W. C. Ward					△
LIEUTENANT					
Charles Calvert	(P)				△
John F. Girardot		2)			△
Hon Lewes W. Milles					△
LIEUTENANT/ADJUTANT					
Hon. Richard Monck					△
LIEUTENANT					
Charles R. Mure					△
Arthur Ponsonby					△
Hugh Robinson					△
Francis G. Stapleton					△
ENSIGN					
Hon Hugh Annesley		3)			△
Hon Barrington R. Pellew	(P)				△
SURGEON					
Alexander Barclay		4)		○	△
ASSISTANT SURGEON					
John Madden	(R)				△
PAYMASTER					
Herbert T. McRae					△
QUARTERMASTER					
Joseph Denton					△
SERGEANT MAJOR					
Thomas Ford					△
QUARTERMASTER SERGEANT					
James Denton					△
COLOUR SERGEANT					
Francis Basford					△
Charles D. Blakeley	(P)				△
Thomas Collum					△
George Garland					△
William McKinley					△
Robert Mortimer					△
William Stubbings		5)			△
John Vance					△
John Welsh		6)			△
BUGLE MAJOR					
Edward Shaughnessy					△
PAYMASTER SERGEANT					
James Faulkner					△
SERGEANT					
Henry Bain					△
Thomas Banks	(P)				△
Joseph Cash					△
James Copeland					△
Richard Dewey					△
Richard Drew					△
Thomas Edwards					△
John Flanders	(P)				△
Samuel Harman	(P)	7)			△
William Hodgins					△
Gains Hubbard					△
Thomas Ingott					△
John Irvine	(R)				△
Walter Macfeat					△

72 South Africa 1853 Medal

		Kaffir Wars 1 2 3			Kaffir Wars 1 2 3
SERGEANT					
Edward McBrien		△	Thomas Adamson	25)	△
William Mills	(R)	△	Benjamin Alder		△
Edward Moriarty	8)	△	James Allen	26)	△
Frederick Schott		△	Peter Allen	27) (R)	△
William Smith	9)	△	David Allerton		△
John Taylor		△	William Anderson	28)	△
William Taylor	10)	△	Thomas Andrews	(R)	△
Charles Thompson		△	Edward Argent		△
Michael Walsh	11)	△	George Ashman		△
Thomas Ward		△	Richard Ashman		△
John Webb		△	Joseph Asplan		△
Thomas Weston		△	Richard Atkins		△
Arthur Williams		△	George Atkinson		△
William Young		△	William Baden		△
			Thomas Bainbridge		△
CORPORAL			Thomas Baker		△
James Allen	12)	△	Robert Baldwin	8)	△
Jonathan Bailey		△	George Bale		△
Charles Barber	(P)	△	Thomas Ballard	(R)	△
Joseph Birmingham		△	Cahrles Banham		△
Thomas Blake		△	Benjamin Barnard		△
Edward Clarke		△	George Barnes	29)	△
William Clarke	13)	△	George Bareham		△
Thomas Collier		△	Henry Baskett		△
Edward Cooper		△	Robert Bayfield	(P)	△
William Crane		△	David Beare		△
George Doyle		△	John Bearn	30) (MRM)	△
Keyron Dunney	14)	△	Michael Beaty		△
Charles Dyer		△	Theophilus Berwick		△
Thomas Fisher		△	Robert Bigsby	31)	△
Edward Francis		△	William Bird		△
Charles W. Galton	(R)	△	William Birmingham		△
William Goodey		△	William Blackler		△
Richard Govier		△	John Blacklock		△
William Grass		△	John Bloomfield		△
William Hallett		△	Robert Body	32)	△
John Harris		△	James Bolcher		△
George Hutchinson		△	James Bonnett		△
James Kingsley	(R)	△	Thomas Bootle	33)	△
Michael Moore	(R)	△	Thomas Bowden	8)	△
William Morris	15)	△	Richard Bowler		△
Allen Murphy		△	George Brackley	34)	△
James Nixon		△	Patrick Brady		△
Robert Offord		△	John Brahm	35)	△
Richard Sawkins	(R)	△	Charles Brazell		△
William Stubbings	16) (R)	△	Benjamin Bream		△
John Toviel		△	John Brennan	36)	△
Cornelius Wade		△	William Bridger		△
John Whibdy		△	William Bridgstock		△
			Benjamin Bright		△
BUGLER			Richard Briggs	37)	△
William J. Anderson	17)	△	George Brown (1)	38)	△
William Arthur		△	George Brown (2)	38)	△
George Barnes	18)	△	Henry Brown	39) (R)	△
James Cawdron		△	William Brown (1)	40)	△
William Farrar	19) (P)	△	William Brown (2)	40)	△
Francis Ginn	20) (R)	△	Richard Bryan		△
George Harrison	21)	△	William Bryant		△
James Kelly	22) (P)	△	William Bulled		△
James T. Lewin		△	John Bullen	(R)	△
Thomas Lomax		△	George Bullock		△
George Lyons	23)	△	Peter Bullock		△
William Manning		△	Love D. Bunker	41)	△
John McMullen	24)	△	Henry Burling		△
John Miles		△	Alfred Burton	8)	△
Samuel Parrett		△	James Busby	42)	△
George H. Peel		△	Thomas Butcher	(MRM)	△
PRIVATE			Martin Byrne	8) (R)	△
George Abbott		△			

South Africa 1853 Medal

Name		Kaffir Wars 1 2 3
Thomas Byrne		△
Edward Callaghan		△
Matthew Callaghan	(MRM)	△
William Campkin		△
Thomas Cardy		△
Isaac Carpenter		△
Charles Carter		△
Henry Carter (alias Moys)		△
James Carter		△
John Carter		△
William Carter (1)	43)	△
William Carter (2) (alias Moys)	43)	△
William Cass	(R)	△
Patrick Cassidy	44)	△
James Catling		△
John Chatfield		△
Richard B. Chester		△
Robert Chilcott		△
John Chipperfield		△
James Clarke		△
William Clarke	45)	△
John Cleary	46)	△
James Cline		△
James H. Cobey		△
Michael Cohen		△
Thomas Coleman		△
John Colfer	(MRM)	△
Samuel Collings		△
James Collins		△
Henry Cooper		△
John Cooper (1)	47)	△
John Cooper (2)	47)	△
Thomas Cooper		△
Patrick Corbett		△
William Cormick	(MRM)	△
Thomas Cosgrove	(R)	△
Samuel Cotterell	48) (MRM)	△
Robert Coulton		△
John Cousins		△
Henry Cox		△
James Cox		△
John Cramer		△
James Crawford		△
John Crawford		△
Charles Creswell		△
Christopher Creswell		△
Matthew Creswell		△
William Crick	(R)	△
John Croughan		△
Thomas Crosbie	49)	△
Thomas Cullen		△
William Cullen	50)	△
Charles Darling		△
Elijah Darling		△
William Darnsday		△
John Daw		△
Josiah Day		△
John Dean	51)	△
Richard Delaney		△
William Dempsey		△
John Dillon		△
Patrick Dillon		△
William Dines	52)	△
Peter Doherty	53)	△
Charles Doman	54)	△
John Donovan	55)	△
John Doyle		
Patrick Doyle	(MRM)	△
Andrew Dunseeth	56)	△
Christopher Dutchfield		△
George Dyer		△
Henry Dyer		△
James Dyer	(R)	△
Charles Eades		△
James Eales		△
William Eastaugh		△
Simeon Easy		△
Richard Eborn	57)	△
William Eccleston		△
Samuel Edgely		△
George Edwards	(MRM)	△
Henry Edwards		△
John Edwards		△
Robert Ellingham		△
William Elner	58) (MRM)	△
James Emms		△
John Evans		△
Thomas Evans	(R)	△
Stephen Evers		△
John Farr		△
James Farrell	(R)	△
William Faulkner		△
John Fenn		△
Henry Finch		△
Dennis Fisher	(MRM)	△
John Fisher		△
Robert W. Flatt		△
Bartholomew Fleet		△
Noah Flood		△
John Fowler		△
John Fox		△
William French		△
James Frost		△
Gamaliel Frummett		△
Thomas Galliver		△
Edward Gardiner	59)	△
Osbert Garland	60)	△
George Gates		△
James Gaynard		△
Patrick Geoghaghan		△
Thomas Gibbons		△
James Gifford	61) (P)	△
Robert Giles		△
William Giles		△
Thomas Gilson	62)	△
Joseph Gladwin		△
George Goddard		△
David Godfrey		△
Richard Golding	63)	△
Thomas Good		△
William Gooding		△
Philip Goodwin		△
Thomas Gray		△
Henry Green	64)	△
Robert Green		△
William Green		△
William Gregory		△
Moses Guthridge		△
John Guttridge		△
Josiah Hales		△
Robert Hall		△
George Hamilton	(R)	△
John Hardwick	65) (P)	△
William Hardy		△
Michael Harnett	66)	△

74 South Africa 1853 Medal

PRIVATE			Kaffir Wars 1 2 3				Kaffir Wars 1 2 3
Thomas Harris			△	Joshua Leader			△
William Harris	67)		△	James Ledger	74)		△
George Harrold		(R)	△	Thomas Lee			△
Isaac Harrold			△	Job Leech	75)		△
James Hart			△	James Lefevre			△
Richard Hart			△	John Leslie			△
William Hart			△	Richard Lewis			△
Henry Hase			△	Henry Lightwing			△
James Hawkes		(R)	△	William Limmer			△
Michael B. Hayde		(R)	△	William A. Lovell			△
Thomas Hayward			△	Thomas Lovegrove			△
Michael Healy	68)	(P)	△	Thomas Loyns			△
John Hearn	69)		△	Robert Lungley			△
Thomas Heatherington			△	Thomas Maggs			△
George Hempstead			△	Robert Manns			△
James Herk	8)		△	William Margetts	76)		△
John Hewitt		(R)	△	Philip Marskell		(R)	△
Thomas Hewlett			△	James Martin	77)		△
James Hewson			△	John Martin	77)		△
Martin Hickey			△	Philip Martin			△
George Hicks			△	George Mash	78)		△
John Hicks			△	James Mason	79)		△
Robert Hills			△	James L. Mason	80)		△
William Hills			△	William Maxwell			△
Charles Hirst			△	George McCombs			△
George Hockley		(MRM)	△	James McCusker	81)		△
David Hogg			△	John McDonnell	82)		△
James Holdcroft			△	Charles McDonough			△
William Holland			△	Thomas McElhoney			△
George Hopgood			△	John McFadden	83)		△
John How			△	Lawrence McGrath			△
William Howard			△	Edward McGuiness			△
Richard Howson			△	John McGuire			△
James Hubbocks			△	Thomas McGuire			△
John Huggins			△	James McHugh			△
David Humphreys			△	Richard McIntosh			△
Patrick Hurley		(R)	△	Hugh McMullen			△
William Hutson			△	William McQuire			△
George Ingle			△	Richard Millard		(R)	△
John Ingle	70)		△	John Miller			△
Allen James	71)		△	Robert Miller			△
Peter Jeffers			△	Samuel Mitchell			△
George Jenkins			△	William Mitchell	84)		△
Henry Jerrald			△	Samuel Moeld			△
Robert Jessopp			△	James Morgan		(R)	△
Thomas Jobson			△	Thomas Morgan			△
Edward Johnstone	72)		△	Michael Moriaty			△
John Johnstone	72)		△	Samuel Morris			△
William Johnstone			△	William Morris	85)	(R)	△
Richard Jones			△	Francis Morrison			△
Robert Jones			△	Simon Mortlock			△
John Jordan			△	George Moseley			△
James Joyce		(R)	△	William Mulrooney			△
Hugh Kabery			△	Patrick Murphy (1)	86)		△
William Keaty			△	Patrick Murphy (2)	86)		△
James Kelly	73)		△	Isaac Murton	87)		△
George Kent			△	William Musk			△
Charles Kerr			△	James Mynott	88)		△
Ralph Kershaw			△	Samuel Nash			△
George Keyworth			△	Alexander Nelson			△
William Kilburn		(P)	△	John Nelson		(R)	△
Thomas Kingsley			△	Charles Nethercott			△
Michael Kinsella			△	David Newell			△
Charles Knowles		(MRM)	△	John Norman			△
George Lackie		(P)	△	John Norris			△
John J. Lappan		(P)	△	George Oaten			△
Emmerson Large			△	George Pack	89)	(R)	△
Edward H. Lay			△	David Palfrey			△

South Africa 1853 Medal

Name	Note	Kaffir Wars 1	2	3
William Palfrey				△
George Palmer	90)			△
Henry W. Palmer				△
Joseph Parker (1)	91)			△
Joseph Parker (2)	91)			△
James Pauling				△
Joseph Payne				△
Stephen Payne				△
William Payne				△
Henry Peacock				△
John Pearce				△
Joseph Pearce				△
George Peck	92)			△
William E. Peel				△
Joseph Pegram				△
Absolom Pelborough				△
Thomas Pelling	(R)			△
Matthew Pentoney				△
Ambrose Perkins				△
William Perkins				△
George Peters	93)			△
John Peters				△
William Piggott				△
Thomas Pink				△
Charles Pinner				△
Thomas Piper				△
William Polly				△
Paul Porter				△
Moses Prior	(R)			△
James Privett				△
Henry Quinn				△
Frank Racher	94)			△
William Radley				△
Edward Rayner				△
William Rayner				△
Benjamin Reece	95)			△
Robert Reeve				△
Charles Reilly				△
Henry Reynolds				△
Joseph Reynolds				△
Samuel Reynolds	(MRM)			△
Charles Rice				△
John Rice				△
James Ridewood				△
James Riley				△
Matthew Ring				△
Noah Rix				△
Jonathan Roberts				△
Thomas Roberts				△
Adam Robson				△
John Rolston				△
John Ross				△
William Rowlingson				△
Thomas Rowson				△
James Rudd				△
Robert Rutter				△
John Ryan	(MRM)			△
John Rynehart				△
George Savours	8) (P)			△
Thomas Scaggall				△
Samuel Scales				△
William Scattergood				△
John Scoll	96)			△
George Seeley				△
John Seerey				△
William Sergeant				△
Edward Sharpe				△
Finlay Shaw				△
James Shaw	97)			△
John Shaw	97)			△
John Shea				△
Edward Shelswell				△
John Simmonds				△
William Skillington				△
Benjamin Smith				△
Joseph Smith	98)			△
John Smithson				△
William Smout				△
John Smyth				△
William South				△
Joseph Southgate				△
Nathaniel Staniford	99)			△
Samuel Stead				△
Robert Stearn				△
Henry Steggles				△
John Stevenson				△
Elijah Stubbings				△
Richard Stroud				△
Thomas Talboys	(R)			△
William Tarry				△
George Taviner				△
George Taylor				△
James Taylor				△
Robert Taylor				△
William Taylor	100) (R)			△
Edwin Terry				△
William Terry				△
Thomas Thompson				△
William Thompson	101)			△
George Thurkell	102)			△
Denis Tiddenham				△
Thomas Tilbrook				△
Charles Timbridge				△
Joseph Tokeley	103) (R)		○	△
George Tolman				△
Timothy Toomey	104) (MRM)			△
Henry Turner				△
John Tyler				△
William Underwood				△
John Varley				△
Jeremiah Vaughan				△
Michael Vaughan				△
William Vaughan				△
James Vines	(MRM)			△
Samuel Vinson				△
Jonas Voice				△
David Wade				△
Robert Walby				△
Joseph Walker				△
William Walker	(R)			△
Sim Wallace	8)			△
Joseph Waller	105) (R)			△
William Walley				△
John Walsh	106)			△
Philip Walsh				△
Thomas Walter				△
James Warburton				△
George Ward				△
Francis W. Wastie	(MRM)			△
Daniel Watkins				△
James Watkins (1)	107)			△
James Watkins (2)	107)			△
Thomas Watson (1)	108)			△
Thomas Watson (2)	108)			△
George Weatherman				△
James Webb				△

76 South Africa 1853 Medal

		Kaffir Wars 1 2 3			Kaffir Wars 1 2 3
PRIVATE					
Jephthal Webb		△	Joseph Williams	(P)	△
John West	109)	△	John Wilson		△
John Weston		△	George Wing		△
Charles White		△	John Woodward	112)	△
John White (1)	110)	△	George Wooldridge		△
John White (2)	110)	△	William Woolfe		△
William White (1)	111)	△	Samuel Worth		△
William White (2)	111)	△	George Wright		△
Job Whitmore		△			
William Wilkinson		△	△ = campaign qualification as WO/100/17.		
Daniel Williams	(MRM)	△	O = campaign which the Rolls fail to credit.		

43RD (MONMOUTHSHIRE) REGIMENT NOTES

1 Commanded the 43rd companies against Mosesh December 1852; see Moodie.
2 A survivor from the 'Birkenhead'.
3 Wounded in operations against the Basutos December 1852; see King.
4 Served with the 91st in the 1846–7 campaign.
5 No 1529 and not to be confused with Cpl Stubbings.
6 Walsh on Roll.
7 Hannan on Roll and medal.
8 Saw his campaign service with the 12th Regiment.
9 No 1904.
10 No 1407.
11 No 1262.
12 2123.
13 No 2065.
14 Keyran Dunny on Roll.
15 No 2347.
16 No 2098 and not to be confused with Col Sgt Stubbings.
17 No 2415.
18 No 2301 and not to be confused with Pte Barnes.
19 Farrer on Roll, Farrar on medal.
20 No 2723, a survivor from the 'Birkenhead'.
21 No 2134 and not to be confused with No 930 George Harrison who survived from the 'Birkenhead' but died in 1854 before the medal was issued.
22 No 1997 and not to be confused with Pte Kelly.
23 No 2688, a survivor from the 'Birkenhead'.
24 No 1193.
25 Also Addimson on musters.
26 No 2262.
27 No 1582, a survivor from the 'Birkenhead'.
28 No shown both as 1613 and 1623.
29 No 2679.
30 Bearne on Roll.
31 Also Bixby on Roll.
32 Note on Roll says 'Medal returned RVA 34 of 8.12.1955'.
33 'Dead' on Roll. Medal sent to sister.
34 No 2712, a survivor from the 'Birkenhead'.
35 Also Braham on musters.
36 Also Brinnan on musters.
37 No 2191.
38 Nos 1099 and 1992; one of these medals is in the Regimental Museum.
39 Saw his campaign service with 12th and received a re-named duplicate medal in 1863.
40 Nos 2269 and 2677.
41 No 2336, a survivor from the 'Birkenhead'.
42 Bushby on Roll.
43 Nos 2146 and 2343.
44 Also Cassiday on musters.
45 No 1226.
46 Also Clarey on musters.
47 Nos 2358 and 2411. One of these medals is in the Regimental Museum.
48 Various spellings on musters.
49 Crosby on Roll.
50 Shown as Culling on Roll, but although a man of this name served with the regiment he joined from the 94th after the 3rd war. I am of the opinion that when the returns were drawn up in 1855, and both men were then serving, a clerk confused them.
51 Deane on Roll.
52 Saw his campaign service with the 2nd Regiment.
53 Dogherty on Roll.
54 Roll has been altered and appears to read Domvan.
55 Donnovan on Roll.
56 Dunscarth on Roll.
57 Eborne on Roll.
58 Elnor on Roll.
59 Also Gardner on musters.
60 Also Ospert on musters. Ex-12th Lancers.
61 Giffard on Roll and medal.
62 Gibson on Roll.
63 Also Golden on musters.
64 No 2260.
65 Hardwicke on Roll and medal.
66 No 2718, a survivor from the 'Birkenhead'. Hornett on Roll but regimental chronicle of 1905 favours Harnett.
67 No 1981.
68 No 2715, a survivor from the 'Birkenhead'.
69 No 2714, a survivor from the 'Birkenhead'. Various spellings on musters.
70 Mistakenly received two medals, one of which was returned and re-named for a man in the 12th Regiment.
71 Although in the original returns his medal was not sent until 1871.
72 Johnson on Roll.
73 No 2617 and not to be confused with Bugler Kelly.
74 Also Leger on musters.
75 Also Leach on musters.
76 Margates on Roll.
77 One of these medals is in the Regimental Museum.
78 Marsh on Roll.
79 No 2589.
80 No 2246.
81 No 1916; John on Roll.
82 No 2717.
83 James on Roll. Saw his campaign service with the 12th.
84 No 1657.
85 No 2416.
86 Nos 1346 and 2520.
87 Minton on Roll.
88 Mynett on Roll.
89 No 2395.
90 Saw his campaign service with the 60th Regiment.
91 Nos 2196 and 2699.
92 No 2179.
93 No 1965, a survivor from the 'Birkenhead'.
94 Racker on Roll.
95 Also Reese on musters.
96 Scott on Roll.
97 Nos 2464 and 2610. One of these medals is in the regimental collection whilst the other was returned to the Mint.
98 No 2213.
99 A medal partly re-named in running script is in a private collection.
100 No 2463.
101 No 1427.
102 Also Thirkell on musters.
103 Saw his campaign service with the Rifle Brigade.
104 Toonney on Roll.
105 Also Wallen on musters.
106 No 2278.
107 Nos 2161 and 2574.
108 Nos 2289 and 2482, one of which is in the Regimental Museum.
109 Not to be confused with 'Birkenhead' survivor Joseph West.
110 Nos 1853 and 2317.
111 Nos 1056 and 2563, one of which was returned to the Mint.
112 No 2557, a survivor from the 'Birkenhead'.

PRO References: WO/12/5605-5606-5607-5608.

45th (Nottinghamshire) Regiment

Both the 1st and Reserve Battalions of the 45th Regiment saw active service on the frontier, but it was the latter who were the more heavily engaged during 1846-7. After the battalions merged in August 1850 the Reserve became the left wing and bore the brunt of the 45th work in Kaffraria during the 3rd war.

The 1st Battalion had arrived in the Cape shortly before Natal was proclaimed a British Colony in May 1843 and during July they were transported from Cape Town to the new colony. The presence of British troops persuaded the restive Boers against any precipitate action and the 45th were mainly occupied strengthening the defences and enlarging their barracks at Durban and Pietermaritzburg.

When the War of the Axe broke out, Capt Seagram's Light Company was detached to Fort Beaufort but whilst en route they were re-directed to the Tarka River and there erected a fort. Being on the extreme left of the British forces they took no part in the Amatola operation but when that failed, the detachment was more actively engaged. In August, Seagram and 80 of his men were part of the force under Capt Hogg (7th DG) who moved against the chiefs Mapona and Mapaisa and in a three days' operation captured over 3,000 cattle besides killing several of the enemy. During December the 45th detachment was engaged in some hard marching through Mapaisa's territory between the Tarka and Shiloh, but without much result.

Capt Blenkinsopp, with 84 officers and men, was sent from Pietermaritzburg during January 1847 to join a force of 300 men proceeding to the southern part of the colony. The objective was to protect some weaker chiefs against chief Foto, and after defeating a party of his warriors, Foto's Kraal was destroyed. A fine of cattle was extracted before the column returned to Pietermaritzburg.

Seagram had been based at Tarka throughout the troubles, and when things quietened on that part of the frontier the forces was broken up in February, but they were especially thanked for their services which, alone among the 1st Battalion, ultimately entitled them to the medal.

The Reserve Battalion had set sail from Gibraltar on July 31st 1845, but because of disturbed affairs in South America they were diverted to the River Plate and there remained for 10 months. Almost exactly a year after leaving the Rock the battalion arrived at Simons Bay and by the end of August 1846 were on the frontier. Two companies remained at Grahams Town while the rest marched to join Col Somerset's division on the Fish River, which they crossed near Fort Dacre to reach Sir Peregrine Maitland's camp at Waterloo Bay. From there, three companies of the 45th under Capts Moultrie, Bates and Parish, operated with Maitland's force to the Buffalo River where the severe weather and short rations caused much sickness among the troops.

The headquarters of the battalion left Waterloo Bay at the end of October 1846 and marched via Fort Beaufort to Fort Hare, which became the main post of the 45th. Soon afterwards Sandili accepted the terms offered him, but in February 1847 cattle were carried off from Block Drift and the situation worsened. In June, 100 of the Reserve Battalion under Moultrie were part of a force sent to arrest Sandili who fled his Kraal and, in spite of negotiations, could not be persuaded to surrender. During September the 45th were split into detachments and constantly harried the Kaffirs, but only a section commanded by Lt Dawson, encountered the enemy.

When hostilities ceased, the Reserve Battalion, apart from a company at Fort Cox and a small detachment at Fort White, were still concentrated at Fort Hare. It was from there that two companies of the regiment marched to take part in the Battle of Boemplaats, where they lost three killed and 19 wounded.

After subduing the Boer opposition of the Orange River Sovereignty the government was faced with serious feuds arising among the natives, and by the middle of 1851 reinforcements under Capt Parish, consisting of two companies of the 45th, 14 of the CMR and 700 Zulus, were sent to deal with hostile natives on one hand, and disgruntled farmers on the other. Eventually, the Sand River convention brought independence to the Transvaal Boers, but before the troops could be ordered back to Natal, another party of the 45th with Lt Coxon had joined Parish.

Meanwhile, British Kaffaria was again boiling over. The left wing of the 45th (the old Reserve Battalion) were still at Forts Cox, Hare and White. On December 20th 1850 a corporal and three men were sent out to escort some sheep but when they did not return 12 more of the 45th were ordered out to look for them and all were massacred. At this time Sir Harry Smith was blockaded in Fort Cox, and when Somerset attempted to relieve him the force, which included some of the 45th, was driven back to Fort Hare with a loss of 20 killed and 15 wounded.

Fort Hare itself then became invested and survived a strong attack on January 28th 1851 before being relieved. During 1851 the 45th were distributed to garrison the advanced posts and seldom took part in the operations of the heavier patrolling columns, but in February 1852 they, with the 43rd, 73rd, some artillery and a few men of the 6th and 60th, were sent to raid the Waterkloof. After a good deal of skirmishing and hard marching the district was subdued and they went on to raid the Amatolas.

During May, three companies of the 45th under Major Preston, with Montague's Horse and some Fingo Levies, left King William's Town to secure Line Drift and establish a fortified post at Tamacka. Other detachments were at Fort Murray, Fort Grey, Fort Pato and Fort Glamorgan, and were holding this line when peace came.

As mentioned elsewhere the bulk of the returns for the 45th Regiment have not survived and the following roll has been reconstructed from the musters. It lists officers and men who appear to be qualified for the medal although some 150 of them undoubtedly did not receive the award. We know from the records at the Royal Mint that at least 694 medals were originally presented to the 45th, and with late issues one can estimate that the total to the regiment was approximately 750.

Where the symbols △ and ○ have been blocked out to show ▲ and ● this indicates service with the Reserve Battalion during the war of 1846-7.

78 South Africa 1853 Medal

		Kaffir Wars		
		1	2	3
LIEUTENANT COLONEL				
Henry Cooper			▲	△
MAJOR				
Charles Hind			▲	
Hallam D. Kyle	(P)			△
BREVET MAJOR				
G. Anthony Blenkinsop	1)			△
John B. Wheatstone			▲	△
CAPTAIN				
William C. Armstrong	2)			△
Robert Bates	(P)		▲	△
Robert Miller				△
Henry W. Parish	3)		▲	△
Charles Seagram				△
Donald W. Tench	4)		▲	
Henry Vialls			▲	
LIEUTENANT				
Drury R. Barnes				△
Sir Robert Colleton			▲	
George S. Coxon	5)			△
William Dawson	6)		▲	△
William Fleming			▲	
Robert J. Garden	(P)		▲	
Trevor Goff	7)		▲	△
Stephen B. Gordon				△
Frederick R. Grantham	9)		▲	
Charles L. Griffin	8)			
John C. G. Halkett				△
George L. Hobbs	10)			△
Robert G. Howard	11)			△
Robert B. Johnstone			▲	
Henry Leach			▲	△
James McCrea	12)		●	
George Morris			△	△
William H. Rowland				△
Arthur Smyth			▲	
ENSIGN				
Charles D. Cameron			▲	
Erskine S. G. Dawson	6)		▲	△
Henry Lucas	13) (P)			△
Frederick H. Suckling			△	
Alexander Walker	14) (P)			△
Wenman L. Woodford			△	
James T. Egan				△
SURGEON				
Francis R. Waring			▲	
ASSISTANT SURGEON				
Fraser O. Barker	15)		▲	●
QUARTERMASTER				
Richard Power	16)			△
COLOUR SERGEANT				
James Beattie			●	○
John Chandler			●	○
Archibald Cunningham			●	○
John Crighton			▲	
John Doig			●	○
Frederick Guernsey			○	○
Titus Hirst			●	○
John Holmes	17) (P)		●	○
John Maslin			●	
Robert Spink	(MRM)		●	○
Joseph White			●	○
SERGEANT				
John Appleton			●	○
Robert Beattie			●	○
Henry Beaumont			●	○

		Kaffir Wars		
		1	2	3
Henry Brady			●	○
John Carleton			●	○
Henry Carrick			▲	
William Clarke				○
Cornelius Coffee			●	○
William Colton				○
Thomas Dodman			●	○
Stephen Doyle				○
John Ellis			●	
Edward Featherstone				○
George Friend	(P)		●	○
George Gordon			●	○
William Green			●	○
George Hallett	(P)		●	○
John Hodge				○
Richard Hood			○	
Richard Irvine			●	○
Richard James			▲	○
Robert Kirk			○	
Norman Mason			○	
Thomas McDermott			●	○
John McFarlane			●	○
James Mayner			▲	
George Milner				○
John Neish			○	
Patrick Quirk			●	○
William Reid			●	
Henry Risewell			●	
Robert Sisson			●	○
Robert Smith			●	○
John Sneddon	18)		△	△
Alfred Soar				△
George Stewart	19) (R)		∧	▲
William Tilbury				○
William Wagstaff			●	○
James Wood			●	○
Thomas Wright			●	
CORPORAL				
Timothy Bathurst			●	○
John Beecham			●	
William Bennett			●	
Charles Bulpitt				○
Martin Cahill				
Robert Crozier				△
James Cruikshank			●	
Thomas Davidson			●	○
Henry Dunn			●	○
William Dunne			●	
Matthew Forsyth				
James Goodale				△
Rowland Heathcote			○	
William Hinchcliffe			●	○
Isaac Holdway			●	○
Robert Leggate	(P)		●	○
Robert Lindsay			○	
Alexander McDowell			●	
Stephen McLaughlin				○
Patrick Mallan			●	○
Samuel Marshall			▲	
George Minal			●	○
Frederick Morris			●	
Francis Murphy			●	
George Newbold				○
Joseph O'Neill	(R)		●	
James Penfold				○
William Ridgeway			●	
Samuel Robinson	(R)		▲	

South Africa 1853 Medal

Name	Note	Kaffir Wars 1	2	3
George Shaw				○
William Smith			●	○
Richard Smithwick			●	
William Waghorn			○	○
Thomas Walker	20)		●	○
John Walters			●	
Joseph Ward			●	
Frederick Welch			●	
William White				○
Joseph Wiggett			●	
Andrew Wilson			●	

DRUMMER

Name	Note	1	2	3
John Brown	21) (P)		●	○
Thomas Dowling				○
Frederick Gannon			●	○
George Goodwin			●	
John Grogan			●	○
William Gudge				○
John Hendry			●	
Edward Horran			●	
George Kennedy			●	
Patrick Murphy			●	○
Joseph O'Gara			●	○
James Paul			●	
Bernard Ralph			●	○
Archibald Stuart				○
Thomas Tye				○
James Watson				○

PRIVATE

Name	Note	1	2	3
Dennis Ahern			●	○
Alfred Alexander			●	○
Charles Alder	(MRM)		●	○
John Allbones				△
Theophilus Allcock	(R)			○
Thomas Allen			●	○
James Allington			●	
Thomas Allspice				○
Charles Amos			●	
Thomas Andrews			●	○
Robert Ansley				○
Joseph Armstrong			●	
Andrew Arthurs				
Richard Asher				○
George Ashmore			●	
Thomas Askey			●	○
Henry Aslett				○
James Attrill			●	
Charles Attenborough			●	○
Benjamin Attewell			●	○
Henry Bacon			●	○
John Badrick			●	○
Thomas Bailey			●	○
Samuel Baker			●	○
George Ball				○
John Ball	(P)			○
William Ball			●	○
John Ballard				○
George Banks			●	○
John Bannerman			●	
William Bannon			●	
Bryan Barden				○
James Barker				○
Robert Barker				○
Thomas Barker				○
William Barker				○
Edward Barkye			●	
Barnett Barlow				○

Name	Note	1	2	3
George Barlow				○
John Barlow				○
Joseph Barlow				○
Jeremiah Barnet				○
Matthew Barr			●	○
Robert Barr			●	○
Denis Barraclough				○
Richard Barrett	(MRM)			○
Christopher Barrs				○
John Barry				
William Bates			●	
Charles Batt			●	○
James Baxter				○
William Bayley			●	○
William Beardshaw			●	○
George Beattie				○
James Beckingham			●	○
John Bellew			▲	△
William Belsher				○
Edward Bennett				
Michael Bigley			●	○
Thomas Bilbie			●	○
Thomas Bingham	(P)		○	○
John Birmingham			●	
James Bishop				○
John Black			●	○
Edward Boardman			●	
John Bond	(P)		●	○
Thomas Bonarlay	22)			△
George Boot				○
Samuel Bowditch			●	○
Walter Bower			○	○
William Bower	(P)		○	○
John Bowyer			○	○
Thomas Boyes			●	○
John Boyd				○
William Boyse	23)		▲	○
Matthew Bracewell	(R)		○	○
John Bradley				○
William Bradley			●	○
William Bramley				○
William Branson			●	○
Alexander Breathet				○
James Brennan			●	○
Michael Brennan			▲	△
William Brewer			●	○
James Briggs				○
William Broad	(P)		●	○
Thomas Broadfoot			○	○
Robert Brodie			●	○
John Brophy			●	○
Colin Brown			●	○
George Brown				○
Henry Brown			●	
James Brown				○
John Brown (1)	24)			△
John Brown (2)	25)			○
John Brown (3)	25)			○
Joseph Brown				
Michael Brown			○	
Henry Brownlow				○
William Bruce			●	
Thomas Buckingham			●	
James Bullas			●	○
Thomas Bullen			●	○
Thomas Burgess				○
David Burke	(R)		●	○
John Burke			●	

South Africa 1853 Medal

PRIVATE		Kaffir Wars 1	2	3				Kaffir Wars 1	2	3
Patrick Burke		●	○		Matthew Cowley	29)		●	○	
Robert Burke		●	○		John Coyle			●		
Thomas Burke			○		Charles Craghill				○	
James Burkinshaw		●	○		Joseph Crane					○
Charles Burns		●			John Crawley			●	○	
Robert Burns		●			William Crosson			●	●	○
John Burrell	(P)	●	○		Thomas Cullen			●		
George Bush			○		William Cullen					○
Thomas Bushell		●	○		Joseph Cullis			●		
James Butler			○		John Cully					○
William Butler			○		William Cummins (1)	30)				○
John Byers		●			William Cummins (2)	30)				○
Thomas Cain			○		Peter Cunningham					
David Cairns		●			William Cunningham			○	○	○
John Camm			○		Francis Curlitt					○
John Campbell	(MRM)		○		George Curtis			○		○
Michael Cantwell			○		Isaac Curtis					
Joseph Card		●	○		Aaron Cutts	(MRM)				○
Patrick Carlian		●			John Dailey			●		
William Carrick			○		Samuel Danson			○	○	
John Carroll			○		John Davey			●	○	
Abraham Carter			○		Frederick Davies			●	○	
George Carton		●			William Davies					○
Thomas Cartwright			○		Edward Davis					○
John Caskey			○		George Davis			●		
James Cassidy			○		James Davis			●	●	○
George Charlton		●	○		John Davis	(R)		△		
Henry Chambers		○	○		William Davis					○
Samuel Chambers		●			James Davison			○		
William Chambers	(M)		○		Henry Day					○
Thomas Chandler		●	○		James Day	(MRM)				○
Joseph Chapman		●			George Deakin	(P)		●		
George Cheany			○		John Deakin			●		
Solomon Cherritt		●	○		William Dennis			●		○
George Clack		●			John Derrycott					○
William Clancy		●			Patrick Desmond					○
John Clark (1)	26)	●	○		John Devlin					○
John Clark (2)	26)	○	○		Patrick Devlin					○
Thomas Clark			○		Robert Dickson			●		○
Robert Clarke			○		James Digby					△
George Clayton		●			Henry Dixon					○
Thomas Clelfold			○		William Dixon	31)		○		
John Clements			○		Charles Dobson			●		○
John Cliff		●	○		George Dobson			●		○
Frederick Clift		●	○		Thomas Dodd			●		
John Cochrane		●	○		Thomas Doe (1)	32)		●		
James Cofield			○		Thomas Doe (2)	32)		●		
James Cole			○		Frederick Doggett			●		○
William Collings	27)	▲			John Donnelly	33)				△
Owen Collins			○		William Donnelly					○
Robert Collins	(R)		○		Arthur Donohue					○
John Colman (1)	28)	●	○		John Dooley			○		
John Colman (2)	28)	●	○		Richard Dooley					○
Thomas Compton			○		William Doonan			●		○
Peter Connelly			○		Edward Dorritty					○
William Connolly		●	○		James Dousee			●		○
John Connor		●	○		Patrick Dowdle			●		○
Frederick Cook			○		Thomas Dowling			●		
William Coombes	(MRM)	●	○		David Draffen	34)		▲		○
William Cooper		○	△		Charles Dunce	35)		▲		○
Benjamin Cope		●	○		W. Wood Dunsfold			●		○
William Corthorn			○		William Dyer			▲		
Thomas Corr			○		Joseph Early					
John Cortys		●	○		Michael Early			●		
James Cottrell	(P)	●			William East					○
John Cousins		●			Arthur Ebbs					○
Edmund Cowdery		●	○		Thomas Ebbs			●		○
					William Ebbs			●		

South Africa 1853 Medal

Name	Notes	Kaffir Wars 1	2	3
John Elliott				O
Thomas Elliott				O
Adam Ellison			●	O
Edmund Ellison			●	O
Samuel Erwin				O
William Ewing			●	O
William Fairburn			●	O
William Falconer			O	
William Fannon			●	
James Farley			O	O
Thomas Farrow			●	O
Lot Farthing				O
John Ferady			O	O
Thomas Ferris			●	O
John Fettyplace			●	
Saul Fielding			●	
John Figgett			●	O
John Fish			O	O
John Fisher			●	O
Thomas Fitzgerald				O
James Fitzpatrick				O
Patrick Flanagan			●	O
James Flanery				O
Thomas Flanery			●	
Edward Flatt			●	
George Flint			●	O
Peter Flynn			●	O
John Foley				O
Richard Ford			●	O
Cunningham Fowler				O
James Fowler		O		
William Fox			●	O
William France				O
Andrew Fraser	(R)		●	O
George Frazer			●	
John Freeman			●	O
William Freeman	(R)		●	O
Francis Fuller			O	
Robert Gally				O
James Galvin				O
John Gannon			●	
Matthew Gannon		△		
Michael Gannon			●	
James Garratt			●	O
Michael Garvey			●	O
Henry George				O
William Ghee				O
Frederick Gibson			●	
Robert Gibson			O	O
William Gilford			●	O
Stephen Goddard			●	
James Goodman		▲		
Michael Gooney			●	O
Michael Gorman			●	O
Roderick Gorman			●	O
Archibald Graham			●	O
Robert Graham				O
John Grant		▲	△	
Jacob Gratton		O		O
Samuel Graves		O		
John Gray				O
William Gray			●	O
George Greatorex			●	
Samuel Greenhill				O
Henry Grinold	(R)		●	O
Thomas Grooms			●	
James Grove				O
Thomas Grover				O

Name	Notes	Kaffir Wars 1	2	3
John Grumley				O
George Guest	(R)			O
Richard Gunay				O
John Habershon			●	O
John Haddon			●	O
George Hall			●	
James Hall			●	O
James Halligan				O
Gideon Hamilton			●	
Ephraim Hammersley	(P)			O
Henry Hammon				O
David Hammond			●	O
Thomas Hammond			●	O
William Hampson			●	O
Terence Hanaway	35)		▲	O
Henry Hands			▲	△
Thomas Hanley			●	O
William Hanley			O	O
Thomas Harper	(P)		●	O
John Harris			●	O
Robert Harris			●	O
John Harrington			●	O
George Harrison (1)	36)		●	
George Harrison (2)	36)		●	
Richard Harman			●	
James Hart			●	
Miles Hart			●	
Thomas Hart			●	
William Harvey			●	
Thomas Hassall			●	
Patrick Hayes			●	O
William Haylock			●	
James Hayter				O
Charles Hayward			●	O
George Hazeldine			●	O
Henry Heather			●	O
Michael Healy			●	O
David Henry				
Thomas Herbert			O	O
Joseph Herrick			●	O
Joseph Herring			O	
Thomas Hessian				O
Thomas Hetherington				O
James Hewitt				
William Hextall			△	
Samuel Heycock			●	O
James Hicks			●	O
Maurice Higgins			●	O
Thomas Higgins				O
Edward Hillier			●	
William Hillier	(P)			O
Charles Hillman			●	
John Hine			O	
James Hoare	(P)		●	O
Thomas Hobbs			O	
John Hodge			O	
John Hodnett				O
Thomas Hoe			O	
Hugh Hogg			●	
William Holehouse				O
James Hollis			●	
John Holmes	37)		●	O
William Holmes	(R)			O
Abraham Hook				O
William Hooley			●	
John Hornor			●	O
Joseph Horton			●	O
William Houghton				O

82 South Africa 1853 Medal

		Kaffir Wars		
		1	2	3
PRIVATE				
George Houlton			●	○
William Howard			●	○
Richard Howells			●	
Michael Hoy				○
Thomas Hudson				○
Ellis Hughes				○
Charles Hurriss			●	○
David Hurst			●	○
Joseph Hurst			○	○
Thomas Hutchings			●	
James Hutt				○
John Ibbotson			●	○
James Inskip			●	○
Raphael Jacob			●	
William Jaffery			●	
John James	(P)			
Richard James			○	○
Thomas Jamieson			●	○
Frederick Jerratt				○
David Job				○
James Johnson				○
Robert Johnson				△
Thomas Johnson			●	○
William Johnson (1)	38)		●	
William Johnson (2)	38)		●	
William Johnstone			●	
Amos Jones				○
James Jones			●	○
John Jones				○
Thomas Jones			○	
Michael Kearns			●	△
Thomas Kearns				○
Adam Keating	39)			○
Alexander Keenan				○
George Kelly			○	
Patrick Kelly				○
William Kelly				○
Thomas Kempthorne			●	
Thomas Kendall			●	○
William Kendall				○
John Kennedy			●	○
Daniel Kenny			●	○
John Kenny			●	○
Andrew Kerr			○	○
Arthur Kerr			●	○
James Kershaw			●	○
Samuel Keward			○	
Thomas Kilbride			●	○
William Kilgour				○
James King			●	
Stephen King				○
William King	(MRM)		●	○
William Kirkby	(P)		●	
William Kirkland			●	○
Robert Knapton				△
John Knox			●	○
Patrick Kyle			●	
John Lamb			●	○
William Lamb			●	○
Benjamin Lane			●	
William Language			○	○
Richard Lanigan			▲	△
John Laurie			●	
Edward Lee	(P)			○
Patrick Lee				○
Thomas Lees			○	○
John Lenaghan				○

		Kaffir Wars		
		1	2	3
William Levell				○
George Leverton	40)		●	○
Thomas Lewin			●	○
Thomas Light			●	○
William Lines				○
Edward Lloyd			●	○
George Lock				○
Thomas Lock			●	○
Owen Logan				○
Theodore Longstreet				○
Edward Luke				○
Levi Lumb			●	○
Thomas Lynch				○
Hugh McAlinden				○
John McCabe				○
Charles McCarthy			●	
John McCarthy	(MRM)			○
Patrick McCarthy			●	
John McClurkin			▲	
Edward McCooey			▲	○
John McCusker			●	
James McCracken				○
James McDermott				○
Thomas McDermott			●	○
David McDonald			●	
Donald McDonald				○
William McDonald			●	○
Alexander McDonnell				○
James McGerritty			●	○
James McGibbon				○
John McGuinness			●	○
Charles McGonnegal			●	
Thomas McGraw				○
John McGrath				○
John McGregor			●	
William McGregor				○
Michael McGuire			●	○
John McKay			○	
Edward McKenna			○	
James McKenna				○
Felix McKeon			●	
John McKeon			●	
Michael McKeown				○
Patrick McKeown				○
John McKilduff	(R)		○	○
Archibald McKinnon				○
James McLaughlin			●	
Stephen McLaughlin			○	
Frederick McLean			●	○
Alexander McLennon				○
Michael McMeara				○
Daniel McMullen			●	
James McNair	(P)			○
James McNea				○
Francis McQuade			●	○
Archibald McVicar			●	○
Robert McVicar			●	○
Francis McWilliams				○
Michael Macnamara			●	○
Richard Magee				○
Daniel Mahoney			●	
Nelson Mallis	(R)		●	○
James Malone			●	
Michael Maloney				○
George Malton			○	
John Mann			○	
James Manning			●	
James Markham				○

South Africa 1853 Medal

Name		Kaffir Wars 1	2	3
John Markham				O
John Marsh			●	O
Andrew Marshall	(MRM)			O
Charles Martin				O
John Martin			●	O
Joseph Martin			O	
Michael Martin				O
John Mason				O
Norman Mason	(P)			O
Alexander Maxwell			O	O
Anthony May			●	O
Thomas Mead				O
Michael Meade				O
William Meany				O
Aldred Medley			●	
Robert Melrose		O		
John Menzies		▲		
George Merrett			●	O
John Metcalf				O
John Michael			●	O
William Midgley			O	
James Miller			●	O
William Mills				O
James Mitchell			●	O
Thomas Moles			●	O
John Molloy			●	O
Peter Moloney			O	O
Felix Monaghan			●	O
Hugh Monaghan				O
William Mooney				O
James Moor				O
David Moore				O
Elijah Moore			●	O
John Moore			●	
Thomas Moore		O		
Bryan Moran				O
Frederick Mordan			●	
John Morehead				O
John Morgan				O
James Morris			●	
John Morris	(R)		●	O
William Morron			●	
John Morrow				O
Alexander Morton			●	O
Thomas Mount				O
Patrick Muldoon				O
Martin Mulhall			●	O
James Mulholland			●	O
Archibald Mulligan			●	O
George Mundy	(P)		●	O
Samuel Murden			O	
Daniel Murphy				O
James T. Murphy			●	O
John Murphy				O
Joseph Murphy		O		
Thomas Murphy			●	O
Patrick Murray				O
Dennis Myham				O
Patrick Nash				O
John Nason		O		
John Naylor	(R)		●	
Samuel Neale			●	
Simon Neale				O
John Newing			●	O
John Newman			●	O
George Newton			●	O
Stephen Norden			●	O
George Norgate		O		

Name		Kaffir Wars 1	2	3
Henry North			●	O
John Norton				O
William Norton	(MRM)		●	O
Nicholas Nulty			●	O
James O'Brien	(R)		●	
Daniel O'Callaghan			●	
John O'Connor			O	
George O'Gee			●	O
Arthur O'Neil			●	
Charles O'Neill	(P)		●	O
Bernard O'Neill			●	O
John O'Neill			●	
George Ong			O	O
John Orr				O
Thomas Orr			●	O
Joseph Orrell				O
John Osborne		O		
Peter Parkin				O
William Parrott			●	O
William Patmore			●	
William Pattison				O
William Peak				O
John Pearce			O	O
Peter Pearson				O
Alexander Peasley	(P)			O
Thomas Peel				O
William Peirpoint			●	O
Edward Penigar			●	O
William Pennell	(MRM)			O
William Persefield				O
Andrew Perry			●	O
Matthew Perry			●	O
William Perry			●	O
George Pervor				O
Thomas Pew				O
Patrick Phelan			●	O
Daniel Phillips				O
James Phillips				O
Richard Pilcher			●	
Richard Platt			O	O
Charles Pocock			●	
Henry Polton				O
William Porke			●	
James Porter				O
Thomas Postings			●	
Charles Potter			●	O
William Poxon			O	O
Thomas Price				O
William Price			●	O
Richard Prince				O
Charles Purton			●	
John Quigley			●	O
Martin Quinn				O
Thomas Race			●	O
Alexander Rafferty				O
Joseph Rafferty				O
George Rafter			O	
William Raggett			O	
Alexander Ranken				O
Moses Read				O
John Reaney			●	O
Martin Redmond			●	O
Alexander Reid			●	O
William Reid				O
James Reilly				O
William Reilly			●	O
William Reynolds			●	O
George Richards			●	O

84 South Africa 1853 Medal

		Kaffir Wars 1 2 3			Kaffir Wars 1 2 3
PRIVATE			Joseph Smith (2)	42)	
Henry Richards		○	Joseph Smith (3)	42)	● ● ○
John Richards		●	Joseph Smith (4)	42)	○
Charles Richardson		● ○	Owen Smith		○
Francis Richens		● ○	William Smith (1)	43)	○
Joseph Rights		● ○	William Smith (2)	43)	●
William Riseberry		● ○	John Soars		● ○
Robert Roach		● ○	Thomas Sonton		○
Frederick Roberts		●	Frederick Spiller		●
George Roberts		● ○	John Stafford		●
James Roberts		○	George Stansfield		○ ○
Joseph Roberts		● ○	George Stephens		○
William Roberts		○	Isaac Sterry		●
Robert Robertson		○ ○	William Stevenson		○
William Robertson		● ○	Robert Stockdale	(P)	○
Henry Robinson		● ○	James Stretch	(P)	● ○
James Robinson		● ○	George Strutt		● ○
Thomas Robinson		● ○	Archibald Stuart		●
Charles Roche		● ○	James Sturman		○
Thomas Roche		● ○	John Summers		○
Patrick Rodgers		● ○	Patrick Summersfield		○
Charles Rodney		○	Daniel Sutton		○
Zachariah Rolfe		○	James Swann		● ○
John Rollins		○	John Sweeney		○ ○
William Rook		● ○	Thomas Sweeney		○
William Rotchford		● ○	William Swindon		○ ○
William Rothwell		○	Edward Tague		○
William Rouse			William Tarrants		○
John Rowell		● ○	William Tate	(P)	○
George Russell		● ○	Francis Tattler		▲ ○
James Ryan	(P)	● ○	George Tattler		● ○
Thomas Ryan		○	James Taylor	(M)	● ○
William Salisbury		○ ○	John Teasel	(P)	● ○
William Savage	41)	△ ○	Francis Turney		○
Elijah Sawyer		○	John Tetley		○ ○
John Saxton		● ○	William Thomas		○
Jeremiah Saynor		● ○	Alexander Thompson		○
John Scott		● ○	James Thompson		● ○
William Searle		● ○	William Thompson	44)	△ △
George Sebourne		● ○	William Thorn		○ ○
Cornelius Secker	(P)		Henry Thorne		○
John Seeley		●	Henry Thornton		●
William Seeth		● ○	Robert Tibbles		●
Edward Shaw		● ○	Robert Tipping		● ○
George Shaw		○	William Tochal		● ○
James Shea		● ○	John Tocock		● ○
Francis Shenton		● ○	William Towler		● ○
William Shilcock		○	Charles Townshend		●
Henry Shipston	(R)	● ○	Michael Trainor		●
John Shrigley		●	John Trowbridge		● ○
Isaac Shrimpton		●	Edward Truswell		○
Patrick Silk		○	Robert Tuck		● ○
James Simpson		○	William Tuckwood		●
John Simpson		● ○	Geoffrey Tuff		○
Robert Simpson	(P)	○ ○	William Tyler	(MRM)	○
Thomas Simms		● ○	Charles Underwood		● ○
John Singleton		●	John Verdon		● ○
Henry Skinner		●	George Wager		● ○
Robert Skinner		○ ○	William Waghorn		○
Thomas Skinner	(P)	● ○	Charles Walding		○
John Slack		○	James Waldron	45)	○
William Slade		● ○	John Waldron	45)	●
Michael Slaine		○	Laughlin Waldron		▲
John Slater		● ○	George Walker		○
Thomas Smallman		● ○	John Walker		○
Benjamin Smith		○	Robert Walker (1)		● ○
George Smith		○ ○	Robert Walker (2)		● ○
Joseph Smith (1)	42)	○	Thomas Walker		● ○

South Africa 1853 Medal 85

		Kaffir Wars							Kaffir Wars		
		1	2	3			Co		1	2	3
William Walker (1)					Charles Wild	(R)					○
William Walker (2)			●	○	John Wilde				●	○	
John Walsh				○	Charles Wildbone				●	○	
James Walsh			●	○	George Williams				●		
Patrick Walsh			○	○	John Willis				●	○	
Philip Walsh	46)		●	△	William Willis					○	
Henry Ward			●	○	Charles Willmott				●	○	
David Wark				○	James Wilson				●		
William Warren					John Wilson				○		
Abraham Waterman	47)		●	○	Joseph Wilson					○	
James Waters			●	○	Peter Wilson				●		
Samuel Waterson			○		Robert Wilson					○	
John Watkinson				○	Thomas Wilson				●		
James Watson			●		Charles Winkworth				●		
Thomas Watterworth				○	Bernard Wood					○	
George Webb				○	Patrick Wood					○	
Oliver Webstock				○	Thomas Wood				●	○	
John West				○	John Woodcraft					○	
William Whalley				○	George Worthington					○	
Charles Wheeler				○	Henry Wright					○	
William Whelan			●	○	Henry Yockney				▲		
George White			●	○	Luke Yorke				●	○	
John White			●	○	James Young	(MRM)					
Richard White			●	○	Thomas Young				○	○	
John Whitehurst	(R)			○							
James Whitelaw			○		△ = campaign qualification as WO/100/17.						
William Wigley			●	○	○ = campaign which the Rolls fail to credit.						

45TH (NOTTINGHAMSHIRE) REGIMENT

1. Commanded a detachment of the 45th at Boemplaats, where he was wounded.
2. Twice shown on the Roll, once credited with 1850-3 and then again with no date and shown as C. W. Armstrong. A note against the latter entry says 'specially entitled by letter from Col Cooper'. It is dated 8.5.56 and a re-named medal was sent to him.
3. Commanded the reinforcements sent from Natal to the Orange River Sovereignty in 1851.
4. Wounded at Boemplaats.
5. Shot through both thighs in action with the Boers and Hottentots in the OR Sovereignty, 1851.
6. Even the 45th musters confused Lt and Ensign Dawson. The Lieutenant's medal was sent in error to E. S. G. Dawson, then a Captain with the 93rd, who had qualified for a medal when with the 45th. The Ensign's medal was then altered for William Dawson.
7. See G and I.
8. Twice entered on the Roll, once among 'Staff' as Garrison Adjutant, but that medal was returned to the Mint.
9. The Roll also credits the 3rd campaign but I can find no evidence that he served in that war and Harts mentions 1846-7 only.
10. When serving with the 91st as a volunteer he commanded their rearguard on December 29th 1850 after they had suffered heavy casualties. For several months Hobbs was Captain of native levies and operated in the Waterkloof and Amatolas. He was again attached to the 91st at the end of 1851 and re-joined the 45th early in the following year.
11. Served at Boemplaats and at Berea.
12. Wrongly credited with 1850-3 on Roll.
13. Medal shows Lukas.
14. Walker frustrated a mass desertion of CMR at Fort Cox in December 1850; See McKay.
15. With Sir Harry Smith at Fort Cox in December 1850.
16. Earned his medal with the 60th Regiment.
17. No 1065 and not to be confused with Pte Holmes No 2708.
18. Snaddon on Roll.
19. According to the Roll he was with the 72nd during the 1st campaign.
20. No 1130.
21. No 1180.
22. Bourley on Roll.
23. Boys on Roll.
24. No 1754; his number appears on the Roll.
25. Nos 3062 and 3203.
26. Nos 1629 and 2555.
27. Collins on Roll.
28. Nos 2446 and 2470.
29. Possibly the 'M. Corsley' shown in the Lt Col Ll. Palmer collection 1914.
30. Nos 2986 and 2992.
31. Also Dickson on musters.
32. Nos 1846 and 2531.
33. Roll gives 146-78.
34. Draffin on Roll.
35. Only credited with 1846-7 on Roll.
36. Nos 1849 and 2566.
37. No 2708.
38. Nos 2155 and 2809.
39. No 3230, the only man of the 45th to survive the wreck of the 'Birkenhead'.
40. Also Loverton on musters.
41. Although credited with 1846-7 on Roll. this has not been confirmed.
42. Nos 2096, 2624, 2690 and 2936.
43. Nos 1960 and 2673.
44. Served with the 90th during the 2nd campaign.
45. One of these medals is in a private collection.
46. Walshe on Roll.
47. One of a handful of soldiers who appear on the Navy Roll.

PRO References: WO/12/5752-5753-5754-5755-5757-5758-5762-5763-5764-5767.

60th (The King's Royal Rifle) Regiment

The six service companies of the 60th arrived off East London on September 27th 1851, but so heavy was the surf the troops were unable to get ashore until October 3rd. Within four days they were at King William's Town and on October 14th moved to Fort Hare. From here Col Nesbitt set out with a 500 strong force, mainly composed of his own regiment, to sweep the Tyumie Valley, but their search for cattle was fruitless and on the 23rd Nesbitt joined with a force under Somerset which attacked enemy positions at the head of the Waterkloof. The Kaffirs were driven from what they considered an impregnable stronghold and the troops returned to King William's Town on the 31st.

Some uneventful patrolling was followed in late November by three companies of the 60th being placed under Lt Col Mackinnon and combining with Somerset's troops in an unsuccessful cattle raid near the Black Kei. Meanwhile, three other companies were part of a 1,000 strong force under Lt Col Eyre (73rd) which saw some sharp action on and near the Great Kei. This column camped at Butterworth as Somerset made a six day march through enemy territory, returning to King William's Town on January 12th 1852. During these operations casualties were light, one rifleman being killed and five wounded.

Some companies were engaged in crop destruction under Col Michel (6th) from January 27th to February 29th and then in early March the regiment was part of Michel's Brigade under Sir Harry Smith which struck at Iron Mountain in the Waterkloof. The 60th led the frontal attack which carried the mountain with the loss of only one man killed and two wounded.

The Brigade returned to camp but was immediately detached via Fort Cox to the foot of Sleyna Mountain. On March 26th they went to support the 45th who were being contained at Wolfs Den and lost five men wounded before the combined regiments drove the enemy from their positions.

During April, the Brigade, now under Nesbitt, had a sharp skirmish at the foot of the Amatolas and the month of May was marked by the regiment being armed by the new Minie rifles, replacements for their Brunswick rifles.

In July, the regiment was bivouacked on the Kroome Heights and, with the Rifle Brigade, occupied on escort duties before joining the four column assault which bisected the Waterkloof. The Battalion concentrated at Fort Hare on October 2nd and two weeks later one man was killed and two wounded when a small wagon escort to Fort White was attacked. Until the revolt was finally put down the regiment was engaged in patrolling and crop destruction. Thereafter the 60th was split into various detachments, largely engaged on roadmaking, and it was while visiting his outposts that Col Nesbitt was drowned in the Keiskamma on October 10th 1853.

		Kaffir Wars		
		1	2	3
MAJOR				
William Bedford	1)			△
CAPTAIN				
Ashton Mosley	2)			△
George Bligh	2)			△
Hon Adrian Hope	3)			△
John McKenzie	2)			△
Gibbes Rigaud	2) (P)			△
William P. Salmon	2)			△
Charles W. H. Sotheby	4)			△
LIEUTENANT				
Robert W. Brooke				△
Henry Cockburn				△
Charles W. Earle				△
Francis Fitzpatrick				△
Stephen Kenny				△
Atholl C. J. Liddell				△
Hugh P. Montgomery				△
William Mure				△
Henry J. Robertson				△
Henry E. Warren	(R)			△
SECOND LIEUTENANT				
C. David C. Ellis				△
PAYMASTER				
William H. Fitzgerald				△
QUARTERMASTER				
Luke Fitzgibbon	5)		△	△
SURGEON				
Thomas Alexander	6)			△
Henry J. Schooles, MD	(P)			△
ASSISTANT SURGEON				
Brinsley Nicholson	(P)			△
SERGEANT MAJOR				
Matthew Tilford	(P)			△
COLOUR SERGEANT				
George Brooks				△
Thomas Carver	7)			△
Patrick Cockrane	8) (R)			△
Daniel McIntyre	(R)			△
James McKay				△
John Moore				△
James Sharley				△
Richard Storey				△
SERGEANT				
David Andrews	9)			△
John C. Bagley				△
Silvey Brown				△
Frederick Carrington				△
Thomas Caldwell	10)			△
Henry Cook				△
William Cook	(MRM)			△
John Coote				△
Ephraim Cox				△
Nathaniel Cullen	(P)			△
William Cragg	(P)			△
John Deacon				△
Edward Dubberley	11) (P)			△
Samuel Dyke				△
Thomas Eady	12)			△
John S. Evans				△
Thomas Fitzpatrick	13)			△

			Kaffir Wars 1	2	3
James Forbes	14)				△
Thomas Fuller	14)	(R)			△
John Fulton					△
Thomas Gleeson					△
Richard Hall					△
William Holmes					△
John Hutton		(R)			△
Charles Hutson	14)				△
Thomas Inglis		(P)			△
John Johnson	15)				△
Daniel Lineham		(MRM)			△
John Lineham					△
James Matthews					△
Charles Meek		(P)			△
Robert Menzies		(MRM)			△
Robert A. Murray					△
Joseph Nicolls					△
Michael O'Brien	16)				△
John O'Farrell					△
Charles Overland					△
Richard Parkins					△
Henry Parsloe					△
John Partridge					△
Edward Phillips					△
William Rossell					△
Solomon Ruderham		(R)			△
James Stickley					△
Edmund Ware	17)				△
CORPORAL					
Joseph Bunting	18)				△
Jesse Collyer		(P)			△
Sydney Day					△
Michael Doyle					△
Robert Edwards					△
Edmund Fraser					△
Edward Fullam	19)	(P)			△
John Gately					△
Charles Hall					△
John Hannan					△
Dennis Harrington					△
John Hart					△
Archelaus Hibbert	20)				△
Henry Hobbs					△
Alexander Hoey					△
Robert Holbrook		(P)			△
Samuel Jackson					△
Patrick Johnson					△
John Keenan					△
Charles Key					△
John King					△
George Marsh					△
James Maxwell					△
John Millar					△
David Nelson		(MRM)			△
Thomas Shipley					△
Thomas Smith					△
William Sommerville					△
John Wiltshire					△
BUGLER					
James Ahern					△
William Bryan					△
Edward Cowden					△
Edward Findley					△
John Kehoe		(R)			△
Maurice Kelehar					△
John Kelly					△
Thomas Kelly	21)				△

			Kaffir Wars 1	2	3
James Parkinson					△
John Rankin					△
James Rowley					△
Thomas Squires		(R)			△
William Thornbury					△
William Tripp					△
Alexander Whiteford		(P)			△
James Woods					△
Robert Woods					△
PRIVATE					
George Adams					△
William Ager					△
J. Henry Ainsborough					△
William Allan					△
William Allcock					△
James Anderson					△
William Andrews					△
John Arkell					△
Enos Arkwell					△
David Armstrong					△
Joseph Arnold		(P)			△
John Ashton		(R)			△
John Atkinson					△
George Attenborough					△
James Bacon					△
Joseph Baker		(R)			△
Samuel Ballafin		(R)			△
Charles Barnett		(P)			△
Henry Barnes	22)	(P)			△
Benjamin Barrett					△
John Bartley					△
George Barton					△
Jacob Baxter					△
William Baxter					△
Thomas Beardsley					△
John Bell					△
Thomas Benson					△
John Beveridge					△
William Bissett	23)				△
John W. Blackley					△
William Blatherwick		(M)			△
Joseph Blease	24)	(R)			△
Henry C. Boehmar					△
John Boland					△
Davis Bolton					△
John Bolton					△
Thomas Bomford					△
Samuel Booth					△
Thomas Booth					△
Sampson Bould					△
John Boyle					△
Patrick Boyle					△
Samuel Bradley					△
Joseph Brairley	25)				△
William Broad					△
George Brown		(MR)			△
Malcom Brown					△
James Bryan (1)	26)				△
James Bryan (2)	26)				△
John Bryan					△
Richard Bryan					△
William Bryce					△
Alexander Buchanan					△
John Bull					△
Robert Bunting					△
John Butler	27)				△
Thomas Caldwell	28)				△

88 South Africa 1853 Medal

PRIVATE		Kaffir Wars 1 2 3			Kaffir Wars 1 2 3
Patrick Callihan	29) (P)	△	William Eborn		△
Edward D. Campion		△	John Ellis		△
Thomas Carrington		△	Joseph Ellison		△
Henry Cartledge		△	Isaac Elson		△
James Casey	(R)	△	James English	(P)	△
James Cashman		△	William Evans		△
William Cassady		△	Samuel Faddes		△
Thomas Chalmers		△	Cornelius Falvey		△
James Chambers		△	Thomas Farmer		△
John Chambers	30)	△	John Finney		△
James Charlton		△	James Fish		△
John Chaseney		△	Patrick Fitzgerald	42)	△
Daniel Chick		△	Thomas Fitzgerald	43)	△
Edward Clarke		△	William Fitzhenry		△
Henry Clarke	31)	△	Patrick Fitzpatrick	(R)	△
William Clarage	32)	△	Peter Fitzpatrick		△
George Clements		△	Thomas Fitzpatrick		△
Thomas Cocking		△	Michael Fitzsimmons		△
John Coffey	33)	△	James Flaherty		△
William Collier		△	Thomas Flannery	(MRM)	△
Daniel Collins		△	James Fletcher		△
John Collins (1)	34)	△	Martin Folay		△
John Collins (2)	34)	△	Henry Foss	44)	△
Christopher Connell		△	George Frankland		△
Dennis Connell		△	Michael Furey	(MRM)	△
Martin Connolly		△	William Garrett	(P)	△
Timothy Connor	(MRM)	△	Patrick Gaskin		△
John Conway		△	William Gee		△
Thomas Cook		△	Alexander Gibson		△
Enoch Cooke	35)	△	David Gibson		△
William Cooper		△	Samuel Gibson		△
Peter Coote		△	John Gilfillan		△
Michael Corcoran		△	Dennis Gleeson		△
Joseph Coughan	(MRM)	△	Daniel Godfrey	45)	△
Joseph Cowan		△	Charles Good		△
William Cox		△	William Gordon	(MRM)	△
Michael Coyle	(M)	△	George Gould		△
Edward Croxall		△	Henry Gould		△
Christopher Cullen		△	William Graham		△
James Culley		△	James Granger		△
James Cummins		△	William Granger		△
John Cunningham		△	Thomas Grant		△
James Daly		△	Francis Gray		△
Thomas Daly		△	James Gray		△
James Dance		△	Charles Greening		△
George Davis	(P)	△	Edward Griffin	(MRM)	△
John Davis (1)	36)	△	James Hall		△
John Davis (2)	36)	△	Patrick Hall		△
Joseph Davis		△	John Halloran	(MRM)	△
William Davis		△	John Hamilton		△
George Dawson	21)	△	Patrick Handcock	(MRM)	△
William Dawson		△	John Harrington	(MRM)	△
John Day		△	Andrew Harris		△
Thomas Deane		△	John Harris	(P)	△
Michael Devlin	37)	△	Richard Hart		△
Thomas Deverill (1)	38)	△	Richard Hartley	(P)	△
Thomas Deverill (2)	38)	△	Henry Hazeldene	(P)	△
William E. Dicks		△	William Head		△
James Doar		△	Jonathan Heath		△
James Doe		△	Henry Henderson		△
Nicholas Donnelly	(MRM)	△	James Henderson (1)	46)	△
William Donoghue	39)	△	James Henderson (2)	46)	△
Thomas Dove	40)	△	William Henderson		△
James Doyle		△	James Henshall	21)	△
Thomas Dulanty		△	Daniel Hickey		△
Thomas Dweesy	41)	△	Henry Hilliard	47)	△
Hugh Eagleston		△	James Hitchmond	48)	△
			Timothy Hobbs	(P)	△

South Africa 1853 Medal

Name	Note	Kaffir Wars 1	2	3
John Holehouse				△
William Hooper				△
Francis Howell				△
Patrick Hughes				△
Terence Hughes				△
James Hunt				△
David Hunter				△
Henry Hurt				△
William Hurt				△
Hugh Hutchinson				△
Alexander Irwin				△
William Jeens				△
William Jeffers				△
John Jelf				△
Francis Jerram				△
James Jessamer	49)			△
James Johnson	50)			△
John Johnson				△
Stephen Johnson	51)			△
James Johnston	21) (MRM)			△
John Johnston	52)			△
Joseph Johnston				△
Thomas Jones				△
Edwin Judd	(P)			△
Nicholas Keane				△
William Kellow				△
Andrew Kelly				△
Michael Kelly				△
Patrick Kelly				△
James Keneybrough	53)			△
James Kenney				△
Charles W. Keppell	54)			△
James Kershaw	55)			△
Mark Killoran				△
David King				△
William Kirkland				△
Thomas Kirkwood	(MRM)			△
Joseph Lalor				△
Michael Lanigan				△
Patrick Leamy				△
Dennis Leary				△
Alexander Leckie	56)			△
George Ley	(MRM)			△
George Litchfield				△
James Lilley				△
William Limbrick				△
George Lindley				△
James Lister				△
Frederick Locke				△
John Locke	(MRM)			△
Patrick Lowney	(R)			△
James Loydal				△
John Lynch (1)	57)			△
John Lynch (2)	57)			△
Joseph Lynch				△
Patrick Maher				△
Edward Mains	58) (P)			△
John Malvay	(MRM)			△
William Manley	59) (P)			△
Patrick Maroney	60)			△
Henry Marsey	61)			△
Patrick Martin	(MRM)			△
Thomas Martin				△
William Martin				△
Harry Mather	62)			△
William McAllister				△
James McCabe	21)			△
Edward McCann				△
Patrick McCarthy	(MRM)			△
Robert McCarthy				△
John McClelland				△
John McCloskey	(MRM)			△
Robert McCrossan	63) (P)			△
John McDanald	64)			△
Michael McDermott				△
William McDonald				△
Andrew McEvoy				△
George McGhie	65)			△
John McGhie	65) (P)			△
David McGill	(MRM)			△
James McGill	(MRM)			△
Michael McGovern				△
William McGrath				△
John McGuire				△
Matthew McGuire	66)			△
Philip McGuire				△
William McHale	(MRM)			△
Duncan McIntosh				△
Patrick McKeon				△
John McMahon (1)	67)			△
John McMahon (2)	67)			△
Hugh McMorland				△
Samuel McMunagle				△
William McMunagle	68)			△
John McNamara				△
Patrick McNamara				△
John McParlin	(MRM)			△
Terence McQuade				△
Thomas Mellor				△
William Mellors	(MRM)			△
Josiah Menlove				△
Henry Merrett				△
John Mew				△
Alexander Mitchell				△
William Mitchell				△
John Molloy				△
John Moorwood				△
William Morgan				△
Thomas Morrice				△
John Morris				△
Thomas Mulholland				△
Owen Mullin	69)			△
George Murdin				△
Archibald Murray				△
James Murray				△
Daniel Naylor				△
James Neal				△
John Neal				△
Joseph Needham				△
Thomas Nelson				△
Edward Newman				△
Thomas Nicholls				△
John Nicholson				△
Isaac Norris				△
Robert Norton				△
Thomas Nuthall	70)			△
Christopher O'Brien	(MRM)			△
John O'Connell				△
James O'Donnell				△
William Ogden				△
James O'Meally				△
James O'Neil				△
Thomas O'Neil	71)			△
John O'Sullivan				△
Timothy O'Sullivan				△
Robert Overland				△

PRIVATE		Kaffir Wars 1 2 3
William Overland		△
James Owen		△
Frederick Palmer		△
George Palmer		△
John Peeling		△
Josiah Perry		△
William Pett	72)	△
George Pheonix		△
Thomas Phillips	(MRM)	△
William Pierces		△
William Piggott	(M)	△
John Pollard		△
John Poole		△
Thomas Pridham		△
Ambrose Purcell		△
William Purvis		△
John Pye		△
Michael Regan		△
William Regan		△
George Reid		△
James Renfrew		△
Charles Reynolds		△
John Reynolds		△
Amos Richardson		△
Adam Ridgeway		△
John Ridgeway		△
James Robertson		△
John Robey		△
James Rodgers		△
John Rogers	73)	△
Henry Rolfe	(P)	△
Joseph Rushworth	(P)	△
John Russell		△
George Rutherford		△
Michael Ryan	74)	△
Richard Ryan		△
James Saunders		△
Moses Saunders		△
George Sayer		△
Murty Scanlon		△
William Scott		△
John Seaburne	75) (MRM)	△
John Seeney		△
John Selby		△
Frederick Sewell		△
Frank Sharley		△
Samuel Sharples		△
Richard Shaw		△
John Shea		△
Michael Sheehan		△
Henry Shelton		△
William Shepperd	76)	△
John Shine		△
James Sim		△
Peter Simmons		△
Thomas Skinner		△
Charles Slann		△
William Slater		△
Thomas Slugg		△
George Smith		△
John Smith (1)	77)	△
John Smith (2)	77)	△
William Smith	78)	△
Willoughby Smith	78)	△
William Souter	79)	△
Robert Stair		△
William Stanage		△
James Steedsman		△
Samuel Stevens		△
John Stokes		△
John Storey		△
Thomas Strong		△
William Sugden	80) (P)	△
John Sullivan		△
David Sutford		△
Lackey Tansey		△
John Tarpy		△
Charles Taylor		△
Hamilton Taylor		△
John Taylor		△
William Taylor		△
Ralph Thirkell		△
John Thompson	81)	△
William Thompson		△
James Thornton		△
Martin Timan		△
William Toft		△
George Towler	82)	△
John Townsend	83)	△
Thomas Townsend		△
William Trollop		△
Thomas Trusler		△
John Tyke		△
James Varndell		△
Frederick M. Wade		△
George Waklin		△
Charles Waller	84) (R)	△
Charles Wallis		△
Francis Wallis		△
Edward Walsh		△
Thomas Walsh		△
Henry Ward		△
Peter Waters		△
Stephen Watson	(MRM)	△
George Watts		△
Edward R. Waugh		△
James Waugh		△
George Wetherall		△
George Webster		△
Charles Weller	85)	△
George Welsh		△
David West		△
James White	(P)	△
William White		△
William Whitelock		△
John Wicksey		△
John Wild		△
Jonathan Williamson		△
Alpheus Wilson		△
James Wilson		△
William Wilson		△
Edward F. Wiltshire		△
William Woodcock		△
Job Workman	(P)	△
Matthew Yuill		△

△ = campaign qualification as WO/100/17.

60TH (THE KING'S ROYAL RIFLE) REGIMENT NOTES

1. Prominent in the attack on Iron Mountain; March 1852.
2. Present in the operation beyond the Kei; December 1851.
3. Engaged in the operations of December 1851 and March 1852.
4. Was in charge of supply wagons travelling from Fort Hare to Fort White when they were attacked on 16.10.52.
5. Although only credited with 1846–7 on the Roll, he served in both the 2nd and 3rd campaigns with the 45th Regt, rising from the ranks. Transferred to the 60th in November 1853.
6. Principal medical officer during the Kei expedition December 1851.
7. No 1947; John on Roll.
8. Medal said to show Cochrane.
9. No 1096, a survivor from the 'Birkenhead'.
10. No 2265.
11. Dubberly on Roll.
12. One of a party of the 60th who sailed to the Depot Companies on 24.1.53 and appear additionally on the Naval Roll, where Eady is shown as Corporal.
13. No 1989 and not to be confused with Pte T. Fitzpatrick.
14. Also on the Naval Roll; see Note 12.
15. No 1272.
16. O'Brien on Roll; see Note 12.
17. Only appears on the Naval Roll; see Note 12.
18. Ex Royal Marines.
19. Also Fulham on Musters.
20. Hibburt on Roll.
21. 'Dead' on Roll.
22. Barms on Roll. Medal correctly shows Barnes.
23. Bessett on Roll.
24. James on Roll.
25. Breirley on Roll.
26. Nos 1425 and 1951.
27. No 2834.
28. No 2264.
29. Cullihan on Roll and medal.
30. James on Roll.
31. Clark on Roll.
32. Clarge on Roll.
33. Coffee on Roll.
34. Nos 1365 and 2778.
35. Cook on Roll and shown as 'Dead'.
36. Nos 1324 and 1631.
37. Develin on Roll.
38. Nos 2537 and 2838.
39. No 1059.
40. Correctly altered from Dore on Roll.
41. Dweesey on Roll.
42. The Regimental Museum is said to have a medal named to F. Fitzpatrick – which is probably this man.
43. No 2975 and not to be confused with Sgt T. Fitzpatrick.
44. No 2677, a survivor from the 'Birkenhead'.
45. I have not been able to identify this man.
46. Nos 1097 and 1434.
47. Hillierd on Roll.
48. Henry on Roll.
49. Correctly altered from Jesseman on Roll.
50. No 2693.
51. Correctly altered from John on Roll.
52. No. 1745.
53. Shown as Frennyborough on Roll! A note on the Roll against Major Rawsthorne (91st) says that a duplicate medal issued in error was returned and re-named 'James Keneybrough' – which may mean the medal named Frennyborough was also returned.
54. William, his second name, is shown on the Roll.
55. Kersham on Roll.
56. No 1061, a survivor from the 'Birkenhead'.
57. Nos 2513 and 2658.
58. The medal in a private collection is engraved and possibly a replacement.
59. 'Dead' on Roll; also Manly on muster.
60. Moroney on Roll.
61. Marsey on Roll.
62. No 2869, a survivor from the 'Birkenhead'.
63. McCrossin on Roll and medal.
64. No 2627 McDonald on Roll.
65. Also McGhee on musters.
66. Two men of this name on Roll but I can only trace No 2642.
67. Nos 2573 and 2703.
68. McMonagle on Roll.
69. Mullen on Roll.
70. No 2151, a survivor from the 'Birkenhead'.
71. O'Neill on Roll.
72. Correctly altered from Pitt on Roll.
73. Rodgers on Roll.
74. No. 2791.
75. Two John Scotts served with the regiment and No. 1110 is undoubtedly the single Scott on the Roll. but the Mint records show a man of this name and regiment applying for a medal on 17.11.63. Whether this was a late claim by Scott No. 2009 or a replacement for Scott 1110 has not been determined.
76. Sheppherd on Roll.
77. Nos 1448 and 2511.
78. One of these medals is in a private collection.
79. No 2150, a survivor from the 'Birkenhead'.
80. Twice on Roll; once as a late claimant in 1861 which may be for a replacement.
81. No 1209; Thomson on Roll.
82. Altered to Fowler on Roll, but musters confirm Towler.
83. Two men of this name on musters, Nos 2674 and 2815.
84. No. 2480 and not to be confused with Charles Weller.
85. No 1313 and not to be confused with Charles Waller.

PRO References: WO/12/6972–6974–6975.

72nd (The Duke of Albany's Own Highlanders) Regiment

The 72nd had been in South Africa since 1828 and was garrisoned at Cape Town when news reached them of the outbreak of the 1st war. No time was lost in rushing support to the overstretched forces on the frontier and on January 2nd 1835 three companies sailed for Algoa Bay. Four days later the Grenadier Company escorted the Governor, Maj Gen Sir Benjamin D'Urban, to the scene of operations while the rest of the regiment marched overland to Uitenhage. A detachment remained there and the remainder moved on to Grahams Town under Lt Col Peddie.

The Light Company, Capt Jervis, soon found employment. Among the troops sent to re-occupy the abandoned Fort Willshire, they were part of the force who set out from there under Maj Cox (75th) to bring in missionaries, traders and settlers who had not been able to reach the shelter of a fort. While they were away the reduced garrison came under attack and three men of the 72nd on cattle guard were killed.

Detachments under Maj Maclean and Capt Murray were with the forces trying to clear the Fish River Bush early in February, and among the casualties were four killed and three wounded from the regiment.

The Highlanders were brought together at Chief Macomo's old Kraal on February 18th and then moved to the Brack River where they were encamped while forces gathered in preparation for the four divisional operations which took place during April. The 72nd were placed in the 1st Division which entered Kaffir territory above Fort Willshire and Executive Drift. The Light Company were despatched to the Upper Amatolas where they captured considerable livestock and killed several of the enemy. On April 3rd they penetrated to the country behind T'Slambies Kop but achieved little and joined the 3rd (Cavalry) Division marching to the banks of the Buffalo.

With three companies of Provisionals, Capt Murray and 100 of the 72nd were sent to intercept 600 Kaffirs under Chief Tyalie who settled on a high and rugged cliff later called Murray's Krantz. The troops scaled the heights under a shower of spears and stones and had several men wounded before the natives fled.

Accompanied by four companies of Provisionals Col Peddie ascended the Isele Berg on April 9th, capturing several thousand cattle and scattering the enemy.

The 1st Division crossed the Kei on April 15th into Hintza's territory. Capt Murray with two companies of the 72nd were part of Col Smith's large patrol which captured 15,000 cattle during a two days' drive and resulted in Hintza agreeing to suspend hostilities.

The regiment marched to Gonubie Hill in mid-May and constructed a post which was named Fort Wellington. Leaving a small detachment as garrison the 1st Division moved to Brownlie's Missionary station, hutted themselves and laid out the plan for the future capital of the province, King William's Town. After the division was broken up in June the Light Company marched to the Poorts of the Buffalo where they erected Fort Beresford. At the same time Capt Lacey and 30 men built Fort Murray and Fort Coke.

During July and August the Kaffirs made desperate efforts and during an attack on Fort Wellington the regiment had a man killed. Major McClean, with 80 Highlanders from King William's Town and Fort Beresford, 200 Provisionals and the Kat River Legion assembled at Fort Cox in July when Tyalie and Macomo were reported to be gathering, but the 72nd seem to have been little concerned in the forays which continued until the peace treaty was ratified.

During October 1835 detachments at Forts Warden and Wellington were replaced by the 75th but the 72nd still manned a number of posts until October 1838 when they returned to Cape Town for the remaining 18 months of their service in South Africa.

		Kaffir Wars 1	2	3
MAJOR				
Charles M. Maclean	1)			△
CAPTAIN				
Charles C. Craven	2)			△
Henry Jervis	3)			△
Thomas E. Lacey	4)			△
LIEUTENANT				
Edward J. Kelso				△
Lewis Xavier Leslie	5)			△
John Wade	4)			△
ENSIGN				
Thomas F. Simmons	(R)			△
ACTING QUARTERMASTER				
William Hume	(P)			△
BANDMASTER				
F. Ricks	6)			△
COLOUR SERGEANT				
William Hume	(P)			△
John Wilson				△
SERGEANT				
Roger Baldwin				△
Charles Coates	7)			△
John Foster				△
Alexander Fraser	8)			△
James Gray	9)			△ △
James Hogg				△
John Kellock				△
James Lindsay				△
Peter McQuade				△
John Milne	10) (P)			△
Thomas Mitchell				△
James Smith	11)			△
George Watson	12)			△
Robert Wilson				△
CORPORAL				
Alexander Abbott				△
James Adams				△
David Dalas				△
Donald Munroe	13)			O
James Ramsay	14)			△
DRUMMER				
Thomas Barclay				△
John Beal				△
James Henderson				△
Alexander Spears	15)			△

South Africa 1853 Medal

PRIVATE		Kaffir Wars 1 2 3			Kaffir Wars 1 2 3
James Alexander		△	Angus McDonald		△
William Allan		△	John McDonald	26)	△
David Anderson		△	John McGregor		△
James Anderson	16)	△	John McIntosh	27)	△
William Avery		△	Solomon McKay	27)	△
William Barr		△	Donald McKenzie (1)	29)	△
William Bell		△	Donald McKenzie (2)	29)	△
William Bennett		△	Kenneth McKenzie		△
Aleander Brown		△	Thomas McLea		△
Henry Brown		△	Peter McNabb	30)	△
John Buchanan	17)	△	Robert Meek		△
Thomas Calder		△	John Meldrum		△
David Campbell		△	William Munro	31)	△
John Campbell		△	William Murray		△
Peter Campbell		△	William Mutch		△
James Clarke	18)	△	Robert Nathaniel		△
Terence Cleary		△	Daniel Neal		△
William Collier		△	John Niddire	32)	△
Adam Colquhoun	(R)	△	John Niven		△
Robert Colston		△	William Rae		△
William Crabb		△	James Reekie		△
Alexander Cunnison		△	Matthew Ridden	33)	△
John Donaldson	(P)	△	George Ritchie		△
John Donat	19)	△	William Ritchie		△
John Duncan		△	John Robertson	34)	△
James Farquharson		△	Donald Ross		△
Alexander Fife		△	John Sinclair		△
John Finlay	20)	△	John Sloan		△
Alexander Fraser		△	Alexander Smith		△
William Gilligan		△	Andrew Smith		△
John Grant	21)	△	Thomas Sommerville		△
James Gray	22)	△	Thomas Steele		△
Alexander Grieve		△	James Stewart (1)	35)	△
Robert Hanna		△	James Stewart (2)	35)	△
David Harrower		△	Roderick Stewart		△
John Henry		△	Ralph Stonehouse		△
Henry Hobson		△	Charles Strachan		△
Alexander Hyde		△	Alexander Sutherland		△
Thomas Hyndman		△	Peter Taylor		△
Thomas Jones		△	George Thompson	36)	△
Andrew King		△	Graham Thompson	37)	△
William King	23)	△	John Thompson	38)	△
William Kirk	24)	△	John Walker (1)	39)	△
John Kirkwood		△	John Walker (2)	39)	△
John Laing	25) (R)	△	James Walsh		△
John Lorimer		△	John White		△
High Love	13)	△	William Wilkie		△
Maxwell Lyon		△	Thomas Williamson		△
William Marshall		△	William Williamson		△
Donald McBean		△	Edward Wilsenham	40)	△
Alexander McCombie		△	Samuel Woods		△
James McCullum		△			
Alexander McDonald		△			

△ = campaign qualification as WO/100/17.

72ND (THE DUKE OF ALBANY'S OWN HIGHLANDERS) REGIMENT NOTES

1 Commanded the regiment throughout the 1st campaign; see Godlonton.
2 Engaged in the operations against Hintza during April and in the expedition to the Buffalo in June. See Godlonton.
3 Commandant at Fort Willshire in February and March 1835; engaged in the operations of June and July and along the Keiskamma during August. See Godlonton.
4 See Godlonton.
5 Employed in the operations of June and July 1835. See Godlonton.
6 Ricks was not a regular soldier. Following the custom of the time he was a civilian musician, appointed Bandmaster by the officers of the regiment and maintained by them. Most highly thought of, he served the regiment from 1829 to 1855 and was the only Bandmaster to receive a medal.
7 Twice on Roll, once as a private. The latter medal is in a private collection.
8 No 66, Frazer on Roll. Was attached to CMR as a hospital sergeant.
9 No 146 and Grey on Rolls; he was discharged at the Cape and may have served in the 2nd war as a volunteer. Not to be confused with Pte James Gray No 407 who returned home with the regiment in 1840.
10 Medal believed not to show rank.

11. Three men of this name served with the regiment but it is likely the recipient was No 293.
12. Schoolmaster Sergeant.
13. Wrongly shown on Roll as qualified for 1846–7.
14. Ramsey on Roll.
15. Spiers on Roll.
16. Two men of this name appear on the musters, Nos 95 and 632.
17. Two men of this name appear on the musters, Nos. 172 and 213.
18. No 766.
19. Douat on Roll.
20. Finley on Roll.
21. Two men of this name appear on the musters, Nos 315 and 660.
22. No 407 and not to be confused with Sgt J. Gray.
23. 'Dead' on Roll. Medal to widow.
24. No 498 and twice shown on Roll.
25. Medal said to show Lang.
26. Two men of this name appear on the musters, Nos 265 and 320.
27. Mackintosh on Roll.
28. McKey on Roll.
29. Nos 206 and 386.
30. No christian name is given on the Roll.
31. Two men of this name appear on the musters, Nos 214 and 743.
32. Niddry on Roll.
33. Reddin on Roll.
34. Two men of this name appear on the musters, Nos 257 and 485.
35. Nos 312 and 456.
36. No 694.
37. No 718.
38. Two men of this name appear on the musters, Nos 514 and 618.
39. Nos 474 and 555.
40. Wilsonham on Roll.

PRO References: WO/12/7948–7949–7954.

73rd Regiment

The six service companies of the regiment embarked at Cork for the Cape in October 1845 but were diverted to South America and saw action against the Argentinians at Monte Video before eventually reaching the mouth of the Great Fish River on August 30th 1846. Their transport, the 'Apollo', was nearly wrecked during a storm but the 73rd finally landed at Port Elizabeth and marched to Grahams Town. The regiment was assigned to Somerset's 2nd Division encamped near the Kei, which, towards the end of the year, operated against Pato. The British forces failed to gather up the chief in their encircling movement and so moved on to Butterworth. There they liberated several thousand Fingoes and attempted to draw chief Kreili into battle but the Kaffirs melted away, leaving some 10,000 stolen cattle to be returned to King William's Town.

Huts were set up for the regiment near the Buffalo in May 1847 and the men constructed a post named Fort Glamorgan, which eventually became East London. Routine patrolling brought little excitement as forward posts were pushed into the Amatolas and the regiment was scattered at Fort White, Fort Grey and Needs Camp. The troops prepared for a drive against Sandili but when that came in September the bird had flown; however, he and his sub chiefs were wearying of the struggle and it was not long before for they surrendered, leaving only Pato in rebellion west of the Kei. It was in these final operations that the 73rd suffered its heaviest loss. The fighting was not severe but on November 13th a small, foolhardy party of officers – four of them from the regiment – went off unescorted, were surrounded and killed.

Shortly after peace had been restored, as far as it ever was on the frontier in those turbulent days, the 73rd found itself in Natal and was quartered here for nearly a year before moving to Cape Town. No doubt garrison soldiering came strangely to men who had been adapting to the demands of frontier warfare. Fortunately their officers had not ignored the need for specialised tactics and when the Kaffirs again broke out towards the close of 1850 Sir Harry Smith must have been thankful to have a tried and soundly taught regiment at his disposal.

The Governor sailed for the frontier in the 'Hermes' on December 5th, accompanied by the 73rd; four days later they landed at the Buffalo mouth and were soon at King William's Town. A detachment of the regiment was with MacKinnon's column when it marched against Sandili and Col Eyre commanded the force ordered to block off a way of escape across the Kei, but on Christmas Eve MacKinnon was caught in Boomah Pass and among the casualties a corporal of the 73rd was killed and two men wounded. Five companies of the regiment formed the backbone of MacKinnon's force which in mid-February 1852 relieved Fort White and drove on to Fort Hare to provide reinforcements for Somerset. Carrying the war to the territory of chiefs Botman, Kona and Tola the 73rd in particular was heavily engaged and although they inflicted severe casualties the British force lost 25 men killed and wounded.

Concentrating on the country of Seyolo, two companies of the regiment were again in the field under MacKinnon later in the month while Eyre commanded a smaller patrol with three companies who, for a shorter time, combined in the same operation. A private of the 73rd was among those killed in escorting supplies to Fort Cox and Fort White in March and on the 13th, when desertion became rife in the ranks of the CMR the 73rd and 6th were lined up on the flanks of the disaffected men while the Hottentot element of the Cape Mounted was disarmed and dismissed.

On April 15th MacKinnon and Eyre struck at chief Stock and met strong resistance in a number of skirmishes. Some 150 Kaffirs were killed but the 73rd lost an officer and five men. The larger operation into the Amatolas during June employed 400 of the regiment in a mixed force but only one man was wounded. By August the 73rd had been so continuously employed that in a General Order, Sir Harry Smith recorded the regiment had marched 2,838 miles, but there was still plenty of work ahead. The majority of the regiment was despatched to Bathurst for the defence of Albany and Grahams Town, while a detachment operated at Committys Heights and in the Fish River Bush. In December one wing was engaged in the Amatolas and the other under Eyre forced the Kei when going to the relief of Fort Butterworth. The Kaffirs had built stone breastworks on the farther bank of the river to resist the crossing but the grenadier company got over higher up and took the enemy on the flank killing 40 of them.

By now the British forces were considerably strengthened by fresh regiments and the 73rd was allowed some time to recoup its strength. Two officers and 55 men sent as reinforcements were lost with the 'Birkenhead' in February 1852 but the 73rd was employed under Eyre during June, and on the 19th stormed a strong Kaffir position in the mountains which are the source of the Buffalo. Next month Cathcart moved into the Waterkloof with three columns and a detachment of the regiment was among those which scaled Fullers Hoek. Having participated in the earliest engagements of the 3rd war the 73rd now joined with the forces which finally subdued Macomo and cleared the Waterkloof, putting to an end all major resistance.

With the exception that is of Mosesh and his Basutos and in November the 73rd marched with Cathcart's force into the Orange River territory. Col Eyre commanded the 2nd Infantry Brigade and at Berea on December 18th the regiment lost one officer and three men killed.

		Kaffir Wars		
		1	2	3
LIEUTENANT COLONEL				
William Eyre	1)			△
C. Jowett Van der Meulen			△	
MAJOR				
Frederick G. A. Pinckney	2)		△	△
George Smith	3)		△	
BREVET MAJOR				
Wyndham E. Bewes	4) (P)		△	△

		Kaffir Wars		
		1	2	3
CAPTAIN				
Philip B. Bicknell			△	
Godfrey Burne				△
Robert Campbell	5)			△
Charles W. Combe	(P)		△	
Christopher Harrison				△
Alfred C. Knox	6)		△	△
Charles Littlehales				△
Maurice C. O'Connell	(P)			△

96 South Africa 1853 Medal

Name	Note	Kaffir Wars 1	2	3
CAPTAIN				
George Renny	118) (P)			△
LIEUTENANT				
Francis Amiel				△
James W. Barnes	7)		△	△
George Davies				△
Edward Evans	(P)			△
John C. Gawler	8) (M)			△
Samuel N. Hall		△	O	
Charles Houghton		△		
Gould A. Lucas	9)			△
Hugh McKenzie				△
Hugh C. Owen		△		
William Peto	(P)	△		
Frederick Reeve	10)			△
Poole F. Shuldham	11) (R)			O
John J. L. Williams				△
ENSIGN				
Richard M. Hickson	12)	△		
PAYMASTER				
John T. Cochrane	(P)			△
QUARTERMASTER				
John Carson		△	△	
SURGEON				
Edward Booth				△
ASSISTANT SURGEON				
William Hodgson		△		
Wellington W. Poole	13)			△
SERGEANT MAJOR				
Francis Rennie		△		
William Rennie	14)	△	△	
J. Gortley Scott		△		
ACTING SERGEANT MAJOR				
William Bayley	15)	△		
QUARTERMASTER SERGEANT				
William Darling		O	△	
John B. Roberts		△		
COLOUR SERGEANT				
James S. Barson		O	△	
Thomas Cosslet		O	△	
James Donnelly		△		
James Fitzgerald	(P)	O	△	
James Holiham		O	△	
James McGlashen		O	△	
Hugh McKay		△		
George Morrison		△	△	
Alexander Rennie		O	△	
Thomas Rowland		O	△	
Alexander Stupart		△		
DRUM MAJOR				
William Conway	117) (P)	O	△	
John Young		△	△	
ARMOURER SERGEANT				
Eyre Hare		O	△	
HOSPITAL SERGEANT				
John Brown	16)	O	△	
ORC SERGEANT				
Henry Burgess	(P)	O	△	
SERGEANT				
Swayne Atkinson		O	△	
Reuben Bird	(MRM)	O	△	
Thomas Bishop		O	△	
David Bromage	17)		O	△
Samuel Bromwich	17)		O	△
William H. Buchanan			O	△
James Darvill			O	△
Hope Duff	112) (P)		△	△
John Flannagan	18)		O	△
William Harris				△
James Hickey			O	△
Thomas Hutchinson			△	△
Thomas Irwin				△
Elias Jones			O	△
William Ketchin	19)		△	△
Bernard Kilkeary	20)			△
Peter Martin			O	△
Alexander McQuarry	21)		O	△
John Murtaugh	22)		O	△
James Norrie			O	△
Matthew Pegler			O	△
Samuel M. Pegler			△	△
Charles Roberts	23) (P)			△
Edward Robins	(P)		O	△
James Rogers	(R)		△	O
William Rowland				△
Dermot Shaughnessy				△
George Shooter	24)		O	△
William Small	25)		△	△
Robert Smith	(P)		O	△
Henry Stafford			O	△
William Walker	(P)		△	
John Ward			O	△
Thomas Watson	(M)		O	△
CORPORAL				
James Arnold			O	△
William Ashfield			O	△
John Carr			O	△
John Connor				△
Patrick Cudihy	26)			△
John Daly	27)		O	△
John Dumbreck			O	△
John Freebairn	(MRM)		O	△
James Gage			O	△
William Garlick			O	△
John Graham			O	△
Terence Green	(MRM)		△	△
Andrew Hallicy			O	△
George Hatch			O	△
John Hawkes			O	△
Daniel Jones				△
John Jordan	28) (MRM)			△
George Lucas			O	△
James McMasters			O	△
Patrick McMenomin	29)		△	△
John Oriel				△
Frederick Perry				△
William Pouldon			O	△
James Powell			O	△
James Robinson			O	△
Matthew Ryan				△
Michael Ryan				△
Herbert Sanderson			O	△
Robert Shaw				△
Alexander Smith				△
Robert Swayne			O	△
John Trydell	30)		△	△
Francis Warman				△
Robert Whitby				△
Samuel Williams				△

South Africa 1853 Medal

Rank/Name	Note	Kaffir Wars 1	2	3
DRUMMER				
John Bennett	31)		O	△
John Best			O	△
William Burke				△
William Coney			O	△
William Flynn	32)		O	△
James Herlihey	33)			△
Amos H. Joice			O	△
George Lever				△
John Murphy			△	△
John Scivier			O	△
John Stretton			O	△
John H. Vicars			O	△
PRIVATE				
George Adby				△
Timothy Ahern				△
James Allen			O	△
Anthony Allibone				△
Charles Ambrose	(P)		O	△
Charles Anderson			O	△
John Anderson	34)			△
John Anderton	35)		△	△
Thomas Archer	(P)		O	△
William Arnold	(P)		O	△
James Bailey			△	△
Richard Bailey			O	△
William Baker				△
James Ball			O	△
John Ballance				△
James Banks			O	△
John Barnett	(MRM)		O	△
Thomas Barry				△
Thomas Bateman			O	△
William Bateman	(P)			△
Robert Beesley				△
John Bettington	(MRM)		O	△
Abraham Bew			△	△
William Bingham			O	△
George Bird				△
Michael Bird				△
John Blackist			O	△
Andrew Bligh			O	△
Alexander Bolton			△	
William Bond			O	△
William Boole			△	△
John Booth			O	△
Samuel Bottoms	36)		O	△
Thomas Bouchier				△
Michael Bourke			△	
William Bowden				△
John Boyde			O	△
William Brazier	(P)		O	△
Thomas Breeas	37)		△	△
William Britton	38)		O	△
George Brocklehurst				△
James Brooker	(MRM)			△
John Browett			O	△
William Brown (1)	39)		O	△
William Brown (2)	39)		O	△
John Buckley				△
James Burke	40)			△
John Burke	41)		O	△
William Burke	42)			△
Patrick Burne				△
George Burnett			△	△
Martin Burns	43)			△
Henry Burrowes	44)		O	△
Thomas Burton			O	△
John Butcher			O	△
John Byrne	45)		O	△
Thomas Byrne			O	△
John Byrnes	46)			△
Matthew Callaghan	47)		O	△
Joseph Campbell	47)			△
Michael Campbell				△
William Campbell			△	△
Samuel Candler			△	O
Charles Cannon			O	△
John Carey				△
Thomas Cargill			O	△
Patrick Carroll	47)			△
Samuel Carson			△	△
John Casey			O	△
Thomas Cash	48)			△
Patrick Cassidy			O	△
Christopher Clarke				△
William Cloves			△	△
Michael Clune			O	△
William Coates			O	△
William Cock			O	△
James Cody	(R)			
Patrick Collevan	(R)		△	△
John Collins				△
Patrick Collins				△
Robert Coney			O	△
Patrick Conlon	49)		O	△
Nicholas Connolly			O	△
James Connors			O	△
Jeremiah Conway			O	△
John Conway	113)		△	O
William Coonan				△
Timothy Cooper	47)			△
John Corcorane				△
Ezekial Corder			O	△
John Corrigan			O	O
William Corrigan	50)			
John Cox	(MRM)		O	△
John Coyne			O	△
John Crawforth			O	
Richard Creedon				△
George Croft	47)			
Joseph Croft			O	△
Lot Cullinan			O	△
Patrick Cusack				△
Richard Dafter			O	△
Peter Dally				△
Henry Daniells			O	△
Nicholas Darsey				△
Thomas Dash	(R)		O	△
Robert H. Dashwood			O	△
Morris Davies			O	△
Manus Day			O	△
William C. Dennis			O	△
Thomas Devane			O	△
John Devitt			O	△
Richard Dickson	51)			△
John Dinan			O	△
James Dobson	52)		O	△
James Donaldson			O	△
John Donohue	53)			△
Thomas Donohue	53)			△
James Doran				△
James Doyle			O	△
Michael Doyle				△
Thomas Drinkwater			O	△

98 South Africa 1853 Medal

		Kaffir Wars 1 2 3
PRIVATE		
Patrick Duffy		△
William Dynan		○ △
John Early		△
David Edwards		○ △
George Edwards		○ △
John Elliott	(R)	○ △
Thomas Elwart		○ △
John Enwright		○ △
Charles Evans	54)	○ △
Edmund Evans	54)	△
Thomas Exell		○ △
Christopher Fearnley	(R)	△ △
Joshua Fell		○ △
Patrick Fenaughty		△
John Finch		△
William Finlay	55)	△ △
John Fisher		○ △
Michael Fitzgerald	56)	○
Thomas Fitzgerald		△
James Fitzpatrick (1)	57)	△ △
James Fitzpatrick (2)	58)	
Joseph Flanagan		△ △
Michael Flanagan		△
Cornelius Fleming	59)	△
Richard Fletcher	(P)	○ △
Thomas Foley		△
James Friend		△
Henry Funnell		△ △
Charles Garrett	(MRM)	○ △
George Gaten		△
Thomas Gibbons	60)	○ △
John P. Gilbert		○ △
Thomas Gill		△
Hugh Gillmore		△
Richard Gobell	(P)	○ △
Thomas Gordon		△
William Gracey		○ △
Patrick Green	9)	△
Robert Greenwood		○ △
William Halfpenny	61)	△
John Hall		△
Richard Hall		○ △
Patrick Halloran		○ △
Michael Hannon	62)	○
Dennis Hare		○ △
John Hare		△
Daniel Hardy		○ △
Thomas Hartrope	63) (MRM)	○ △
James Haughey		○ △
Frederick Hawkins		△ △
William Hawkins	(P)	○ △
Patrick Hayes		△
Charles Hayman		△ △
Edward Hazlehurst	64)	○ △
Daniel Heavey		○ △
William J. Henley		△ △
James Hennessy		△
Joseph Henry		○ △
Michael Herlihey		△
Patrick Herrick		△
William Hezlehurst	65)	○ △
William Higgins		△
Charles Hill		△ △
Thomas Hill		○ △
William Hilliard		○ △
Joseph Hoddoway		○ △
Edward Hogan (1)	66)	○ △

		Kaffir Wars 1 2 3
Edward Hogan (2)	66)	△
Patrick Hogan		△
Edward Holihan		△
James Holihan	67)	△
John Holihan		○ △
George Holton		○ △
William Hooker		○ △
John Hopkins		
James Hopper		○ △
James Horan		○ △
John Hoskin		△ △
Michael Howley		△
Henry Huntley		○ △
John Ibbett		△
James Ilsley	(R)	○ △
Joseph Ingram		○ △
James Irwin		○ △
James Jackman		○ △
William James		△ △
Cornelius J. Joice		△
William Jones		○ △
John Jordon		○ △
Patrick Jordon		△
James Kedwell		△
Daniel Kelliher	68) (MRM)	△
John Kelly		○ △
John Kent		○ △
Michael Kerr		○ △
James Kerry		○ △
John Kildea		△
Michael King		○ △
George Knott		○ △
Stephen Lacey		△
Frederick Ladds		○ △
George Lane	69)	○ △
Frederick Lawes	70)	○ △
Robert Lawrence		△
John Lawrie	71)	△ △
Michael Leary		○ △
James Legate		△
Edward Lester	72)	○
John Lewin		△
Patrick Lewin	114) (P)	△
Richard Lewis		○ △
John Lindsay		○ △
John Lines		○ △
Henry Loal		○ △
Peter Lock		○ △
John Lockhart		△ ○
Abraham Lockwood		○ △
William Longstaff	73)	○ △
Samuel Lord	(MRM)	△
John Lough		△
Brian Loughrinn		△
William Lunnon		○ △
George Lye		○ △
James Lynch		△ △
Patrick Lynch	74)	△
John Maddagan		△
Patrick Maddigan		△
Daniel Mahoney		
John Malone		△ ○
Daniel Maloney	75) (MRM)	△
Patrick Maloney		○ △
William Manley	76)	○ △
James Martin		○ △
Michael Martin		△
Alexander Mathieson	77)	○ △

South Africa 1853 Medal

Name	Ref	Note	Kaffir Wars 1	Kaffir Wars 2	Kaffir Wars 3
Patrick May	78)				△
John Mayes					△
John McCann					△
Daniel McCarthy (1)	79)				△
Daniel McCarthy (2)	79)				△
Thomas McCombe	80)				△
Alexander McDonald				O	△
Peter McGlashen				△	O
John McGrath					△
Michael McGrath	81)				△
John McGrigor				O	△
Patrick McKearney				O	△
James McKinlay	82)				△
Robert McKinlay				O	△
William McLean				O	△
James McMahon (1)	83)			O	△
James McMahon (2)	83)				△
Bernard McNally					△
John McNally					△
Dennis McNamara					△
Thomas McNamara	84)				O
Martin McTigue	85)	(MRM)			△
George Merchant					△
Stephen Miles				△	O
John Miller				△	△
William Mills				O	△
Alexander Milne		(M)		O	△
George Mitchell				O	△
Samuel Moffatt				O	△
John Mongavon					△
James Moore				O	△
Peter Moore		(MRM)		O	△
John Moran					△
Patrick Moran (1)	86)				△
Patrick Moran (2)	86)				△
John Morgan				O	△
Samuel Morgan				O	△
William Morgan	87)				△
William J. Morwood		(MRM)		O	△
Malcolm Muirhead				O	△
Michael Mulloy	88)				△
David Munger	89)			O	△
Daniel Murnane	90)				△
Patrick Murphy	91)				△
John Murray				O	△
Patrick Murray				O	△
Thomas Musgrave				△	
George Muspratt				O	△
James Neal				△	O
Robert Neal					△
James Newton				O	△
Thomas Nolan	92)				△
Anthony Norman					△
Edmund O'Brien	93)			O	△
James O'Brien				O	△
Martin O'Brien	94)			O	△
Thomas O'Brien					△
Matthew O'Connor				O	△
William O'Donohoe		(MRM)		O	△
John O'Grady					△
Patrick O'Reilly	9)				△
James Page				O	△
Robert Parfeet	95)			O	△
Patrick Parker		(MRM)			△
John Parkinson				O	△
John Payne		(P)		△	△
Robert Payne		(P)		O	△
George Peate					△
George Penrose				O	△
Robert Pettitt				O	△
John Popple					△
Thomas Powell				O	△
Michael Prendergast					△
Richard Proudley				O	△
Charles Prosser					△
John Quill					△
William Quilter		(MRM)			△
Richard Rawley		(MRM)			△
William Renny				O	△
Michael Reynolds				O	△
John Rice					△
John Rich				O	△
Richard Richards					△
David Riley	96)				△
Rimmy Roach					△
Meredith Roberts		(P)		O	△
John Rooney					△
Edward Rorke				O	△
Patrick Ryan	97)			O	△
William Salsbury					△
Henry Salt					△
Robert Saunders				△	△
James Scannell					△
Jesse Seymour				O	△
John Shanahan					△
Peter Shannon				O	△
James Sharkey		(MRM)		O	△
Daniel Sheehan					△
Michael Shruan				△	△
George Shuttle					△
Charles Simms	98)	(R)		O	△
George Simms	99)	(P)		O	△
Thomas Sinclair				O	△
William Sinnott				O	△
Michael Slattery				O	△
David Smith				△	△
George Smith		(MRM)			△
Henry Smith				O	△
John Smith (1)	100)			O	△
John Smith (2)	101)			O	△
William Snell					△
Charles Soper					△
George Sparkman				O	△
Charles Spier				O	△
John Steel				O	△
William Steel				△	△
James Stewart					△
Robert Stewart				O	△
Philip Stockdale		(MRM)		O	△
Noah Stoneham	102)			△	△
Daniel Sullivan	103)				△
John Sullivan	104)				△
Murtey Sullivan					△
Patrick Sullivan					△
Timothy Sullivan					△
David Swarton				O	△
Thomas Sweeney				O	△
William Swonson				O	△
Benjamin Taylor				O	△
Patrick Taylor	105)				△
William Thomas	106)			O	△
Alexander Thompson					△
William Thompson		(MRM)		O	△
Israel Thorndyke		(P)			△
Jeremiah Thorndyke		(P)		O	△
John Tilley				O	△

100 South Africa 1853 Medal

		Kaffir Wars					Kaffir Wars		
PRIVATE		1	2	3			1	2	3
John Trendall			○	△	John Watt			○	△
John Trowell	107)		○		Daniel Weadock				△
Josiah Trump	108)			△	William West			△	△
James Trydell	76)		○	△	James White			○	△
Adam Turnbull				△	Patrick White				△
Edward Turner			○	△	James Wilgram			○	△
John Turner				△	Frederick Williams			○	△
David Vincent				△	John Williams			○	△
David Viney			○	△	Joseph Williams	100) (P)			△
Godfrey Walker			△		Frederick Williamson	76)		○	△
James Wallace	109)		○		Frederick Wilson				△
John Wallace				△	John Wilson	111)		○	△
John Walsh	76)			△	Henry Wiltshire	116) (P)		○	△
Joseph Walsh			○	△	William Witham			△	△
Thomas Walsh	115) (P)			△	Joseph Wood			○	△
George Walton				△	Samuel Woolcott			○	△
William Ward			○	△	Isaac Wright	(MRM)			△
John Waterman			○	△	John Wright			○	△
James S. Waters			○	△					
Thomas Watkinson			△	○	△ = campaign qualification as WO/100/17.				
Aaron Watson			○	△	○ = campaign which the Rolls fail to credit.				

73RD REGIMENT NOTES

1 Divisional Commander.
2 See Moodie.
3 Wounded, April 1847.
4 Served with the 45th during the 2nd campaign; see G and I; Moodie.
5 Took part in the Trans-Kei expedition and operations in the Waterkloof, October 1851, March and September, 1852.
6 At Berea.
7 Served with the native levies during the 2nd campaign, accompanying the expedition into Tambookie country in August 1846.
8 Commanded the Light Company in all the principal actions and was at Berea. At different times served as Field Adjutant and DAQMG to the divisions under Eyre. See King.
9 A survivor from the 'Birkenhead'.
10 Twice returned, once wrongly as Captain, and may have received two medals.
11 Not on Roll although musters confirm qualification.
12 Roll wrongly shows initials as B.M.
13 Staff Asst Surgeon before being appointed to the 73rd in January 1853.
14 Later an Ensign and listed among officers on Roll.
15 Later received a commission. Musters also show Bailey.
16 No. 1792.
17 These two men were the bane of orderly room clerks, David Bromage is given as Bromwich on Roll, but never on musters. Samuel Bromwich is correctly named on Roll but occasionally given as Bromage on musters.
18 Also Flanagan on musters.
19 Kitchen on Roll.
20 No 2740, a survivor from the 'Birkenhead'.
21 Also McQuarrie on musters; McQuerrie on Roll
22 Murtough on Roll.
23 No 2221; wounded in the face 17.4.51.
24 Shorter on Roll.
25 A staff officer's servant who travelled home to England with Sir Harry Smith in 1852.
26 Cuddihy on Roll.
27 Also Daley on musters.
28 No 2133.
29 McMenomie on Roll.
30 No 978.
31 No 1786; appears twice on Roll, once as a private, credited with 1846–7 only.
32 Flinn on Roll.
33 Herlehy on Roll.
34 No 979.
35 No 790; received a re-named replacement in 1858.
36 Died; medal returned.
37 Brias on Roll.
38 Shown as Button on the 'Black Watch Medal Roll'.
39 Nos 1663 and 1665.
40 No 2574.
41 No 2214.
42 No 2828, a survivor from the 'Birkenhead'.
43 Dead: medal returned.
44 Burrows on Roll.
45 No 2198.
46 No 2242.
47 The careless use of ditto symbols on the Roll has led to these men being wrongly identified as drummers.
48 No 2754, a survivor from the 'Birkenhead'.
49 Conlan on Roll.
50 Carrigan on Roll.
51 Dixon on Roll.
52 No 2210.
53 Donoghue on Roll.
54 Evens on Roll.
55 Finley on Roll.
56 Roll wrongly credits 1846–7.
57 No 812; given a re-named replacement after the War Office lost the original.
58 No 2839, a survivor from the 'Birkenhead'.
59 Flemming on Roll.
60 Gibbens on Roll.
61 No 2810, a survivor from the 'Birkenhead'.
62 Hannen on Roll.
63 Harteope on Roll.
64 Haslehurst on Roll.
65 Hazlehurst on Roll but consistently Hezlehurst on musters.
66 Nos 1210 and 2351.
67 Hoolihan on Roll.
68 Keliher on Roll.
69 Dead; medal returned.
70 Also Laws on musters.
71 Lowrie on Roll.
72 Wrongly credited with 1850–3 on Roll.
73 Lingstaff on Roll.
74 No 2564, a survivor from the 'Birkenhead'.
75 No 2698, a survivor from the 'Birkenhead'.
76 'Dead' on Roll, medal returned.
77 Matheson on Roll; variously spelt on musters.
78 No 2845, a survivor from the 'Birkenhead'.
79 Nos 2390 and 2416; one of these medals was returned to the Mint.
80 Also McCoombe on musters.
81 No 2792.
82 McKinley on Roll.
83 Nos 1254 and 2480.
84 No 2582; wrongly credited with 1846–7 on Roll.
85 Easily mis-read as McSigne as is shown on the 'Black Watch Medal Roll'. The Mint also misconstrued the returns and perhaps because the regiment could not trace a soldier of that name the medal was returned to the Mint.
86 Nos 2512 and 2639.
87 No 2035.
88 Molloy on Roll.
89 Mungar on Roll.

90 Murnance on Roll and shown as 'dead'.
91 May have received two medals as he was also returned by the CMR to whom he transferred.
92 Nolon on Roll.
93 Christian name given as Edward on the 'Black Watch Medal Roll'.
94 O'Bryan on Roll. Mint records show a replacement (?) issued on 5.2.61 'at the expense of Col Smith'.
95 Parfett on Roll.
96 Riley earned and was awarded a medal with the 91st Regiment, but Mint records show another was issued on 5.2.61 'at the expense of Col Smith'.
97 No 1191.
98 Sims on Roll; both spellings on musters.
99 Also Sims on musters.
100 No 1401.
101 No 2799; served with the 6th Regiment during the 1846–7 campaign.
102 Twice recorded on the same page in the Roll.
103 No 2337, a survivor from the 'Birkenhead'.
104 No 2831, a survivor from the 'Birkenhead'.
105 No 2812, a survivor from the 'Birkenhead'.
106 No 1965.
107 Wrongly credited with 1846–7 only on Roll.
108 Medal sent to his widow.
109 Not on Roll, but Mint records show medal applied for 22.3.64.
110 No 2248.
111 No 1860.
112 No 870; appointed Hospital Sergeant, 29.11.45.
113 No 1903.
114 No 60.
115 No 2807.
116 No 2039.
117 No 1140.
118 Served in the operations in the Amatolas, Fish River, Waterkloof and Trans-Kei expeditions. Wounded at Keiskamma 16.4.51. Commanded the advance guard at the passage of the Kei 3.12.51.

Note: – An Alexander Irwin is shown on the Roll and repeated in the 'Black Watch Medal Roll', but he does not appear on the musters, and a medal reference against his name makes it clear that Irwin was a soldier of the 60th Rifles.

PRO References: WO/12/8028–8029–8033–8034–8035.

74th (Highland) Regiment

After passing through some very heavy weather on their voyage from Queens Town the 74th Highlanders arrived safely at Algoa Bay in March 1851.

Marching to Grahams Town the regiment was re-equipped with canvas blouses, leather peaked forage caps, lightweight pouches and veldtshoen instead of boots. Only trews remained of regulation issue and because of a similarity between the Lamont tartan and tortoiseshell colouring the Kaffirs called the men of the 74th 'the tortoises', a name they grew to like. Consequently, the regiment began its campaigning more suitably equipped from the outset for guerilla warfare than any other regular unit. Col Fordyce also practised his men in movements made to bugle calls and the opportunity to test these innovations came when the Highlanders were sent to deal with some deserters from the CMR and Fingo levies who had gathered at a missionary station 40 miles south of Grahams Town. It was an easy introduction to the field for the dissidents were quickly dispersed.

Hardly had the regiment returned to camp than it was ordered to take part in the Amatola operations during June. In assaulting Victoria Heights the 74th lost three men killed and several wounded, but the enemy, having been driven from the crest, took up the fight from the forest. Some days were spent scouring the bush before the British force retired from the scene and moved to Fort Hare. From here the regiment was promptly transferred to the Koonap River and on July 14th a detachment was sent against Macomo. Two men were lost in the subsequent operations which did little to curb Kaffir activities.

In September, Fordyce commanded a force of the 74th, CMR and Fingo levies to attack Macomo's stronghold on the western Kroome. The heights were scaled without difficulty but the enemy then gathered in such numbers they threatened to over-run the advanced guard of the 74th and it was decided to withdraw down the steep winding pass. As the troops descended along the narrow path Kaffirs swarmed from the thick forest and for a while it was every man for himself. Gradually, some order was restored from the confusion and the attackers suffered heavy losses before the regiment emerged from the bush at the foot of the pass. During the savage fighting the Highlanders lost 15 men and one officer killed and 14 men wounded; not the least lamented was their German bandmaster who was dragged off alive and cruelly tortured to death.

After retiring to camp at Reitfontein, patrolling was kept up until the regiment withdrew to recuperate at Fort Beaufort. Fordyce kept the troops occupied with his inevitable drilling and was given command of the 2nd Brigade when Somerset moved into the Waterkloof during October. For two weeks the troops were in the field without any covering from the heavy rains; subsisting on short rations they endured some hard marching and were ragged and often bare-footed. The continual skirmishing cost them a number of casualties before they went into camp on the Blinkwater – but their rest was short.

On November 4th the 74th returned to the mountains through the Blinkwater Pass and, upon reaching the head of the Waterkloof, came under fire. While leading an encircling movement, Fordyce was mortally wounded and, when the men showed some uncertainty about orders their colonel had been giving, the Kaffirs swept down upon the confused companies. But the troops rapidly recovered and some well-directed volleys drove the enemy back to the bush. During the engagement seven officers and men were killed in addition to Fordyce and six were badly wounded.

These operations temporarily cleared the Waterkloof and the Highlanders went into camp at Fort Retief before all but a company returned to Fort Beaufort. From here, Fort Hare and other smaller outposts patrolling was kept up during the winter of 1851–2, often with the purpose of crop destruction. Then came the dismal news that 50 officers and men of the 74th, among them Col Seaton, had been lost with the 'Birkenhead'. Only 18 of the regiment's reinforcements survived.

In March 1852 troops were assembled for another drive into the Waterkloof. The 74th, 91st, a detachment of CMR and some levies formed the 1st Division and in the subsequent sweep the Highlanders lost eight men killed and wounded. The effects of the operation were no more decisive than those which preceded it and by July it became necessary to again launch an attack on the mountains. This time the troops scoured parts of the bush not previously explored and a detachment of the 74th joined with the 43rd and 73rd in the assault on Fullers Hoek. Yet it was not until October that resistance in the Waterkloof was finally subdued by an expedition which included part of the 74th.

In November the regiment accompanied Cathcart's force which marched into Basutoland; being placed in the 1st Brigade. Following the failure of negotiations with Mosesh the 2nd Brigade, with two companies of the 74th, advanced on the Berea mountains. After the British cavalry had gathered up Basuto cattle the Highlanders played a big part in repulsing the desperate attempts which were made to recapture them.

By mid-January 1853 the regiment was back at Fort Beaufort and for most of the year was stationed there, until in November they set forth for India.

		Kaffir Wars 1	2	3
LIEUTENANT COLONEL				
John McDuff	1)			△
MAJOR				
George W. Fordyce	2)			△
George Monkland	2)			△
Walter D. P. Patton	2)			△
CAPTAIN				
Robert Bruce	2)			△
Lewis A. Brydon	2)			△
James Duff	2)			△
William F. L. Hancock	2)			△
William Ross King	3)			△
Henry W. Palmer				△
LIEUTENANT				
Sir David Baird	2)			△
William W. Bruce	4)			△
John J. Corrigan	5)			
James Falconer	2)			△

South Africa 1853 Medal

		Kaffir Wars 1	2	3
Thomas W. Lawson				△
Robert H. D. Lowe	2)			△
Philip Philpot	2)			△
Charles Sherlock				△
LIEUTENANT ADJUTANT				
Frederick Thackeray	2)			△
ENSIGN				
Anthony Bell	(R)			△
Robert Cathcart				△
Bedford Davies	6)			△
QUARTERMASTER				
Charles Daines				△
PAYMASTER				
Ferguson Dunbar	(R)			△
SURGEON				
James Alexander Fraser	7)		O	△
ASSISTANT SURGEON				
Arthur Bell	(P)			△
SERGEANT MAJOR				
George Watson				△
QUARTERMASTER SERGEANT				
James Davidson				△
George Johnston				△
COLOUR SERGEANT				
George Baskett				△
William Everleigh	2) (R)			△
John Glass				△
William Henderson	8) (MRM)			△
Thomas Matthews	9)			△
John McCabe	2)			△
Charles McLagan	2)			△
James Murray	2)			△
George B. Raleigh	2) (R)			△
Archibald Whimster	2)			△
DRUM MAJOR				
Samuel Young	10)			O
PIPE MAJOR				
William McKay				△
ARMOURER SERGEANT				
Robert McKenzie				△
HOSPITAL SERGEANT				
Joseph Cook	(P)			△
SERGEANT				
John Alexander				△
John Bryan	2)			△
Thomas Bryant				△
Alexander Burns				△
John Cleary	2)			△
William Doorley				△
James Duff	(R)			△
James Dunn				△
William Finnie				△
Robert Gillespie				△
Charles Gray				△
John Harrold	11)			△
John Lockheart	12)			△
Thomas Lowney				△
Robert MacNab				△
James MGuire				△
James McHarge	13)			△
David McIntyre	2)			△
John Miller				△
John Pook				△
James Quinlan	2)			△
Andrew Shand				△
James Stevenson	14)			△
John Stewart				△
CORPORAL				
Robert Allister				△
James Anderson				△
Edward Doonan				△
John Drummond				△
James Effingham	15)			△
James Elvin				△
Edward Evertaion	16)			△
James Galbraith				△
Edward Guirey				△
James Harley	2)			△
Robert Hartley	17)			△
James Henderson	17)			△
John Hill				△
Patrick Hynes				△
Thomas Inglis				△
Martin Kelly				△
George Kyd	18)			△
John Kyd	(P)			△
John Little				△
John Morrison				△
William Slater				△
Donald Smith				△
George Vincent	(MRM)			△
Jeremiah Vincent	(R)			△
James Whitelaw				△
DRUMMER				
Alexander Anderson				△
William Brown	19)			△
Douglas Chambers				△
Robert J. Harrison				△
Joseph Holbrook				△
John Nelson	20)			△
James Owens	(P)			△
PIPER				
David Clark				△
John Doran				△
George Wattie	(MRM)			△
PRIVATE				
Robert Adams				△
Edward Aden				△
John Affleck	21) (R)			△
James Aitken	22)			△
John Aitken	23)			△
David Anderson	(MRM)			△
Hugh Anderson				△
John Anderson				△
William Angus (1)	24)			△
William Angus (2)	24)			△
William Arlow	(MRM)			△
Archibald Armstrong	2)			△
John Armstrong				△
Thomas Armstrong				△
John Arnott	25) (MRM)			△
John Atkin				△
George Baird				△
John Barcley	26)			△
David Barr				△
John Barr	27)			△
George Bason	28)			△
Samuel Bear				△
John Beaton				△
William Beattie				△
James Begbie				△

South Africa 1853 Medal

		Kaffir Wars 1 2 3
PRIVATE		
Robert Bell		△
William Bell		△
Alexander Beveridge	(R)	△
Andrew Bishop	(P)	△
William Blackie		△
John Bone		△
James Bonner		△
Thomas Born		△
Alexander Bowden		△
Samuel Boyd		△
Walter Bray		△
George Brechin		△
Charles Brewer		△
John Brown	29) (R)	△
William Brown	30)	△
William Browning		△
Thomas Brunkard		△
James Brunton		△
Francis Buchanan		△
Christopher Burke	31)	△
Michael Burns	32)	△
William Byass	33) (MRM)	△
James Cairnes		△
Robert Caldwell		△
Dougald Cameron		△
William Cameron	(MRM)	△
James Campbell (1)	34)	△
James Campbell (2)	34)	△
John Campbell		△
Peter Campbell		△
Thomas Campbell		△
William Campbell		△
Duncan Carmichael		△
Cornelius Carroll	35) (R)	△
John Carson		△
Thomas Carson		△
Samuel Carter		△
Patrick Cassidy	(MRM)	△
Edward Cavan	2)	△
George Chalmers		△
Frederick Chapman		△
George Cherry		△
James Christie		△
William Christie		△
Bryan Christy	(R)	△
Hector Claugher	36)	O
William Clearkin		△
Thomas Cleary	36)	O
John Clements	36)	O
John Clindinning	36)	O
David Coghill	36)	△
John Comb	36)	△
Joseph Considine	36)	O
William Cook	36)	O
James Cooper		△
John Cooper		△
William Cooper	(R)	△
John Cope		△
John Cormiskey	37)	△
James Cornie	38)	△
Archibald Cowan		△
Henry Cowan		△
Patrick Coyle		△
Peter Craig		△
William Croome		△
James Curdie		△
Thomas Cunningham		△

		Kaffir Wars 1 2 3
Robert Dahms		△
Edmund Daly	39)	△
William Davis		△
Abraham Davidson		△
Alexander F. Davidson		△
Robert Davidson		△
John Dawson		△
James Devlin		△
Hugh Dick		△
James Divine		△
Peter Dixon		△
William D'Kinross	40)	△
Felix Donnely		△
Charles Dougherty		△
William Douglas	(MRM)	△
William Drummond	2) (MRM)	△
John Drysdale		△
Patrick Duffy		△
Thomas Duggan		△
Hugh Duncan		△
Edmund Dyer		△
William Dykes		△
John Edwards		△
William Edwards		△
John Eland		△
Alexander Elder		△
George Farr		△
Alexander Ferguson (1)	41)	△
Alexander Ferguson (2)	41)	△
Charles Ferguson	42) (R)	△
Matthew Ferguson		△
John Finlay		△
John Fisher		△
Edward Fitzpatrick		△
William Flannigan		△
Thomas Fletcher		△
Thomas Florence		△
Thomas Floyd		△
William Floyd		△
Arthur Forbes	(MRM)	△
Alexander Forrest		△
James Forsyth		△
William Frail		△
Henry France	2) (P)	△
John Francis		△
John Friend		△
Daniel Garraghty	43)	△
John Gayner	44)	△
Henry Gemmell	45)	△
John Geven	46)	△
John Gibbons	(R)	△
Thomas Gibbs		△
William Gibson		△
John Gilchrist		△
David Gilfillan		△
David Gilmour	47)	△
James Gilmour	48)	△
William Gilmour	49)	△
Edmund Gleeson		△
James Glendinning		△
George Goodall	(R)	△
Thomas C. Goodier		△
Robert Gordon		△
John Gorman		△
James Grafton		△
Alexander Grant		△
Samuel Grimes		△
David Gunn		△

South Africa 1853 Medal 105

		Kaffir Wars				Kaffir Wars
		1 2 3				1 2 3
John Guy	50)	△	John King			△
William Guy	50)	△	Henry Kinsley			△
James Hackett		△	David J. Kirkwood			△
William Hackett		△	George Kittlety			△
Hugh Haddan	51)	△	John Laing	67)		△
Alexander Haddock	(R)	△	Edward Lappin	68)		△
James D. Haines		△	John Latta			△
Hugh Hall	(P)	△	Edward Lee		(R)	△
John Halpin		△	Michael Leggett	69)		△
Andrew Hamilton		△	Ebenezer Leitch		(R)	△
James Hamilton		△	James Liddell			△
William Hamilton		△	James Lindsay	70)		△
Shadrach Hannam	52)	△	Henry Lithgow			△
Robert Harkins		△	Samuel Livicy	71)		△
William Harkness		△	Charles Long			△
Joseph Harper		△	Alex Lyttle			△
William Harper		△	William Mahagan			△
Edward Harrison		△	Robert Makin	72)		△
Robert Harvey		△	Thomas Mallett			△
Edward Hayes		△	Robert Manson	73)	(P)	△
Patrick Heffernon		△	James Marshall (1)	74)		△
Francis Henderson	(R)	△	James Marshall (2)	74)		△
George Henderson		△	John Marshall			△
James Henderson	53)	△	Thomas Marshall		(MRM)	△
John Henderson		△	Archibald Martin			△
William Henderson	54)	△	John Martin			△
John Hendry	55)	△	Peter Martin		(R)	△
Alexander Hill		△	Alexander Mathieson	75)		△
John Hill	56)	△	William Mathieson	75)		△
William Hinds		△	John McAusland			△
Thomas Hogbine	57) (MRM)	△	William McCabe			△
Charles Hogg		△	Archibald McCallum	76)	(MRM)	△
James Hogg	58)	△	David McCausland			△
Robert Horn		△	James McClelland			△
Charles Howell		△	Thomas McColl	77)		△
Bernard Hughes		△	John McCulloch			△
John Hughes		△	Archibald McDonald			△
Daniel Hurley		△	Donald McDonald			△
William Hurley		△	John McDonald			△
Lawrence Hutcheson		△	Dugald McDougald			△
John Hutton	(MRM)	△	Alexander McDougall			△
Samuel Irvine		△	Duncan McDougall			△
Ramsay Jack	59)	△	David McFarlane			△
John Jackson		△	Walter McFarlane		(R)	△
William Jackson		△	Archibald McFee			△
John James		△	Hector McFee		(R)	△
John Jenkins		△	Robert McFee			△
Francis Johnston		△	Frederick McGavan	78)		△
Philip Johnston	60) (R)	△	James McGough			△
Thomas Johnston		△	Felix McGready			△
William Johnston (1)	61)	△	David McGregor			△
William Johnston (2)	62)	△	George McGregor			△
John Jones		△	James McGregor	79)	(MRM)	△
William Jones		△	Peter McGregor			△
James Joss		△	Hugh McHardie			△
David Karrigan	2)	△	Donald McInnis			△
James Kay		△	James McInnis			△
John Kay		△	Donald McIntosh			△
John Keane	63)	△	Duncan McIntyre		(R)	△
William Keane	63) (MRM)	△	John McIntyre			△
John Kearns		△	James McKay (1)	80)		△
William Kearns		△	James McKay (2)	80)		△
John Keiley	64)	△	John McKechnie			△
James Keith		△	John McKenny			△
Festus Kelly		△	John McKenzie			△
John Kennedy		△	Michael McKever	81)	(MRM)	△
William Kerr	65) (P)	△	John McKie	82)		△
William Kevins	66)	△	John McKnight			△

106 South Africa 1853 Medal

		Kaffir Wars 1 2 3			Kaffir Wars 1 2 3
PRIVATE			Peter Porteous	(R)	△
Daniel McLaughlan		△	John Potter		△
James McLaughlan		△	Robert Prescott		△
John McLean		△	William Price		△
Donald McLeod		△	Michael Quinn		△
Hugh McLeod		△	John Ramsay	101)	△
Neil McLeod		△	George Randall		△
Torquil McLeod		△	Patrick Ready	(R)	△
Luke McManus		△	Matthew Reid		△
Thomas McMillan	83)	△	Lawrence Reilly	102)	△
Duncan McNab		△	Patrick Reilly	103)	△
Alexander McNeil		△	John Rennie		△
James McNeil		△	Solomon Roach		△
William McNeil		△	Thomas Roberts		△
Archibald McNevin	84)	△	James Robertson		△
Arthur McQueen		△	Walter Robertson		△
William McQueen	85)	O	Thomas Robinson		△
Hugh McQuetters	86)	O	William Ronald	104)	△
Hugh McTaggart		△	Alexander Ross		△
John McVicar		△	James Ross (1)	105)	△
John McWilliams		△	James Ross (2)	105)	△
James Miller		△	Alexander Russell		△
John Miller		△	Alexander Ryan		△
Joseph Miller		△	John Ryan		△
William Miller (1)	87)	△	Ralph Scott		△
William Miller (2)	87)	△	James Shankie		△
Alexander Milne (1)	88)	△	John Sharp	106)	△
Alexander Milne (2)	88)	△	David Shaw	107)	△
John Mitchell	(R)	△	Archibald Sinclair	(P)	△
William Mitchell		△	Robert Sinclair		△
William Moore	(MRM)	△	Joseph Skiffington		△
Alexander More	89)	△	David Skinner		△
James More	89)	△	James Slater		△
William Morris		△	Archibald Smith		△
Henry Morrison		△	James Smith (1)	108)	△
William Morrison		△	James Smith (2)	108)	△
Daniel Mulholland		△	James Smith (3)	108)	△
James Mullins		△	John Smith	109)	△
Dennis Murphy		△	Samuel Smith		△
John Murray		△	Stewart Smith	110)	O
William Murray		△	William Smith		△
James Nairne		△	George Soares		△
Archibald Nathaniel	90)	△	William Somerville		△
James Neagle	91)	△	John Souden	111) (MRM)	△
John Neilson	92)	△	Nathaniel Spence		△
Robert Neilson		△	Samuel Stacey		△
John Nelson	92)	△	Charles Starks	(P)	△
Thomas Niblock		△	John Steel		△
Donald Nicholson	93)	△	Charles Stevenson		△
William Nixon		△	Daniel Stevenson		△
John Nowlan	94)	△	John Stevenson		△
Peter O'Brien		△	Arthur Stewart	112)	△
John O'Hara	(MRM)	△	Charles Stewart (1)	113)	△
Patrick O'Neill	95)	△	Charles Stewart (2)	113)	△
William O'Reilly	96)	△	James Stewart		△
James Orrock (1)	97)	△	Thomas Stone	(R)	△
James Orrock (2)	97)	△	John Stuart		△
Joseph Park		△	Norman Stuart	114)	△
Robert Park		△	Robert Stuart	114)	△
Levi Parrot	98)	△	William Stuart	114)	△
Frederick Parslow		△	James Symington		△
John Patterson (1)	99)	△	George Tait		△
John Patterson (2)	99)	△	Jabez Tart		△
William Patterson		△	George Taylor	115)	△
James Peters	2)	△	James Taylor		△
Andrew Phillips (1)	100)	△	Walter Taylor	116)	△
Andrew Phillips (2)	100)	△	Thomas Templeton		△
James Pittendreigh		△	Andrew Thompson		△

South Africa 1853 Medal

Name	Ref	Kaffir Wars 1	2	3
David Thompson	(P)			△
Graham Thompson				△
James Thompson (1)	117)			△
James Thompson (2)	117)			△
John Thompson				△
Thomas Thompson				△
William Thompson	118)			△
William J. Thompson	119)			△
David Thorn				△
Michael Thorndell	120)			△
Henry Thornhill				△
Samuel Tibbey	121)			△
Edward Timmon	122)			△
Broome Tipples	(MRM)			△
William Trail				△
Patrick Trenor				△
William Troup	123)			△
John Turnbull				△
William Turnbull				△
William Ure				△
John Waddell	124)			△
Alexander Walker	125)			△
Angus Walker	125)			△
Charles Walker	126)			△
James Walker	(P)			△
William Wallace				△
James Ward				△

Name	Ref	Kaffir Wars 1	2	3
John Watson	127) (P)			△
Robert Watson				△
George White				△
John White	128)			△
Robert White				△
Alexander Whitehouse				△
John Whyte	129)			△
George Wilkins	(R)			△
John Wilkinson				△
Andrew Wilson				△
James Wilson	130)			△
John Wilson	131)			△
John C. Wilson	132)			△
Mervyn Wilson				△
Robert Wilson (1)	133)			△
Robert Wilson (2)	133)			△
Michael Winters				△
William J. Wolsey	134) (R)			△
Edward Woodlock				△
John Wright				△
James Young	110)			O
William Young (1)	135)			O
William Young (2)	135)			O
George Stewart				△

△ = campaign qualification as WO/100/17.
O = campaign which the Rolls fail to credit.

74TH (HIGHLAND) REGIMENT NOTES

1. Commanded the 1st Infantry Brigade under Cathcart in the expedition against Moseh. See King; McKay and Moodie.
2. See McKay.
3. Author of 'Campaigning in Kaffirland'. See McKay.
4. Wounded 28.6.51. See G and I.
5. Slightly wounded; see McKay.
6. Served with the CMR throughout the 3rd campaign. Commander at Trompetters Drift Post.
7. Served as a Staff Surgeon during the 2nd war. Not to be confused with Alexander J. Fraser, who was a Staff Surgeon during the 2nd campaign and briefly with the 73rd during 1850.
8. No 2136 and not to be confused with Pte Wm. Henderson. See McKay.
9. Mathews on Roll.
10. Wrongly credited with 1846–7 on Roll. See McKay.
11. No 1608, a survivor from the 'Birkenhead'. See McKay.
12. Also Lockhart on musters. See McKay.
13. McHarg on Roll.
14. Stephenson on Roll.
15. Shown on Mint records as receiving a medal, possibly a replacement, on 17.11.63.
16. Consistently spelt thus on musters, but Everton on Roll.
17. Nos 2835 and 3213 respectively, both survivors from the 'Birkenhead'.
18. Was transferred to the CMR after the 3rd campaign and is on the Roll for both regiments. His CMR medal is in a private collection.
19. No 2277 and not to be confused with Pte Wm. Brown.
20. No 144 Neilson on Roll.
21. Afleck on Roll.
22. No 1929.
23. No 2812.
24. Nos 2777 and 3080.
25. Arnot on Roll. See McKay.
26. Bartley on Roll.
27. No 3160.
28. Beeson on Roll.
29. No 1978.
30. No 3297.
31. Also Burk on musters. See McKay.
32. Also Burnes on musters.
33. No 3188, a survivor from the 'Birkenhead'. Byas on Roll.
34. Nos 2859 and 3249.
35. Carrol on Roll.
36. A number of surnames beginning with 'C', have been obliterated on the Roll. By process of elimination I have concluded that these are the men concerned.
37. Commaskey on Roll; Commiskey in McKay.
38. Cormie on Roll.
39. Daley on Roll.
40. Shown thus on Roll; musters show No 3064 William Douglas, alias Kinross.
41. Nos 2830 and 2875.
42. No 3211, a survivor from the 'Birkenhead'.
43. Garaghty on Roll.
44. Gaylor on Roll.
45. Gummell on Roll.
46. Gavan on Roll.
47. No 3057; see McKay.
48. Gilmore on Roll.
49. Transferred to CMR and is also shown on their returns.
50. Gay on Roll.
51. Hadden on Roll.
52. Hannen on Roll.
53. No 1426 and not to be confused with Cpl James Henderson.
54. No 2950 and not to be confused with Col Sgt Wm. Henderson.
55. Henry on Roll.
56. No 2408 and not to be confused with Cpl John Hill.
57. Also Hogbin on musters.
58. No 2418.
59. Ramsey on Roll, and apparently not a reversal of christian and surnames.
60. Also Johnson on Roll.
61. No 1922, Jonston on Roll.
62. No 2087.
63. Kean on Roll.
64. Keilley on Roll.
65. No 2874; received a re-named medal originally issued to a 2nd Regiment deserter.
66. Kevans on Roll.
67. Leing on Roll.
68. Died and medal sent to WD.
69. Leggate on Roll.
70. Lindsey on Roll.
71. Livisy on Roll.
72. Maiken on Roll.
73. Note on Roll says 'See cancelled list' but medal in a private collection.
74. Nos 3045 and 3108.
75. Matheson on Roll.
76. McCallam on Roll.
77. Fingers amputated after being wounded; see King.
78. McGavin on Roll.
79. No 3214, a survivor from the 'Birkenhead'.
80. Nos 1374 and 3024; the latter received a re-named medal issued to a deserter of the 6th Regiment. Sgt

James McKay No 2865, author of 'Reminiscences of the Last Kaffir War' does not appear to have claimed a medal.
81 McKiver on Roll.
82 No 3214, a survivor from the 'Birkenhead'.
83 No 2894, a survivor from the 'Birkenhead'.
84 McNiven on Roll.
85 Wrongly credited with 1846–7 on Roll.
86 No christian name is given on the Roll which wrongly credits 1846–7 only.
87 Nos 1915 and 3122.
88 Nos 3090 and 3121.
89 Moore on Roll, but musters consistently show More.
90 No 3166, a survivor from the 'Birkenhead'.
91 Also Nagle on Roll.
92 Nos 2753 and 2217; the latter shown as Neilson on Roll.
93 Also Nicolson on musters.
94 Nolan on Roll.
95 O'Neil on Roll.
96 O'Reilly on Roll; various spellings on musters.
97 Nos 1517 and 2576. Orrlock on Roll; one of these medals was returned to the Mint.
98 Parrat on Roll.
99 I have only managed to trace No 1581, though it is possible his name was entered twice in error.
100 Nos 1313 and 3314, the latter received a re-named medal originally issued to a deserter of the 6th Regiment.
101 Ramsey on Roll.
102 Also Riley on musters.
103 Reilley on Roll, also Riley on musters.
104 Ronnald on Roll.
105 Nos 3069 and 3092.
106 No 3159, a survivor from the 'Birkenhead'. Also Sharpe on musters.
107 No 3168, a survivor from the 'Birkenhead'.
108 Nos 1693, 2806 and 3138.
109 No 1844, a survivor from the 'Birkenhead'.
110 Roll wrongly credits 1846–7.
111 Soudon on Roll.
112 No 2286, Steward on Roll.
113 Nos 2866 and 2924.
114 Stewart on Roll.
115 No 3179, a survivor from the 'Birkenhead'. See McKay.
116 No 3220, a survivor from the 'Birkenhead'.
117 Nos 1075 and 3136.
118 No 1669.
119 No 3295.
120 Thorndale on Roll.
121 Tibby on Roll.
122 Timmons on Roll.
123 Troop on Roll.
124 Waddle on Roll.
125 One of these medals is in the Regimental Museum.
126 No 3186, a survivor from the 'Birkenhead'.
127 No. 2641.
128 No 3317.
129 No 3141.
130 No 3313.
131 No 3868.
132 No 3065.
133 Nos 1385 and 2715.
134 Welsay on Roll, Welsey on medal.
135 Nos 1492 and 1641, both of whom are wrongly credited with 1846–7 on Roll.

PRO References: WO/12/8104–8105–8106.

75th Regiment

The service companies of the 75th arrived at the Cape in August 1830 but did not move up to the frontier for two years. Once at Grahams Town they were distributed to various posts and, as the only regular infantry, it was upon them that pressures fell as depredations increased in 1834. But when the Kaffirs swept through the districts of Albany and Somerset in December, some of the fortified posts were abandoned as their garrisons withdrew to Grahams Town.

Hastening to the frontier and reinforced by the 72nd Regiment Lt Col Harry Smith soon took a firm grip on the situation at Grahams Town and organised two columns ready to take the field to carry the war into the enemy's country. The 75th supplied 100 men to what was designated as the Left column and 150 men – a third of whom were mounted – to the Right column. A further 50 men of the regiment were set to being trained as artillerymen but during January Grahams Town was felt to be under threat. Small forces were sent out to bring in isolated groups of settlers who had joined together for mutual protection but were of insufficient strength to risk a dash for safety.

As the marauders drifted back to their own territory, posts were gradually re-established by volunteer forces, often under command of officers of the 75th, and Major Cox was sent to attack the Kraal of Chief Eno. When that had been destroyed Cox joined with a column under Major Burney (CMR) to march upon the Kraals of Chiefs Tyali and Macomo. Eager to assume an offensive Harry Smith ordered Lt Col England (75th) to gather information on enemy positions and, with a detachment of 300 men, England penetrated the rugged kloofs on Committys and Trompeters Drifts. After some skirmishing the force returned with a number of captured cattle and acting upon the intelligence, Smith moved to clear the area in early February. Combining with a force under Somerset, he pursued the Kaffirs through the tangled thickets and although suffering a number of casualties, much higher losses were inflicted upon the enemy. Nevertheless, when the troops returned to Grahams Town it was with feelings of frustration that they had not been able to pin down the elusive Kaffirs.

In March, a central camp was established at Fort Willshire, from which operations along the Keiskamma could be controlled and the army was reorganised into four divisions. At the end of the month these divisions launched an attack on the foothills of the Amatolas, but while a number of the officers of the 75th were placed in command of various levies attached to the invading columns, the bulk of the regiment was put to defend an inner line from Winterberg to the sea. Even with some levies and burgher forces at his command Col England could not entirely police such distances and raiders continued to murder and rob settlers, but the aggressiveness of the government forces was already encouraging some rebel chiefs to surrender.

Macomo, Tyali and other dissidents beyond the Kei chose to continue the struggle and were quick to cut off any stragglers from patrols which harried them. The 75th was concentrated at Fort Cox – named after their Major – and that energetic officer played a prominent role in the operations which led to a suspension of activities in August. Towards the end of the year the regiment was moved to King William's Town and its vicinity, replacing the 72nd at Forts Warden and Wellington, but many men suffered from scurvy as a result of the poor diet they had endured during their campaigning.

In April 1842 preparations were made to return home, but these arrangements had to be abandoned and it was not until July 1843 that the 75th set sail, which meant they had spent almost precisely 13 years in South Africa.

			Kaffir Wars 1 2 3
LIEUTENANT COLONEL			
Richard England	1) (P)		△
MAJOR			
William Cox	2) (R)		△
CAPTAIN			
J. Boys			△
Peter De Lancey			△
Robert D. Hallifax	1)		△
Charles Tyssen			△
Charles A. Young			△
LIEUTENANT			
William Brummell	1)		△
John Forbes			△
Henry J. Gold			△
ENSIGN			
William Brookes	3)		△
Charles E. P. Gordon	(P)		△
COLOUR SERGEANT			
William Dillon	4)		△
James McFarlane			△
Alexander Rutherford			△
SERGEANT			
William Cash			△

			Kaffir Wars 1 2 3
Donald Davidson			△
John Elphinstone			△
Patrick Feekery			△
Thomas Flood			△
Robert Forsyth			△
Jeremiah Howe	5)		△
John Jones	6)		△
John Nowlan	7)		△
John Peel		(P)	△
James Simpson	8)		△
Henry Walsh			△
Henry Williams			△
CORPORAL			
Thomas Hopkins			△
Patrick Kinsela			△
Peter McFarlane			△
Gregor McGregor		(P)	△
John O'Brien	9)		△
Peter Toan	10)		△
DRUMMER			
Thomas Corne			△
PRIVATE			
John Amos			△

South Africa 1853 Medal

		Kaffir Wars					Kaffir Wars		
PRIVATE		1	2	3			1	2	3
Dennis Bannon				△	Dennis Kelly				△
William Barnett	11)			△	Michael Keogh	24)			△
John Bartie				△	Peter Kilgour				△
Patrick Bermingham	12)			△	Bryan Lee	25)			△
John Blackwood				△	William Leslie				△
Patrick Bleany				△	Jabez Lowrie	26)			△
Matthew Boyle	(P)			△	Michael Lowrie				△
John Bradford				△	Martin Lynch				△
Patrick Britt				△	James McArthur				△
James Brock				△	Malcolm McCallum	27)		△	△
John Buchanan	13)			△	Luke McGuire				△
Michael Buckley				△	Lachlan McInnes				△
John Campbell				△	Thomas McLey	28)			△
Andrew Carr				△	Andrew McManus				△
James Cavanagh				△	James McMinn				△
Edward Chapman	14)		△	△	George Maconatt				△
Edward Colbert				△	Francis Mahon	29)			△
Thomas Curboy	15)			△	Francis Martin				△
Lawrence Delaney	(R)			△	Henry Martin				△
John Devine				△	William Melville				△
William Dillon	16)			△	John Metters	30) (P)			△
Andrew Dixon				△	John Mohan				△
John Doherty				△	John Molloy	31)			△
Thomas Donaghoe	17)			△	John Moran	32)			△
James Ducker	(P)			△	Thomas Moran				△
John Dullanty	18)			△	Matthew Moran				△
John Dwyer	(R)			△	Owen Morris				△
James Eaton				△	Daniel Murray	(R)			△
Thomas Farrell				△	David O'Neill				△
Thomas Ferguson				△	Washington Paterson				△
John Fife				△	James Patterson				△
Robert Findlay	19)			△	Thomas Quin	33)			△
William Fitzgerald				△	James Quinlisk	(P)			△
Patrick Fitzgerald	20)			△	John Robertson	34)			△
William Fletcher				△	William Ryall				△
Charles Gallagher				△	John Saddler				△
William Gean	(P)			△	William Sessions				△
James Gorman				△	John Shea	(P)			△
Thomas Hernon				△	Cornelius Sheehan				△
Denis Hines	21)			△	Thomas Shortle				△
Richard Hogan				△	James Smith	35)			△
Thomas Hopkins				△	William Walker				△
Daniel Horan	(P)			△	John Walsh	27)		△	△
Michael Hughes				△	Charles Watson				△
Robert Hutton				△	John West				△
Thomas Jones	22)			△					
Patrick Joyce	23)			△					

△ = campaign qualification as WO/110/17.

75TH REGIMENT NOTES

1. See Godlonton.
2. 'The most useful and active officer under my command' – Sir Harry Smith. The medal in the Regimental Museum is re-named. See Godlonton.
3. Brooks on Roll.
4. No 435; not to be confused with Pte William Dillon.
5. No 505.
6. No 239.
7. Shown twice on Roll, once as Nowlain accompanied with note – 'duplicate medal sent to Mint to cancel and engrave'.
8. No 27.
9. No 739.
10. Easily mistaken for Joan on Roll.
11. Note on Roll says 'Ex-45th' but I have not been able to trace this man.
12. Also Birmingham on musters.
13. Buchannon on Roll.
14. Transferred to 91st (Res Batt) and then to 1/91st in June 1847.
15. Corboy on Roll.
16. No 621, not to be confused with Sgt Dillon.
17. Donahoe on Roll. Various spellings in musters.
18. Also Dulanty on musters.
19. Various spellings on musters.
20. No 356.
21. No 479; Hynes on Roll.
22. No 690.
23. No 682; Joice on Roll.
24. No 405; also Kehoe on musters.
25. This man's medal appears to have been cancelled and re-named for a soldier of the 90th.
26. Lawrie on Roll.
27. Served with the 91st (Res Batt) during the 2nd campaign.
28. Also McLay on musters.
29. No 672; twice entered on Roll.
30. Medal believed to show Methers.
31. No 457; Mulloy on Roll.
32. I have not been able to trace this man but a James Horan did serve with the regiment, and this could be his medal.
33. Two men of this name were with the regiment, Nos 401 and 517. See Gardyne.
34. No 153.
35. No 593; Smyth on Roll.

PRO References: WO/12/8146–8147–8148–8155.

90th (Perthshire Volunteers) Regiment

After years of service in Ceylon the headquarters companies of the 90th arrived at Simons Bay on April 3rd 1846; stepping immediately into the 2nd Kaffir War. Ordered to sail on to Algoa Bay, they had by the 25th reached Grahams Town and their first duty was to recover the body of a volunteer officer killed a few miles from the town on the day of their arrival.

Moved forward to Fort Beaufort as part of the escort for a supply convoy, the wing was split up in May. Commanded by Capt Eld, 100 men occupied Fort Brown, Lt Lecky and a company were posted to Koonap Drift to keep open communications, and a small detachment under Capt Bringhurst returned to Grahams Town. The latter were engaged in foraging until they were brought up to company strength and then they were sent to carry supplies to Fort Peddie. The enemy were met in such numbers the convoy could not advance beyond Trompetters Drift and was held up for two weeks before the march was resumed. With the assistance of a troop of the 7th DG the train safely reached its destination and the 90th detachment stayed on at Fort Peddie for some time.

By now three more companies of the regiment were serving on the frontier. These men had survived a terrible voyage which cost many lives when their transport the 'Maria Somes' had all but been lost in a storm and, since their arrival in the Cape, had been engaged on outpost duty. On June 23rd they were made part of Sir Peregrine Maitland's force which set off down the coast from the Fish River to find suitable landing places. The troops outstripped their supplies and were nearly starving before provisions reached them at the selected site at the mouth of the Buffalo in mid-July.

In August all the detached companies were brought together and the 90th moved to the permanent camp at Block Drift on the Tyumie River where a force was being assembled. Capt Bringhurst and two companies of the regiment were despatched across the Keiskamma River to harass the enemy but found it impassable when they tried to return and for three days had to bivouac without cover and few rations before being able to cross.

In September part of the regiment was employed on the Fish River and in October, under Lt Col Slade operated inland until the principal chiefs surrendered.

On January 6th 1847 the 90th were ordered to England but after marching to Port Elizabeth no ship awaited them. It was not until February 3rd that the 'Thunderbolt' appeared but scarcely had they been taken aboard than the ship went aground and eventually had to be abandoned. The regiment was carried to Cape Town in the 'President' but while they awaited passage home affairs on the frontier had deteriorated and the 90th again headed east. The Left Wing (three companies) under Eld landed at the mouth of the Buffalo from the 'Rosamon' at the end of July and advanced to Goolah Heights. The Right Wing was caught in a hurricane and driven into Algoa Bay before eventually landing on the Buffalo. Two companies under Capt Gale were left here while the remainder pushed on to join Eld. The regiment remained near the coast until January 1848 when they returned to Cape Town and subsequently reached England on April 18th.

		Kaffir Wars 1 2 3
LIEUTENANT COLONEL		
Marcus Slade		△
MAJOR		
Frederick Eld		△
CAPTAIN		
John H. Bringhurst		△
Marcus Geale	1) (P)	△
Robert Grove		△
William V. Johnson		△
John B. Mann		△
Thomas Meredith		△
Purcell O'Gorman		△
Richard Wyvill		△
LIEUTENANT ADJUTANT		
Thomas DeCourcy Hamilton		△
LIEUTENANT		
John M. Walter		△
QUARTERMASTER		
Samuel Williams		△
ASSISTANT SURGEON		
William Maclise		△
SERGEANT MAJOR		
David Jackson	2)	△
QUARTERMASTER SERGEANT		
George Barnes	3)	O
Thomas Barnes		△
COLOUR SERGEANT		
Edward Harper	(P)	△
Richard Hughes		△
BUGLE MAJOR		
Francis Fitzpatrick		△
SERGEANT		
James Arnold		△
William Bailey	4)	△
John Bishop		△
Charles Bungey	5)	△
George Eve	6)	△
Henry Edmonds	7)	△
Richard Hyde		△
James Isherwood	8)	△
Henry Johnson		△
George McQuade		△
Henry Peter	9)	△
William Postlethwaite		△
Jesse Rich	10)	△
Edward Sampson		△
William Stevens	11)	△
Thomas Williams		△
CORPORAL		
James Baring		△
Joseph Broom	12)	O
Daniel Cameron		△
Thomas Efford	13)	△
William Gurney		△

112 South Africa 1853 Medal

		Kaffir Wars		
		1	2	3
CORPORAL				
Henry Hill				△
John Rye				△
William Thomas	14)			△
Enoch Watkins				△
BUGLER				
William Ainsworth				△
Thomas Bridges				△
George Laugher				△
William Letter				△
Francis Murray				△
James Mathews				△
William Thomas	14)			△
PRIVATE				
John Abbott				△
Richard Arnold				△
James Ashenton	15)			△
Thomas Ayres	16) (M)			△
John Baker (1)	17)			△
John Baker (2)	17)			△
William G. Baker				△
Fenton Balden				△
John Ball	18)			△
William Ball				△
Richard Balmer				△
John Banger				△
William Barry				△
William J. Beachey	19)			△
Charles Beauchamp				△
William Beckwith				△
Samuel Benister	20)			△
Thomas Bentham				△
Joseph Bloxam				△
Matthew Bohan				△
John Bolkham				△
James Bottrill				△
Edward Bradley				△
Patrick Brett				△
William Broady	(P)			△
James Brockbank				△
John Brown (1)	21)			△
John Brown (2)	21)			△
William Brown	22)			△
Timothy Bryant				△
James Bucklish				△
William Bush				△
Richard Byrne	(P)			△
Allen Cameron	23)			O
James Cannon				△
James Carruthers	24)			O
James Carson	24)			O
George Carey	24)			O
John Chatters				△
William Church				△
William Clancey	26)			△
Jacob Clarke	27) (P)			O
John Clucas	24)			O
Cornelius Collins				△
James Cook	24)			O
William Cook	24)			O
James Cooper	25) (R)			O
William Craig				△
James Crawford (1)	28)			O
James Crawford (2)	28)			△
John Crump	(P)			△
Thomas Dakin	(P)			△
Herbert Davies				△
Michael Delaney	29)			△
James Dennis				△
John Devine				△
John Duckett				△
Alexander Dunbar				△
Charles Eaton				△
Richard Edwards				△
Arthur Ellis				△
John Ellis				△
Thomas Evans				△
Thomas Fahey				△
James Farley				△
William Farley				△
James Filmer	30)			△
Peter Flood				△
John Ford				△
Richard Foulkes				△
Alban Fowler				△
Thomas Fox	31)			△
Richard Glasspool				△
John Gleeson				△
Robert Glendenning				△
Thomas Goodwin	32)			△
Edward Griffiths				△
Evan Griffiths				△
John Griffiths				△
Joseph Gunn				△
James Hall				△
Thomas Handy				△
Richard Harris				△
James Hart				△
Philip Hazell	33)			△
Michael Healy	(R)			△
Thomas Heeney	34)			△
Samuel Heiford				△
David Herbert				△
John Hill				△
Humphrey Hockeday				△
William Hogan				△
Lewis Holmes				△
John Holness				△
Robert Howarth				△
William Howden				△
William Howlett	(R)			△
Joseph Jackson				△
Thomas James				△
Isaac Jecks	35)			△
James Jeffrey				△
James FitzJennings				△
Charles Johnson				△
Edwin Johnson				△
William Johnson	(R)			△
Edward Jones				△
Thomas Jones	36)			△
William Jones	37) (P)			△
William Kellett				△
John Kenney	38)			△
William Kiddy				△
Marcus Kilkelly				△
Thomas King	(R)			△
Richard L. Kirby	39)			△
Stephen Lacey	40)			△
John Lancaster				△
James Laverty				△
Robert Leech				△
David Lloyd				△
John Lomax				△
William Long	(P)			△

South Africa 1853 Medal

			Kaffir Wars 1 2 3			Kaffir Wars 1 2 3
James Loveday			△	John Rudrum		△
Joseph Manders			△	George Ryland		△
Edward Martin	41)		△	Richard Saker	(MRM)	△
Thomas Martin	42)		△	William Saker		△
Andrew McDonald			△	Anthony Shiels	48)	△
James McIntosh			△	John Silcock	49)	△
Bernard McKerry			△	William Simpson		△
George McLuckie	(MRM)		△	William Slater		△
Andrew Melrose			△	Edward Smith		△
Edward Melton			△	John Smith	50)	△ O
Isaac Milsome	43) (MRM)		△	William Souter	51)	△
William Monck	44) (P)		△	Joseph Sparrow		△
Joseph Moore			△	Richard Springate		△
George Moss			△	Peter Stapleton	52)	△
James Murphy			△	Robert Stavert		△
Edward Murray			△	David Stevenson		△
Thomas Needs			△	William Stell	53)	△
John Newcombe			△	Stephen Switzer		△
John Nicholson			△	William Tappin	54)	△
James Nunn	45)		△	Edward Tempest		△
Edward Oram			△	Edward Timmins		△
John Orr			△	James Timms		△
Oscar Osbaldiston			△	James Tooley	55)	△
George Paddock			△	George Tulk		△
Joseph Palmer			△	Joseph Vincent	(R)	△
David Parry			△	Felix Walters	56)	△
William Payne			△	Henry Warr		△
Joseph Peacock			△	William Waters	57)	△
John Penfold			△	William Watts		△
Samuel Pond			△	Joseph Weeding	(P)	△
Thomas Poole			△	Charles Weeks		△
William Price			△	Richard Welsh	58)	△
George Purkiss			△	James Wilkinson		△
John Rankins			△	James Williams	(MRM)	△
Charles Ransley			△	Benjamin Wilson		△
Patrick Rawley			△	James Wilson		△
Thomas Reason			△	John Wilson		△
William Reghel			△	Joseph Wogan		△
George Rigby			△	James Worley		△
Matthew Riordon	46)		△	William Wright	59)	△
John Robertshaw			△	Thomas Young		△
John Robertson	(R)		△			
James Robinson			△			
John Roddy			△			
William Rodgers	47)		△			

△ = campaign qualification as WO/100/17.
O = campaign which the Rolls fail to credit.

90TH (PERTHSHIRE VOLUNTEERS) REGIMENT NOTES

1 Gale on Roll.
2 Listed under officers on the Roll as he was a Quartermaster when the list was submitted.
3 Wrongly credited with 1834-5 on Roll.
4 Bayley on Roll; an Armourer Sergeant.
5 Bungy on Roll.
6 An Orderly Room Sergeant.
7 Edmunds on Roll; a Hospital Sergeant.
8 A Schoolmaster Sergeant.
9 Also Peters on musters.
10 Christian name given as Jessie on Roll.
11 Stephens on Roll.
12 Broome on Roll and qualifying date obliterated.
13 No 367; may have received two medals as he is twice returned on the Rolls, once as a private.
14 Cpl Thomas No 1349 and Bugler No 1440.
15 Asherton on Roll.
16 Ayre on Roll; medal correctly named.
17 Nos 1263 and 1366.
18 I have not traced this man.
19 Beachy on Roll.
20 Barister on Roll.
21 Nos 504 and 1649.
22 Probably No 1741.
23 No christian name or initial is shown on the Roll but no other Pte Cameron appears with the regiment. Qualifying date is obliterated.
24 Qualifying date obliterated from Roll.
25 Cary on Roll and date obliterated.
26 Clancy on Roll.
27 Also Clerk and Clerke on musters.
28 Nos 484 and 805, one of whom received a re-named replacement.
29 Delany on Roll.
30 Filmen on Roll.
31 Twice entered on Roll and may have received two medals, one of which was returned to be altered after being incorrectly impressed as Cox.
32 Also Goodwing on musters.
33 Hazel on Roll.
34 Heeny on Roll.
35 Also Jacks on musters.
36 Two men of this name served with the regiment, Nos 395 and 1591.
37 Two men of this name served with the regiment, Nos 1694 and 1826.
38 Kenny on Roll.
39 Kerbey on Roll.

40 Lacy on Roll.
41 Also Edmund on musters.
42 No 1100.
43 Milsom on Roll.
44 Also Monk on musters.
45 May have won his medal with another regiment. No 2647.
46 Also Rierdon on musters.
47 Also Rogers on musters.
48 Shields on Roll.
49 Silcocks on Roll.
50 No 1617 – sometimes shown as 1615; served with the CMR during the 3rd campaign and then transferred to the 7th DG.
51 Also Soutar on musters.
52 Also Stappleton on musters.
53 Still on Roll.
54 Also Tapin on musters.
55 William on Roll but No 1358 James Tooley is the only man of this surname on the musters.
56 Walter on Roll.
57 Walters on Roll.
58 Also Welch on musters.
59 Two men of this name served with the regiment, Nos 560 and 1357.

PRO References: WO/12/9207–9208–9212.

91st (Argyllshire) Regiment

1st Battalion

The 1st Battalion of the 91st was sent to the Cape of Good Hope from St Helena in 1839 and, with the headquarters at Grahams Town, furnished detachments for outposts on the eastern frontier. The service was uneventful until June 1843 when a detachment took part in a punitive expedition against the Kaffir Chief Tola who had been stealing settlers' cattle. After a skirmish which wounded one man of the 91st the force returned to the colony with the cattle they had recovered.

In December 200 Argylls were with the troops ordered to the Colesberg district when Boers began to give trouble to the authorities. The display of force was enough to prevent any rebellion but more trouble sprang up beyond the Orange River early in 1845 when Boer farmers attacked Griqua villages. The natives appealed to the British Government and a detachment of the 91st was involved in the brief clash which put an end to the disturbances. At the end of the year the 1st Battalion was told to be prepared for a return to England but the move was postponed and the 91st were still at Grahams Town when the War of the Axe erupted.

Headquarters were established at Fort Peddie and from there detachments were sent to Post Victoria and Trompeter's Drift. On May 22nd 1846, 60 men of the 91st were escorting 42 supply wagons between Fort Peddie and Trompeter's when they came under heavy attack. The convoy stretched for some three-quarters of a mile and it being found impossible to protect such a long line of wagons, most had to be abandoned to the Kaffirs.

At the end of the month a considerable force of the enemy attacked Fort Peddie and the Fingoes sheltering close by. Skirmishing took place around the fort for two days before the Kaffirs were driven off with the loss of several hundred killed and wounded.

In June 120 men served with the force under Sir Peregrine Maitland which explored the coast as far as the mouth of the Buffalo in search of a new landing place. They were in the field for three months before falling back to Waterloo Bay for supplies. When Somserset moved into the Amatolas a detachment from the 1st Battalion was with the column under Col Johnstone (27th Regiment) which joined in the movement to drive the Kaffirs from those mountains.

The troops suffered from exposure and hard marching to little purpose for the expedition was no great success.

During 1847 the 1st Battalion of the 91st took no part in active operations and were occupied only by patrolling and escort duties until hostilities petered out. In January 1848 the Argylls prepared to go home. Some transferred to the Reserve Battalion, while others chose to stay in the colony as settlers in the military villages. The remainder marched to Port Elizabeth where four companies embarked on February 23rd. Three other companies followed on March 10th and by May 11th all had arrived at Gosport.

Reserve Battalion

The Reserve Battalion was formed only two months before sailing from the Cape in the transport 'Abercrombie Robinson' on June 2nd 1842. Upon arriving at Table Bay towards the end of August the battalion received orders to relieve the 1st Battalion on the frontier and, instead of disembarking, remained on the ship as she lay at anchor. During the night of the 27th a strong gale blew up and the 'Abercrombie Robinson' was parted from her anchors. In a fearful storm heavy seas swept over the ship and she began to break up before being driven onto a sandbank near the mouth of the Salt River. A cutter managed to reach the beach and surf boats were hurried to the spot on wagons. After the disembarkation of women and children the troops drew lots by companies and after many hours of imminent danger some 700 people reached safety. Only 400 yards away a convict ship in a similar predicament lost nearly 160 soldiers and prisoners.

The battalion eventually reached the frontier in March 1843 and were stationed with the 1st Battalion at Grahams Town. Here they stayed for nearly a year before proceeding to Fort Beaufort which became the headquarters of the Reserve Battalion for four years. It was the headquarters company commanded by Maj Campbell who first saw action in the war of 1846 when Col Richardson (7th DG) led an expedition into the Amatolas. On April 16th the men of the 91st were in danger of being overwhelmed by vast numbers of the enemy and lost six men killed and wounded when fighting their way through the woods of the Amatola Hoek to join with other troops under Col Somerset on the heights above.

The following day the force moved towards Burns Hill to join up with the wagons left there under Maj Gibson (7th DG). Early that morning Gibson's camp came under attack and eight men of the 91st detachment with the wagons were killed or wounded before the Kaffirs were driven off. A convoy of 125 wagons then moved out to meet Somerset but a dash upon the centre of the long train split the column. Forced to withdraw to Burns Hill, Gibson abandoned many of his wagons and although 80 men of the 91st under Capt Scott, who had been sent ahead from Somerset, tried valiantly to restore the situation, the numbers against them were too great and the Argylls had to fight their way back to rejoin the brigade.

On the 18th the entire British force retired to Block Drift. Most of them had not eaten for two days and the column was constantly threatened by the enemy. Scott's company formed the advance guard and Capt Rawstoorne protected the rear. Lt Cochrane was wounded and two men were killed during the march to the Tyumie River where the 91st held the Drift during the crossing. Some time afterwards, when troops again entered the Amatolas, they came across the remains of an Argyll who had been tortured and burned to death tied to the wheels of a wagon.

Emboldened by their successes the Kaffirs poured down upon the colonists and the 91st, scattered along the various outposts, suffered a number of men killed and wounded. But everywhere the enemy were repulsed with heavy losses. Patrols, some penetrating deep into the Amatolas, seemed to convince the Kaffirs of the benefits of peace and in December 1846 the Reserve Battalion moved to Fort Beaufort. Hostilities were resumed in July 1847 and the battalion was assigned to Col Hare's 1st Division. Striking into the Amatolas from Fort Cox the division pursued the enemy through the kloofs and hills and up to the foothills of the Buffalo Mountains, returning to Fort Cox on August 7th. At the same time, 81 men of the 91st accompanied the force under Capt Hogg (7th DG) to punish Tambookie Chief Mapassa. They were engaged in several skirmishes and were thus employed until mid-October when the force went to Fort Beaufort. The detachment continued to act

under Hogg at various places until arriving at Post Victoria on December 9th.

On August 23rd 100 men of the Argylls had been engaged in rescuing a patrol of Hottentot and Fingo levies out from Fort Cox, which was in danger of being overwhelmed. From September the Reserve Battalion was concentrated at Fort Cox and kept the area clear of the enemy with frequent patrols. On the 17th Chief Macomo came in to Campbell (now a Lt Col) to sue for peace and in subsequent months the 91st was heavily involved in operations in the Amatolas and Tab Indoba Mountains under Campbell which led to Chief Sandili surrendering at Fort Hare. Two companies of the battalion under Capt W. G. Scott and Capt C. Campbell joined the force under Sir Geo. Berkeley and operated with Somerset's division on or near the Kei River until peace was concluded in December.

The Reserve Battalion moved from Fort Beaufort in January 1848 to Grahams Town. In July two companies under Capt Rawstoorne marched to Colesberg and joined Sir Harry Smith's force against the rebel Boers. The detachment played a prominent part in the Battle of Boemplaats and had six officers and men wounded. The troops marched some 1,200 miles during the expedition and the men of the 91st returned to Grahams Town in mid-October where the battalion remained for two years.

At the outbreak of the 3rd war the Reserve Battalion of the 91st marched to Fort Hare and from here patrols were sent out to offer protection to nearby settlements. On December 29th a detachment of 150 men led by Col Yarborough set out to re-open communications with Fort Cox. Meeting formidable resistance the force was compelled to abandon the attempt and a reinforcement of a 100 men was sent from Fort Hare under Ensign Squirl to Yarborough's assistance. In a severe struggle two officers and 20 men of the 91st were killed and 18 other ranks wounded; two of whom died later.

A small detachment of the Argylls was at Fort Beaufort when it came under attack from a large enemy force under Hermanus. The rebel leader was killed and by defeating the attackers a welcome success was registered at a time when the tide was running against the settlers. On February 24th 1851 a force of several thousand Kaffirs and Hottentot rebels approached Fort Hare and tried to carry off Fingo cattle being sheltered in the vicinity of the fort, but a detachment of only 100 men under Squirl was sufficient to repel the enemy.

In the following months detachments of the regiment were regularly employed on patrolling and suffered several casualties. During June Major Forbes, with 126 officers and men, served under Somerset in his drive into the Amatolas and a detachment under Lt Rae was in action with a force commanded by Col Michel which operated out from Fort Peddie. The series of attacks into the Waterkloof which commenced on October 13th incorporated 318 officers and men of the 91st. Considerable fighting took place in the almost impassable forests and ravines and continued for some three weeks. During this time the regiment suffered a number of casualties, but only one man was killed and an Ensign died of wounds. Other regiments lost more heavily.

At the end of December 71 men under Lt Mackenzie joined a patrol under Maj Wilmot, RA. Whilst searching some Kaffir huts Wilmot was killed and when the enemy began to swarm around the British troops Mackenzie was compelled to withdraw to Fort Peddie. Late in January 1852 Col Yarborough marched out of Fort Hare with 416 officers and men of the 91st. For a month they were employed in crop destruction in the Amatolas and then, after a few days rest, took part in the combined movements in the Waterkloof. On March 5th they drove the Kaffirs from strong positions and five men were killed or died of wounds. Two officers and 15 other ranks were wounded.

Meanwhile, 75 officers and men of the Argylls were in the field for several weeks under Maj Kyle (45th). Ravishing the crops in Seyola's country the force was engaged in several skirmishes and worked its way to King William's Town before returning to Fort Peddie. On March 10th a force commanded by Lt Col Napier, consisting of the 91st, 74th, some Cape Mounted Riflemen and Levies, entered the Waterkloof Valley. The fighting was short but sharp and the 91st, who covered the rear, had 10 wounded – two of whom died. A week later the 91st was searching out enemy cattle and destroying crops in the country between the Blinkwater and Thomas River, but the whole operation achieved little, even though the battalion was in the field until the middle of May.

Further operations in the Waterkloof Mountains were undertaken in July and involved a detachment of Argylls. Capt Wright, with only 23 men, was at Elands Post when invested by several hundred of the enemy, but as the British troops moved out to meet them they were joined by some levies and the Hottentots were driven off with some loss. At the end of the month the battalion was engaged across the Kei under Maj Forbes, and striking through the territory of Chief Kreli, captured thousands of cattle. The 91st was back at its camp at Blinkwater on August 30th and after two weeks rest marched again to join Gen Cathcart's final operations in the Waterkloof. Contributing some 400 men to the force of 3,000 the Highlanders supplied four companies to the detachment on the northern heights while others moved along the Fullers Hoek Ridge and the three days' operation swept Kaffir and Hottentot marauders from their secluded places, bringing the insurrection virtually to an end.

The headquarters of the regiment was now established at Fort Fordyce from where detachments continued to be sent to various frontier posts. In November 1853 a move was made to Fort Beaufort and here the Reserve Battalion remained until ordered to return home in June 1855. The officers and men of the 91st had marched farther, seen more action and suffered greater casualties than any other regiment in the Kaffir Wars. The long service on the frontier of the two battalions had particularly identified the regiment and it was said the colonists regarded them as friends as well as defenders.

Where the symbols △ an ○ have been blocked out to show ▲ and ● this indicates service with the 1st Battalion. Where a man transferred between the battalions during the war of 1846–7 I have tried to give the battalion in which the recipient saw the major portion of his campaign service.

		Kaffir Wars		
		1	2	3
LIEUTENANT COLONEL				
John F. G. Campbell	1)			△
Martin G. T. Lindsay	2)			▲
MAJOR				
David Forbes	3)		○	△
Charles C. Yarborough	4) (P)			▲ △

		Kaffir Wars		
		1	2	3
BREVET MAJOR				
John G. Rawstorne	5)		○	△
CAPTAIN				
Frederick Bayly	(P)			▲
Colin Campbell			△	△
James D. Cochrane	6)			▲

South Africa 1853 Medal

		Kaffir Wars		
		1	2	3
Robert H. Howard	7)			△
Alexander W. McKenzie				△
Robert F. Middlemore	8) (P)		●	△
William T. L. Patterson	7)		▲	
Henry J. Savage	9)		●	
William G. Scott	10)			△
John Ward	11)		▲	
Edward W. C. Wright	12)		○	△

LIEUTENANT

		1	2	3
John T. Bethune			△	
Robert Borthwick	13)			△
John Bruce				△
Richard S. Cole			▲	
Robert H. Crampton	14)			△
Edward Dickson	15)		△	
W. George C. Gordon				△
Francis G. Hibbert	16)			△
Henry C. Metcalfe	17)		△	
James Owgan	18)		△	
James M. Pennington	18)		△	△
Charles H. Pickwick	19)			△
Edward J. Rae	20) (P)		△	△
William Squirl				△
Robert Stein			▲	

ENSIGN

		1	2	3
William Aitchison	21)		▲	
Henry A. Bond	22)			△
Ormond Fitzgerald	23) (P)		△	
Thomas T. Lane				△
William M. Mill	24)		▲	
Lloyd H. Thomas	25)			△

PAYMASTER

		1	2	3
G. Haddington Dalrymple			▲	

QUARTERMASTER

		1	2	3
James Paterson	26) (P)		○	△

SURGEON

		1	2	3
William Arden				△
Samuel M. Hadaway			△	
Francis Reid				△

ASSISTANT SURGEON

		1	2	3
Alexander B. Morgan	27)			△
William Munro	28)		▲	
John O'Nial				△

SERGEANT MAJOR

		1	2	3
John Bishop			○	△
William Grant	29)		●	△
John Starrett	(P)		△	

QUARTERMASTER SERGEANT

		1	2	3
William McKay			▲	
Peter Murray	30)		○	△
John Peggie			▲	

COLOUR SERGEANT

		1	2	3
James Anderson			▲	
John Barnett			▲	
William Cameron			○	△
Donald Campbell			▲	
William Gilmour	(P)		▲	
James Gray	31)		○	△
John Kingkeade				△
Daniel Mason			○	△
George McDonald	32)		▲	
Donald McKay	33)		▲	
James M. Murray			▲	
Jacob O'Neil	34)		▲	
Thomas Ormsby			○	△

		1	2	3
George Russon			○	△
George Stewart			▲	
George Taylor			▲	
Joseph Trotter			○	△

DRUM MAJOR

		1	2	3
Thomas Bentley				△
James Cameron	35) (R)		▲	
Roderick Gollan			▲	
Thomas Graham			○	△

ARMOURER SERGEANT

		1	2	3
Charles Hillman				△

HOSPITAL SERGEANT

		1	2	3
William Grant			△	○

PAYMASTER SERGEANT

		1	2	3
John Crozier	36)			△

SCHOOLMASTER SERGEANT

		1	2	3
James Fairlie	(MRM)			△

SERGEANT

		1	2	3
Timothy Begley	37)	○	○	△
Thomas Bunting			○	△
George Burnett	(P)		△	△
Edward Burns				△
Archibald Carmichael				△
William Challiner			△	△
John Coplan			▲	
David Coulter	38)		▲	
Robert Duncan			○	△
Ewan Ferguson	39)		○	△
James Goudie	40) (P)		▲	
John Halmarack			○	△
James Haxton			○	△
Joseph Hickie			▲	
James Hood				
Andrew Huggan			△	△
William Kilpatrick			○	△
Edward King			○	△
James Lawless			○	△
Alexander Leitch	(P)		○	△
John Lyons				△
Samuel Norman			○	△
Thomas Porter	41)		▲	
Francis Prior	42)		○	△
Henry Rodgers			△	△
John Ross	43) (P)		○	△
Thomas W. Saunders	44)		○	△
Samuel Smith	45)	△	▲	
William Smith	46)		▲	
James Steel			○	△
Thomas Stirling	47)		○	△
John Strange	48)		○	△
Peter Sturrock	49)		▲	
William Thorburn				△
John Treasurer			○	△
William Wallace				△
William J. Whitehead				△
William Wright	50)			△

CORPORAL

		1	2	3
John Adam	51)		○	△
Thomas Andrews				△
Joseph Baxter				△
John Betts			○	△
Robert Boyd				△
John Burnside	52)		△	○
John Cameron			▲	
Samuel Clayton	(P)		△	△
Owen Carnin	53)			○

118 South Africa 1853 Medal

Rank/Name	Note	Kaffir Wars 1	Kaffir Wars 2	Kaffir Wars 3
CORPORAL				
Daniel Carpenter	53)		O	
William Clarke	54)		O	O
William Deacon				△
George Duncan			O	△
Edward Dwyer			△	
David Farquharson				△
John Frame				△
John G. Freer			O	△
Martin Halloran	55) (P)			△
William Hamilton			O	△
Patrick Harrington				△
Charles Hoskins			O	△
Neil Hughes			O	△
James Hutton				△
William Jaffery	56)			△
William Johnston	(MRM)			△
Matthew Knight				△
John McManus	57)		O	△
Henry McMullin			O	△
James McPherson			O	△
William Murray			▲	
John Newman	(P)			△
Robert Orkney			▲	
Charles Pigram				
Alexander Rose			△	
Thomas Strachan				△
Matthew Strang			△	
William Wilkings				△
George Wilson	58) (R)			△
Adam Wragg			O	△
James Wright				△
DRUMMER				
Robert Carrick			△	O
Andrew Cook	53)		●	O
Thomas Doyle	59)		O	△
Andrew Forrest			O	△
John Galvin	60)			△
William Gibb			O	△
James Gardiner			△	
Joseph Harvett				△
Frederick A. Hoare				△
John McBain	(P)		O	△
Peter McGowan				△
John McLevie			O	△
David Redman			O	△
William Reid			▲	
James Rennie			▲	
Charles Staker				△
James Young			O	△
PRIVATE				
Edward Abbott			O	△
Charles Abernethy			●	△
James Adam			O	△
John Adamson			O	△
William Addison	61)		●	
James Aitken	62)		▲	
Thomas Aitken	62)		▲	
William Aitkin				△
James Alcorn	61)		●	
Alexander Alderdice			O	△
William R. Alderdice	(P)		▲	
Kenneth Alexander	63)		●	△
Robert Alison			O	△
John Allan	64)			△
Adam Allen	65)		O	△
Andrew Allen	65)		O	△
John Allen	66)		O	△
William Alsop	67)		O	△
George Anderson			O	△
John Anderson	68)		●	△
William Anderson	69)		▲	
Thomas B. Andrews	70)		▲	
John Arnott			▲	
Archibald Ash				△
Edwin Atkinson			O	△
Richard Badby				
Thomas Bailey	71)		O	△
William Bain			O	△
Patrick Baker			O	△
William Barker			O	△
Robert Barnett			O	△
George Barnwell			O	△
John Barry	72)		▲	
James Bartlett				△
John Battersby				△
Charles Beattie			O	△
David Bell			▲	
Robert Bell			▲	
George Bennett				△
John Bennett			▲	
James Bennison			O	△
John Berrill				△
John Betts	73)		△	O
James Beveridge	74) (P)			△
William Bird	75)			△
John Bolton				△
William Bonnyman			O	△
John Boulton	76)		O	O
Thomas Bowman	(P)		O	△
Robert Boyce			O	△
James Boyle	77) (P)		O	O
Neil Bradley			▲	
Patrick Breen				△
Thomas Britton	78)		O	△
Peter Broadfoot			▲	
Anthony Brown			O	△
David Brown			▲	
George Brown				△
John Brown	79)		▲	
Richard Brown			▲	
Thomas Brown			▲	
John Brownlee				△
William Bruce			▲	
Martin Bryan	80)		O	△
Andrew Buist	81)		△	△
Henry Burgess			O	△
John Burke				
Charles Burnett				△
Thomas Burns			△	
Andrew Burnsides	82)			△
Henry Butt				△
Samuel Butt			▲	
John Byrne	83)			△
Patrick Byrnes				△
Thomas Caisey			▲	
Henry Callaghan	53)			O
Charles Cameron			▲	
Donald Cameron			▲	
James Cameron	53)		O	O
James Campbell	53)			O
Malcolm Campbell	53)		O	O
William Campbell			O	O
Patrick Cannon	53)		O	O
Thomas Capper			O	△

South Africa 1853 Medal   119

Name	Ref	1	2	3
David Carey	84)			○
William Carey	(MRM)		△	
Thomas Carlin	(MRM)			△
Samuel Carmichael			○	△
John Carney			○	△
John Carrahill			○	△
James Cartey			○	△
Allen Cassidy	(P)		▲	
Peter Cassidy			○	△
William Catterill	85)		○	△
James Chapman	86)		○	△
John Chapman	87)	○	△	
Thomas Chipps				△
William Christie	88)		○	△
Ebenezer Clark	(P)		△	○
George Clark			○	△
James Clark	89) (R)		▲	
John Clark			△	
William Clark	90)		▲	
Thomas Clarkson			○	△
William Clay			○	△
James Collary	91)		○	△
Thomas Colgan			○	△
John Connechan	92)			△
Laurence Connor			○	△
Brian Connors			●	△
James Cook				△
John Cook		△		
William Cook			○	△
Alfred Cooper			△	△
George Cooper				△
Robert Cooper			○	△
James Copland			▲	
William Corby			△	
Charles Corns	93)		○	△
Robert Cornwall				△
John Costello				△
Alexander Coull		△	○	
David Coutts			▲	
William Craig			○	△
Alexander Crammond			●	△
Thomas Cray	94)			○
William Cray				△
William Creighton	95)	△	○	
Thomas Crookshanks			○	△
James Cruickshanks	96)		▲	
Luke Culverwell			○	△
Alexander Cummings			△	
Luke Cunniff			○	△
Alexander Cunningham			○	△
Robert Currie		△	○	
Patrick Daly	97)			△
Philip Daly	97)			△
Richard Darlington			○	△
Francis Davidson			○	△
John Davidson				△
George Davies			○	△
William Davies	98)		△	
Patrick Devaney				△
David Develin				△
David Dewane				△
James Dick				△
Henry Dickson				△
Robert Dickson			○	△
James Dobbie			○	△
Bernard Docherty				△
Patrick Docherty	99)		○	△
David Doig			○	△
George Dollar				△
Charles Donnell			△	
Michael Dooley			△	△
John Dougall			△	
William Dougall			△	○
John Dougherty				△
Alexander Douglass			○	△
Thomas Doyle			○	△
William Doyle			○	△
James Drage			○	△
Francis Drew			○	△
John Drummond			▲	
James Drury			○	△
James Dunbar			▲	
Michael Dunbar				△
Andrew Dundas	100)			○
James Dunlop				△
John Edmonds				△
Thomas Egan			○	△
John Ellis			●	△
Samuel Ellis			▲	
John Evans			○	△
James Ewing			▲	
James Eyesenbell	101)		○	△
Edward Fair				△
William Fallick	102)		○	△
Alexander R. Falls			▲	
Robert Farmer			○	△
John Feeney			▲	
Alexander Ferguson			○	△
Duncan Ferguson				△
John Ferguson	103)		▲	
Henry Fielding				△
James Fitman				△
George Fitzgerald			▲	
Peter Fitzgerald			○	△
Bartholomew Fitzsimmonds				△
Patrick Flaherty				△
James Fleming	104) (R)			△
John Flemming			▲	
William Flockton			○	△
John Flynn (1)	105)			△
John Flynn (2)	105)		○	△
John Flynn (3)	105)			△
Michael Flynn			●	△
Peter Flynn	106) (P)			△
James Forrest				△
Henry Francis				△
Alexander Fraser	107)		○	△
Robert Fraser			●	△
Thomas Frazer			○	△
James Fynes			○	△
Peter Gallagher				△
John Gamble	(MRM)			△
Thomas Gardiner			▲	
Thomas Garrigan	(MRM)			△
Joseph Gavin			○	△
William Gibson			○	△
Patrick Gillespie				△
Thomas Gillett			○	△
John Gilmour	108)		○	△
John Glassford			○	△
Patrick Glennon			○	△
John Goldsmith			○	△
William Gordon			○	△
Hugh Gorman			○	△
Philip Gorman				△
Jeffrey Gotcher	109)		○	△

120 South Africa 1853 Medal

		Kaffir Wars 1	2	3
PRIVATE				
James Goudie	110)			
John Grant		▲		
Robert Grant		▲		
Archibald Gray			O	△
Thomas Gray	111)			△
Edward Greally			O	△
William Greives	112)		△	O
Francis W. Greenalsh				△
John Greenan				△
Owen Griffin				△
William Griffin				△
James Hagan			O	△
John Haggart	113)			△
William Haggart	114)			△
John Hall			O	△
George Halse	115)		O	△
Douglas Hamilton	116)			△
George Hamilton				△
Michael Hand				△
William Handley			O	△
William Hannah		▲		
Henry Harlen	117)		O	△
Daniel Harper			O	△
Thomas Harrington			O	△
George Harris (1)	118)			△
George Harris (2)	118)			△
Mitchel Harris			O	△
Alexander Harrold				△
William Harrower			O	△
Charles Hart			O	△
John Hay		▲		
James Healy		▲		
Andrew Henderson		▲		
David Henderson		▲		
James Henderson				△
Thomas Henderson				△
William Henderson			O	△
Lawrence Hendrick				△
James Hepburn				△
John Hepburn			O	△
Robert Hewitt			O	△
William Hickson				△
John Higgan	119)			△
Ruben Higginbottom			O	△
Michael Higgins			O	△
Patrick Higgins		▲		
Robert Hill			O	△
Thomas Hill		▲		
George Hinton			O	△
John Hogan				△
Henry Hogg			O	△
James Holden	120)			
William Hoole			O	△
William Hopkins				△
James Houlihan				△
Mark Hudson	121)			△
William Hunt				△
Alexander Hunter				△
James Hunter	122)	△		
Robert Hunter			O	△
Thomas Hunter			O	△
William Hurts		△		△
William Hyde	123)		O	△
Thomas Ingram				△
John Ives			O	△
James Izatt			O	△
John Jack		▲		

		Kaffir Wars 1	2	3
John Jackson		▲		
Alexander Jamieson			O	△
William Jellings				△
Stephen Jelly	124)			△
James Jenkins				△
John Jenkins			O	△
Thomas Jennings				△
Joseph Johnston			O	△
Thomas Johnstone	125)		O	△
James Jolly		▲		
Charles Jones		▲		
Martin Jones			O	△
Samuel Jones			O	△
William Jones				△
John Joyce	126)			△
Edward Justice		▲		
Thomas Kain				△
William Kanes				△
Michael Kavanagh				△
William J. Kedian				△
Francis Keen				△
James Kelly				△
Henry Kemble			O	△
John Kenny			O	△
Thomas Kenny			△	O
Francis Kightley	127)			△
William Kinnaird		▲		
Robert Kirkland				△
James Laggan			O	△
George Lanceley				△
James Land				△
Patrick Laven	128)			△
David Law			O	△
John Lawlor	129)		O	△
Patrick Lawlor	129)		O	△
James Lawrence		△		
Simon Leary	130)			
John Lement			O	△
John Lennon				△
James Lennon	131)			O
Samuel Lethem	132)		O	△
James Lewis		▲		
Adam Leyden			O	△
Edward Lilley				△
Alexander Lindsay	(P)	▲		
John Little			O	△
David Lloyd			O	△
William Lock	133) (MRM)	▲		
William Loman			O	△
John Lonie			△	O
Stephen Love			O	△
Hugh Lowrie			O	△
John Loxton				△
John Lunn				△
Thomas Lynch			O	△
William Lyons				△
Daniel Manderson	134)	△	O	
Joseph Mapletoft			O	△
James Marsh			O	△
William Marsh			O	△
William Martin			O	△
George Mason				△
James Mason (1)			O	△
James Mason (2)	135)			△
James Mathie	135)	▲		
Adam Mathieson	136)		O	△
Anthony Matthews	137)		O	△
Robert McAlpine				△

South Africa 1853 Medal 121

Name	Ref	Kaffir Wars 1	2	3
John McAndrews				△
Duncan McArthur			▲	
James McArthur			△	
William McBride			○	△
James McCamley				△
John McClellan	138)			△
Andrew McConnell			○	△
James McConnell			○	△
John McCormack	139)		△	
Patrick McCormack			△	
Michael McCormick			△	○
Alexander McCraith	140)		○	△
Patrick McDaid			○	△
John McDaniel				△
Philip McDermott				△
Donald McDonald			●	△
George McDonald	(P)		○	△
James McDonald (1)	141)		▲	
James McDonald (2)	141)		○	△
John McDonald	142)		○	△
Peter McDonald			○	△
Kernan McDonnell			○	△
James McDowall			▲	
Bernard McElvouge				△
John McEvoy			○	△
Isaac McEwan			▲	
Alexander McFarlane			○	△
Patrick McFarlane	143)		▲	
Samuel McFedries			▲	
Alexander McGarr			○	△
John McGavin				△
Alexander McGhee			○	△
William McGibbon			▲	
Thomas McGill			▲	
Alexander McGregor			○	△
James McGregor				△
Patrick McGonnell	(P)		▲	
John McGorlick				△
John McGowan				△
James McHugh			○	△
Duncan McIntosh			○	△
Dougald McIntyre			○	△
Findley McIntyre				△
Alexander McKay	144)			△
Archibald McKay	145)			△
Colin C. McKay	146)			○
John McKay			○	△
John McKean	147)		△	△
James McKee	148)		▲	
James McKeen	149)		○	△
William McKeevor			○	△
Donald McKenzie			▲	
John McKerroll	150)		○	△
Henry McKey				△
Charles McKinnon			○	△
John McKinnon			○	△
Allen McLean				△
John McLean			▲	
John McLeod	151)		▲	
Robert McLeod			○	△
Hugh McLoughlin			○	△
Michael McLoughlin	(MRM)			△
Daniel McMillan				△
Colin McRae				△
John McRae				△
David McWhirter			▲	
George McWhirter			▲	
Charles McWilliams			○	△

Name	Ref	Kaffir Wars 1	2	3
Henry McWilliams			○	△
John Meldrum				△
Charles Michie			○	△
William Middleton				△
James Miller (1)	152)		○	△
James Miller (2)	153)		▲	
John Miller	154)		▲	
Thomas Miller				△
Thomas Mitchnor	155)			△
William Moffatt			▲	
Alexander Mollison			○	△
Hugh Monaghan				△
Robert Monteith			△	○
Robert Moody	156)		△	○
Edward Moore	(P)		○	△
William Mortimore	202) (P)			△
George Moseley			○	△
James Mounser	157)			△
Andrew Muir			△	○
Phelim Muldoon				△
Patrick Mullins	158)		○	△
John Munro (1)	159)		○	△
John Munro (2)	159)		▲	
Donald Munro	160)		▲	
William Munro	160) (MRM)		▲	
John Murphy				△
James Murray (1)	161)		▲	
James Murray (2)	161)		○	△
John Murray (1)	162)		○	△
John Murray (2)	162)			△
Peter Murray	163)		○	△
John Napier			△	○
George Nelson			○	△
John Newall			▲	
William Newman				△
John Newton			△	○
John Nicholson			○	△
James Nicol				△
William Nicol	164) (R)		▲	
Thomas Nodwell	(MRM)			△
James Norrie			○	△
John Norrie			○	△
William Norris				△
William North				△
Thomas Nugent			○	△
William Nugent			○	△
Jeremiah Nunan			○	△
Patrick O'Brian	165)		○	△
Bartholomew O'Donnell	166)		○	△
John O'Neil	167)		○	△
George O'Rourk				△
James Orr	(MRM)			△
Joseph Orr			○	△
Joseph Osborne			▲	
Patrick O'Toole				△
Patrick Parlane	168)		○	△
James Parry			○	△
John Passmore			○	△
Robert Paterson	116)			△
Edward Patterson			○	△
Walter Patterson			▲	
James Paul	169)		▲	
George Pearce			○	△
Thomas Pearse				△
Thomas Pearson				△
James Penrose				△
Robert Peters	(R)		○	△
Daniel Pettigrew			▲	

122 South Africa 1853 Medal

		Kaffir Wars		
		1	2	3
PRIVATE				
Robert Phillips				△
James Poole			O	△
William Price			O	△
Thomas Pringle			O	△
Nathaniel Randles			O	△
Thomas Randles			O	△
Thomas Rayne			△	O
Thomas Reddle	116)			△
Adam Reid				▲	
Andrew Reid			O	△
Archibald Reid			O	△
James Reid			▲	
Luke Reilly	170)			△
Michael Reilly			▲	
Thomas Reilly	171)		O	△
Thomas Reynolds			▲	
David Riley	172)			△
Joseph Robb			△	O
James Robertson (1)	173)		O	△
James Robertson (2)	173)		O	△
John Robertson	174)		O	△
Robert Robertson			O	△
John Robinson	175)			△
James Rodgers			O	△
John Rodgers			▲	
Thomas Rodyham			△	O
Jesse Rolfe			O	△
William H. Rose			O	△
David Ross			△	O
William Ross			△	△
James Rossiter			O	△
Patrick Rowe				△
John Roy				△
Michael Scanlan	(MRM)			△
William Scott			O	△
Edward Scurr			O	△
Colin Shand			▲	
Charles Sharp			O	△
Joseph Shaw			O	△
Christopher Shears				△
Hugh Sheeran				△
John Sherkie	176)			△
William Shields			▲	
Joseph Short				△
Patrick Shreening				△
James Singer			O	△
Daniel Smith			O	△
Emmanuel Smith			O	△
James Smith (1)	177)		▲	
James Smith (2)	177)			△
John Smith (1)	178)	△		
John Smith (2)	178)		O	△
Peter Smith				△
Richard Smith			O	△
Robert Smith			▲	
William Smith (1)	179)			△
William Smith (2)	179)		O	△
William Smith (3)	179)		O	△
Peter Smyth				△
Patrick Spain			O	△
David Speirs			O	△
Charles Spence			▲	
John Spencer			O	△
John Spittal			O	△
Michael Stack				△
William Stangwood			O	△
George Stenhouse			▲	
George Stephens			▲	
Adam Stevenson	180)		▲	
Joseph Stevenson				△
Alexander Stewart			▲	
Allan Stewart			O	△
James Stewart			▲	
John Stewart	181)		▲	
Ronald Stewart	182)		▲	
William Sulliver	183)		▲	
Eli Summers				△
Joseph Sumner			O	△
Michael Swiney	184)		O	△
Daniel Taylor				△
James Taylor				△
William Taylor			O	△
William Thomas				△
James Thompson		△		
William Thompson			O	△
James Tibbles				△
Joseph Tinsley			O	△
Samuel Torrence				△
Thomas Torrence	185)		▲	
Philip Travers	(R)		▲	
Benjamin Treadwell			O	△
George Truin				△
Thomas Turley	186) (P)		▲	
James Turnbull			▲	
Samuel Turner			▲	
John Twaddell				△
William Tyndall				△
John Urie				△
George Vanner			O	△
Andrew Waddell			●	△
Edward Walker			O	△
James Walker				△
John Walker				△
Samuel Walker (1)	187)			△
Samuel Walker (2)	187)			△
Peter Wallace			▲	
John Walsh	188)			△
Thomas Walsh	189)		O	△
Lawrence Ward			O	△
John Watchorn	190)		O	△
Daniel Watson			O	△
James G. Watson			▲	
William Watson			O	△
Robert Watts				△
Thomas Welsh	191)		△	△
Edward Whigham	192)			△
James Whitehouse			O	△
William Whiteside			△	
David Williams			O	△
Henry B. Williamson			O	△
Andrew Wilson			O	△
George Wilson			O	△
Hugh Wilson			△	O
Samuel Wilson				△
William Wilson (1)	193)		O	△
William Wilson (2)	193)		O	△
William J. Wilson	194)		O	△
John Winn				
Frederick Winterbottom	195) (MRM)			
David Woddam	196)		△	△
Alexander Wood				△
John Woodrow			●	△
Henry Wragg			●	△
James Wright			O	△
Joseph Wright			▲	

		Kaffir Wars				Kaffir Wars		
		1	2	3		1	2	3
William Wright (1)	197)			▲	Donald Young		○	△
William Wright (2)	198)		○	△	George Young			▲
John Wylie	199)		○	△				
William Wylie	200)		○	△	△=campaign qualification as WO/100/17.			
Henry Yateman	201)			△	○=campaign which the Rolls fail to credit.			
Henry Yore			○	△				

91ST (ARGYLLSHIRE) REGIMENT NOTES

1. Commanded the Reserve Battalion throughout the 2nd campaign. Horse shot from under him while helping a wounded man in April 1846.
2. Commanded the 1st Battalion during the 1846–7 campaign.
3. See G and I; and King.
4. Wounded during the operations in the Waterkloof 4.5.52. See G and I; Moodie.
5. Wounded at Block Drift in April 1846 and was present at Boemplaats. Also listed with Staff and received two medals, one of which he returned on 7.1.58; this was re-named for James Keneyborough, 60th Regt.
6. Severely wounded by a shot through the body during the withdrawal to Block Drift 18.4.46.
7. A Lieutenant during the 2nd war.
8. Said to have been present at every affair the battalion was engaged in – which seems a little difficult to believe.
9. Served at Boemplaats. Roll wrongly shows 1850–3 qualification.
10. Served as Deputy Adjutant and QMD to the 1st Division.
11. Wrecked in the 'Abercrombie Robinson' in 1842. Appointed Commandant of Fort Beaufort in 1847.
12. ADC to General Hare during the 2nd war. Promoted for his heroic conduct during the sinking of the 'Birkenhead'.
13. Wounded at Fort Hare in December 1850. His life was saved by QM John Gordon who was assegaied whilst placing Borthwick on his own charger.
14. Lost use of his right arm after being wounded at Boemplaats.
15. Horse killed under him on 21.5.46. See Goff.
16. Wounded 4.5.52.
17. Commended for his conduct at Tyumie Post 19.4.46.
18. Present at Boemplaats.
19. Wounded 27.6.51.
20. Twice on Roll, once credited with 1846–7 and then with 1850–3, when he commanded the Fort Peddie Fingo Levy. See Goff.
21. Had his horse shot from under him on 21.5.46.
22. Narrowly escaped with his life in March 1852. See Goff.
23. Distinguished himself in October 1847 on an expedition against Chief Mampassa.
24. Severely wounded at Boemplaats. To CMR 30.4.47.
25. Participated in all the Waterkloof operations in which the 91st were engaged.
26. Promoted from Sgt Major October 1847.
27. On half-pay until employed as Staff Asst Surgeon and attached to the 91st.
28. Author of 'Records of Service and Campaigning in Many Lands'.
29. A gallant soldier who rose to Captain. Served in all the actions in the Amatolas during the 2nd war and against the Tambookies. Was at Boemplaats and engaged in all the major actions of the 3rd campaign.
30. No 1085. Later a Quartermaster.
31. No 1528.
32. No 293.
33. Severely wounded; see Munro. Was one of the party to represent the 91st at Wellington's funeral.
34. No 509; O'Neile on Roll.
35. No 2078.
36. Apart from the first letter of his surname and his rank, the entry for this man is obliterated on the Roll, but it is not difficult to deduce the recipient.
37. Served with the 75th in the 1834–5 campaign.
38. Although his name is largely indecipherable I conclude it is Coulter who was at one time a Drum Major.
39. No 1209; see Goff, where his christian name is given as Evan.
40. This man's name is shown thus on the Roll, but, following a late claim by Pte James Goudie (No 661), mention is made that Sergeant Goudie's number was 1220. This attempt to avoid confusion only complicates matters, since No 1220 was Pte James Fraine. However, a Sgt David Goudie, sometimes shown as Gowdie, had the number 1200.
41. No 863. Shown as also qualifying for 1834–5 on Roll, but I have not been able to confirm this.
42. Acting Hospital Sergeant.
43. No 1192.
44. No 1748; also Sanders on musters.
45. No 2030; with the 75th in the 1834–5 campaign.
46. No 989.
47. Also Sterling on musters.
48. Also Strang on musters.
49. See Goff, where he is wrongly named Sherrock.
50. No 269 and not to be confused with two Privates of the same name.
51. No 1867; Adams on Roll.
52. Received two severe assegai wounds near Fort Hare on 29.12.50. One entered his back and passed entirely through his body.
53. A section of the Roll listing men whose surnames began with 'C' has been obliterated. These men have been identified by process of elimination.
54. No 960; mentioned in General Orders by Sir Peregrine Maitland. Clark on Roll.
55. Medal said to show Haloran.
56. Also Jeffrey on musters.
57. No 1967; appears to read Manns on Roll but as no man with this name was with the regiment, the entry was probably meant to be Manus, itself a mistake.
58. No 2462; not to be confused with Pte George Wilson.
59. No 1714 and not to be confused with Pte Thomas Doyle.
60. Also Galvan on musters.
61. Wrongly credited with 1850–3 on Roll.
62. Aitken on Roll.
63. Christian name given as Kesuth on Roll.
64. No 2609; Allen on Roll.
65. Also Allan on Roll.
66. No 1889.
67. Allsop on Roll.
68. No 1103.
69. Two men, Nos 309 and 693 of this name were with the 1st Battalion.
70. No 2057.
71. Baily on Roll.
72. Barrie on Roll.
73. Later to the CMR.
74. Dangerously wounded on 4.3.52 at the Waterkloof.
75. Received gunshot wound in the leg 4.10.51 at the Waterkloof.
76. No qualifying dates indicated on Roll.
77. No 1803. No qualifying dates given on Roll.
78. Bretton on Roll.
79. No 363.
80. Brain on Roll; also Brien on musters.
81. Slightly wounded near Fort Hare 29.12.50 and dangerously wounded in the Waterkloof 4.3.52.
82. Believed to be related to Cpl Burnsides.
83. Transferred to the CMR after the 3rd war.
84. No 2500; a survivor from the 'Birkenhead' whose name is probably one of those obliterated on the Roll.
85. Cattreill on Roll. Various spellings on musters.
86. No 1370.
87. Served with the 75th during the 3rd campaign.
88. No 1850.
89. No 235.
90. No 420.
91. Colary on Roll.
92. Cormachan on Roll. No 2795, a survivor from the 'Birkenhead'.

93 Cornes on Roll.
94 Wrongly credited with 1846–7 on Roll.
95 Crichton on Roll.
96 Cruikshank on Roll.
97 Daily on Roll, and occasionally on musters. One of these medals was returned to the Mint.
98 Davis on Roll.
99 No 1050. Dougherty on Roll and occasionally Doherty on musters. Ex-75th Regiment.
100 Wrongly credited with 1846–7 on Roll.
101 Eyesnbell on Roll.
102 Falleik on Roll.
103 Two men of this name were with the regiment Nos 680 and 1056.
104 Flemming on Roll, both spellings on musters.
105 Nos 1931, 1757 and 2501 respectively.
106 No 2791, a survivor from the 'Birkenhead'.
107 Also Frazer on Roll.
108 Gilmore on Roll.
109 Also Goatcher on musters.
110 No 661 and not to be confused with Sgt Goudie.
111 This man probably earned his medal with another regiment.
112 Greaves on Roll.
113 No 2567, a survivor from the 'Birkenhead'.
114 Hagger on Roll.
115 Helse on Roll.
116 I have not been able to trace this man and assume he earned his medal with another regiment.
117 Also Harlane on musters.
118 Nos 2100 and 2167 respectively.
119 Higgin on Roll.
120 No 2746, a survivor from the 'Birkenhead'.
121 No 2163, a survivor from the 'Birkenhead'.
122 One of the 91st Escort at Wellington's funeral.
123 Hide on Roll.
124 Also Jelley on Roll.
125 Johnston on Roll.
126 Joice on Roll.
127 Keightley on Roll.
128 Lavin on Roll.
129 Lawler on Roll.
130 Also Learie on musters.
131 Wrongly credited with 1846–7 on Roll.
132 Also Letham on musters.
133 The Roll notes that this man also served with the 2nd European Levy.
134 Manderstone on Roll.
135 Nos 1206 and 2994 respectively.
136 Matthieson on Roll.
137 Mathews on Roll.
138 McClellin on Roll.
139 Probably Patrick John McCormack, No 2024. John McCormack No 2190 does not seem to have gone to the Cape.
140 Also McCreath on musters.
141 Two men of this name Nos 780 and 1000 served with the 1st Battalion during the 2nd war. No 1768 served with the Reserve Battalion in both campaigns.
142 No 1248.
143 McFarland on Roll.
144 No 1811.
145 No 2715, a survivor from the 'Birkenhead'.
146 Wrongly credited with 1846–7 on Roll.
147 No 793; McKane on Roll.
148 No 576.
149 No 1040; also McKee on musters.
150 Also McKerrill and McKurrell on musters.
151 Died; medal sent to widow.
152 No 2026; also Millar on Roll.
153 Probably No 380 but possibly No 2802.
154 Two men of this name in the 1st Battalion Nos 160 and 401.
155 Mitchner on Roll.
156 Moodey on Roll.
157 Mouncer on Roll.
158 No 2751, a survivor from the 'Birkenhead'. Mullin on Roll.
159 Nos 1340 and 1341 respectively.
160 Munro on Roll.
161 Nos 940 and 113.
162 Nos 1773 and 2608.
163 No. 1311.
164 Nicholl on Roll; Nicol on musters and medal.
165 O'Brien on Roll.
166 O'Donald on Roll.
167 No 1703, a survivor from the 'Birkenhead'.
168 Parlance on Roll.
169 Pawl on Roll.
170 Reily on Roll.
171 See Goff.
172 Reily on Roll. He later transferred to the 73rd and the Mint records show him receiving another medal in the name of Reilly, possibly as a replacement.
173 Nos 1139 and 1359 respectively.
174 No. 1250.
175 No 2743, a survivor from the 'Birkenhead'.
176 Gallantly saved the life of Lt Bond in January 1852. Called Sharkie by Goff.
177 Nos 435 and 2307 respectively.
178 Nos 236 and 1393 respectively.
179 Nos 936, 1451 and 1990 respectively.
180 Stephenson on Roll.
181 No. 561.
182 No 1215.
183 No 1178; Sullivan on Roll.
184 No 1870; also Sweeney on musters.
185 Torvance on Roll.
186 Turlay on Roll, but medal correctly impressed.
187 Nos 2414 and 2591.
188 No 2456.
189 No 1640.
190 Watehorn on Roll.
191 A late applicant who I failed to trace on musters. Possibly the same man as Thomas Walsh.
192 I have failed to trace this recipient.
193 Nos 380 and 1400.
194 No 162.
195 No 2802, a survivor from the 'Birkenhead'.
196 Woodham on Roll.
197 Two men of this name served in the 1st Battalion, Nos 155 and 1315.
198 No 1269.
199 Also Wyllie on musters.
200 Wilie on Roll.
201 Also Yeatman on musters.
202 Also Mortimer on musters. Severely wounded in the elbow at Boemplaats.

PRO References: WO/12/9279-9280-9281-9282-9283-9289-9290-9291-9292.

1st Battalion Rifle Brigade

Carried in two transports the 1st Battalion sailed from Gibraltar in October 1846 and by Christmas was encamped on the Kei River as part of Somerset's 2nd Division. Before the end of the year a patrol lost one rifleman killed and another wounded and during January 1847 several detachments who were engaged in action suffered a number of casualties. Towards the end of the month the regiment marched to King William's Town and from there was split up among several posts. Two companies under Lt Hardinge joined Col Michel's expedition into the Fish River bush and early in February a patrol under Lt Oxenham killed and wounded 18 of the enemy near Grahams Town when intercepting a party of cattle thieves.

One company of the 1st Riflemen served at Fort Coke while another was sent to Goolah Heights until mid-September. Other detachments operated across the Buffalo and Keiskamma Rivers but by September 17th the battalion joined together for the expedition into the Amatolas and was engaged in the pursuit of the Kaffirs in the Keiskamma basin. It was to Col Buller that Sandili and his principal leaders surrendered themselves on October 19th. This terminated the campaign in the Amatolas but one company of Riflemen was called upon to assist in the sweeping up which was still going on at the Kei River before the 1st RB was re-united in King William's Town at the end of the year.

When the Boers rebelled in 1848 two companies from the regiment were part of the force under Buller which fought at Boemplaats and they lost 17 officers and men killed and wounded.

By 1850 the 1st Battalion had been abroad for 10 years and preparation was made for a return to England. Part of the regiment embarked at Cape Town on June 6th but the remainder had to wait until July 12th before they left for home and it was not until late September that the battalion again came together. But within three months the Kaffirs had again risen in revolt. As 1851 wore on it was obvious they were not to be easily put down and the 1st RB was at Dover when told to make ready to reinforce the colony. On January 2nd 1852 the whole battalion was packed into the 'Megaera' and commenced a voyage which was a nightmare. The overcrowded ship encountered severe gales and survived fire aboard before limping into Simons Bay two months after it had set out, but the troops could later reflect that they might well have been transported by the ill-fated Birkenhead.

Appointed to Gen Somerset's 1st Brigade the Riflemen were just in time to join the expedition to the Waterkloof which set out from Fort Beaufort on April 22nd. Within a few days Russell's, Woodford's and Somerset's companies were in action trying to feel out the enemy and had one officer and three men wounded.

From their camping ground at Bears Farm frequent patrols kept up a harassment which resulted in several skirmishes during May and June and the regiment lost two killed and seven wounded. As a base from which to launch the assault the 1st RB was employed in building two redoubts at Mount Misery and on July 24th the battalion with their forces under Buller's command attacked the Kaffirs at Mundell's Kranze. Arms and ammunition were destroyed and horses and cattle captured. Two Riflemen were wounded.

At the end of the month the 1st Battalion was back at Fort Beaufort and, during August, re-equipped in preparation for the final drive to clear the Waterkloof. Four divisions carved into the valley and met little opposition. The Rifle Brigade marched on September 15th and successfully joined up with the 73rd Regiment. Subsequent days were spent scouring the gorges for fugitive rebels and a company at a time was employed on roadmaking through enemy territory as operations drew to a close. But for Rooper's company there remained Cathcart's expedition to punish Mosesh. Ninety Riflemen under Lt Curzon accompanied the force as camp bodyguard and in the bitter fighting against the Basutos on and around the mountain of Berea the Brigade lost three men killed before the troops withdrew.

The 1st RB returned to England in October 1853 before being committed to the Crimea.

		Kaffir Wars 1	2	3
LIEUTENANT COLONEL				
Alfred H. Horsford	1) (R)		△	△
MAJOR				
Charles DuPre Egerton			△	
BREVET MAJOR				
Lord Alexander Russell	2)		△	
CAPTAIN				
Aubrey A. Cartwright	3)		△	
Hon Gilbert Elliott	4)		△	△
Julius Glyn	5)		△	△
Henry Hardinge	6)		△	△
Alexander Macdonnell			△	
Charles Oxenden			△	
Edward Rooper			△	△
Edward A. Somerset	7)		△	
Charles J. Woodford	8)		△	
LIEUTENANT				
Coote Buller	9)		△	
Edward M. Buller			△	△

		Kaffir Wars 1	2	3
LIEUTENANT ADJUTANT				
William B. Brewster			△	
LIEUTENANT				
Charles H. S. Churchill			△	
Hon Henry Clifford	10)			△
Augustus H. Clifton			△	△
Hon Leicester Curzon	8)			△
Arthur W. Godfrey				△
Charles Hale				△
Hon George B. Legge				△
Henry G. Lindsay	11)			△
John Nicholl	(P)			△
SECOND LIEUTENANT				
Thomas H. Bramston	12) (R)			△
Claude T. Bourchier	13) (R)		△	△
ENSIGN				
John Brett	14)		△	△
PAYMASTER				
John E. Large	15)			△

126 South Africa 1853 Medal

			Kaffir Wars		
			1	2	3
QUARTERMASTER					
Henry Peacocke	16)			△	△
Richard Taylor	17)				△
SURGEON					
Robert Bowen	18)				△
Evan G. Lloyd				△	
ASSISTANT SURGEON					
Joshua Paynter				△	
James E. Scott	19)			△	△

Note; Col George Buller, wounded at Boemplaats and a divisional commander during the 3rd campaign, is listed under Staff.

			1	2	3
SERGEANT MAJOR					
Francis Green		(P)			△
William Stillwell				△	
William Webb				△	
QUARTERMASTER SERGEANT					
Foster Hewison				△	
William Young				△	
COLOUR SERGEANT					
George Ackerman				△	△
William Bond		(R)		△	
John Brett		(R)		△	△
Richard Cornelius				△	△
George Garner	20)			O	△
Edward Harris				△	
William Higgins				△	△
Jonathan Palmer				△	
Charles Tapp				O	△
Abraham Trew				△	
Henry Tucker				O	△
Charles Ward				△	
Albert T. Wood	21)	(R)		△	
BUGLE MAJOR					
Alexander Miller				△	△
William Money				△	
SERGEANT					
William Ackerman	22)			△	
William Bentley		(MRM)		△	
William Cornelius			△	△	
George Drowley				△	
William Evans				△	△
David Flory	23)			△	△
Paul Gibson		(P)		△	
William J. Gibson	24)			△	
John Green	25)			△	
John Hicks				△	△
Robert Hills	26)	(R)		△	△
Charles Hiscock				△	△
Joseph Holdom		(P)		△	
George Jerrome	27)			△	△
William Jerrome				△	
John Judge					△
William Knight				△	△
James Malden				△	
Job Mason	28)			△	
Thomas McCullen				△	△
William McDonald		(P)		△	
John McGrotty	29)			△	
Charles McNalty	30)			△	△
Matthew Meech				△	
William Miller		(P)		O	△
David Milne					△
Timothy Murphy				△	△
David Osborne				△	△

			1	2	3
William Patstone					△
Frederick Pearson	31)			△	△
James Peirce	32)			△	△
William Price				△	△
Donald Robertson					△
William Rudkin	33)	(P)		△	
George Seldon				△	△
John Spriggs				△	△
Patrick Tinneny	34)			△	
William Ward				△	
CORPORAL					
William Bass					△
George Bateman				O	△
Daniel Burns				△	
William H. Clayton					△
William Cook	35)			△	△
William Cooke	36)			△	△
John Cross	37)			△	
Thomas Davey				△	
Charles Douglas					△
George Drury					△
John Evans	38)			△	
John Fisher	39)				△
Henry Fothergill					△
Charles Goddard				O	△
Thomas Hall				△	
William J. Hamilton					△
Charles Lambert					△
Thomas Mackay					△
James Maloney					△
George Mascall				△	
James Mason		(R)			△
George R. Nosely	40)				△
David Peachy		(R)		△	△
James Powell					△
Matthew Rice				△	△
John Round	41)				△
James Rudling					△
Lucas Saunders					△
Samuel Smith				△	
William Stent				△	
Charles Stroulger					△
George Taylor	42)			△	△
John Vaughan					△
Maurice Walsh				△	△
Edward Warren					△
Wilmer Webb	43)				△
Alfred Willson					△
BUGLER					
George Ackerman	44)				△
Thomas Clements				△	△
Richard Cummins					△
William Gardner				△	△
Michael Harding					△
James Judge	45)			△	
John Kennedy					△
James Kerns	46)				△
John McLynchy	47)			△	△
Arthur McWilliam				△	△
Richard Pope				△	
Charles Stewart					△
Robert Stewart					△
PRIVATE					
Edward Abery				△	
George Abery				△	
Mark Abraham	48)			△	
Richard Ackerman					△

South Africa 1853 Medal

Name	Note		Kaffir Wars 1	Kaffir Wars 2	Kaffir Wars 3
William Ackerman	49)				△
Edward Adams				△	
Richard Adams					△
Martin Ahearn				△	△
William Allchin	50)			△	
George Aldridge					△
David Allcock					△
John Allen (1)	51)			O	△
John Allen (2)	51)				△
Thomas Allen	52)			O	△
Thomas Allum					△
Michael Ambrose					△
Stephen Amer			△		
Daniel Andrews					△
Nathaniel Arthur					△
John Atkins			△		
Thomas Atwell	(P)				△
Robert Austin					△
William Aylett			△		
George Bailey					△
Henry Bailey (1)	53)				△
Henry Bailey (2)	53)				△
William H. Baker	54)				△
John Barham	(P)			△	△
Mark Barker	55)				△
Henry Barley				△	△
Henry Barnes			△		
John Barry					△
Thomas Bartley					△
Samuel Barwell					△
Henry Bassett					△
Herbert Batchelor	(P)				△
Charles Bate			△		
Stephen Bates	(MRM)				△
Horace Batkin					△
George Bax	56)		△		
Joseph Baxter					△
Joseph Bayliss	(P)				△
Matthew Beadel	57)				△
Robert Beale					△
Frederick Beard					△
William Beatty					△
Edwin Beaumont					△
Francis Bell	58)			△	
Nelson Bell				△	
Robert Bell	(R)			△	
George Bennett				△	△
Francis Bevege	59)			△	△
Henry Bibby					△
Richard Binskin				△	△
George Birch					△
George Bishop				△	
John Blaber				△	
James Blackwell					△
Edward Blake				△	△
John Blanks				△	△
Richard Blanks	54)				△
Anthony Blount					△
Henry Boulton					△
John Boyce					△
Thomas G. Bradbury					△
William Bradford					△
Thomas Bray					△
Alfred Breed					△
William Bridport					△
James Broadway	(P)				△
James Brooks	60)				△
John Broome					△

Name	Note		Kaffir Wars 1	Kaffir Wars 2	Kaffir Wars 3
Patrick Brophy					△
Charles Brown				△	
James Brown	61)				△
John Brown	62)	(P)			△
Joseph Brown	63)				△
William Brown					△
Robert Bruce				△	△
William Bruce				△	O
Michael Bryan					△
Thomas M. Buckmaster				△	
William Bucknall				△	
James Budden					△
James Buller				△	△
William Bulloch					△
William Burden				△	
Thomas Burley				△	△
William Burnett					△
James Burns				△	
Michael Burns					△
John Burrows					△
Benjamin Burton					△
William Burton					△
James Butcher				△	△
Thomas Cain	64)				△
John Calderbank					△
Thomas Cane	65)			O	△
George Cann					△
John Carroll				△	
Patrick Carroll				△	
William Carroll					△
Eli Carson				△	△
Francis Cash					△
Charles Catchpole	66)				△
Henry Chamberling	67)				△
George Chapman	(R)				△
Horatio Chapman					△
John W. Chapman					△
Robert Chapman				△	
William Claridge				△	
Alfred Clarke				△	
Edmund Clarke					△
George Clarke					△
Thomas Clary	68)				△
James Clayton					△
William B. Clerke	69)				△
Cornelius Clews					△
George Clothier					△
John Coates					△
Simon Cockbill				△	△
Isaac Cole				△	
John Coleman					△
John B. Collins					△
Samuel Collins					△
William Compton					△
John Connolly					△
Patrick Connolly					△
Michael Conron					△
Charles Constable					△
Samuel Cooke				△	
Edward Coombes				△	△
John Cooper	(R)			△	△
Thomas Cooper					△
Horace Cornelius	70)				△
Robert Coulter	(P)				△
Stephen Coulter				△	
John Cowan					△
George Cramp				△	
Caleb Croft					△

128 South Africa 1853 Medal

PRIVATE		Kaffir Wars 1	2	3
William Crosswaite			△	
Thomas Cryer				△
Michael Dahoney	71)			△
John Daley		△		
John Dalgety	72)		△	
Matthew Dalrymple	73)	△		
Walter W. Davies				△
Richard Davies	74)			△
William Davis (1)	75)			△
William Davis (2)	75)			△
James Davison				△
John Demit			△	△
Thomas Dennis				△
Hugh Devlin	(P)		△	O
George Doel	76)		△	
Hugh Donnelly	77)			△
John Doonan		△		
William Doran				△
John Dornin		△		
James Dowling	(MRM)			△
James Dowsell				△
John Drowney	78) (MRM)	△		
William Druse	79)			△
John Duggan				△
Patrick Dunn			△	△
Robert Dunn				△
John Dunt	80)		△	△
George Durant				△
John Eagle	(P)			△
Walter N. Eagle	(R)			△
Peter Easton				△
Thomas Edwards	(P)		△	△
William Edwards			△	
William Egleston	81)		O	△
Francis Evans				△
Joseph Eveleigh		△		
Samuel Eyres	82)			△
John Fallon				△
Edward Farley		△		
George Farnes		△		
Christopher Farrell				△
Henry Farris	83) (P)			△
John Fearn			△	△
Joseph Fergy				△
William Ferriss	(P)			△
Prince F. Finch				△
Edward Fitzgerald				△
John Fitzgerald		△		
Richard Fitzgerald				△
John Flanagan	84)			△
Richard Fletcher		△		
John Float		△		
William Flower	85)			△
John Floyd				△
John Flynn	(MRM)			△
Thomas Flynn				△
Henry E. Ford				△
James Fox (1)	86)			△
James Fox (2)	86)			△
Robert Frary				△
James Freeman				△
Simon Frindle			△	△
Thomas Geddes			△	
Henry George			△	△
Charles Gibbons				△
Alfred Gibbs				△
Thomas Gibbs			△	△

		Kaffir Wars 1	2	3
Robert Gillespie			△	
Charles Glazebrook			△	△
Michael Gleeson				△
Charles G. Goad				△
George Goodall				
Henry Goodman				△
William Gore	(R)		△	△
George Gorham			△	△
George Goring				△
Charles Gorton				△
George Gould				△
James Graham			△	△
William Graham				△
Samuel Gray				△
Mark Green				△
Robert Green	(R)			△
William J. Green		△		
Hugh Gregory		△		
Terence Grey	88)			△
Abraham Grigg				△
Charles Groves	89)			△
George Haines			△	△
Charles Haggerty				△
George Hall				△
Robert Hall				△
William Hall	90)			△
William Halls	91)			△
Edward Hallows			△	△
George Halliwell	92)			△
John Hamblin			△	△
George H. Hammond				△
Edward Hampton				△
Michael Hanify				△
Hugh Hannan	93)			△
Robert Hannan	94)			△
John Harding				△
William Hargraves	95)		O	△
Matthew Harley		△		
William Harper				△
William Harris				△
Richard Hartland				△
William Harward				△
George Hatcher				△
Moses Haycock	96)			△
William Hayward	97)			△
Robert Head				△
Edward Heath	48)	△		
Henry Heather			△	△
James Hedger			O	△
Daniel Heimsath				△
Samuel Henderson		△		
George Herd		△		
Daniel Herlihy		△		
William Hermitage				△
James Herring				△
Edward Higgins	(R)			△
John Higgins			△	△
Edwin Hill	98)	△		
Henry Hill				△
Richard Hill			△	△
William Hill				△
William Hodges				△
Edward Hogan		△		
John Hogan	99)	△		
Alfred Holdin				△
Henry Hollingsworth				△
Burrell Holmes				△
Thomas Holyland			△	△

South Africa 1853 Medal

Name	Ref		Kaffir Wars 1	2	3
Joseph V. Hooke	100)				△
Charles Hooper				△	△
Philip Hooton					△
Thomas Horan				△	△
Arthur Howard					△
James Howshaw				○	△
Edwin Hudson					△
John Hudson					△
David Huggett			△		
Henry Hughes					△
Augustus F. Humphreys	101)				△
Titus Hurst	98)	(R)	△		
James Hussey					△
Elijah Huston					△
John Hutchinson				△	△
William Huthwaite	102)				△
James Jackson				○	△
Philip Jenkins		(P)			△
Richard P. Jenkins	103)				△
Robert G. Jenkins	104)				△
Christopher Jesson					△
Walter Jesson					△
Benjamin Johnson			△		
Henry Johnson					△
John Johnson					△
William Johnson (1)	106)			△	
William Johnson (2)	106)			△	○
Thomas Johnston	107)			△	△
Edward Jones					△
Henry Jones				△	△
Robert Jones					△
William Jones (1)	108)			△	△
William Jones (2)	108)			△	△
George Jordan	109)				△
Henry Josling					△
Alfred Judd			△		
Peter Keating					△
John Kelly					△
William Kelly		(P)		△	△
Robert Kent					△
Robert Kerr					△
Henry Kibby				△	△
John Kiely				△	△
John Kilroe					△
John King (1)	110)		△		
John King (2)	110)				△
Thomas King					△
William King (1)	111)	(P)		△	△
William King (2)	111)			△	△
James Kingsman					△
Charles Kirsey					△
Thomas Knight				△	△
Robert Knott					△
James Labdon					△
Peter Laffarty	112)				△
George Laidler	113)				△
Edward Lamb					△
John Lambert					△
Robert Lambert					△
Richard Lanning					△
John Latchford		(P)		△	△
Alfred Lavell					△
Richard Law					△
Charles Lawrence					△
John Lawrence			△		
Thomas Lawrence					△
William Lawrence			△		
Edward Laws					△

Name	Ref		Kaffir Wars 1	2	3
Edward Leaver	114)			△	△
John Leech		(P)			△
Horatio Legg				△	
Thomas Leighfield				△	△
John H. Lewis				△	
William Lewis					△
Thomas Liggins				△	
George Lines					△
James Linnett				△	
Richard Lloyd					△
George Lockton					△
James Mack	115)				○
George Macklin				△	△
Thomas Makepiece					△
William Manclarke					△
John Martin					△
Thomas Martin	116)			○	△
William Martin					△
John Masfield					△
James Masters				△	△
Frederick Matthews	117)				△
John Maythe					△
John Maxwell				△	
Patrick McCann					△
John McCarthy					△
Hamilton McGalligan	118)			△	
Joseph McGee					△
Patrick McGee					△
Patrick McGough					△
Arthur McGrath	115)				○
Michael McGrath	115)	(P)			△
Benjamin McGuinty					△
Alexander McIntyre					△
Andrew McKee					△
John McKenna				△	△
Patrick McKeown					△
William McKnight		(MRM)			△
Bernard McMahon		(MRM)		△	△
John McMullen				△	△
Anthony McNalty	119)				△
Patrick McNalty	120)				△
John McNeal	121)				△
George Melhuish					△
Joseph Merritt		(P)		△	△
William Merritt	98)			△	
Philip Milgate	122)				△
Robert Millen					△
Joseph Miller					△
Reuben Mills				△	△
Thomas Mills					△
James Mineham				△	△
John Minter					△
George Mitchell					△
Timothy Monger	123)				△
James Moon					△
Henry Moonan					△
John Moran				△	△
John Morgan (1)	124)				△
John Morgan (2)	124)			△	△
William Morgan		(P)		△	△
George Morrison					△
Christopher Murphy					△
Michael Murphy (1)	125)				△
Michael Murphy (2)	125)				△
Joseph Murray					△
Robert Murray					△
John Musgrove					△
Job Neal				△	

130 South Africa 1853 Medal

PRIVATE		Kaffir Wars 1 2 3			Kaffir Wars 1 2 3
Amos Nevard		△	Edward Rooney		△
Charles New		△	John Rooney		△
James Newbanks		△	Richard Rowland		△
Henry Nightingale	(P)	△	Robert Russell	(P)	△
William Nomilie		△	John Saltmarsh	115)	△
Frederick Nurse		△	Lucas Saunders	115)	○
Thomas Oakey		△	John Scannell	141)	△ △
Thomas Oakman	(R)	△ △	Henry E. Scott		
Joseph Ogden		△	George Scully	115)	○
Thomas Onley		△	George Seath		
George Ostler		△	Henry Seppings	142)	△ △
George O'Sullivan	126)	△	William Serge		○ △
Charles Otaley	127)	△	Abraham Shaw		△
Thomas Packer	128) (P)	△	Samuel Shaw		△ △
William Page		△	John Shean	143)	△
Thomas Palmer	115)	○	John Shroeder		△
William Palmer		△ △	William Silk		△
William Parsons	115)	△	William Simms		△
William Pascoe		△	George Simpson		△
Thomas Patchett	129)	△ △	Thomas Simpson		△
John Patey	130)	△	James Skinner		△ △
Holford Pavitt		△	Frederick Smith		△
Thomas Payne		△	George Smith	48)	△
George Pepperall		△ △	Henry B. Smith		△ △
Alfred Percival		△	Joseph Smith	115)	○
Henry Perey	131)	△	Mark Smith		△
Edward Perrett	(R)	△	Richard Smith		△
Henry Philpott		△	Robert Smith		△
Joseph Pickering		△ △	William Smith (1)	144)	△
William Pierce	132)	△ △	William Smith (2)	144)	△
John Pine		△	James Snow		△
Richard Pinnock	(R)		Frederick Soden		△
John Plumridge	133)	△ △	Peter Sparks		△
William Pocock		△	Martin Spencely	(P)	△
Edward Porter		△	William Sprackett	(P)	△
Thomas Power		△	James Stanley	145)	△
George Potter		△ △	William Stanton	146)	△
Thomas Price		△ △	James Steadman	147)	△
Edwin Prichard	134)	△	George Stephenson		△
Henry Prompby		△	Alfred Stevens	148)	○
John Prout		△	Henry Stokes		△
James Purcell		△	George Stubbs	115)	○
William Putman		△ ○	John Stuckey		△
Thomas Quinlan	(P)	△	Peter Sutton	115)	○
Felix Quinn		△	George Swain		△
Thomas Radcliffe		△ △	John Swanscott		△
William Rainey		△	Edward Tainsh		△
James Rawe	135)	△	Thomas Tapley		△
John Read	136)	△	Richard G. Tarrant	149)	△
John Readhouse		△	David Taunton	150)	△
James Reid		△	William Taunton		△
William Reith		△	George Taylor	151)	△
Charles Remnant	137)	△	James Taylor	152)	△
George Reston		△	John Taylor	153)	△
Joseph Riley	138)	△	Thomas Taylor		△
Elias A. Richards	139)	△ △	William Taylor		△
John Richards	115)	△	William Teed	48)	△
Thomas Richardson		△	William Telford		△
William Ricketts	11)	△ △	Thomas Temperley	154)	△ △
James Ridgway	140)	△	William H. Thompson		△
John Ridout		△	Frederick Thornhill		△
Andrew Ritchie		△	James Tierney		
George Roberson		△	Thomas Tillby	155)	
Joseph Roberts		△	James Tinneny	156)	△ △
James Robertson	(P)	△	James Tobin		△ △
William Robinson		△ △	Abraham Tomkinson	(P)	△
Bartholomew Rock		△ △	Richard Tomlin	157)	△
Richard Ronan		△	Henry Tonks		△

South Africa 1853 Medal 131

Name		Kaffir Wars 1 2 3	Name		Kaffir Wars 1 2 3
Charles Tumber		△	Thomas Whelan		△
Robert Turley		△	Richard Whitaker	163)	△ △
George Turner		△	Richard K. Whitaker	164)	△ △
John Turner		O △	William Whitaker		△ △
Thomas Turner		△	Henry White		△
William Turner		△ △	John Whiting		△
James F. Traylen		△	Thomas Whittle		△
Charles Twining		△ △	Richard N. Whymark		△
Joseph Underwood		△	James Wild		△
John Vanson		△	Richard Williams		△
Stephen Vast		△	Thomas Williams		△
William Wackley		△ △	William Williams		△
James Wain	158)	△	Andrew Williamson		△
William Wainwright	48)		John Williamson		△
William Wakeham		△ △	Robert Williamson		△
John Waldron		△	William Williamson		△
John Walker		△	John Willis		△
Joseph Walker (1)	159)		Joseph Wilson		△
Joseph Walker (2)	159)	△	William Wilson	165) (P)	△
Joseph Wallace		△	John Wines	166)	
Edwin Wallington	160)	△	William Winter		△
George Wallington		△	George Wolfe		△
William Wallington		△ △	Joseph Wood		△
John Walmsley	161)	△	Thomas Woodhall		△
John Walsh		△	Thomas Woods		△
Nicholas Walton			William Woods (1)	167)	△
Samuel Ward		△ △	William Woods (2)	168)	△
William Ward	(R)		Samuel H. Woolfe	(P)	△
Thomas Warner		△	George Worley	169) (MRM)	△
Henry Warren		△	Samuel Wormleighton		△
James Warren		△ △	William Wrake		△
Wonfred Waterman		△	John Wren		△
Henry Webb		△	George Wright		△
George Weeks		△	Thomas Wright	170)	△
Thomas Wellding	162)	△	Esau Yewen		△
George Weller		△	Henry Pigot		△
John Wells	(P)	△	Henry Pound		△ △
William Wheadon		△			
Francis Wheatley	(R)	△ △	△=campaign qualification as WO/100/17.		
Robert Wheatley		△	O=campaign which the Rolls fail to credit.		

1ST BATTALION RIFLE BRIGADE NOTES

1 Horseford on Roll.
2 Served as DAQMG to the 1st Division and was present at Berea.
3 Wounded at Boemplaats. See Bissett.
4 ADC to Cathcart; served at Berea.
5 Field Adjutant at Boemplaats. ADC to Cathcart. Served at Berea.
6 Slightly wounded at Boemplaats.
7 Although credited with 1846–7 on Roll I have been unable to confirm participation in that campaign. Harts only mentions the 3rd war.
8 As in the case of Edward Somerset the Roll wrongly credits 1846–7 and again Harts only mentions the 3rd campaign. Served at Berea.
9 Yet another officer mistakenly credited with 1846–7 on Roll when he was undoubtedly at the depot in England.
10 Shown on the Roll as qualified for the 2nd war but in December 1847 he was on leave from the depot awaiting orders to join the service companies. Present at Boemplaats. See King.
11 Distinguished himself at Berea.
12 Credited with the 2nd war on Roll but he was not in fact commissioned until 1849. Sketches made by Bramston in the field are in the possession of the Regimental Museum.
13 Although I have not been able to confirm his qualification for the 2nd war, Bourchier seems to have been with the commissariat before being commissioned in 1849 and may have served in that capacity. Harts only credits 1850–3.
14 Severely wounded at Boemplaats. Served in the ranks at both the 2nd and 3rd campaigns before being commissioned in July 1854.
15 The Roll credits 1846–7 but he was with the 76th Regiment at that time and Harts only mentions the 3rd campaign.
16 Peacock on Roll. Served in the ranks at Boemplaats and was commissioned in 1849.
17 Went on half-pay in 1849 and I have been unable to confirm qualification for the 3rd war as shown on Roll.
18 Wrongly credited with 1846–7 on Roll when he was with the 48th Regiment. A survivor from the 'Birkenhead' he joined the RB from Staff in February 1852.
19 Although joining the RB in June 1847 I have not been able to confirm his qualification for the 2nd campaign. 'Medical Officers of the British Army' only credits 1850–3.
20 Medal returned for alteration after wrongly being named Gardner.
21 Orderly room clerk.
22 No 1622 and not to be confused with Pte Wm. Ackerman.
23 Also Florey on musters.
24 No 2414.
25 No 2575; had a lucky escape when a bullet struck the brasses of his waist belt in July 1852.
26 Hospital Sergeant.
27 No 2086, Jerrom on Roll.
28 Christian name given as Jacob on Roll.
29 McGorthy on Roll.
30 McNulty on Roll.
31 Paymaster' clerk.

32 Pearce on Roll.
33 Twice shown on Roll, once as a private.
34 Tinnany on Roll; a paymaster's clerk.
35 Cleyton on Roll.
36 No 2666; served with the 73rd during the 2nd campaign. Also Cooke on musters.
37 No 1519; Cook on Roll.
38 Also credited with the 3rd campaign on Roll.
39 See the 'United Services Magazine' 1898.
40 Christian names shown as Robert George on Roll.
41 Raund on Roll.
42 No 1951 and not to be confused with Pte George Taylor.
43 Christian name spelt Willmer on Roll.
44 No 3269, and not to be confused with Col Sgt George Ackerman No 956.
45 No 2177; twice entered on Roll, once credited with 1846–7 and then incorrectly with 1850–3 when in fact he was at the depot. Not to be confused with Sgt John Judge.
46 Also Kernes on musters.
47 McLynchey on Roll.
48 Also credited with 1850–3 on Roll but he was sent to the depot when the regiment sailed from Dover.
49 No 2770, and not to be confused with Sgt William Ackerman. Although shown as Private on the Roll he was a Bugler when the returns were made and this may be shown on the medal.
50 Alckin on Roll.
51 Nos 1671 and 2748.
52 No 2066.
53 Nos 744 and 2909.
54 'Dead' on Roll.
55 No 3031; Baker on Roll.
56 Roll can be read as Box.
57 Beadle on Roll.
58 Twice returned on Roll.
59 Beavage on Roll.
60 Brookes on Roll.
61 No 3315, he joined the regiment as a 'Boy' at the depot 9.2.53 and so was not properly qualified for a medal.
62 No 2162.
63 No 2881.
64 No 2170.
65 No 1128.
66 'Died' and medal believed to have been returned.
67 Chamberlain on Roll; to Grenadier Guards 1854.
68 Also Clarry on musters.
69 Clarke on Roll; to 2nd Battalion February 1854.
70 Cornellius on Roll; to 2nd Battalion February 1854.
71 Dahony on Roll.
72 Dalgetty on Roll.
73 Dalrympe on Roll.
74 Davies on Roll; to RA February 1854.
75 Nos 2573 and 2728; also Davies on musters.
76 Also Doell on musters.
77 Also Donnolly on musters.
78 Drawney on Roll.
79 Druce on Roll.
80 Dant on Roll.
81 Also Eagleston on musters; to 2nd Battalion February 1854.
82 Eyers on Roll.
83 Ferriss on Roll.
84 Also Flannagan on musters.
85 Also Flowers on musters; to 2nd Battalion February 1854.
86 Nos 1924 and 2961.
87 Christian names also given as John William on musters.
88 Also Gray on musters.
89 A note on the Roll says medal was given to a man who falsely representing himself as Groves and forged a receipt.
90 No 2612.
91 No 2233.
92 No 2432; Halwell on Roll.
93 Hannon on Roll; to 2nd Battalion February 1854.
94 Hannon on Roll.
95 Also Hargreaves on musters.
96 Heycock on Roll.
97 No 2175; distinguished himself in the fighting against Mosesh.
98 Wrongly credited with 1850–3 on Roll.
99 I have been unable to trace this recipient.
100 Hook on Roll.
101 Humphries on Roll.
102 Huthwait on Roll.
103 No 2762.
104 No 2874.
105 Twice entered on Roll, once as Johnstone. The musters show both spellings.
106 Nos 1320 and 1758.
107 Johnson on Roll.
108 Nos 1640 and 1848; one of these medals is in a private collection.
109 Jordon on Roll.
110 Nos 2024 and 2629.
111 Nos 1135 and 1722.
112 Lafferty on Roll; all his campaign service was with the 74th.
113 Leidler on Roll.
114 Lever on Roll.
115 Wrongly credited with 1846–7 on Roll.
116 No 2041.
117 The Roll has been altered and appears to read Matheros.
118 McGilligan on Roll.
119 Also McNulty on musters. To 2nd Batt 28.2.54.
120 McNulty on Roll.
121 McNeil on Roll and credited also with 1846–7.
122 Also Millgate on musters.
123 Manger on Roll.
124 Nos 969 and 1306.
125 Nos 2339 and 2756.
126 O'Sulivan on Roll.
127 Otley on Roll.
128 Christian names given as John Thomas on musters.
129 A Schoolmaster Sergeant during the 2nd campaign.
130 Paitey on Roll and credited also with 1850–3.
131 Altered on the Roll from Perey to Percy but musters show the former.
132 Also Peirce and Pearce on musters.
133 Plumeridge on Roll.
134 Died 21.9.54 – before the GO was issued.
135 No 2939; Rowe on Roll.
136 No 2254; twice entered on Roll, once wrongly as Reid and when this medal went astray the application for a duplicate was made as Read.
137 Rennant on Roll.
138 No 2005. Roll could be interpreted as Ribey.
139 Musters give christian names as Alfred Elias.
140 Ridgeway on Roll.
141 Scarnell on Roll.
142 No 2730; Shepping on Roll.
143 Sheen on Roll.
144 Nos 2780 and 2934.
145 Also Standley on musters.
146 No 2810; Staunton on Roll.
147 Stedman on Roll.
148 No 2983; Stephens on Roll and wrongly credited with 1846–7.
149 Christian name of Richard has correctly been inserted on the Roll but may not show on the medal.
150 Christian name given as Daniel on Roll.
151 No 1680 and not to be confused with Cpl G. Taylor.
152 No 2596.
153 No 2574.
154 Also Timperley on musters.
155 Also Tillbey on musters.
156 Tinnery on Roll.
157 Tamlin on Roll.
158 Waine on Roll.
159 Nos 1787 and 2868; one of these medals is in the Regimental Museum.
160 No 3336; all his campaign service was with the 73rd.
161 No 2530 and correctly altered on Roll from Warmsley.
162 Welding on Roll.
163 No 1323.
164 No 1821; Whittaker on Roll.
165 No 2722. After being in Chatham Military Prison was sent to the depot when the regiment sailed from Dover in January 1852 and does not seem to be qualified for the medal.
166 Roll correctly altered from Whies.
167 No 1201; also credited with 1850–3 on Roll.
168 No 2899; Wood on Roll.
169 Whorley on Roll.
170 Mint records show he received a replacement in 1863.

PRO References: WO/12/10079-10080-10084-10085.

Cape Mounted Riflemen

The Cape Mounted Riflemen were designated as such from 1828 and had grown out of a corps of Hottentot scouts employed to assist in policing the frontier. Only a few years before the force had been called 'the infamous Cape Hottentot Regiment' and its loyalty to the government was somewhat fragile. Nevertheless during the 1st war Sir Harry Smith was impressed by the speed with which this volatile people could be trained as soldiers. In later years he was still reluctant to believe ill of them, blaming much of the discontent in the CMR upon the newspaper 'Zuid African', a copy of which was found to be circulating among the men in 1849. In March 1851 many deserted, but although the numbers have been put at nearly 350 this seems an unearned slur on the regiment, for the pay lists reveal only a fifth of this number actually took the side of the Kaffirs. As provisional companies were raised at times of emergency – formed of Hottentots who were horsed, armed, equipped and subsisted but not paid – it is likely the bulk of the defectors were provisionals whose appearance made them indistinguishable from regulars of the CMR. However, the warning was enough and the proportion of men of European extraction in the regiment was rapidly expanded.

Apart from the officers and some senior NCOs, the CMR consisted wholly of Hottentots and men of mixed race in 1828. The total strength was under 300 and they were organised into three companies. The complement had fallen slightly by 1835 and it was not until well after the close of the 1st campaign that the number of companies was increased. Many men transferred to the Cape Mounted from regiments returning to England and were formed into all white companies. Even after the provisionals raised for the 2nd campaign had been stood down in April 1847 the regiment mustered over 40 officers and some 570 men.

The high proportion of officers, several of whom had lived all their lives in the Cape, was called for by the nature of the services of the regiment. Principally used for skirmishing and scouting, CMR companies were scattered all along the frontier before being split into detachments. No force was as widely employed and only regiments long exposed to bush warfare could approach the experience built up by the Cape Mounted over many years. On small active horses and wearing blue forage caps, green cloth jackets and brown buckskin trousers, they were armed with short double-barrelled carbines which were ideal for close fighting whether on horseback or afoot. Their use as mounted infantry was increasingly appreciated during the war of 1850–3 when the strength of the regiment was held at over 900 officers and men.

Between the Kaffir campaigns Cape Mounted Riflemen found little rest on the frontier. A detachment was with Capt Smith on his expedition to Natal in 1842; they fought the Boers at Boemplaats in 1848 and were involved in untold minor skirmishes at other times. The regiment well deserved its medals.

Name	Note	Kaffir Wars 1	2	3
LIEUTENANT COLONEL				
John Bissett	1)	△	△	△
George Napier	2)		△	△
Charles H. Somerset	3)	○	△	△
William Sutton	4) (P)	○	△	△
MAJOR				
Alexander B. Armstrong	5)	△	△	
William Burney	6) (P)	△		
Thomas Donovan	7) (P)		○	△
George J. Carey	8)		△	△
CAPTAIN				
John Armstrong	9)	○	△	△
Richard J. Bramley	10)		△	△
Frederick K. Campbell	11)	△		△
Henry Crause	12)	△		
Thomas W. Goodrich	13)			
Thomas Hare			△	△
Abraham P. Keynon	14)			△
Arnold M. Knight	15)		△	△
Edward G. Mainwaring	16) (P)		△	△
John O'Reilly	17)	○	△	
Charles Ross	18)	△		
Joseph Salis	19)		△	△
Archibald H. Stuart-Wortley	20)			△
George S. Whitmore	21)		△	△
John S. Warren	22)			△
Price B. Manners Wood	23)	○		
LIEUTENANT				
Charles H. Bell	24)			△
John Borrow				△
John Bourke	25)		△	△
James Boyes	26)		△	△
William Goodison			△	△
Edward L. Green	27)		△	△
John Harvey	28)	△	△	△
John M. Isaac	(P)			△
Francis Le Touzel		△		
Thomas J. Lucas				△
John McDonnell	29)		△	
Henry Palmer	30)			△
Charles E. Phillpots				△
Francis Smyth	31)		△	△
Robert M. Sparks	32)		△	
Ralph L. Thursby	33)			△
ENSIGN				
John P. Cox	34)			△
Latham Thomson	35)	○		
Arthur Fowler	36)			△
Walter Gill	37)			△
Edward M. Jones			△	
Daniel Mackenzie	38)			△
Walter Musgrave				△
William Peel	39) (P)			△
Patrick Robertson	40)			△
Richard Rorke	41)			△
William W. Simkin	42) (P)			△
PAYMASTER				
Benjamin D. Wemys				△
QUARTERMASTER				
Michael Rorke	43)	○	○	△

134 South Africa 1853 Medal

Name	Ref		Kaffir Wars 1	Kaffir Wars 2	Kaffir Wars 3
SURGEON					
William C. Eddie	44)			O	
James C. Minto	45)			△	△
ASSISTANT SURGEON					
Robert Allen				△	
Henry B. Hassard	46)				△
William Singleton	47)			△	△
VETERINARY SURGEON					
John Kingsley				△	△

Note: Maj Gen Sir Henry Somerset (Commander) and Ensign Henry G. E. Somerset (ADC) are both returned under staff.

Name	Ref		1	2	3
SERGEANT MAJOR					
Thomas Argent	48)				△
Charles B. Marshal	49)			O	△
Francis McGuire	50)		△	△	
QUARTERMASTER SERGEANT					
Roland Heathcote					△
Alexander Wilmore	51)		O	O	△
COLOUR SERGEANT					
James Davidson					△
John Grimes	52) (P)			O	△
John Hobson	53)				△
Richard Hood	53)				△
Alexander Ingram	54)			O	△
Edward Kelly	55)			O	△
Charles Smith	56)				△
William Tucker	57)			O	△
John F. Williams	59)			O	△
FARRIER MAJOR					
Felix O'Neill					△
TRUMPET MAJOR					
William Hough				O	△
ARMOURER SERGEANT					
Richard Furmidge				O	△
HOSPITAL SERGEANT					
Thomas Aitken	59) (P)				△
PAYMASTER SERGEANT					
George Gordon	60) (P)			O	△
SCHOOLMASTER SERGEANT					
Robert Swanston	61)				△
SERGEANT					
William Adams	62)			O	△
Jacob April	63)			O	△
Robert Arnold	64)			O	△
Nathaniel Barrell	65)			O	△
Jantjie Booy				O	△
Henry Bradshaw	57)				△
Martin Cahill	66)		O	O	△
Class Class	67)			O	△
Jacobus Coetzie				O	△
George Curry			△	O	
–. David	68)			O	△
Daniel Dimmus	69)		△	△	△
Robert M. Fletcher					△
Jeptha Golliet	70)			O	△
Daniel Hartoh				O	△
Thyse Hendrick	71)		△	△	△
William Isaac	(P)			O	△
April Jantjies				O	△
Nicholas Jass				O	△
Matthew Kelly	72)			O	△
David Kettles					△
John Knight	73)		O	O	△
Appolis Leawe	74) (P)		O	O	△
William Long	75)		O	O	△
Patrick Lyons	65)				△
Hugh Manson	76)			O	△
Bernard McCabe	50)				
Benjamin Milbarrow	77) (M)		O		△
Charles Nicks					△
Fortein Okkers	78)				△
John Oliver	79)			O	△
George Pitt			△	△	△
John Pollock	76)			O	△
James Richardson	80)		O	O	△
Henry Rowland				O	△
Sampson Sampson				O	△
James Seery	81) (P)				△
Thomas Shepard					△
Richard Simpson	65)			O	△
William Smit			△	△	
Hugh Stewart	82)			△	△
Martin Stewart	83)			O	△
James Thompson	84)				△
Adam Uitholder				O	△
Piet Van Wyngardt			△	O	
William Van Wyk	85)			O	△
Michael Wheelan	86)			O	△
CORPORAL					
Class Adams	87)			O	△
Thomas Argent	88)				△
John Ashcroft	89)				△
Cupido Batjies					△
Thomas Batts	52)			O	△
William Blake	90)				△
Edward Boyde	91)				△
James Brown	92)				△
William Clements	93)			O	△
Hendrick Dragooner	94)			O	△
Cobus Fisher				O	△
Whiteboy Flink				O	△
Thomas Freeman	56)				△
Thomas Galley					
William Gerrell	95)			O	△
Frederick Goddard	95)			O	△
Charles E. Greenacre	84)				△
William Hanna	89)				△
John Harkins	96)			O	△
David Hendrick	97)				△
Class Hendricks	98)				△
Jacob Kerval					△
Saayer Lambert	99)			O	△
Thomas Lee					△
John Leets				O	△
James Lowden	56)				△
Edward Martin	64)			O	△
Robert McMahon	100)				△
John Morrison	59)				△
Patrick Mulcahy	53)				△
James O'Reilly	101)				△
Henry Porzeyn	102)				△
Moss Sampson					
Cobus Tellemachus					
Adam Tigerflesh	103)				△
Frederick Uithalder					△
James Wadden	104)				△
Thomas Washbrook	56)				△
August Williams					△
Patrick Woods	76)			O	△
Abraham Wynn					

South Africa 1853 Medal

Name	Ref	Kaffir Wars 1	2	3
TRUMPETER				
Daniel Adonis	105)			△
Thomas Bell			○	△
Caleb Chitty	77)			△
Dedrick Hatting	106)		○	△
Piet Herman				△
Charles F. Howard				△
Gaspard Jager	107)		○	△
John McLoughlin				△
Thomas Reynolds				△
Jacob Steerman			○	△
William Vandermerwe	108)			△
James Wilson				△
Andries Windfogle	109)	△	△	
PRIVATE				
Abel Able	110)			△
Carolies Abraham	111)			△
Christian Abraham	112)	△		
Johannes Abram	113)		○	△
Adam Adams (1)	114)		○	△
Adam Adams (2)	114)			△
Cobus Adams			○	△
David Adams				△
Jacob Adams				△
Moss Adams				△
Thomas Adams	59)			△
William P. Adams	115)			△
Paul Adonis	116)			△
Africa Africander				△
John Africander				△
William Ahearn	117)			△
Ian Alexander	118)			△
George Allen	119)			△
John J. Allen			○	△
David Andries	120)		○	△
Dirk Andries	121)			△
Hans Andries				△
Martinus Andries				△
Carel Anthonison			○	△
John Apple				△
Henry Appleford	84)			△
David April	122)		○	△
James April				△
George Arendse				△
Andries Aries				△
Booy Arnoldus			○	△
Henry J. Ashton				△
Wildshut Asson	123)			△
Thomas Atcheson	124)		○	△
Andries August	125)	○	○	△
Hans August				△
Tobias August			○	△
William Aunger	119)			△
Robert Austin	126)			△
Hendrick Baart				△
Thomas Batjies	127)			△
Joseph Bales	56)			△
James Barnes	95)			△
Thomas Barnett	36)			△
Jacob Bartman		△		
Christian Beale				△
Thomas Beattie	128)			△
Thomas Beavan	84)			△
Hendrick Beaves			○	△
David Beherns	129)			△
James Bennett	84)			△
Adrian Bergman	130)			△
Booy Bergman	130)		○	△
John Berry	60)			△
William Berry				△
Thomas Bickett	104)			△
Class Bier			○	△
William Bird	131)	△		
James S. Birkby	132)			△
John Bleach	104)			△
James Bloice	104)			△
Edward Boardman				△
William Boddey	133) (MRM)			△
David Boer	134)			△
Charles Boniface				△
Boosack Boosack				△
Platjie Boosack				△
Peter Booy	(P)			△
William Bourke	56) (P)			△
Henry Bowles	135) (MRM)		○	△
John Bowyer	136)			△
James Boyle	137)		○	△
John Boyle	138)	○	△	△
Francis Brady	139)			△
Williamd Brander			○	△
Jacob Breastneur	140)			△
Samuel Brewin	56) (MRM)			△
John Briggs				△
–. Brittania	141)		○	△
Hanse Britz			○	△
Class Bromer				△
John Brooks (1)	142)		○	△
John Brooks (2)	143)			△
James Brown	144)			△
Robert Brown			○	△
Thomas Brown	90)			△
Thomas Burke	60)			△
William Burn	74)			△
Kevit Bushman	145)		○	△
John Butler	128)			△
Jacob Buys		△	△	
John Byrne (1)	53)			△
John Byrne (2)	128)			△
Nathaniel Callaghan	128)		○	△
Thomas Callory	100)			△
Thomas Campbell (1)	146)			△
Thomas Campbell (2)	147)			△
John Campe	100) (MRM)			△
Michael Camphor			○	△
James Carr	89)		○	△
William Carson	128)			△
Hugh Carvill	148)			△
Henry Cass	56)			△
James Cauley	149)			△
Michael Chambers	104)			△
G. Chapman	136)			△
Daniel Clancy	100)			△
George Clarke (1)	150)			△
George Clarke (2)	151)			△
Joseph Clarke	53)			△
Stephen J. Clarke				△
William Clarke	52)		○	△
Armood Class				△
Martinus Cleinboy	152)	○	○	△
Markin Cloete	153)			△
Alfred Cluney			○	△
Edward Coates				△
John Cody	89)			△
Christian Coetzie			○	△
John Coleman	89)			△

South Africa 1853 Medal

PRIVATE		Kaffir Wars 1	2	3
Patrick Coleman	128)			△
Edward Collum	154)			△
Michael Conlon	104)			△
John Connery	100)			△
Patrick Connolly	128)		○	△
Jager Conraad	155)	△	○	
Class Conraad	156)		○	△
Cobus Constable				△
Henry Cook				△
William Cooper				△
George Copping	89)			△
William Corbitt	128)			△
Jacob Cornelious			○	△
William Cornelious	104)			△
James Corr	157)			△
Jan Corridan	158)	○	○	△
Frederick Cory	89)			△
Jackson Coward	84)			△
T. Cowling	159)			△
Alexander Cox	60)			△
Adam Cramer				△
Robert Cross	84)			△
Patrick Cunningham	89)			△
Class Cupido				△
William Cushley	119)			△
Edward Daley		△		△
Adrian Damon				△
Jonker Danster		△		△
Class Danster	156)		○	△
Cobus Danzer	160)		○	△
James Darling	339)		○	△
Booy Darris			○	△
Hans Darris	161)		○	△
Andries David				△
Florris David	162)	△		
Thomas David	163)		○	△
Clement Davids			○	△
Solon Davids			○	△
Willem Davids	164)		○	△
William Davids			○	△
Stratford Davoren	165)			△
Richard Dawson	166)		○	△
William Dawson	157)			△
James Day	167)		○	△
Hans Dedrick	168)	△	△	
Hendrick Dedrick	169)		○	△
John Deeley	128)		○	△
Adrian Delour				△
Hans Demas			○	△
William Dempsey	93)		○	△
John Diamond				△
Peter Dinimanza	170) (P)		○	△
Class Dirk	171)		○	△
Petros Dirk	172)		○	△
Joseph Doge	89)			△
William Dolan	173)		○	△
Thomas Donnolly	56) (MRM)			△
Sylvester Douglass	174)		○	△
John Dove	175)	△	△	
Patrick Dowdall				△
James Downey	136)			△
Hendrick Dragooner	176)		○	△
George Driscoll	56)			△
Dederick Drooy	177)	△	△	△
John Droy	178)	△	△	△
John Dudley	179)			△
William Dunn			○	△

		Kaffir Wars 1	2	3
John Dwyer	104)			△
Jesse Edesion	180)			△
Stoffle Edwards				△
Timothy Egan	166)		○	△
Abram Esau	181)			△
Henry Etherington	128)		○	△
George Evans	104)			△
Cornelius Everson	182)		○	△
Hendrick Ekstein	183)	○	○	△
Spillman Faltyn	184)		○	△
Hendrick Faunce				△
Edward Fenn	185)			△
Alexander Ferguson	59)			△
Samuel Ferguson	89)			△
Abram Fester			○	△
Jan Fester	186)			△
Thomas Fields	187)			△
Hendrick Figland				△
John Figland	188)	○	○	△
Hieronymus Filmalter			○	△
Swartboy Filmink	189)	△		
Robert Firman	56)			△
Simon Fisher				△
Thomas F. Fleming	89)			△
Jager Flora	190)	○	○	△
Frederick Floris	191)			△
Cobus Fortuin	192)		○	△
Elias Fortuin	193)		○	△
Saul Fortuin	192)		○	△
Dragooner Frederick	194)	○	○	△
Hendrick Fredericks			○	△
James Fury	128)		○	△
Isaac Gardner	195)			△
John George				△
Martinus Gert				△
William Gerts	196)		○	△
John Geswint				△
James Gilles	100)			△
William Gilmore	197)			△
James Gilmour	198)			△
George Glasgow	84)			△
Daniel Gleeson	199)	△	△	
Piet Goes				△
Dirk Gogelman				△
John Golding	200)		○	△
Thomas Golding	201)		○	△
Sampson Golliard				△
Hans Gordon		○	○	△
James Grady	157) (MRM)			△
Robert Graham				△
William Greathurst	140)			△
John Green				△
Thomas Green	93)		○	△
Frederick Griffin				△
Lawrence Grimes	56)			△
Abram Growenwaldt			○	△
Stoffel Grovers	202)			△
John Gunn			○	△
John Guy	203)			△
William Guy	204)			△
Robert Guyatt	89)			△
Hermanus Gurzar	205)		○	△
Thomas Haggard	157)			△
Thomas Hall	100) (P)			
James Halloran	100)			△
January Hans				△
John Hans		△		
Kees Hans	206)			△

South Africa 1853 Medal 137

Name	Ref	Kaffir Wars 1	2	3
Leuter Hans	207)		△	△
Ebdol Harris				△
William Harris (1)	208)			△
William Harris (2)	209)			△
James Hart				△
Daniel Hartwick			△	
Michael Harty	210)			△
Robert Harvey	59)			△
Henry Hawkins	64)		O	△
David Hayland				△
John Healy				△
Henry Heath				△
Jacob Helen	(P)			△
David Hendrick	211)		O	△
Hendrick Hendrick	212)		△	△
Cobus Hendricks	212)		O	△
Henry Henshaw	104)			△
John Hetherington	213)		O	△
Joseph Hickman	214)			△
George Hicks	84)			△
Edward Higgins	104)			△
John Higgins	64)		O	△
William Hill	100) (MRM)			△
William Hilliard	104)			△
Frederick Hiscox	104)			△
Thomas Hodgetts	100)			△
Thomas Hodby	215)			△
Stephen Holman	104)			△
Christian Holmes	216)		O	△
James Hore	217) (P)		△	△
Henry Horton	84)			△
James Howell	104)			△
John Hudson	128)		O	△
Ellis Hughes	60) (MRM)			△
Patrick Hughes	218)			△
John Hunt	84)			△
John Husey	219)			△
James Innis			O	△
Andries Isaac				△
Isaac Isaac	220)		O	△
–. Jack	221)			△
Isaac Jackson			O	△
James Jackson				△
John Jackson (1)	222)			△
John Jackson (2)	222)			△
Joseph Jackson	89)			△
Andries Jacobs			O	△
Brander Jacobs			O	△
Class Jacobs (1)	223)		O	△
Class Jacobs (2)	223)		O	△
Jeptha Jacobs				△
John Jacobs				△
November Jacobs				△
Raynor Jacobs	224)		O	△
William Jacobus		O	O	△
Cobus Jager			O	△
John Jager (1)	225)		O	△
John Jager (2)	225)		O	△
John James	204)			△
Abram Jansen				△
Arnoldus Jansen			O	△
John Jansen (1)	226)		△	
John Jansen (2)	227)			△
Steerman Jansen	228)			△
Armood Jantjies	229)			△
Hendrick Jelande				△
Thomas Jenkins	60)			△
William John	230)		O	△

Name	Ref	Kaffir Wars 1	2	3
Isaac Johns				△
James Johnston	100)			△
John H. Johnstone	231)			△
Joseph Johnstone	132)			△
Henry Jones	233)		△	△
James Jones	56)			△
Patrick Jones	89)			△
Thomas Jones	234)			△
William T. Jones	235)		△	
Hendrick Jonker				△
Jan Jonker				△
Michael Joyce	236)			△
Jonker Juman				△
John Jummaar	237)		O	△
Kevido Junie			△	
Thyse Juries			O	△
Hugh Kain	89)			△
Thomas Kavanagh	128) (MRM)		O	△
James Kay	59)			△
James D. Kay	238)			△
Patrick Kean	239)		O	△
Denis Keaton				△
Lot Keefe	100) (P)			△
Robert Kendall	100)			△
John Kenny	157)			△
Charles Kerrigan	56)			△
Jeptha Kevido	240)		O	△
Andries Kevitt	241)		O	△
Frederick Keyser	242)	O	O	△
James Kilbride	89)			△
Andries Klass	243)		O	△
Piet Klass				△
Thomas Klass	244)		O	△
Platjie Kleinfeldt				△
William Kleinfeldt				△
John Kleinboy	245)			△
Hans Knapsack			O	△
James Knight	104)			△
Hans Kock	246)	O	O	△
Baart Koopman	247)		O	△
Bernard Koopman	248)			△
Cornelius Koopman	248)		O	△
Jurie Koopman				△
Michael Koopman	248)			△
David Kriel			O	△
George Kyd	204)			△
Michael Laffey	100)			△
Gert LaFleur				△
James Lamb	89)			△
William Lambert	(MRM)			△
Carolus Lambo			O	△
John Lancey	89)			△
William Landman	249)		O	△
Patrick Lawless	185)			△
Adonis Lawrence				△
Carol Lawrence	250)		O	△
John Lenaghan	185)		O	△
John Leonard	65)		O	△
Michael Leonard	128)		O	△
William Leonard	65)		O	△
James Lindsay	251)			△
William Lloyd	100)			△
John Lockie	76)		O	△
John Logan	252)			△
Frederick Lowe	185)			△
Garret Lucas	89)			△
John Lucas				△
Henry Luckman	185)			△

138 South Africa 1853 Medal

PRIVATE			Kaffir Wars 1	2	3
Adonia Lynx				○	△
Johannes Lynx					△
James Lyons					△
Robert Lyons	89)				△
Jacob Maart				○	△
John Magahey	253)				△
Carel Magerman		(M)			△
Stephanus Magul	254)			○	△
Michael Maher	64)			○	△
Alfred A. Main	265)				△
John Main	255)				△
Peter Main	255)				△
Thomas Peter Main	255)				△
George Maisey	65)			○	△
Daniel Makin	166)			△	△
Michael Maleady	128)			○	△
Peter Malone	89)				△
Thomas Manewell	90)				△
Richard Mansfield	84)				△
Thomas Manson	93)			○	△
David Manuel	256)			○	△
John Mara	104)				△
Peter Marcus					△
Charles Marquis					△
George Marston	257)				△
John F. Martin				○	△
Appollus Mortinus				○	△
Arnoldus Martinus				○	△
John Masterhouse					△
Hendrick Mattross			△		
Stoffle Mattross				○	△
Alexander McAlister	56)				△
George McBean	258)			○	△
William McCabe	259)	(P)			△
William McCaffery	56)				△
James McCalden	89)				△
Alexander McCleeve					△
Alexander McDermott					△
Kenneth McDonald	59)				△
Michael McGrath	157)				△
William McGonnell	59)				△
John McGregor	260)			○	△
Henry R. McKean	53)				△
Edward McKey	89)				△
Alexander McLean	59)				△
James McNerney	261)				△
Francis McQuiggen	128)			○	△
Andrew McQuillen	262)				△
James McShea					△
Michael Meade	60)				△
Francis Meades	263)	(M)			△
James Meehan	264)				△
William Meldrum					△
George Menlouf	128)	(MRM)			△
Lodwick Mentor	265)				△
Isaac Meyers	266)				△
Class Meyers					△
Steerman Meyers			△		
Cornelius Michaels	267)	(P)			△
Richard Middleton					△
Joseph Miller	93)			○	△
Thomas Mooney	100)	(MRM)			△
James Moore					△
Carle Moss	268)			○	△
John Mouatt	269)	(P)			△
John Mulcahy	157)				△
John Mulloy	104)				△
Matthew Murphy	100)				△
Patrick Murphy	157)				△
James Naughton	89)				△
Robert Nevergeldt					△
Hendrick Newkirk				○	△
Edward Newman	104)				△
David November				○	△
John Nunan	100)				△
Murty O'Brien	157)				△
Patrick O'Brien					△
John October					△
George O'Dell	84)				△
John O'Neil	52)			○	△
William Ongewaght	270)	(MRM)			△
George Onverwaght	271)				△
Faltyn Opperman				○	△
Skeeman Opperman	272)		△	△	△
James Pamberton	104)				△
Charles Parker	100)				△
James Parker	84)				△
Alexander Pastina				○	△
John Pearil				○	△
James Percy	100)				△
Gert Peters				○	△
Hermanus Peters				○	△
John Peters	104)	(MRM)			△
Philip Peters (1)	273)			○	△
Philip Peters (2)	273)			○	△
Frederick Peterson					△
Peter Peterson	274)			○	△
Frederick Peterus	275)			○	△
Piet Peterus	276)			○	△
Isaac Petro	277)				△
Windfogle Philip	278)		○	△	△
Kambries Phillips	279)				△
Thomas Phillips	100)				△
Jantjie Piet	280)		△	△	△
Booy Platjies	281)			○	△
Edward Platjies	282)				△
Jacob Platjies	282)				△
John Platjies	282)				△
Joris Platjies	282)			○	△
Marcus Platjies	282)		○	○	△
Martinus Platjies	282)			○	△
Piet Platjies	282)				△
Sedras Platjies	282)				△
William Platjies (1)	283)			○	△
William Platjies (2)	283)			○	△
Otto Pohl	284)				△
James Pomeroy	128)				△
Class Pommer					△
Charles Poole					△
–. Poonah	221)			○	△
John Powlis					△
John Pretorious	285)				△
James Price	100)				△
Africander Prince					△
Piet Prince				○	△
Stoffel Prince	257)		○	○	△
William Pugh	90)	(P)			△
Frederick Rademeyer	286)			△	△
James Ralph	104)				△
Henry Randell	287)				△
John Rasoe	288)			○	△
Kevit Rasow	289)			○	△
John Ratcliff	100)				△
John Redican	64)			○	△
George Redmond	100)				△
Thomas Reilly	230)				△

South Africa 1853 Medal

Name	Number	Kaffir Wars 1	Kaffir Wars 2	Kaffir Wars 3
John Reuter			○	△
Thomas Reynolds	100)			△
Charles Richards	157) (P)			△
Samuel Richardson	157)			△
George Riley	291)		○	△
George P. Rillett	104)			△
William H. Roberts	104)			△
Solomon Roda				△
Class Roman				△
John Rooey	292)		○	△
Richard Rose	128) (P)			△
James Ross	59)			△
Roman Rooy				△
Michael Ruberry	293)		○	△
Jasper Rutherford				△
Adam Ruyters				△
Windfogle Ruyters			○	△
Michael Ryan (1)	294)			△
Michael Ryan (2)	295)			△
Patrick Ryan	90)			△
Abraham Sabola				△
David Saturday			○	△
John Scattergood	100)			△
Hendrick Scheepers			○	△
Klass Scheepers				△
Storm Scheepers				△
Abraham F. Scholtz	296)			△
Charles J. Schroeder				△
John Scott	84)			△
Thomas Seaman	104)			△
Christian Sevas				△
John Sharrocks	100)			△
Patrick Shaughnessy	297)			△
William H. Shaw			○	△
Isaac Shelton	84)			△
Matthew Shelvey	84)			△
William Slavin	298)			△
Cobus Slinger				△
Christian Smith				△
George Smith				△
Hendrick Smith				△
James Smith			○	△
Martinus Smith				△
William Smith (1)	299)		○	△
William Smith (2)	300)			△
Whiteboy Sneeman			○	△
Frederick Soldat			○	△
John Soldat	301)	○	○	△
Abraham Solomon			○	△
Frans Solomon				△
Jonas Soranna	302)		○	△
Africa Speyer			○	△
John Spillman	303)			△
Philip Spillman	304)		△	△
William Steele	100)			△
Africa Steerman	305)	○	△	△
Class Steerman	306)	○	○	△
Hendrick Steerman	307)		○	△
Isaac Steerman			○	△
George Stephens	308)			△
Alfred Steward	309)			△
George Stiles	191)			△
Dragooner Stoffle	310)			△
James Stoll			○	△
Hendrick Storm	311)	○	○	△
Conrad Strouble			○	△
Jacob Sturman	312)		○	△
John Subdan	100)			△
John Summer	313)			△
Eugene Sweeney	56)			△
John Sweeney				△
Robert H. Sweetman				△
Thomas Sykes	100) (MRM)			△
Kevitt Tallie				△
John Tallman				△
Isaac Tamboor			○	△
William Tamboor			○	△
Henry Taylor				△
Jan Tedore	314)		○	△
Andries Tellemachus				△
Dolly Tellemachus			△	
Jacob Tellemachus	315)		○	△
John Thomas			○	△
William J. Thompson	59)			△
Jan Tigerflesh	316)		○	△
Patrick Timmins				△
Class Tobee				△
–. Tomate	317)			△
James Tomlinson	318)			△
George C. Tracy	319)			△
Patrick Trainor	320)			△
Jacob Trental	321)		○	△
Michael Tromp			○	△
William Troup	59)			△
William Trowbridge	104)			△
Edgar True				△
Solomon Trump				△
Booy Uithalder			○	△
Hendrick Uithalder (1)	322)	○	○	△
Hendrick Uithalder (2)	323)		○	△
William Upton	104)			△
Abel Valtyn	136)			△
Class Van Ardt	324)	○	○	△
John Van Ardt			○	△
Martinus Van Bullen			○	△
Ragooner Van Fore			○	△
Owen Vanna	325)			△
Dedrick Varry				△
William Vaughan	104)			△
Piet Vertuyn	326) (P)		○	△
Toon Vertuyn			○	△
Abraham Vigland				△
Jacob Vigland				△
Ruyter Vogle			○	△
Jonas Volmink				△
John Vries			○	△
John Walmsley	89)			△
Michael W. Wall				△
Thomas Wall	56)			△
Patrick Walsh	60)		○	△
Manuel Wanson	327)		○	△
Hugh Ward	128)		○	△
Lando Webber				
Charles Weeks	328)			△
Theodorus Welling	329)			△
George Wells	(MRM)			△
Hector D. Wentzel				△
Charles White	84)			△
George W. White	60)			△
Gert Whiteboy			○	△
Joseph Whiteboy				△
Steerman Whiteboy			○	△
Joseph Whitehead	100)			△
James Whitmarsh	53)			△
George Wilderman				△
Barend Wildshut			△	△

		Kaffir Wars					Kaffir Wars		
		1	2	3			1	2	3
Platjie Wildshut	330)		△	△	Jacobus Windfogle				△
Andries Williams				△	Madoor Windfogle			O	△
Frederick Williams	331)	O	O	△	Spillman Windfogle				△
George Williams	332)		O	△	Whiteboy Windfogle	337)		△	△
Golliett Williams	333)		O	△	William Windfogle			△	△
John Williams			O	△	George Wise	157)			△
Kevitt Williams (1)	334)		O	△	William Woods	93)		O	△
Kevitt Williams (2)	335)			△	Thyse Zealand			O	△
William Williams	185)			△	–. Zoora	338)			O
Edward Wills	336) (P)			△					
William Wilson	84)			△	△ = campaign qualification as WO/100/17.				
Danster Windfogle			O	△	O = campaign which the Rolls fail to credit.				

CAPE MOUNTED RIFLEMEN NOTES

1 Twice on Roll, once credited with the 1st and 2nd campaigns and then for 1850–3 only. Only 15 years of age when he served with the Bathurst Volunteers in 1835. Bissett was also with the Corps of Guides and native levies. Accompanied Capt Smith on the expedition to Natal in 1842. DAQG during the 2nd war when he was twice wounded. Again wounded, this time severely, at Boomah Pass in December 1850. Rose to Maj Gen. Author of 'Sport and War, or Recollections of Fighting and Hunting in South Africa; 1835–1867'.

2 Son of Sir George Napier. Commanded the regiment at Gwanga and throughout the 2nd and 3rd wars. Present at Boomah Pass and Berea.

3 South African born, he was volunteer ADC to his father during 1834–5 and ADC to Berkely in the 2nd campaign.

4 Twice on Roll, once as Asst QMG. With the 75th when Field Adjutant to Cox in 1835. Commanded the Burgher Forces of the Eastern Divn during the 2nd war and the Kat River Burghers during the attack on the Amatolas in 1846. Commanded a Division in 1847. Successfully defended Fort Beaufort against overwhelming odds at the commencement of the 3rd campaign. Served with the 1st Division in 1851.

5 Initial altered from 'J' on Roll – presumably a confusion with John Armstrong. He had a long and distinguished military career on three continents. Participated in the defence of Grahams Town in 1819. Commanded the Kat River settlement in 1834–5. Present in the attack on the Amatolas in April 1846.

6 Commanded a column against Macomo in January 1835 – see Godlonoton; Moodie.

7 Although with the Cape Regiment from 1827 he was on leave in Europe during the 1st war. Commanded the advance guard which forced the Fish River in May 1846. Slew two adversaries single handed when faced by four Kaffirs. See G and I; Moodie; Bissett.

8 Twice entered on Roll; once credited with 1846–7 and then for 1850–3. At Block Drift and Gwanga when he was wounded during the 2nd war. Military secretary on the Staff as well as Acting Brigade Major in the 3rd campaign. Served at Boemplaats and Boomah Pass. See G and I; McKay; Stewart; Bissett; King.

9 Served as a Provisional Ensign in 1834–5 with the CMR before being appointed to the 72nd Regiment. Field Adjutant and then ADC on Somerset's Staff in 1846–7, having returned to CMR. Severely wounded at Boemplaats, he commanded Armstrong's Horse of Irregulars during the 3rd war. Rose to Maj Gen. See G and I: Moodie.

10 Wounded at Boemplaats. Served in the expedition against Mosesh. See Moodie; Lucas.

11 A volunteer Provisional Ensign during the 1st war he commanded a troop of the CMR against the Zulus in 1844. He missed the 2nd campaign being attached to the 1/45th in Natal but was engaged in the Amatolas and across the Kei during the 3rd war. He commanded a Squadron against Mosesh.

12 Shown as Crouse on Roll. Served in the 1st Provisional Battalion and commanded the three companies who accompanied Col Harry Smith's force into the Buffalo Mountains in April 1835. See Godlonton; Moodie.

13 Commanded the detachment of Cavalry at Berea. See Moodie.

14 A veteran of Waterloo where he served with the 2nd Life Guards.

15 With the 7th DG during 1847 after having been at Aliwal with the 16th Lancers. Commanded the escort of Sir Harry Smith during both the 2nd and 3rd campaigns.

16 His service record in the CMR succession book gives his christian name as Edwin. At Boemplaats, he saw all his campaigning with the 91st and joined the Cape Mounted in 1854. Mint records show him applying for a medal in 1865 probably as a spare for a medal in a private collection is properly named. See G and I; Goff.

17 Served as a Provisional officer during the 1st campaign. Shot through both thighs at Bushmans River in January 1835. Resigned the same year but rejoined the CMR in 1837. See Godlonton; Moodie; Appleyard.

18 Commanded the CMR detachment which was with Smith when Hintza was killed, April 1835. See Godlonton; Moodie.

19 Dangerously wounded in the arm at Boemplaats. Riding Master of the CMR. See G and I; Bissett; Moodie; Lucas.

20 Commanded the cavalry attached to Buller's division during operations in the Waterkloof. Present at Boomah Pass. See Bisset.

21 At Boemplaats and Boomah Pass. Was with the 2nd division during the 3rd campaign and commanded Sir Harry Smith's escort from March to November 1851. Was Brigade Major to the cavalry at Berea. See Lucas.

22 At Boemplaats; transferred to the 91st before retiring in 1854.

23 Wrongly credited with the 3rd campaign on the Roll. He qualified for the medal through his service with the 73rd during the war of 1846–7 and went to Europe on leave in October 1850 before retiring.

24 Served as Field Adjutant on Somerset's Staff (1st Division). Commanded the CMR detachment at Fort Hare when the Kaffir attack was repulsed in January 1851. See G and I.

25 Wrongly credited with the 2nd campaign. He transferred from the 17th Regiment in August 1847 but was on leave until September 1848 before joining the CMR.

26 One of the few South African born officers. Was at Gwanga and Boomah Pass. See G and I; Moodie; Bisset.

27 Twice entered on Roll. Once as 1846 and then for 1850–3 as DAQG. Severely wounded 20.11.47.

28 Rose from the ranks and was serving on commandos as early as 1827. Frequently engaged during the 1st war when he was a corporal. With Somerset's division in 1846–7 and was at Gwanga. Adjutant to the CMR detachment under Napier in the 3rd campaign. See Appleyard.

29 Correctly altered on Roll from McDonald. With Berkeley in the Amatolas. Commanded the CMR at Boemplaats after Armstrong was wounded.

30 See G and I.
31 See G and I.
32 Wounded December 1834. See Godlonton; Moodie.
33 With the force which attacked Seyolo's territory in March 1851. Wounded at Fish River 9.9.51. See G and I.
34 Present at Berea.
35 Not on Roll but according to Hart's he received a medal. Served as a Provisional between February 1835 and March 1838.
36 Present at the taking of Fort Armstrong. With the 1st Division during operations in the Waterkloof and Amatolas where he received serious injuries.
37 Appointed Commandant of Fort Brown after defeating an attack on the Post on 9.4.51. See G and I.
38 Born at the Cape in 1804 but he did not enter the Army until 1851 when 47 years of age.
39 See G and I.
40 A Field Captain in Armstrong's Horse. Had his mount killed under him in April 1851. See G and I, Lucas.
41 Son of Q/Master Rorke; he was born at Fort Beaufort and served as a volunteer during 1851. Present at the storming of Fort Armstrong. Commanded the bodyguard of the CIC at Berea.
42 Served at Berea. See McKay.
43 Rose from the ranks and was a Sgt Major during the 1st campaign.
44 Wrongly credited with 1850-3 on the Roll.
45 Twice returned on the Roll, once among later claimants. A hospital assistant as early as 1827, he joined the CMR from Staff in 1840 but served as Staff Surgeon 2nd class during the 1846-7 campaign. Must not be confused with his son of the same name who received a medal after serving as a volunteer with the Graaf Irregular Horse and joined the CMR as an Ensign in August 1853.
46 Had his horse killed under him in August 1851.
47 Served as Asst Staff Surgeon during the 2nd campaign. Present at Berea.
48 No 1920 and not to be confused with Cpl Argent. Served with the 1/45th during the 2nd war.
49 Shown on the Roll under officers as he was an Ensign in 1855. Served with the 7th DG and was with them at Berea and Boemplaats.
50 Served with the 27th during the 1st campaign.
51 Also Willmore on musters. Was with the 75th during the 1st campaign but attached to the Provisionals.
52 Served with the Reserve Batt 45th during the 2nd war.
53 Served with the 1/45th during the period of the 2nd war.
54 To the CMR from the 91st in July 1847.
55 Served with the 91st in the 1846-7 campaign. See G and I.
56 Saw all his campaign service with the 12th Regiment.
57 Also served with the 7th DG.
58 Also served with the 7th DG. See Moodie.
59 Saw all his campaign service with the 74th Regiment.
60 Saw all his campaign service with the 45th Regiment.
61 Saw all his war service with the 91st. Although shown as Sgt Major on Roll he was in fact a Schoolmaster Sgt and it would seem that the WO Clerk has misconstrued the abbreviation S/M.
62 No 586 and not to be confused with Pte Wm. P. Adams.
63 No 223.
64 Served with the 27th during the 2nd campaign.
65 Served with the 90th during the 2nd campaign.
66 Served with the 27th during the war of 1834-5.
67 No 432.
68 No 945; musters show he had no other name.
69 No 270. Dinimus on Roll.
70 Also spelt Golliad and Golliat on musters.
71 No 230.
72 With the 27th in 1846-7 and probably the man mentioned by G and I.
73 Served with the 75th during the 1st campaign and was with Smith on the Natal expedition of 1842.
74 No 399. Musters also record name as Leuive, Leive and Liewe. The Dutch for lion is Lieuw which may have been what was intended.
75 Paymaster's clerk. Originally with the 27th.
76 Served with the 91st during the war of 1846-7.
77 Also served with the Rifle Brigade. Discharge papers spell his name Milborrow.
78 Musters also show Ockers. Christian name spelt Fortun on Roll.
79 No 375. Also shown on musters as Jan Olivier.
80 No 215; a Hospital Sgt.
81 An Orderly Room Clerk.
82 Also Stuart on musters. Served with the 73rd during the 2nd campaign.
83 Also served with the 27th Regiment.
84 Saw all his campaign service with the 12th Lancers.
85 No 778. Name not entirely legible on Roll.
86 Whielan on Roll. Also served with the 90th.
87 No 551, a number which is mistakenly altered to 351 in later musters.
88 No 2185. Also shown as Argeant on musters. Entire campaign service was with the 2nd Regiment whose musters also use this common alternative. Not to be confused with Sgt Major Argent.
89 Saw all his campaign service with the 91st.
90 Saw all his campaign with the 1/RB.
91 Bloyde on Roll. His entire campaign service was with the 6th.
92 No 2071.
93 Served with the RB during the 2nd campaign.
94 No 482 and not to be confused with Pte Dragooner. During the 2nd campaign he saved the life of Col Bisset who seplls his name Dragonder.
95 Also served with the 90th.
96 No 1092.
97 No 1337 and not to be confused with Pte D. Hendrick.
98 No 694.
99 Also Sayen Lamberts on musters.
100 Saw all his campaign service with the 60th Regiment.
101 O'Rielly on Roll. His entire war service was with the 73rd.
102 Shown as Posyn on Roll.
103 Also Tigerflee on musters.
104 Saw all his campaign service with the 2nd Regiment.
105 No 1728. Name on Roll could be interpreted as Adams.
106 Christian name shown as Dederick on Roll.
107 No 462. Casper Yaager on Roll - and later musters.
108 One of the most extreme mis-spellings on the Roll, where the name is shown as Merwe W. Vander.
109 No 228. A later applicant who is shown on the Roll as Bugler but he was in fact a Private during the 1st war and a Corporal in the 2nd.
110 No 1406. Able Able on Roll.
111 No 2003; Carolus Abrams on Roll.
112 No 1410; Abram on Roll, which also credits 1850-3.
113 Also Abrams on musters.
114 Nos 463 and 1347.
115 No 2012 and not to be confused with Sgt W. Adams.
116 No 1193; also shown on musters as Ardonis and Ardones.
117 Aherne on Roll and CMR musters, but saw all his campaign service with the 12th Regiment when his name is spelt Ahearn.
118 Christian name given as Jan on Roll.
119 Also served with the 45th Regiment.
120 No 428.
121 No 1891. One of these medals is in a private collection.
122 No given as 1139 and 1239 on musters.
123 Wildshuit Assan on Roll.
124 Atchieson on Roll. His entire war service was with the 45th.
125 No 286.
126 Austen on Roll. His entire war service was with the 91st.
127 Baatjies on Roll.
128 Saw all his campaign service with the 6th Regiment.
129 Behearns on Roll.
130 Also Berghman on musters.
131 As he was once a deserter and had been charged with horse stealing, he was fortunate to receive a medal.
132 Received a re-named medal previously cancelled to a man discharged with ignominy.
133 Boddy on Roll. Saw his entire war service with the 2nd.
134 No 1532.
135 With the 7th DG during the war of 1836-7.
136 I have not been able to trace this man.
137 Saw his entire campaign service with the 91st. His number with that regiment was 2560 and he should not be confused with Nos 176 or 1803.

138 No 999. Served with the 75th during the 1st campaign.
139 Shown as a Farrier on Roll. His entire war service was with the 91st.
140 Breastmere on Roll.
141 No 1503. Musters show he had no other name.
142 No 2469. His entire war service was with the 6th who usually spelt his name Brookes.
143 No 2270. His entire war service was with the 12th.
144 No 2071.
145 No 1287; also spelt Boshman and Bosheman on musters.
146 No 2058.
147 No 2158. Saw all his war service with the 91st.
148 Saw his entire war service with the 73rd (No 2311).
149 Canley on Roll; all his war service was with the 12th Regiment.
150 No 1884.
151 No 2273; his entire war service was with the 12th Regiment.
152 Clemboy on Roll.
153 Marcus on Roll. Although with the CMR during the 2nd war he seems to have been in Capetown and not in the field.
154 No 1927. Cullum on Roll.
155 Also credited with 1850–3 on Roll.
156 Christian name spelt Klass on Roll.
157 Saw his entire campaign service with the 73rd.
158 No 185; also John on musters.
159 I have been unable to trace a man of this name, and it may be an error for Thomas Conling, No 2051.
160 Also Danzar on musters.
161 Darries on Roll.
162 Flores on Roll.
163 No 1546. Servant to Capt Salis and with him when the Captain was Paymaster to the Land Transport Corps in the Crimea.
164 Probably one of two William Davids Nos 1175 and 1414.
165 Also Davoran on musters. All his war service with the 73rd.
166 Served with the 7th DG during the war of 1846–7.
167 Although with the 1/45th during the 2nd campaign he was attached to the Reserve Battalion and so qualified for that war.
168 Diederick on Roll.
169 Dederick on Roll.
170 Also Denemanza and Dinnimanza on musters.
171 No 1385.
172 Also Peter and Petrus on musters.
173 Dolamn on Roll. Medal believed to show 'M. Dolon'. His entire war service was with the 6th.
174 Also Douglas on musters. Served with the 91st during the 2nd campaign. See G and I.
175 Also served with the 72nd Regiment.
176 No 754; not to be confused with Cpl H. Dragooner.
177 No 201. Droy on Roll.
178 No 176. This is probably the same man who is named as Draay before the use of regimental numbers. He was a later applicant who I failed to trace on any wartime musters, but during the 2nd campaign there is a note referring to extra pay for a John Drooy. Possibly he was a provisional.
179 Dudly on Roll.
180 Edeson on Roll. His entire war service was with the 60th.
181 Esaw on Roll.
182 Broken service gave him two regimental numbers, 1055 and 1895.
183 No 368; Extein on Roll. Musters also show Eksteen and Exteen.
184 Christian name spelt Spilman on Roll.
185 Saw all his war service with the 43rd.
186 Christian name given as Ian on Roll.
187 Field on Roll.
188 No 353.
189 Also credited with 1850–3 on Roll.
190 No 231.
191 Flories on Roll.
192 Also Fortein on musters.
193 Also Alias Fortein and Fortain on musters.
194 No 333; once a Trumpeter.
195 Gardiner on Roll.
196 Girt on Roll.
197 Saw all his service with the 74th who also listed him among their returns on the Roll.
198 Also Gilmour on musters. Saw his entire campaign service with the 60th.
199 Served with the 75th during the war of 1834–5.
200 No 1009; also Goulding on musters. Another Golding/Goulding, No 1805 deserted, as did this man at a later date.
201 No 1898. Goulding on Roll and on service papers, but he signed his name Golding. Served with the 6th during the campaign of 1846–7. See 'Letters of Col/Sgt Golding'.
202 Also Groves on Roll.
203 No 2143. Saw his entire war service with the 74th who also returned him on their list of applicants; that medal is in a private collection.
204 Also returned by the 74th Regiment, with whom he saw all his war service.
205 No 1381. Hermames Gurzoa on Roll. Musters also show Gurzzar.
206 Christian name spelt Keis on Roll.
207 Christian name also spelt Louther on musters.
208 No 1941.
209 No 2115.
210 A survivor from the 'Birkenhead' who saw all his campaign service with the 6th.
211 No 1380; not to be confused with Cpl D. Hendrick.
212 Surname also Hendricks on musters.
213 With the 90th during the 2nd campaign. Wounded in the right hand 29.8.48 at Boemplaats.
214 Also served with the 1/RB. Wounded in the arm by an assegai 20.12.52.
215 Hodley on Roll. A 'Birkenhead' survivor who saw all his war service with the 6th.
216 Also Homes on musters.
217 Served with the 73rd during the campaign of 1846–7.
218 His entire war service was with the 6th, his regimental number being 2793.
219 Hussey on Roll.
220 No 1468.
221 Musters show he had no other name.
222 Nos 2085 and 2449.
223 Nos 1353 and 1481.
224 Christian name spelt Raynoor on Roll. Musters also spell it Rayner.
225 Nos 494 and 1508. One of these medals was returned to the Mint.
226 No 1843.
227 This man's number 2424 suggests he joined the regiment too late to qualify for the 3rd war. However, another John Jansen, No 1289, served during the 2nd campaign.
228 Christian name spelt Sturman on Roll.
229 Christian name spelt Ormoed on Roll.
230 Also Johns on musters.
231 No 2057; Johnson on Roll.
232 Johnston on Roll.
233 No 1420. Part of his service during the 2nd war was with the 73rd.
234 Saw his entire war service with the 45th, being with the 1st Battalion during the 2nd campaign.
235 No 1012 shown as Thomas W. on musters. A trumpeter during the 2nd war and is credited with 1850–3 on Roll.
236 Joice on Roll. Saw his entire war service with the 6th.
237 Christian name given as Jonker on Roll.
238 No 1930.
239 No 1988. Shown as Kain on Roll. Much of his service was with the RB.
240 Christian name given as Japta on Roll.
241 No 443; served with Smith on his expedition to Natal in 1842.
242 No 249.
243 No 1443.
244 No 1258.
245 Klemboy on Roll.
246 No 259. Also Kok on musters.
247 Bartholomew Kopman on Roll.
248 Kopeman on Roll.
249 Also Landsman on musters.
250 Christian name given as Carel on Roll.
251 Lindsey on Roll. His entire war service was with the 74th.
252 Also Longan and Lougan on musters. His entire war service was with the 12th.
253 Magahy on Roll. His entire war service was with the 6th.
254 No 495. Also shown on musters as McGull.
255 These men were all of one family. The Roll shows that the father possibly Peter (No 1921) was discharged on pension 7.12.54 and collected all the medals for his family. Thomas Peter, No 1918 is shown on the Roll simply as Peter. Alfred's No was 1922 and John's 1197. One of the few Sir Harry Smith medals is named to the latter.
256 No 1243.
257 A farrier.
258 No 1401. McBain on Roll.
259 Also served with the 12th Regiment.
260 Saw his entire war service with the 91st and was wounded in the left elbow 29.12.46.
261 McNierney on Roll. Saw all his war service with the 74th.
262 McQuillan on Roll.

263 A re-named Sir Harry Smith medal bears the name of Meades.
264 Mehan on Roll. Saw his entire war service with the 6th.
265 Christian name spelt Lodewyk on Roll.
266 Meyer on Roll.
267 Michael on Roll.
268 No 1083. Moos on earlier musters.
269 Saw his entire war service with the 6th. There survives a Sir Harry Smith medal named to Mouatt.
270 Died in 1858.
271 Onferwaght on Roll.
272 No 285.
273 Nos 445 and 1362.
274 Christian name also Piet on musters.
275 No 608. Also Peiters on Roll.
276 Petrus on Roll.
277 No 1632. Also Petero on musters.
278 No 320. Twice entered on Roll, once as 1850–3 only.
279 Philip on musters.
280 No 181.
281 Also Platjie on musters. Served with Smith in Natal in 1842.
282 Also Platjie on musters.
283 Nos 696 and 1383. One of these men is shown with the Christian name Wilham on Roll.
284 At one time a Saddler Sergeant.
285 Christian name Jan on Roll.
286 No 1266. Raddeymere on Roll.
287 Randal on Roll. Saw his entire war service with the 12th Lancers.
288 No 1276. Also shown as Roson, Rasone, Rassau and Rassone on musters.
289 Also shown as Rassow and Rasson on musters.
290 Reily on Roll, and also Reilley on musters. Saw his entire war service with the 6th.
291 No 1340. Also Reilly on musters.
292 No 1285. Rooi on Roll.
293 Rueberry on Roll. Served with the 91st during the 2nd campaign.
294 No 2261. Saw his entire war service with the 6th, where his number was 3083 and should not be confused with No 2647 of that regiment.
295 No 2316. Saw his entire war service with the 60th.
296 No 2041. Scholes on Roll.
297 Shaughenssy on Roll. Saw his entire war service with the 60th.
298 Slevin on Roll. Saw his entire war service with the 91st.
299 No 1209.
300 No 2317. Saw his entire war service with the 60th.
301 No 391.
302 No 1251. Soranno on Roll.
303 Spilman on Roll.
304 Spilman on Roll. His qualification for the 3rd campaign remains in doubt.
305 No 343; a farrier.
306 No 232.
307 No 1338.
308 Stevens on Roll. Saw all his war service with the 45th.
309 Stewart on Roll. Saw all his war service with the 12th Lancers.
310 No 1635. Stoffels on Roll.
311 No 308.
312 No 1462. Also Sturmin on musters.
313 No 1956. Sumnar on Roll.
314 Christian name also shown as John on musters.
315 No 477; a corporal during the 2nd war. See Bisset.
316 No 1137. Also John Tigerflee on musters.
317 No 1411. Tomatt on Roll.
318 Tomblinson on Roll. Saw all his war service with the 12th.
319 Tracey on Roll.
320 Also Trainer on musters. Saw his entire war service with the 6th.
321 No 721. Tarental on Roll. Served with Smith on the Natal expedition in 1842.
322 No 356.
323 No 497.
324 No 347.
325 Venna on Roll. Saw his entire war service with the 91st.
326 No 780. Also Vertoon on musters. Was with Smith in Natal in 1842.
327 Also Wansen on musters.
328 A shoeing smith with the CMR who saw his entire war service with the 2nd.
329 Christian name given as Theodore on Roll.
330 No 730. Twice entered on Roll, once credited only with 1850–3.
331 No 294.
332 No 1432.
333 No 400.
334 No 951.
335 No 1694. Kevett on Roll.
336 Wells on Roll. Saw his entire war service with the 12th.
337 Christian name given as Witboy on Roll.
338 Spelling on Roll not positive and no qualifying dates are mentioned.
339 Served at Boemplaats.

PRO References: WO/12/10561–10563–10564–10567–10570–10572–10573–10574–10575.

Staff

I would have preferred to show Lt Gen Sir Harry Smith at the head of the Staff but I felt I had no choice other than to present those who served on the Staff, in the Commissariat, with the Medical Services, the Colonial forces and the Levies alphabetically. WO/100/17 lumps them together but to facilitate checking I have classified them under separate headings.

Where an officer listed as 'Staff' on the Roll has also been returned by his regiment I have shown him with the latter. When the officer has not been returned by his regiment even though it was actively employed his name is shown with the Staff as the medal may not show his regiment.

			Kaffir Wars		
			1	2	3
Capt Sir James Alexander	ADC	1)	△		
Bvt Capt Sir George Beresford	ADC	2)	△		
Lt Col Charles A. Fitzhardinge Berkeley	Military Sec	3)		△	
General Sir George Berkeley, KCB	Commander	4)		△	
Col George Buller	Div Commander	5)		△	△
Col Sir A Josias Cloete	Quartermaster Gen	6)	△	△	△
Major Hon Richard W. P. Curzon	ADC	7)			△
Col William H. Dutton	Military Sec	8)	△		
Col John Garvock	ADC	9)			△
Capt Arthur Greville	ADC	10)			△
Major Edward Holdich	ADC	11)			△
Col George MacKinnon, CB	Div Commander	12)		O	△
Capt Charles Maitland	Asst Military Sec	13)		△	
Major Henry L. Maydwell	Military Sec	14)			△
Col Edward E. Napier	On particular service	(P)	△		
Lt Col George Nicholls	On particular service		△		
Lt Col John O'Grady	On particular service			△	
Major Anthony A. O'Reilly	Brigade Major	15)	△	△	O
Lt Henry B. Ramsbottom	Acting ADC	(P)			△
Lt Gen Sir Harry G. Smith, GCB	Governor and C-in-C	16)	O		△
Major Hugh Smith	ADC	17)			△
Capt John C. Smith	Asst QMG	18)		△	
Maj Gen Sir Henry Somerset, KCB	Commander	19)	△	△	△
Ensign Henry G. E. Somerset	ADC	20)		O	△
Lt Col Henry Storks	Asst Adj General	21)		△	
Maj Gen Charles Yorke	Commander	22)			△

Note: Lt C. Griffin (Garrison Adj) and Lt Col O. Robinson (Acting ADC) were both returned by their regiments as well as being listed among Staff on the Roll.

△ = campaign qualification as WO/100/17.
O = campaign which the Rolls fail to credit.

NOTES ON STAFF

1. ADC to Sir B. D'Urban. Author of 'A Campaign in Kaffirland' and 'Narrative of a Voyage'. Alexander prompted the extension of the award for the 1st and 2nd wars. Captain in the 14th Regiment.
2. ADC to Sir B. D'Urban. Captain in the 7th Regiment.
3. Secretary to Sir George Berkeley. Was Captain in the Scots Fusilier Guards during the period of the 2nd war.
4. C-inC until the arrival of Sir Harry Smith in November 1847.
5. Received the surrender of Chief Sandili in 1847. Was severely wounded at Boemplaats. Commanded a Division in the Waterkloof during the 3rd campaign. Colonel in the Rifle Brigade.
6. Commanded the troops sent to Natal to relieve the beseiged Captain Smith in 1842.
7. Roll simply shows W. P. Curzon. ADC to Sir George Cathcart. Major in Grenadier Guards.
8. No initials shown on Roll.
9. Private Secretary to Sir Harry Smith. Served at Boemplaats.
10. ADC to Sir Harry Smith and Cathcart.
11. Holdick on Roll. ADC to Sir Harry Smith. Was at Boemplaats. Major in the 80th Regiment.
12. AQMG during 1846-7. Commanded the 2nd Division December 1850 to April 1852.
13. Secretary to Sir P. Maitland. Captain in Grenadier Guards.
14. Secretary to Sir Harry Smith. Major in the 41st Regiment.
15. Brigade Major at the Cape in 1819. DQMG and Commandant of Grahams Town. Settled as a farmer in 1848 but became Civil Commander of the townspeople and Grahams Town Volunteers at the request of Sir Henry Somerset in June 1851. See WO/1/451 for interesting correspondence.
16. Although the major figure of the Kaffir Wars Sir Harry is only credited with 1850-3 on the Roll. DQMG at the Cape in 1828 he commanded a Division under D'Urban in the 1st campaign. Appointed Governor of the Cape late in 1847 he arrived in Table Bay on December 1st. By the middle of the month he had called at Grahams Town and King Williams Town and although not active in the field it might be argued he should be credited with 1846-7. Commanded the forces at Boemplaats. Was replaced by General Sir George Cathcart in April 1852.
17. ADC to Sir Harry Smith and General Yorke. Major in the 3rd Regiment.
18. Served with the 2nd Division.
19. Somerset had a long and distinguished career in the Peninsular. Was at Waterloo and went to the Cape in 1818 where he was actively employed for the next 25 years. Colonel of the CMR.
20. ADC to his father Sir Henry and also with the CMR.
21. On the Roll as H. C. E. Storks.
22. 33rd Regiment.

CHAPLAINS

			Kaffir Wars		
			1	2	3
Rev Herbert Beaver	Mil Chaplain	(P)		△	△
Rev George Dacre	Asst. Chaplain	(P)			△
Rev F. Fleming	Mil Chaplain				△

△ = campaign qualification as WO/100/17.

"Odd Men" of the Regular Army

Only four Other Ranks, serving with regiments not generally employed, received the medal. Three of them were soldiers of the 98th Regiment, which was left to garrison Cape Town during the campaign of 1834–5, but the musters offer no explanation as to how the medals might have been earned.

Perhaps they were part of an escort with despatches to the frontier; or did they accompany Major Gregory, 98th Regiment, who served as a Volunteer with the Albany Levy under leave of absence and was thanked in GO No 6, 18.2.35. We are unlikely ever to know.

Returning to England in 1847, after taking part in the 1st Sikh war, the 62nd Regiment left a detachment in the Cape. They were not called upon and soon came home but an officer, Capt C. W. Sibley and Pte Kent stayed behind. It would seem that Sibley performed some service in the War of the Axe and Kent probably accompanied him, perhaps as his servant.

		Kaffir Wars		
		1	2	3
SERGEANT MAJOR James Ramsey	98th Regt		△	
SERGEANT John Wright	98th Regt		△	
PRIVATE William Curll	98th Regt	1)	△	
John Kent	62nd Regt			△

△ = campaign qualification as WO/100/17.

(1) Curle on Roll.

Staff Medical Services

The Cape of Good Hope was one of the healthier stations for British troops but the wars on the frontier imposed considerable strain on medical services. The regimental surgeons could usually provide adequate care for their particular charges and regiments short of medical officers were able to call upon Staff Surgeons, but there was an insufficient number to serve with the Colonial forces and Native Levies.

Early in 1851 attempts were made to recruit civilian doctors who were prepared to expose themselves to the discomforts and hazards of the frontier. Not altogether surprisingly there was a poor response and the Government was driven to seek men who, while not properly qualified physicians, had some experience of medicine. The Colonial Office correspondence shows at least three applicants were interviewed, one was a Frenchman, and at least one received an appointment as an Acting Assistant Surgeon with Native Levies. This was Henry Smith, a shop assistant with a Cape Town chemist who had once studied at Bristol Infirmary. His contract ran for six months and at its expiry he was replaced by a Staff Surgeon newly arrived in South Africa. The Hon John Montague, secretary to the Governor, afterwards confirmed that Smith '... performed his duty with advantage to the service and credit to himself...' but DIG John Hall had opposed an extension to the period of the original engagement which suggests a reluctance to rely upon non-qualified personnel a moment longer than necessary.

	Campaign Status	Kaffir Wars 1	2	3
SURGEON 2ND CLASS				
Thomas Atkinson	Staff Surgeon 1)	△	△	
Thomas Barrow	Staff Surgeon		△	
Thomas Best	Staff Surgeon		△	
William T. Black	Staff Asst. Surgeon	O	△	
ASSISTANT SURGEON				
John Campbell	Staff Asst. Surgeon 2)		△	
SURGEON				
William Cameron	Staff Surgeon		△	△
Thomas Cotton	Staff Surgeon (MRM)		△	
SURGEON 2ND CLASS				
Collis J. Delmege	Staff Surgeon 3)		△	
John Forrest	Staff Surgeon		△	
ASSISTANT SURGEON				
Alexander John Fraser	Staff Asst. Surgeon 4) (MRM)		△	
SURGEON 2ND CLASS				
Alexander Gibb	Staff Surgeon		△	△
ASSISTANT SURGEON				
James S. Grant	Staff Asst. Surgeon 5)		△	
DEPUTY INSPECTOR GENERAL				
John Hall	Deputy Insp Gen of Hospitals 6)	△	△	
DOCTOR				
Ralph Holden	Native Levies 7)		△	
ASSISTANT SURGEON				
Edward T. Mandeville	Staff Asst. Surgeon 8)	△	△	
SURGEON 2ND CLASS				
Duncan McDonald	Staff Surgeon 9)			△
DEPUTY INSPECTOR GENERAL				
Alexander Melvin	Deputy Insp Gen of Hospitals		△	
ASSISTANT SURGEON				
Nicholas O'Connor	Staff Asst. Surgeon		△	△
George Peake	Staff Asst. Surgeon		△	△
SURGEON				
William Sall	Staff Surgeon (P)		△	
ASSISTANT SURGEON				
Henry R. Smith	Native Levies 10) (P)		△	
George W. P. Sparrow	Staff Asst. Surgeon	O	△	

△ = campaign qualification as WO/100/17.
O = campaign which the Rolls fail to credit.

NOTES ON STAFF MEDICAL SERVICES

1. Twice returned, once as Thomas Atkinson credited with 1850–3 only, and then as T. M. Atkinson credited with 1846–7. He served in both wars and was at Boemplaats remaining in the field with the wounded while the Army pursued the Boers. Was in charge of the Hospital and Garrison of Grahams Town from January 1851 to March 1852.
2. Was with the expedition across the Kei in August 1852. Present at the last attack on the Waterkloof and at the Battle of Berea.
3. During the early part of the 2nd war was with the 27th Regiment.
4. On Roll as Frazer. Should not be confused with James Alexander Fraser of the 74th. Both men were Staff Surgeons in the Cape during the 2nd war. Alexander John F. was with the 73rd from April 1850 to December 1850 and it was from the 73rd that his medal was returned to the Mint. As he was employed by the Foreign Office on special service after resigning from the Army and survived to 1866 he may have owned another medal.
5. Initials wrongly shown on Roll as M. S. Was accidentally shot in the shoulder and later went to the 53rd Regiment.
6. Head of the Medical Department during the 2nd campaign. Served at Boemplaats and was Principal Medical Officer of the Army 1850–3.
7. A civilian employed by the Army owing to the shortage of Doctors and Surgeons. Served with the 43rd Regiment as well as the native levies.
8. In medical charge of all native levies 1846–7. Was at Boemplaats and present during the Kaffir attack on Fort Brown 1.10.51.
9. With the 25th Regiment at the taking of Natal in 1842. Served with the 73rd throughout the 3rd war. Was Senior Medical Officer on the expedition to Kreli's country in 1851.
10. Not on Roll. An Apothecary's assistant who was appointed Acting Assistant Surgeon 15.1.51 and did duty with the 1st Corps Native levies until 30.6.51. See WO/1/450 for interesting correspondence relating to Smith.

The Commissariat

A forerunner of the Royal Corps of Transport, the Commissariat was responsible for providing and paying for everything necessary for the subsistance and transport of an army. During the period of the Kaffir Wars the Commissariat was a civilian department under the direct control of the Treasury and, in the field, had custody of the Military Chest. Nevertheless the uniform worn by Commissariat officers was laid down by a General Order from the Horse Guards on August 1st 1834.

Comparative ranks were:

Commissary General as Brigadier General

Deputy CG as Major (and after three years Lt Col)

Assistant CG as Captain

Deputy ACG as Lieutenant

Clerk as Ensign.

Name	Rank	Note	Kaffir Wars 1	2	3
James Bailey	Clerk	1)			△
Robert Baker	DACG				△
Henry Bartlett	DACG	2)		△	△
H. de Beer	Clerk	(P)			△
George B. Bennett	DACG	3)			△
Lathan W. Blacker	DACG				△
H. Blackmore	Ordnance Clerk				△
William Blake	Ordnance Clerk				△
Charles G. Blanc	DACG				△
J. Blunden	Asst. Storekeeper			△	
W. Boyce	Ordnance Clerk				△
S. A. Branette	Ordnance Clerk			△	
J. Callaghan	Clerk Storekeeper				△
Luke R. Castray	Clerk	4)		△	
J. Chambers	Clerk Storekeeper	5)(P)			△
Charles W. Charlier	Clerk				△
Henry Clarke	Asst. CG				△
J. O'Connor	Clerk				△
J. Cox	Supt Mule Train				△
Charles Coxen	?				△
Percy Crause	Clerk				△
Robert Cumming	DACG	6)		△	△
Henry Curll	DACG			△	
H. DeMeillon	Clerk			△	
I. Van Dyke	Messenger				△
P. Egan	Storekeeper				△
B. Fitzpatrick	Storekeeper				△
Robert M. Gardiner	DACG				△
E. George	Asst. Storekeeper				△
W. Gordon	Writer				△
Thomas Graham	DACG	3)			O
B. Grayson	Deputy Ordnance Storekeeper (MRM)		△		
A. M. Green	Clerk				△
Henry Green	Asst. CG				△
William Green	DCG			△	△
Henry Hall	Clerk of Works			△	△
W. Hall	Supt Mule Train				△
F. Hawkes	Asst. Storekeeper				△
V. W. L. Hawkins	DACG			△	
Bulmer Hedley	Acting DACG				△
J. Hemming	Writer	(M)			△
George Horne	DACG			△	
Charles Hudson	Ordnance Clerk				△
Arthur Kay	DACG	7)			O
W. Kelly	Issuer				△
John Kent	Asst. CG	(MRM)			△
W. Kilpatrick	Asst. Storekeeper	(MRM)			△
John Knight	Asst. Storekeeper				△
W. F. Liddell	Clerk				△
W. F. Lissing	Conductor				△
J. F. Lonsdale	Clerk	(P)			△
R. Lynch	Asst. Storekeeper				△
Donald Maclean	DACG				△
Sir George Maclean	Commissary General				△
W. Macleod	Clerk				△
J. Mansfield	Messenger				△
Joseph Marsh	DACG	(P)			△
Theodore E. McLintock	DACG	8)			△
Thomas F. Moore	DACG				△
W. Muggleton	Asst. Storekeeper				△
C. A. Nesbit	Clerk				△
Henry Nesbitt	Clerk	9) (MRM)			△
W. Nettleton	Clerk				△
Kean Osborne	DACG				△
Charles Palmer	DACG	10)			△
William Palmer	Asst. CG	10)			△
Conrad F. Potgieter	DACG		△	△	△
William Tyrone Power	DACG				△
C. Pritchard	?			△	
R. S. Pryce	Clerk			△	
W. Rawstorne	Writer				△
Geo. Rennie	DACG				△
J. Richards	Asst. Storekeeper				△
Henry Robinson	DACG				△
Thomas T. J. Rorke	Commissary				△
Randolph Routh	Asst. CG				△
John H. Sale	DACG	11)		△	△
H. N. Salis	Ordnance Clerk				△
E. C. Saunder	Ordnance Clerk				△
John Charles Saunder	Ordnance Storekeeper	12)	△	△	△
J. Scott	Clerk				△
W. H. H. Scott	Ordnance Clerk	13)			△
Charles H. Sheil	DACG				△
F. Short	Ordnance Storehouseman				△
George A. Skinner	DACG			△	△
Johannes de Smidt (1)	Asst. CG				△
Johannes de Smidt (2)	Clerk				△
Charles B. Smith	DACG			△	△
David Smith	Clerk			△	
Robert H. Smith	DACG				△
W. B. Smith	Clerk				△
David Standen	DACG				△
Thomas Strickland	Clerk			△	
H. Taylor	Ordnance Clerk				△
W. Taylor	Asst. Storekeeper				△
Justus H. Thompson	DACG			△	△
Titus	Issuer	14)			△

		Kaffir Wars						Kaffir Wars		
		1	2	3				1	2	3
M. Tracey	Asst. Storekeeper			△		Robert Wolfe	Clerk of Engineers' Dept		△	△
James H. Tubby	DACG		3)	O		Arthur Wood	DACG		△	
James Whitmore	Asst. CG			△		J. N. Wynne	Clerk			△
James D. Watt	Asst. CG			△						
Fitzjames E. Watt	DACG		3)	O						
Henry Williams	Commissary			△		△ = campaign qualification as WO/100/17.				
Thomas Williams	DACG			△		O = campaign which the Rolls fail to credit.				
G. Willmore	Storekeeper			△						

NOTES ON THE COMMISSARIAT

1. Became DACG January 1854.
2. See King.
3. Not on Roll but received the medal according to Hart's.
4. See Appleyard.
5. Medal shows 'Commy Storekeeper'.
6. See Appleyard.
7. Stationed at Grahams Town 1852–3.
8. Served with the force against Mosesh.
9. Later an Ensign in the 12th Regiment.
10. 'Charles' has been altered to 'William' on the Roll but as William Palmer is also entered elsewhere on the Roll I am inclined to think someone has attempted to check William's medal and, only being able to find Charles, has jumped to the conclusion that the entry is in error. In fact the Roll is correct, for there were two Palmers, Charles and William. Another Charles Palmer who was ACG in 1815 and Deputy CG in 1837 and served in the Cape for many years does not appear to have received a medal.
11. See Godlonton and Irving.
12. Saunder's name appears on Sappers and Miners accounts and requisitions at Grahams Town during the 3rd war.
13. Was Acting Ordnance Storekeeper at Grahams Town in 1852–3.
14. No other name is given.

The Colonial Forces and Native Levies

Ever since mankind began to live in groups the able bodied have felt bound to turn out in the common defence of life and property. This maxim has always been well understood among pioneering communities and has nowhere been better demonstrated than in Southern Africa. During the frontier wars volunteers banded together under titles which indicated the districts where the forces were originally raised. To attract recruits, names were sometimes adopted which had a ring to them, such as the Albany Mounted Sharpshooters. Occasionally units took the names of their commanders; Catty's Rifles, Graham's Horse, Read's Volunteers and Lakeman's Volunteer Corps are a few examples. The latter had been formed by Sir Stephen Lakeman, author of 'What I saw in Kaffirland' and were more properly known as the Waterkloof Rangers. Doubtless to the envy of others, Sir Stephen contrived to equip his volunteers with Minie rifles, but most of the European levies carried their favourite personal weapons.

The longer they served the more uniform and practical became their dress. Initially some levies sallied forth as a motley collection of individuals. Capt Jervois, RE, writing in his diary at Simons Town on July 6th 1846, recorded '. . . saw the Burgher Guard at drill – a splendid sight severally – some without shoes or stockings, some with spicy frock coats, some with Malay handkerchiefs round their heads and indeed one might see every variety of Cape costume'. Such a sight was not a rarity as can be seen by an illustration in King's 'Campaigning in Kaffirland'.

Generally Europeans, Hottentots, and Fingos were in separate levies. They were commanded by regular officers seconded to the levies, retired officers living in South Africa, men of standing in the communities and officers from regiments in India who were on leave in the colony. Leave could be spent in the Cape on full pay rather than the half pay which applied when officers made the long journey to England and so those going home via the Cape had a financial incentive to stop off and gain some campaign experience.

Settlers with farms to run and families to support could not afford to offer their services for an unlimited time. Wives and children of the volunteers received rations and privates were paid 6d a day, but colonists at the seat of the troubles were often in such reduced circumstances that they were unable to serve and those in more comfortable areas were not disposed to rouse themselves. Consequently the Government had difficulty in raising sufficient forces for the levies and to keep up their strength in the field. When the Hon John Montague raised a levy in Cape Town in 1851, the recruits contracted for six months' service and few were willing to re-engage after the expiry of this term. As an inducement, Hottentots were promised a liberal allowance of cattle at the termination of the campaign. In time some units were stood down or absorbed by others; the Grahams Town European Levy was disbanded at the suggestion of the town Commandant, Major Burnaby, RA, within a month of formation, and few survived throughout 1851 and '52 without change in structure and organisation.

Contingents from Port Elizabeth, Uitenhage, Grahams Town and other frontier localities marched overland to the scene of operations, but the bulk of them went by sea from the western district of Cape Town, George, Swellendam and Riversdale and were landed at the Buffalo mouth. Military settlers, men who had spent all their lives on the frontier and those Boers who suppressed their dislike of the British by recognising that they too had a stake in the country, often fought magnificently; it was men such as these who had to absorb the initial shock of each uprising. Those from long settled districts were not always so hardy and reliable. They lacked discipline and the doggedness necessary for long campaigning in the field and the regulars tended to view them with disapproval.

The native levies were mainly used as a skirmishing screen to trigger off any ambush and to follow in pursuit of a fleeing enemy after the backbone of resistance had been broken by regular troops. It was dangerous work shared by the mounted Europeans employed on scouting and they deserve more credit for these hazardous duties than is generally accorded to them.

As the General Order announcing the award of the SA 1853 medal referred only to 'Regular Forces', men who served with the Levies must have felt that for them to apply would have been to invite a rebuff. But once some applications had been supported by certain personages of rank and met with a favourable response, precedents had been established which could have removed the barriers to hundreds of volunteers no less worthy. That the War Office was not swamped by claims suggests that the news of the success of the few was not widely spread abroad. Only a handful of men who served with the Levies are listed on the Roll, but medals to others are known to exist and I have no doubt that more will surface from time to time.

In the PRO there can be found the pay lists of Levies which operated during the 3rd campaign. They are not complete, but it may be of interest and of use to researchers, to list them here. Where known, their approximate strengths are shown in brackets.

Albany Native (Hottentot) Levy (170)
Albert Fingo Levy (200)
Alice Fingo Levy (100)
Alice Levy (150)
Armstrong's Horse (45)
Beaufort West (Hottentot) Levy (115)
Fort Beaufort Fingo Levy (700)
Fort Beaufort Mounted Troop (50)
Burghersdorp European Levy (20)
Burghersdorp Native Levy (90)
Burghersdorp Volunteers (25)
Cape Town Levy (500)
Cattys Rifles (320). Replaced the 2nd European Corps of Levies late in 1851.
Colesburg Hottentot Levy (45)
Cradock (European) Levy (20)
Cradock Fingo Levy (150)
Cradock Hottentot Levy (50)
1st European Levy (450)
2nd European Levy (400). Replaced by Cattys Rifles
Fingo Free Companies (1st and 2nd)
George (Hottentot) Levy (380)
Graaf Rienet Burgher Levy (30)
Graaf Rienet (Hottentot) Levy (30)
Graaf Rienet Mounted Troop (100)
Grahams Town European Levy (30)
Grahams Town Mounted Rangers (90)
Grahams Town Fingo Levy
Grahams' Horse (40)
Kamastone Levy
Kat River Fingo Levy

Kat River Levy
Mancanza Fingo Levy
Montague's Horse (50)
North Victoria Burghers
North Victoria Levy (800)
Fort Peddie Fingo Corps (500)
Port Elizabeth Fingo Levy
Port Elizabeth Levy
Read's Volunteers

Riversdale Levy
Shilo Fingo Levy
Somerset Fingo Levy
Somerset Rangers
Waterkloof Rangers (80)
Whittlesey Fingo Levy (200)
Whittlesey Levy (35)
Whittlesey Mounted Burghers

OFFICERS AND MEN WHO SERVED WITH THE COLONIAL FORCES OR NATIVE LEVIES AND OTHERS NOT CLASSIFIED

Name	Unit	Ref	Kaffir Wars 1	2	3
Lt Richard Babington	2nd European Levy	1) (P)			△
Lt Edward R. B. Barnes	Cape Town Levy	2)		△	
Lt Alfred F. D. Broughton		3)		△	
Ensign Charles G. Buckner	Fingo Levy	4)			△
Capt Thomas Cassidy	Cape Town Levy	5) (P)		O	
— William Gordon Corfield	Waterkloof Rangers	6)			△
Lt/Adj Edward Bowers Doggett	1st Native Levy	7)		△	
Lt William P. Finlay	Native Levy	8)		△	
Lt Crofton H. Fitzgerald	Cattys Rifles	9)		△	△
Capt William Fisher	Barrack Master	10)			△
— C. D. Griffiths		11)			O
Pte James MacPherson	Cattys Rifles	12)			△
Lt James C. Minto	Graaf Irregular Horse	13)			△
Pte John Morgan	Cattys Rifles				△
Lt George Newdigate	Native Levy	14)		O	
Capt Henry M. Orpen	Native Levy	15)		△	
Lt George F. Pocock	Riversdale Levy	16)			△
Capt Henry Reynolds		17)		△	
— William Sampson	Native Levy				△
— Charles L. Salis		18)			△
Lt/Col James P. Sparks	Grahams Town Volunteers	19)	O	△	
Lt J. D. Simmonds	Colonial Levies	20) (P)			
— J. T. Thomas	Mounted Burgher Corps	20) (P)			

△ = campaign qualification as WO/100/17.
O = campaign which the Rolls fail to credit.

THE COLONIAL FORCES AND NATIVE LEVIES NOTES

1 An officer in the 4th Madras Native Infantry, he landed at East London 18.2.51 and resigned from the 2nd Europeans on 3.4.51. The medal is engraved. See G and I.
2 Sent to the frontier with the Capetown Levy on 14.1.51. Barnes accompanied the 1st patrol to leave King Williams Town on 30.1.51. He was a regular officer of the 3rd Regiment.
3 Broughton is shown in the musters as a sergeant with a troop of Mounted Burghers which was part of the 1st Corps Native Levy. He was appointed a Lieut in Montagu's Horse 22.11.51 and later became a Lieut in the 33rd Madras Native Infantry.
4 Attached to the 1st Corps Native Levy and later commissioned into the 56th Regiment.
5 A Col Sgt with the 1/45th in Natal during the period of the 2nd campaign, Cassidy rose to become Q/Master and went on half pay in 1850. In January 1851 he was given the pay of a Captain and appointed to assist in organising the raising of the Cape Town Levy. He did not serve on frontier and in May became Q/Master in the 21st Regt.
6 Probably not a settler as his medal was sent to Queen's Terrace, Haverstock Hill, London NW. Roll shows period of service as 'till peace was proclaimed'. A Sgt George Corfield was also with the Waterkloof Rangers.
7 Landed at East London on 10.3.51 and originally served with the 2nd European Levy. To the 1st Corps Native Levy on 1.11.51.
8 Resigned 31.3.52.
9 Also served with Hottentot Levies and was present at operations in the Waterkloof and Amatolas. Fitzgerald was with Cattys Rifles until the close of the 3rd campaign.
10 Commander at Eland's Post and Barrack Master at Fort Beaufort. A captain in the 94th Regiment.
11 Griffiths' medal, believed to be engraved, and with a clasp for 1877-8-9, is in a South African museum. Shortly after the 3rd campaign he served on the Staff of Sir Walter Currie, commander of the Frontier Armed & Mounted Police and in the 1860s was Magistrate at Queens Town. In 1877 Griffiths was Colonel in command of the Colonial Forces.
12 Served from 1.12.51 to 30.4.52.
13 The son of the surgeon of the CMR he served with the Graaf Rienet Mounted Troop and secured an Ensigncy in the CMR in August 1853. Minto later transferred to the 97th Regiment.
14 Although not shown on the Roll, Newdigate's service is mentioned by Harts and it seems he may have received a medal. He appears on the musters for the George Levy late in 1851.
15 Musters show him with the Colesberg Hottentot Levy.
16 Rose from private in the Mounted Burghers.
17 An officer in the 2nd Regiment who later transferred to the 58th, he served as a volunteer and was with the force which crossed the Kei.
18 Attached to the CMR he appears twice on the Roll but one medal was returned to the Mint.
19 Sparks happened to be visiting his family in Grahams Town upon the outbreak of the 1st war; he served with the 49th and 38th Regiments. See Moodie.
20 Not on Roll but probably served during the campaign of 1850-3.

PRO References: WO/13/3718-3719-3720-3721-3722-3723-3724-3725.

Diagrammatic Chart of Medals Awarded

	ARMY OFFICERS						OTHER RANKS				
	1834–5	1846–7	1850–3	1834–5 and 1846–7	1846–7 and 1850–3	1834–5 1846–7 and 1850–3	Total	1834–5	1846–7	1850–3	1834–5 and 1846–7	1846–7 and 1850–3	1834–5 1846–7 and 1850–3	Total

	1834–5	1846–7	1850–3	1834–5 and 1846–7	1846–7 and 1850–3	1834–5 1846–7 and 1850–3	Total	1834–5	1846–7	1850–3	1834–5 and 1846–7	1846–7 and 1850–3	1834–5 1846–7 and 1850–3	Total
Staff	3	8	8	—	3	3	26	—	—	—	—	—	—	—
Staff Med Services	—	5	9	—	8	—	22	—	—	—	—	—	—	—
7th Dragoon G	—	20	—	—	—	—	20	—	—	—	—	—	—	150†
12th Lancers	—	—	27	—	—	—	27	—	149	—	—	1	—	340
Royal Artillery	1	5	6	—	2	—	14	—	—	339	—	1	—	212*
Royal Engineers	1	7	12	—	1	—	21	—	—	—	—	—	—	244*
2nd Regiment	—	—	24	—	—	—	24	—	—	577	—	—	—	577
6th Regiment	—	10	16	—	12	—	38	—	47	175	—	378	—	601
12th Regiment	—	—	25	—	—	—	25	—	—	510	—	—	—	511
27th Regiment	9	8	—	4	—	—	21	26	70	—	84	—	—	180†
43rd Regiment	—	—	24	—	1	—	25	—	—	585	—	—	—	585
45th Regiment	—	17	13	—	10	—	40	—	—	—	—	—	—	711*
60th Regiment	—	—	23	—	1	—	24	128	—	553	—	—	—	553
72nd Regiment	10	—	—	—	—	—	10	—	—	—	1	—	—	129
73rd Regiment	—	11	17	—	6	—	34	—	27	180	—	327	—	534
74th Regiment	—	—	25	—	1	—	26	—	—	558	—	—	—	558
75th Regiment	12	—	—	—	—	—	12	116	—	—	—	—	—	116
90th Regiment	—	14	—	—	—	—	14	—	243	—	—	1	—	244
91st Regiment	—	21	15	—	9	—	45	—	179	222	2	355	1	759
1st Rifle Brigade	—	9	14	—	11	—	34	—	161	420	—	150	—	731
CMR	7	7	20	2	16	1	59	—	22	471	5	271	36	805
							561							8,540

*Estimated.
†Including one of uncertain date.

ROYAL NAVY	831 Officers and men
ROYAL MARINES	93
ROYAL MARINE ARTILLERY	40
COMMISSARIAT	118
Others	27
TOTAL	10,210

The Mint records show that 10,558 medals were struck between April 24th 1855 and March 31st 1862. This number includes two patterns which were presented to Queen Victoria. The difference between the figures of 10,558 and 10,203 is accounted for by those issued to deserters and later cancelled, replacements, duplicates and others of which we have no record.

Sir Harry Smith's Medal for Gallantry

Early in 1853 the War Department was asked by the Paymaster of Local Levies in the Cape to settle a debt of £59 18s 2d which had been incurred in the production of some silver medals. It was explained that, during his term as Governor of the Cape Colony, Sir Harry Smith had announced in a General Order that medals were to be awarded to men of the Levies who had distinguished themselves. The Duke of Newcastle, indignant at the thought that Sir Harry had exceeded his authority, called upon the hero of Aliwal to explain the matter. On February 6th Sir Harry, now Commander of the Western District, wrote from Devonport. As the Queen's representative in the Cape he had, he said, deemed himself authorised to grant such a distinction to Local Corps. At the outbreak of the 3rd war he had been in a difficult position. The allegiance of the native population was uncertain from one end of the Colony to the other; open rebellion existed on the eastern frontier, the CMR were wavering and 50 had actually deserted to the enemy, while the regular troops were few in number and scattered over extensive country. Consequently, as Commander he was prepared to resort to every expedient to preserve loyalty and hold his position, the abandonment of which would have been destructive to the Colony. He '... issued a General Order granting medals to those who nobly and gallantly distinguished themselves, a measure attended with great success'. In the exigencies of the moment, continued Sir Harry, he had neglected to report what he had done to the Secretary of State for the Colonies. The letter ended '... no officer could more desire than myself to act with humility and not to trespass on the Queen's prerogative by granting honorary distinctions'.

It was a persuasive letter but I am not convinced that Sir Harry Smith was being absolutely frank. Could he seriously have thought in 1851 that a few medals might affect the rebellion in any way whatsoever? I find it curious too that when the debt came to be adjusted to £60 9s od it was mentioned as being charged up to March 31st 1852. By then the campaign was no longer in a critical phase even though it was far from over, and if Sir Harry was still distributing his medals it could hardly have been with the hopes of improving the war situation.

Any doubts the War Department may have had were stifled. The Colonial Office was informed that a satisfactory explanation had been forthcoming and it was recommended that the charge be borne by the Colonial Funds.

No mention is made in this correspondence of the number of medals that had been struck – although the expenses indicate that there must have been very few – and as no Roll has ever been discovered collectors have always wondered who received the medals and how they were earned.

Dr Frank K. Mitchell, a South African authority, has compiled a list of 30 Sir Harry Smith medals which are known to exist or have been recorded. In the course of my research I kept in mind the names given by Dr Mitchell and tried to ascertain whether there is any substance in the assertion that the medals were distributed to men of the CMR who escorted the Governor when he broke out from the beseiged Fort Cox early in the 3rd campaign. I found nothing to support this belief and only one of the men listed was serving with the Cape Mounted at that time. However, there is always the possibility that others served with attached Provisional Hottentot Companies and so are not shown on the pay lists.

Whatever may have been his intention when he conceived the idea I am inclined to the opinion that Sir Harry simply handed out his medals as recognition of some particular service which had been rendered to him. We can scarcely doubt that the medal named to 'Capt Skead, RN' was once owned by Francis Skead, 2nd Master of HMS 'Dee', and the Governor could hardly have needed to encourage the loyalty of one of Her Majesty's Naval officers!

No two of the medals named are similarly engraved and as 11 of those surviving are unnamed it is reasonable to assume that they were presented in this state. Until the appearance of the SA 1853 medal, Sir Harry Smith's medal must have been a most desirable memento of the fighting on the frontier and it is likely some changed hands, subsequently being engraved with the names of men who had not received them from the hands of the Governor. Even after the issue of the campaign medal it must have been nice to possess another which had inscribed on it 'for Gallantry in the Field'.

See 'African Notes and News' June 1955, Vol XI No 7, where Dr Mitchell discusses the origin and design, the dies and manufacture of the medal.

SIR HARRY SMITH MEDALS HAVE BEEN RECORDED AS NAMED TO THE FOLLOWING

— Paul Arendt		(P)
— Piet Jan Cornelis		(P)
RSM William Richard Dakins	1)	(P)
— Thomas Dicks		(P)
— Thomas Duncan		(P)
Sapper R. Dunning, RE	2)	(P)
— Henry Evans		(P)
— David Faroe		(M)
— Hendrik Ferara		(P)
— Fundi	3)	
— J. Hassall		(P)
— John Keiberg		(P)
— John Main	4)	(P)
— H. McKain		(P)
— John McVarrie		(P)
— Francis Meades, CMR	5)	(M)
— J. Mouatt, CMR	6)	(P)
Capt Skead, RN	7)	(M)
— Adrian Strauss		(P)

SIR HARRY SMITH'S MEDAL FOR GALLANTRY NOTES

1 Possibly Sgt Major John R. Darkin, 2nd Regiment.

2 Served with the 9th Company. Must have been named after 1855, otherwise the Corps would have been given as the Royal Sappers and Miners.

3 Recorded by Gordon and said to be a native policeman.

4 See the Roll for the Cape Mounted Riflemen.

5 No 1743.

6 Joined the CMR 1.11.53 after service with the 6th Regiment.

7 Francis Skead, 2nd Master of HMS 'Dee'.

Ranks and Rates in the Royal Navy. 1853

The year of 1853 saw the creation of a 'Standing' or 'Regular' Royal Navy and other supporting administrative arrangements – all aimed to improve the conditions of sailors on the lower deck and professionalism in the Service.

The traditional 'jobbing' system of employment was abolished – a centuries old method whereby the crew were hired for the commission of a ship which usually lasted three years, and then found themselves without a berth when their vessel was paid off and placed 'In Ordinary'. From now onwards, suitable sailors could be certain of continuity in employment by signing a Continuous Service Engagement to serve for 12 years from the time they became aged 18 – cooks, stewards and other 'idlers' (day-workers) excepted. These CS men could also re-engage for a further period to complete their time for pension.

Prior to 1853 a small body of specialist sailors had for some years had the opportunity to be continuously employed, albeit not with the same longevity or certainty as offered by the new rules. These were men who had been trained aboard HMS 'Excellent' and become Seaman Gunners ('SG' on some medals). In 1859 this same group of men were to gain an advantage never equalled by another branch in the Navy, when they were to be allowed to count six years service for every five years that they actually performed – possibly earning a LS & GC medal well before the '21 yrs' engraven on their award.

Implicit in the new contract of employment was the advantage of being granted leave with pay between commissions, which in due course led to 'Baggage Stores' in ports from whence men proceeded home. The creation of a floating population of men for whom they were responsible brought about the construction of RN barracks in home ports.

The new rules bolstered up the creation of a Regular Navy by the instruction allowing Petty Officers to retain their rate when 'paid off', and carry it to their next ship. In the fullness of time the Shore Authorities had more POs than sea billets to fill. Formerly many beached and unpaid ex-Petty Officers had to take on any duty they could obtain in a ship being newly commissioned, and often found themselves with no alternative but that of accepting the humbler duties of Able Seaman.

Now that the seamen of the Navy were to be a single collective body of men, the control for the manning of ships was to pass from the commanding officers of ships to shore based authorities. This system led to ships being manned speedily from a pool of ratings, rather than lying idle for up to six months whilst crews were collected to form the full ship's company.

The opportunity was also taken at this time to grant the most senior ratings of the Navy a new title. The highest rate which a seaman could attain on the lower deck had been Working First Class Petty Officer, but from now onwards certain of the duties performed by such men were to be upgraded and their holders given the title of Chief Petty Officer. This prefix was to remain for over a century. But in the Victorian era some age old customs took a long time to die, and it was usual to continue the traditional procedure of expressing a rating's title as his 'duty' aboard ship, rather than as his rate as PO or CPO. It was to be about 30 years before the rate of Chief Petty Officer appeared on the rim of medals. In many ways the retention of the older method of identifying sailors by the duties – amply portrayed on so many medals – has made the award more meaningful to a collector, who most likely would prefer to see that the recipient was the Admiral's Coxswain or Chief Captain of the Forecastle, rather than the generic words of Chief Petty Officer.

Two other changes were made to the content of the structure which formed the basis for promotion within the seaman branch. The title and rate of Landsman was abolished and this most junior of adult rates was classified as 2nd Class Ordinary Seaman – a group which already existed whose duties corresponded in large measure with those previously performed by Landsmen.

The other innovation brought in at this time was a new rate to fit between Able Seaman and Petty Officer, when the title of Leading Seaman was chosen in preference to Able Seaman First Class. The exact duty performed by each individual with this new title is invariably hidden by its general application – as it was to be with CPOs in later years. To confuse the purist, as can be seen in the forthcoming List of Rates, the title and rate of Leading Stoker is completely contradictory. This nomenclature had already been assigned for a number of years to the most senior ratings of the emergent engineering branch of the RN. It carried with it the style and status of Petty Officer and such men were senior (except in military command) to, and considerably better paid than Leading Seamen. Many years were to pass before this anomaly was overcome by the institution of Stoker Petty Officer and a reversion of Leading Stoker to equal status with other leading rates of the various branches in the Navy.

TABLE OF RANKS AND RATES IN ORDER OF SENIORITY

Captain (three distinguishing stripes until 1861, then four)

Commander (two distinguishing stripes until 1861, then three)

Lieutenant (one distinguishing stripe until 1861, then two)

Master (the Navigator)

Chaplain (sometimes 'Chaplain and Naval Instructor')

Medical Inspector of Hospitals and Fleets

Surgeon

Paymaster (sometimes expressed as 'Paymaster and Purser')

Clerk in Charge (a Clerk who had passed examination for 'Paymaster')

Mate (old title was 'Master's Mate'. In 1861 to be Sub Lieutenant and wear one distinguishing stripe)

Assistant Surgeon

Second Master

Subordinate Officers
Naval Instructor
Midshipman
Master's Assistant
Clerk
Clerk's Assistant
Naval Cadet

Warrant Officers
Gunner
Boatswain
Carpenter
Inspector of Machinery
Chief Engineer (1st to 3rd Class)
Assistant Engineer (1st to 3rd Class)

Chief Petty Officers
Master at Arms
Chief Gunner's Mate
Chief Boatswain's Mate
Chief Captain of the Forecastle
Admiral's Coxswain
Chief Quarter Master
Chief Carpenter's Mate
Seaman's Schoolmaster
Ship's Steward
Ship's Cook

1st Class Working Petty Officers
Ship's Corporal
Gunner's Mate
Boatswain's Mate
Captain's Coxswain
Captain of the Forecastle
Quarter Master
Coxswain of the Launch
Captain of the Main Top
Captain of the Fore Top
Captain of the Afterguard
Captain of the Hold
Sailmaker
Ropemaker
Carpenter's Mate
Caulker
Blacksmith
Leading Stoker

2nd Class Working Petty Officers
Coxswain of the Barge
Coxswain of the Pinnace

Captain of the Mast
2nd Captain of the Forecastle
2nd Captain of the Main Top
2nd Captain of the Fore Top
Yeoman of the Signals
2nd Captain of the Afterguard
Captain of the Mizzen Top
Sailmaker's Mate
Coxswain of the Cutter
Cooper
Armourer
Caulker's Mate
Musician
Head Krooman

Leading Rate and below
Leading Seaman
Shipwright
Yeoman of Storerooms
2nd Captain of the Hold
Painter
Sailmaker's Crew
Blacksmith's Mate
Armourer's Crew
Carpenter's Crew
Cooper's Crew
Stoker/Coat Trimmer
Able Seaman
Sick Berth Attendant
Bandman
Tailor
Butcher
2nd Head Krooman
Flag Officer's Domestics
Captain's Steward
Captain's Cook
Ward/Gun Room Steward
Ward/Gun Room Cook
Ship's Steward's Assistant
Secretary's Servant
Subordinate Officer's Steward
Subordinate Officer's Cook
Ordinary Seaman
Cook's Mate
Barber
2nd Class Ordinary Seaman
Commander's Servant
Krooman
Ship's Steward's Boy
Boy 1st Class
Boy 2nd Class

www.ingramcontent.com/pod-product-compliance
Lightning Source LLC
Chambersburg PA
CBHW080054200426
43197CB00054B/2725